R.A. East

Supermarine Aircraft

since 1914

The rejuvenated Spitfire Mk F.XIV with the Rolls-Royce Griffon 65 engine, disclosing its superb control in roll as demonstrated by Supermarine chief test pilot Jeffrey Quill. The picture was taken by Supermarine photographer F. H. Burr from the open doorway of a Dragon Rapide.

Supermarine
Aircraft

since 1914

C F Andrews
E B Morgan

PUTNAM

ISBN 0 85177 800 3
© C. F. Andrews & E. B. Morgan 1981
Printed in Great Britain for
Putnam, an imprint of
Conway Maritime Press Ltd,
24 Bride Lane, Fleet Street,
London EC4Y 8DR
by Thomson Litho Ltd, East Kilbride
Set in Linotron 202 Times
First Published 1981
New edition 1987

Dedicated to the memory of
Reginald J. Mitchell and
Joseph Smith—design
engineers of distinction.

CONTENTS

Foreword by
SIR PETER MASEFIELD

SUPERMARINE—a name hallowed in the archives of aeronautical history—will forever be associated with Reginald Mitchell's inspired design of the Spitfire and, before that, with its illustrious forebears, the S.5 and S.6 Schneider Trophy winners.

Originally, however, in its origins before the First World War, Noël Pemberton Billing's imaginative 'sobriquet' was conceived in the context of marine aircraft. How appropriate that was, is evident from the fine sequence of Supermarine flying-boats as well as from the successive Supermarine winners of the greatest international seaplane contest of all time.

Occupying, as it did for more than 50 years, such a remarkable place in the story of British aviation, we have had to wait too long for a definitive history of the Supermarine Aviation Works, its people and its products.

Now, that wait is well rewarded, and the gap well filled, by this meticulously assembled story, compiled with so much care and authority by Charles Andrews and Eric Morgan.

I take special pleasure in having been invited to write a Foreword to this important contribution to the chronicles of British aircraft manufacture; a pleasure for two reasons. Firstly, the story of Supermarine is a classic example of the history of the British Aircraft Industry as a whole—from tentative beginnings around the ideas of a pioneering enthusiast, along a hard and often stony path between the Wars to a period of brilliance and expansion before and during the Second World War. During that time, successive mergers gave strength but also, it cannot be denied, sapped some of the special character of a highly individual concern. And so on to eventual absorption and extinction in, what seemed, inevitable industrial coalitions.

Truly, a bright Spring, a bountiful Summer, and then a hard, cold, Winter softened by warm memories of great days now gone.

The second reason for my pleasure in this book is not only for the way in which it rescues from oblivion, and from the almost-forgotten past, so many of the imaginative efforts and stern endeavours which brought, from drawing boards, through the shops and into the air, such a flowering of the best of their day in design, in manufacture and in flying qualities; but, also, because this book engenders bright memories of blue and sunlit waters lapping around the hulls of Southampton flying-boats, the exhilaration of a bumpy take-off in open cockpits, through a shower of spray, translated suddenly into the smoothness of flight, with thundering, uncowled, engines only feet away. With all of it, there was a combination of fresh air and open waters which is wholly lost from the enclosed and pressurized high-flying aircraft of today; rich as they are in creature comforts and in technological attractions.

Quite different, again, was the feeling of power and mastery in the cockpit of a Spitfire, with its massive, deep-throated, Merlin in front, giving life to its elegant, elliptical wings—however difficult they were to build.

Nor would anyone who saw them ever forget the delight of the sight and sound of the Schneider Trophy seaplanes sweeping low over the Solent in 1929, at speeds which promised even greater things to come; promise so well fulfilled.

The names of the generations of Supermarine aircraft read like a roll-call of the champions of British aeronautics; Sea Eagle, Seagull, Sea Lion, Southampton, S.5, S.6, Scapa, Walrus, Stranraer, Spitfire, Seafire, Swift, Attacker, Scimitar and many more—with a great succession of Rolls-Royce, Napier and Bristol engines.

Less well-known, less remembered, but the originators of them all, are the names of the men who inspired and built the Supermarine Aviation Works; the eccentric Noël Pemberton Billing; the sturdy James Bird and Hubert Scott-Paine; the elegant Victor Paine; brave and brilliant Reginald Mitchell; with Alan Clifton and Beverley Shenstone and loyal and dogged Joe Smith; all of them in company with that gallant band of test pilots—prominent among them Henri Biard, George Pickering, Jeffrey Quill and Mike Lithgow.

These men and their machines will be remembered with pride and respect whenever the tale is told of the small design and manufacturing industry in Britain which enthusiastically embraced the new art and science of man-made flight and, in the space of 50 years, produced aircraft which changed the course of history.

Charles Andrews and Eric Morgan have added an important dimension to that history in this story of great achievements around a famous name.

P.G.M.

Acknowledgements

Because of the unusual and chequered history of the Supermarine archives, starting with the bombing of Woolston Works during the Battle of Britain, much reliance has had to be made by the authors on outside sources of invaluable information. They are indeed grateful to so many people for filling in pieces of the jig-saw although regretfully they cannot all be mentioned by name. Especially, however, thanks must be rendered to Hugh Scrope of Vickers House for access to Company records dealing with the Supermarine Division of Vickers (Aviation) Limited and for his zeal in practical sponsorship. Also to S. J. Paine for his authoritative summary of the recognized Spitfire variants culled from the official Air Publications; and to Norman Parker for his able description of the Spitfire Dispersal production in the Southern region, with the assistance of the late Leonard Gooch of Supermarine. But without the help of the 'Men on the spot' Alan Clifton and Ernest Mansbridge, this book would never have appeared. Acknowledgement must also be accorded to John Bagley, Ronald Harker, Harry Robinson and Fred Underwood for their specialist contributions, technical and photographic. We also have to thank the widows of Supermarine pilots Henri Biard, George Pickering and Mike Lithgow for making records and flying logs available. Last but not least, the assistance of Charles Burnet in smoothing the airflow around the 'sound barrier' was thankfully accepted in relation to Supermarine types, and to Norman Jackman for his carefully compiled précis of the emotive Swift story.

As regards academic bodies, we acknowledge permission of the Royal Aeronautical Society to quote from their vast collection of authoritative Lectures in the secure custody of their Librarian, to the Smithsonian Institution of Washington, D.C., for a similar sortie and to Leo Schefer, of British Aerospace Inc at Dulles International Airport, Washington, and to the Royal Air Force for making this possible. To the Air Historical Branch of the Ministry of Defence, to the Royal Aircraft Establishment Library, and Air-Britain (Historians) Ltd we pay tribute to their vital help in filling in many gaps in the Spitfire production details, caused by the circumstances already mentioned. We must thank E. W. Fice and his graphic artists, and Darby Childerhouse and his photographers, all of Weybridge Works, for completing the expert work of the late L. E. Bradford on the line drawings, not forgetting the labours of the solo typist Mrs Linda Parsons, who waded through some quarter of a million words of original and corrected text. Finally a tribute to our long-suffering wives for their forbearance.

Pemberton Billing under private instruction from Harold Barnwell of Vickers Flying School at Brooklands. The aircraft is a secondhand Boxkite.

Introduction

In October 1913 Noel Pemberton Billing (who first entered aviation in 1904 when he built a man-lifting glider) decided to build 'boats that will fly, and not just aeroplanes with floats'. 'Supermarine', the name registered as his telegraphic address, expressed his aim—to build the antithesis of the submarine.

In the previous year, Pemberton Billing had made a wager with Frederick Handley Page, another aviation pioneer, that he would learn to fly and obtain a Royal Aero Club Aviator's Certificate within 24 hours. In fact he did it between 5.45 am and breakfast one morning.

Pemberton Billing's first flying-boat, the Supermarine P.B.1. with a single tractor engine mounted between the wings and above the cigar-shaped hull, was shown in public for the first time in March 1914. At the outbreak of the war that August, Pemberton Billing decided to build a single-seat fighting aeroplane. This machine, Supermarine's first landplane and distant ancestor of the Spitfire, will go down in history as the aeroplane that was designed and built in nine days. Officially, it was known as the P.B.9, but unofficially, and slightly inaccurately, as the 'Seven Day Bus'.

1

PEMBERTON-BILLING, Ltd.

IN FLIGHT

ILLUSTRATIONS DEMONSTRATING THE LATEST TYPE OF

"SUPERMARINE"

(FLYING LIFEBOAT)

Telephone : No. 38, Southampton.   *Telegrams : "Supermarine."*

BUILT UNDER PEMBERTON-BILLING'S PATENTS AT HIS SOUTHAMPTON WORKS

AFTER ALIGHTING— THE WINGS DETACHED

SOUTHAMPTON, ENGLAND

Advertisement for Pemberton Billing's patent slip-wing flying-boat to proceed with under-water propeller in case of emergency.

Early picture of the Supermarine Works on the River Itchen at Woolston, Southampton, showing Billing yacht basin on the left and the flying-boat works on the right with an A.D. flying-boat ready for launching.

This picture from Supermarine's 1919 catalogue shows an Avro 504E (*top left*), Sopwith seaplane (*top right*), Bristol T.B.8 (*bottom left*) and Avro 510/519 (*bottom right*). The Avro 510/519 had been sent to Supermarine for modification.

Hubert Scott-Paine was appointed works manager in 1914 and at the end of 1916 became managing director of the renamed company—The Supermarine Aviation Works Limited.

During the war the factory, at Woolston beside the River Itchen, Southampton, did repair and experimental work for the Admiralty. Perhaps the best remembered of these experiments was the 1915 Push Proj single-seat pusher scout. In 1916 two large quadruplane landplanes, designed for the interception of German airships, were made. Much more important, in the same year, the man who was to design the Schneider Trophy winners and the Spitfire, Reginald J. Mitchell, joined the firm.

A diminutive pusher flying-boat, the Supermarine N.1B Baby, was probably the firm's most successful design of the war years. A 200 hp Hispano-Suiza engine gave it a top speed of 116 mph (186·6 km/h) at sea level, but the war ended before it saw any action.

Despite the immediate postwar slump in aviation, 1919 saw the emergence of a new commercial flying-boat, the Channel Type, developed from a wartime design and powered at first by a 160 hp Beardmore engine and later by 240 hp Siddeley Puma. With accommodation for three passengers in an open cockpit ahead of the pilot, Channels were used in South America, Bermuda, Norway, Japan and Chile, as well as in the south of England.

From these beginnings it is possible to trace the continuity of four main types of aircraft in the firm's historical development. A basic series of general-purpose single-engine amphibians began with a design for an Air Ministry Competition and with the first Seagull of the early 1920s and ended with the unique variable-incidence amphibian Seagull ASR.I of 1948.

A second series started with the graceful twin-engined Southampton flying-boat of 1925 and terminated with the Stranraer of 1936 (although the firm worked on later design studies for a large flying-boat).

The third type was the series of clean-line monoplane racing seaplanes built for the Schneider Trophy contests of 1925–31. By winning this Trophy on three successive occasions, Britain, under the rules, became the permanent holder. The final version, the Supermarine S.6B, was the first aeroplane ever to exceed 400 mph when it created a world speed record of 407·5 mph in 1931.

Woolston 'hard' towards the end of the flying-boat era, with Southamptons in various stages of overhaul and the first Stranraer awaiting its engines.

4

Reginald Joseph Mitchell (*left*) as a young aeroplane designer, and Henri Biard a Channel Islander who was Supermarine's first chief test pilot.

The last series, single-engined single-seat fighters, began in 1934 with the unsuccessful Air Ministry specification F.7/30. But Reginald Mitchell, assisted by a highly efficient technical team, in a private venture incorporating the many lessons learned on the Schneider Trophy seaplanes, began the design of what was to become the Spitfire. With revolutionary thin, elliptical wing, retractable under-carriage and enclosed cockpit, the first prototype Spitfire took off from Eastleigh on 5 March, 1936, in the hands of Vickers chief test pilot, J. 'Mutt' Summers.

Supermarine's first experience of the Schneider Trophy contests was in 1919, when they entered a Sea Lion I single-engine pusher flying-boat. However, it was damaged by striking a floating obstruction at take-off. Italy won the race in 1920 and 1921 and had only to win it once more to retain the Trophy. The Italians and French, but not the British, were helped in their Schneider Trophy efforts by Government financial assistance. However, Supermarine, rather than let Italy win the Trophy outright, financed a British entry themselves in 1922. Based on the six-year-old N.1B Baby hull, a high-speed pusher flying-boat was designed by Mitchell. This Sea Lion II, flown by Supermarine test pilot H. C. Biard, beat the Italian entry with an average speed of 145·7 mph. Biard received a tumultuous welcome when he arrived back in England.

The same aeroplane with clipped wingtips and other modifications was beaten in the 1923 contest at Cowes by the American Curtiss CR-3 twin-float seaplane flown by a US Navy pilot at 177·4 mph. The same year, 1923, saw the birth of the Sea Eagle flying-boat specifically designed for airline passenger carrying, with a six-passenger cabin. It was powered by a 360 hp Rolls-Royce Eagle IX driving a four-blade pusher propeller.

A larger amphibian flying-boat, later known as the Swan, and powered by two Rolls-Royce Eagles, made its debut in 1924. In the same year twelve Scarab amphibians, similar to the Sea Eagle, were built for the Spanish Air Force. Design versatility was demonstrated at the 1924 Lympne Light Aeroplane Meeting by the appearance of a little two-seat sesquiplane, the Sparrow.

Technically, 1925 was a highlight in the fortunes of the Supermarine Works. The Southampton, probably the most beautiful biplane flying-boat that had ever been built, made its appearance. It had a hull of most alluring line, triple fins and rudders, and two Napier Lion engines which gave it a speed of 108 mph at sea level. There was provision for a crew of five in open cockpits.

R. J. Mitchell's drawing office staff in 1923. Top row left to right: Arthur Shirvall, Frank Holroyd, George Kettlewell and Joe Smith. Bottom row: Miss Haines and Miss Attwater (tracers) and Mr Harris who, in the early days of Supermarine aircraft design, put all Mitchell's schemes on paper.

This eventful year also produced the first of the racing seaplanes, the S.4. Years ahead of its time by virtue of a completely unbraced cantilever midwing, and floats carried on cantilever struts, it achieved a speed of 226·75 mph at Calshot on 13 September, 1925, a British seaplane record. It was powered by a 700 hp Napier Lion. After a series of misfortunes the S.4 crashed into the sea near Baltimore on the eve of the 1925 Schneider Trophy race. The cause of the crash was never determined, and the Supermarine pilot, Biard, was lucky to escape with his life.

In July 1926 two Southamptons flew from Plymouth to Egypt and back. The Air Ministry by then had decided to standardize on all-metal construction. The new metal hulls for the Southampton II were lighter than the dry weight of the wooden hulls which, in addition, absorbed 300 lb of moisture after remaining for any time in the water. Perhaps the most memorable Southampton flight was the Far East Cruise in 1927. Four Southamptons flew from Plymouth to Australia, round Australia and then back to Singapore—a total distance of 27,000 miles.

The Schneider Trophy event in 1927 brought great prestige to the British aircraft industry. The Government at last supported the event and ordered seven

Sir Robert McLean (left) chairman of Vickers (Aviation) 1928–37 and then managing director. He played a significant part in the direction of Supermarine and his forthright attitude led to the successful development of the Spitfire and Wellington, and (right) Alan N. Clifton, head of the Supermarine technical office from the early 1920s, and chief designer after Joseph Smith. (*Lefthand photograph Bassano and Vandyke*)

special high-speed seaplanes. Three of these, S.5s, were developed from the S.4, designed and built by Supermarine. In the Schneider Trophy race of that year at Venice, an S.5, powered by an 875 hp geared Napier Lion, came first averaging 281·65 mph and another came second at 273·01 mph. Later in the year an S.5 created a new British speed record of 319·57 mph.

In 1928 the Nanok, a new flying-boat, intended as a torpedo-carrier for the Danish Navy, was built. Basically a Southampton hull but with three Armstrong Siddeley Jaguar engines mounted between the wings, it was never taken over by Denmark. Ultimately, it was converted into a civil machine, given the name Solent and sold to the Hon A. E. Guinness who used it as a luxury aircraft. Southampton flying-boats, in the same year, were sold to Japan, Argentina and Turkey. Late in 1928 the Supermarine Aviation Works Limited was acquired by Vickers (Aviation) Limited, thus linking Supermarine with the varied and extensive Vickers group of companies.

1929 saw the birth of the Rolls-Royce/Supermarine partnership. A new Rolls-Royce R engine developing some 1 900 hp became available and Mitchell was quick to make use of it. These engines were installed in two new racing seaplanes being built for the Schneider Trophy race, the S.6s. Generally, the S.6 followed the proven form of the S.5, but it was larger and the noselines were blended round the different engine shape. At Spithead the 1929 Schneider race resolved itself into an Anglo-Italian duel with an S.6 winning at a speed of 328·63 mph. A few days later, on 12 September, the same aircraft created a new world speed record at 357·7 mph, although not ratified.

Between 1929 and the next Schneider Trophy race in 1931, a luxuriously fitted parasol-wing monoplane flying-boat with three engines was built for the

7

Hon A. E. Guinness and was always referred to as the Air Yacht. Also, an entirely new three-engined sesquiplane flying-boat was built and given the name Southampton MkX.

Supermarine seaplanes had won the Schneider Trophy for Britain on two successive occasions and had only to win it a third time, in 1931, for Britain to retain the Trophy. Inexplicably, the Air Ministry decided not to finance the 1931 attempt. The cost was too great for the Supermarine Company alone and the position looked hopeless. Suddenly, the late Lady Houston offered £100,000 to cover the cost of building and entering a British team.

With only about six months to go to the date of the race, Supermarine designed and built two improved versions of the S.6, known as the S.6B. Rolls-Royce supplied an improved racing engine which actually developed 2,300 hp for a very short guaranteed period. Radiator area for the coolant was provided by double-skin radiators on both surfaces of the wing and on the top of the floats. The Italians proved unable to produce a suitable competitor in time and Great Britain won the Schneider Trophy finally in a 'fly-over' at 340·08 mph. Later the S.6B, fitted with a special sprint engine, created a new world speed record of 407·5 mph.

The Schneider Trophy races were quasi-sporting events but they have been recounted here and later on in some detail because of the background they provided to Supermarine's endeavours in the field of high-speed fighter development—in particular to Mitchell's approach to the original Spitfire design.

Between the final Schneider Trophy success in 1931 and the beginning of the Spitfire story in 1934, there were other experiments and new ventures. In 1931, a standard Southampton was given two Rolls-Royce Kestrel engines in place of the Napier Lions. In 1933, a new private venture single-engined amphibian, the Seagull Mk V, appeared. Capable of being catapulted from naval vessels, it later saw extensive war service under the famous name Walrus.

The Scapa flying-boat emerged as a result of the 1931 Kestrel-engined Southampton and was adopted by the RAF. Towards the end of 1934, a Scapa successor was launched—a much larger twin-engined flying-boat then designated Southampton V but renamed Stranraer.

Then the Spitfire story began. In 1934 Mitchell designed a single-seat fighter, which was to have been known as the Spitfire, to fulfil an unimaginative Air Ministry specification, F.7/30. Powered by a Rolls-Royce steam-cooled Goshawk, it had a wing span of 45 ft 10 in, a cranked wing, and a fixed trousered undercarriage. Its top speed was only 228 mph and it was not surprising that the project was a failure.

Supermarine, however, started work on a new design project as a private venture. Nothing like it had been seen before. At much the same time a brilliantly-conceived Air Ministry specification F.5/34, calling for eight wing-mounted machine-guns, was issued and, also, Rolls-Royce produced their PV.12 liquid-cooled twelve-cylinder vee engine with a promise of 1,000 hp for production engines.

Mitchell set out to design the smallest cleanest aircraft that could be built round the PV.12, the pilot, and the eight machine-guns. The fuselage still bore the unmistakable lines of the Schneider racers but the wing was altogether new, with its thin aerofoil section, small area and elliptical planform.

The Spitfire was the fighter pilot's dream, fast, deadly, but docile. It was to fulfil many roles with wings clipped, extended, or varied slightly in shape, but the classical outline always remained, proof of the fundamental correctness of this first design.

King George VI being informed of the promise of the Spitfire fighter at a prewar demonstration from Eastleigh aerodrome by Supermarine pilots George Pickering (centre) and Jeffrey Quill (left). (*Portsmouth Evening News*)

Work on the prototype continued rapidly and on 5 March, 1936, the first Spitfire flew from Eastleigh. With a maximum speed of 349·5 mph it was then the fastest military aircraft in the world. An initial order for 310 Spitfires was placed by the Air Ministry.

Tragically, R. J. Mitchell, CBE, who had fathered the creation of a weapon that was to do more than any other single type in the coming war, died in 1937 at the age of 42. Design was then in the hands of his successor, Joseph Smith, who led the Supermarine team throughout the extensive, varied and invaluable wartime development of the Spitfire and on into the transonic age which followed.

It was in 1938 that No.19 Squadron, RAF, was the first to be equipped with the Spitfire I, which had a speed of 362 mph. In the same year both the Supermarine Aviation Works (Vickers) Limited and their parent company Vickers (Aviation) Limited of Weybridge were taken over by Vickers-Armstrongs Limited. They gained the advantage of unified command while retaining their individual approaches. In the main, Vickers of Weybridge built bombers, notably the Wellington, while Supermarine specialized in fighters and marine types.

In 1939, while Spitfire production was building up and an aircraft shadow factory was under construction at Castle Bromwich for Lord Nuffield (but eventually taken over by Vickers), a replacement for the Seagull/Walrus, the Sea Otter amphibian, was produced. Because of large Spitfire commitments, production of the Sea Otter and later Walrus IIs was sub-contracted to Saunders-Roe of Cowes in the Isle of Wight.

The first battle successes of the war were obtained by Spitfires against the sporadic hit-and-run raiders of the early period. The Battle of Britain saw the Spitfires Mk I and II at the height of their glory. The two-position propellers of the Mk I were replaced by constant-speed types, and the Merlin II engine by the Merlin XII. These changes still further increased the superiority of the Spitfire over the opposing German fighters. The introduction by the Germans of armour on their aeroplanes was combated with striking success by replacing four of the Spitfire's eight machine-guns with two 20 mm cannon.

9

Hursley Park, Winchester, requisitioned from Sir George Cooper of Strongs Breweries, as the design and administrative headquarters of Vickers-Supermarine after the bombing of the Woolston Works.

Following heavy raids in September 1940 by the Luftwaffe on the parent factory at Woolston, the firm's headquarters and design staff were eventually transferred to a large country house at Hursley Park near Winchester. By 1944, Spitfire production was spread over some 63 dispersals.

Two Mk III Spitfires were built as a private venture, with clipped wingtips, from which many lessons were learned. A Spitfire was also produced specifically for photographic reconnaissance.

During 1941 and 1942 the Mk V (developed from the Mk III) was the mainstay of Fighter Command and took part in numerous massed sweeps over France. It was powered by a 1,300 hp Rolls-Royce Merlin.

In 1942 the Mk VI, the first fighter ever to be fitted with a pressurized cockpit, was hurriedly produced to combat the high-flying German Ju 86Ps. The Mk VII which followed had an improved airframe to take the Merlin 61 engine with two-stage supercharger and extended wingtips to maintain performance at altitude. The Mk VIII was an interim type, virtually an unpressurized Mk VII. Many were used in the Middle East.

One of the most successful Spitfires of the war, the Mk IX, was rapidly developed to combat the German Fw 190. With a new two-stage supercharged Merlin 61 with inter-cooler, it had a top speed of 402 mph and a rate of climb not far short of 5,000 ft/min. Well over 5,000 Mk IXs were built.

The Mk X and XI were photographic reconnaissance types while the Mk XII was developed from the Mk IV, with the new 2,000 hp Griffon III to combat the Fw 190s that in 1942 were diverted to low-level fighter bombers. The Spitfire Mk XIII dealt with specialized low-level photographic reconnaissance. The Mk XIV, an interim type, was used in the invasion of Europe and against the V1

10

flying bombs. Top speed was 442 mph, rate of climb 4,900 ft/min, and ceiling 43,000 ft. Many variants appeared.

There were no Mk XV and XVII Spitfires. The Mk XVI was basically a Mk IX fitted with a Packard-built Merlin 66. The Mk XVIII was a Mk XIV with strengthened wings and increased fuel tankage. The Mk XIX fulfilled the need for a proper photographic reconnaissance machine and was based on a Mk XIV airframe. Only one Mk XX, fitted with the magnificent 1,770 hp Griffon IIB engine, was made, but the experience gained with it contributed greatly to the development of the Mks 21 and 22—the peak of Spitfire wartime development.

The Mks 21, 22 and 24, were the last links of the Spitfire chain. Powered by 2,050 hp Griffon 61, 64, or 85s, with completely redesigned larger, stronger wings, and in some cases, six-blade counter-rotating airscrews, they had a top speed of 450 mph.

So, from the time of the first prototype in 1936 to the Mk 22 in 1945, Spitfire speeds increased from 350 mph to 450 mph, rate of climb from 2,500 to 4,900 ft/min and fire power from 4 to 12 lb per sec. Altogether, 20,351 Spitfires were manufactured, as well as 2,408 Seafires—the naval version of the Spitfire which was developed from the standard Mk VB Spitfire.

When, towards the end of the war, the significance of compressibility shock-wave troubles was becoming apparent, it was realized that, at last, a new fighter was needed to replace the Spitfire. High-speed flight had entered a new phase of evolution. Designated the Spiteful XIV, it had a similar but stronger and deeper fuselage to the Spitfire. The wing, however, was completely new, straight-tapered, and of laminar-flow form, with an inward retracting undercarriage. The power unit was the famous Rolls-Royce Griffon.

The war ended before the Spiteful saw action but by 1947 a top speed of 494 mph was achieved with a Spiteful prototype—the second highest measured level speed ever achieved by a piston-engined aircraft. Naval variants with sting hooks were called Seafangs.

Navy personnel with Supermarine executives on the occasion of the Seafire's entry into full service with the Royal Navy. Admiral (Air) Sir Denis Boyd with, on his right, Jeffrey Quill and Joseph Smith, and on his left Sir James Bird and Ernest Mansbridge (flight test controller).

11

Spitfire F.VIIIs of No.136 Squadron and squadron personnel in the Cocos Islands after the end of the war. No.136 was the 'crack' squadron of South East Asia Command, with 100 victories.

But now, overshadowing every previous major change affecting fighter aircraft design, came the gas-turbine. The first Supermarine jet fighter, the Attacker, soon followed and was first flown in July 1946 by chief test pilot Jeffrey Quill, who had done a remarkable job in flying the various Spitfires from the original prototype in 1936. The Attacker had a speed of 590 mph, was powered by the Rolls-Royce Nene and entered naval squadron service in August 1951. In February 1948, piloted by M. J. Lithgow, the original Attacker broke the international record for the 100 km closed-circuit at 564·881 mph.

Apart from a full postwar programme of high-speed fighter research aircraft, Supermarine found time to sell many Spitfires abroad. A two-seat trainer Spitfire was introduced, and a number of Sea Otters were converted for civil use in various parts of the world.

An interesting amphibian flying-boat of advanced design, a new Seagull, appeared in 1948. Of exceptionally clean design these Griffon-powered monoplanes embodied a variable-incidence wing and high-lift devices resulting in the excellent speed range of 54–260 mph.

On 28 December, 1948, the first flight was made of the Type 510, a high-speed research aircraft featuring sweptback wings and tail surfaces on what was virtually an Attacker fuselage. It created a sensation at the 1949 SBAC Show at Farnborough in the hands of Mike Lithgow, then chief test pilot. Later, it was modified by the addition of an A frame deck-arrester hook and, on 8 November, 1950, became the first fully sweptback jet fighter in the world to land on an aircraft carrier.

A second prototype, the Type 528, was modified to accommodate an afterburner. Subsequently, a nosewheel undercarriage was fitted and, as the Type 535, it appeared at the 1950 SBAC Show with even more speed than the 510. On 1 August, 1951, the first flight of the Type 541, or Swift, took place. A new development of the 535, this aeroplane was powered by the Rolls-Royce Avon in place of the older Nene.

12

By sheer bad luck, on the eve of the 1951 SBAC Display, it had to be force landed. Test pilot Dave Morgan made a masterly belly landing but the damage sustained prevented a comparison with the Hawker 1067, later the Hunter.

The production type Swift appeared at the 1952 SBAC Display and came into squadron service with the Royal Air Force that year.

On 5 July, 1953, in the Mk 4 Swift, M. J. Lithgow broke the London to Paris speed record, averaging 669·3 mph for the 212½ mile journey. Later, on 25 September, 1953, in the same aircraft, he established a new World Air Speed Record of 737·3 mph, at Tripoli in Libya, but for a few days only, being beaten shortly after by an American aeroplane.

In service with the RAF in West Germany, Swift FR.5s distinguished themselves by twice winning the low-level photographic reconnaissance competition against other Allied aircraft. The strength of the Swift airframe was amply proven in the turbulent gust conditions at tree-top heights and this experience was invaluable later on when types such as Scimitar, the TSR 2 and the Tornado came to be evolved. Similarly, the accumulated knowledge gained in the design and operational service of the last solo design of Supermarine, the Scimitar naval fighter, was of value in pioneering new methods of airframe construction such as the extensive use of titanium components and removal of surplus metal in surface skins by chemical etching.

Other promising project designs of advanced technical merit were on the drawing board as defined herein but how the specific Supermarine contribution to aeronautical progress came to an end is really a matter for a more political appraisal. No one can deny the excellence of its technical team throughout its history as recorded in this book. Its achievements spanned half a century. During this epoch aeronautics had come from the simple wooden construction quite adequate for slow-speed flight to the stringent structural demands of the supersonic age—to which Supermarine bequeathed an exceptional and valuable heritage.

Supermarine executives after the Second World War. Left to right: Jeffrey Quill (chief test pilot and then military liaison), Joseph Smith (chief designer after Mitchell), Mike Lithgow (chief test pilot after Quill), and Stanley P. Woodley (superintendent Vickers-Armstrongs Works, South Marston). (*Southern Daily Echo*)

Noel Pemberton Billing with his P.B.1 at the 1914 Olympia Aero Show. The rebuilt P.B.1 is illustrated on page 354.

Pemberton Billing

Perhaps the most eccentric of the early British aviators was the 'incredible' Noel Pemberton Billing, as one writer called him. He was the genius who founded a little aircraft company at Woolston, Southampton, before the First World War, an enterprise that in later decades was to play an important part in aviation history.

Pemberton Billing took an early interest in aeronautics and in 1904 nearly succeeded in killing himself in the classic mode by jumping off the roof of his house in a home-made glider. His first efforts at making a successful flying machine also followed precedent with qualified failure but he was a man with big ideas and in 1909 attempted to establish a large aviation complex and flying ground at South Fambridge in Essex. Although this enterprise attracted other pioneers, including Howard Wright, Weiss and McFie, it failed before a full year of operation probably because of marshy terrain and a transverse ditch across the take-off zone.

Pemberton Billing's marine interests were mainly centred on dealings in yachts which his friend C. G. Grey of *The Aeroplane* thought was a dubious business. With capital accrued from this and other sources and with a financial backer, in 1912 he purchased a site next to Woolston Ferry on the River Itchen at Southampton for a factory to produce fast launches and marine aircraft and work started there in 1913. Billing was so obsessed with the idea of flying over the sea instead of ploughing through it that he coined the word Supermarine for his telegraphic address, as the antonym of submarine for underwater craft. This word was to prefix many famous aircraft names at later dates even when the proprietary name of Vickers was officially prefixed after 1928.

14

Even before the company was officially registered on 27 June, 1914, a striking biplane flying-boat had emerged from the Woolston Works and had been exhibited at the Aero Show at Olympia in London in the previous March. This was labelled the Supermarine P.B.1 and revealed a rakish fish-like hull with flared sponsons or fins, with the bottom planes attached to and built integrally with the upper frames of the hull. These features were the work of Linton Hope, a marine architect of some distinction, who introduced advanced yacht design techniques into flying-boat hull design which stood the test of time and found many applications later. Another novel feature of the P.B.1 was the rotary engine mounted power-egg fashion forward of the wings (the pilot was located aft) driving a three-blade propeller, with an upward thrust line to induce take-off performance. In fact, this characteristic had the reverse effect, that is, poor take-off caused mainly by the very low power delivered by the alleged 50 hp Gnome. Two attempts to fly this 'boat failed, the second after a redesign and rebuild.

Undaunted, Pemberton Billing went ahead with his plans and secured an order from the Admiralty for twelve Short S.38 dual-control school biplanes. From the multiplicity of project designs he was busy hatching, Billing did secure an option from Germany for two P.B.7 flying-boats, intended for the 225 hp Sunbeam engine, on his pet slip-wing theory. In the event these were abandoned on the

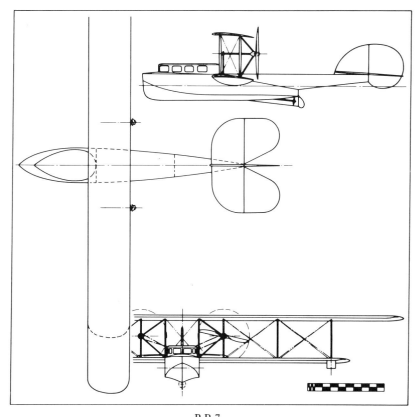

P.B.7

15

outbreak of war in August 1914 and the hulls subsequently used as flying-boat tenders. The slip-wing idea of shedding the wings of a seaplane crippled by engine failure and proceeding on the surface by an auxiliary marine engine and water screw was persevered with in other PB 'paper' designs but none ever reached the hardware stage, though the modified P.B.1 was used for this concept as a test vehicle.

Billing was hardly the man to be satisfied with producing other people's designs such as the S.38 and proceeded to the rapid evolution of a private-venture single-seat scout of simple construction, which has become legendary as the 'Seven Day Bus'. It had now become obvious that Pemberton Billing used the exercise of designing and building a small aeroplane of this type to create a political lever capable of influencing the sensitive emotions of the British public during the confusions of a democracy going to war. In fact, he did parade the aeroplane around his campaign area when standing for Parliament during by-elections, when his plan was to demolish the War Office aviation policy of the day, aided and abetted by C. G. Grey.

Under the stress of the time, exaggerations were probably excusable and so PB must be accorded the licence of his contemporary statements, such as that he did the drawings himself in a day and that the machine was built from scratch within seven days and so on. A great deal of research has been done by Philip Jarrett, an aeronautical writer, into the real truth about the P.B.9, as the aeroplane was first classified, and the facts disclose that Billing had at least a lap start when his rush programme was initiated. E. C. Gordon England has said since that in the effects of the then defunct Radley-England enterprise, which had been making 'water-planes', was a set of wings complete, intended for a small pusher aeroplane designed by himself and which were bought by Pemberton Billing.

This purchase of redundant aircraft parts from Radley-England is confirmed in the balance sheet of Pemberton Billing Limited, dated December 1914. It was a comparatively simple matter to design a straightforward fuselage and tail unit to match the Gordon England wings, particularly as these were of one-piece design. The fuselage in fact merely rested on the bottom wing and was attached by U bolts, the inner struts standing proud of the body, there being no orthodox centre section. A reproduction of the P.B.9 fuselage drawing shows that it was done by C. Vasilesco which seems to dispose of PB's claim that he did the drawings himself

The P.B.9 'Seven Day Bus' with, left to right Hubert Scott-Paine, Victor Mahl and C. Vasilesco.

16

The P.B.9

or that the whole design was done on the factory walls, apart probably from a rough scheme. The structure appears to have been of the braced mortise and tenon type, the sort of thing that could have been produced in any reputable joiner's shop. This was in fact Billing's idea, namely quick reproduction by furniture makers and so on.

In the event, the P.B.9 performed creditably on its first test flight on 12 August, 1914, in the hands of Victor Mahl and it had a reported top speed of 78 mph and a climb of 500 ft/min. No order resulted but the one example served as a naval trainer at Hendon. The internal history of the Woolston Works here becomes misty, for because of uninterested official reaction to his Seven Day Bus, PB went off in a huff to do some service with the naval air arm and left Woolston in the charge of Hubert Scott-Paine, an up-and-coming young man with red hair. How much control the founder actually retained can only be a matter of conjecture but it became clear that Scott-Paine and the Air Department of the Admiralty gradually came more and more into the picture while PB himself became absorbed in his various political crusades. With his election as member of Parliament for East Herts on 10 March, 1916, Pemberton Billing gave up his interests in the company and a new one was formed as the Supermarine Aviation Works Limited.

Before that, however, two original designs had emerged from Woolston which were constructed as distinct from the bewildering series of unorthodox project ideas that poured from the fertile brain of Pemberton Billing. One was a little pusher scout, the P.B.23E*, originally known as the Sparklet and later as the Push-Proj which apparently was short for pusher-projectile. The other was a large ungainly quadruplane designed to attack the Zeppelin airships which had started to bomb Britain in January 1915.

The P.B.23E was a clean and simple design reducing drag to a minimum and was most probably inspired by Harold Bolas of the Air Department of the Admiralty, with whose chief, Murray Sueter, Pemberton Billing was in close

---

*The suffix E undoubtedly stood for Experimental as in the Government designed B.E., F.E., R.E. and S.E. series of military aircraft and other designs of the time.

The original P.B.23E Push-Proj.

contact at that time. In the prototype's flight trials at Hendon, in September 1915, instability was encountered, caused by the excessive rearward centre of gravity. By introducing an 11 degree sweepback to the wings a measure of correction was achieved in the improved redesign as the P.B.25 but pilots' unsatisfactory reports of its handling characteristics persisted. Other modifications included inversely-tapered ailerons and an increase in fin area. An elliptical cross-section fabric-covered nacelle replaced the metal-covered version of the earlier machine, but it proved unpopular with the pilots, who feared its flimsy structure in the event of a nose-over landing.

As far as is known, none of the twenty P.B.25s produced was used operationally although the type was flown at Eastchurch and others were at the Isle of Grain and Killingholme. At a time when fighting scouts with a free field of fire were in short supply against the 'Fokker scourge' on the Western Front, more might have been made of them but no doubt shortage of engines and time for more development precluded any practical effort in that direction, especially in view of the

This view of the P.B.25 shows the sweepback to adjust the centre of gravity.

P.B.25 production without outer wings and engines—then in short supply.

political climate in regard to aircraft procurement for two competitive Services. One opinion expressed at a much later date was that the type was intended by Pemberton Billing as a short-range escort fighter for his anti-airship patrol quadruplane, of which a description follows.

In 1915 the bombardment of Britain by the German airships posed a real threat to national morale, however minimal the total effect was in comparison with similar action in the Second World War. In consequence, anti-Zeppelin measures were introduced and one of these was to encourage the design and construction by Pemberton Billing of a slow-flying aeroplane of offensive capability. This was the P.B.29E, a quadruplane of large wing area and high aspect ratio to promote high flying. The somewhat crude appearance of this aeroplane is shown in the picture

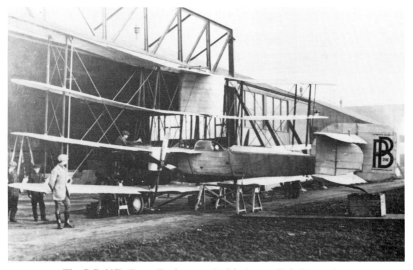

The P.B.29E 'Zeppelin destroyer' with Austro-Daimler engines.

19

P.B.31E NightHawk with Anzani tractor engines. The star louvres in the nose admitted cooling air to the auxiliary power unit.

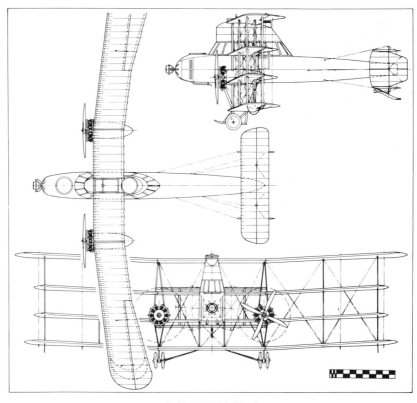

P.B.31E NightHawk

but its improved version, the P.B.31E, presented a more sophisticated outline and concept, with every known aid incorporated to improve its combat efficiency. Although the P.B.31E, better known as the Supermarine NightHawk, could scarcely be described as a weapons system in the modern sense, a fleet of such aircraft might have settled the airship threat further afield than was eventually accomplished by conventional short-range aeroplanes and anti-aircraft weapons.

The NightHawk is interesting because in fully-equipped form it embodied the Davis non-recoil gun firing a $1\frac{1}{2}$ pound shell and a Lewis machine-gun on a Scarff mounting, both on the top wing, with another Lewis, similarly mounted, in the fuselage nose. A gimbal-mounted searchlight was located in the front end of the fuselage and was probably the first instance of such a use. Similarly, the installation of auxiliary power for the searchlight, by means of a 5 hp ABC flat-twin engine and generator, was probably the first example, certainly in British practice. Two NightHawks were ordered by the Admiralty, with serial numbers 1388 and 1389, but only the first was built. Before its completion the company had been reconstituted as the Supermarine Aviation Works Limited in which control passed to Hubert Scott-Paine.

The P.B.29E crashed soon after its first flight, but the P.B.31E had greater success during its tests in the hands of Clifford B. Prodger at Eastchurch. The NightHawk proved to be underpowered with its two 100 hp Anzani radial engines but reached 75 mph top speed with a landing speed of only 35 mph, the latter an essential characteristic at that time for night operation.

Pemberton Billing continued to evolve unorthodox concepts for aircraft and aids to flying, such as his idea for a mechanical height indicator for the landing approach, later revived at the RAE, Farnborough. A type list of the Pemberton Billing projects is given in the appendices as far as they properly come in the purview of Supermarine history. The story of his colourful career outside those interests is not within the scope of this study although he certainly achieved notoriety in political and juridical matters.

P.B.9—One 50 hp Gnome. Single seat.
　　Span 26 ft (7·9 m); length 20 ft (5·09 m); height 8 ft 3 in (2·51 m); wing area 205 sq ft (19·04 sq m).
　　Empty weight 560 lb (254 kg); loaded weight 750 lb (340 kg).
　　Maximum speed 78 mph (125·5 km/h); climb 540 ft/min (164 m/min); duration 3 hr.

P.B.23E—One 80 hp Le Rhône. Maximum speed 90 mph.

P.B.25—One 100 hp Gnome Monosoupape or 110 hp Clerget. Single seat.
　　Span 33 ft (10·05 m); length 24 ft 1 in (7·34 m); height 10 ft 5 in (3·17 m); wing area 277 sq ft (25·73 sq m).
　　Empty weight 1,080 lb (489 kg); loaded weight 1,576 lb (761 kg).
　　Maximum speed 99 mph (159·2 km/h) at sea level, 83·5 mph (134·3 km/h) at 10,000 ft (3,048 m); stalling speed 40 mph (64·4 km/h); climb to 6,000 ft (1,828 m) 11 min, to 10,000 ft (3,048 m) 21 min; duration 3 hr.
　　Armament. One 0·303-in Lewis machine-gun in front of nacelle.

P.B.29E—Two 90 hp Austro-Daimler.

P.B.31E—Two 100 hp Anzani. Two pilots, supernumeraries optional.
　　Span 60 ft (18·28 m); length 37 ft (11·27 m); height 17 ft 8½ in (5·39 m); wing area 962 sq ft (89·37 sq m).
　　Empty weight 3,677 lb (1,667 kg); loaded weight 6,146 lb (2,787 kg).
　　Maximum speed 75 mph (120·7 km/h); landing speed 38 mph (61·1 km/h); normal duration 9 hr; maximum duration 18 hr.
　　Armament. One 1½ pdr cannon and 20 rounds of ammunition and two Lewis guns.

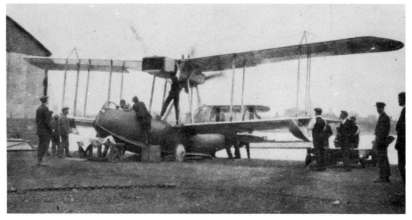

The prototype A.D. Boat with 150 hp Sunbeam engine.

The A.D. Designs

After the departure of Pemberton Billing for pastures new, which seems a novel way of describing the House of Commons, the Supermarine Works concentrated on working directly for the Admiralty, under Hubert Scott-Paine as managing director. The new company had been registered as the Supermarine Aviation Works Limited on 20 September, 1916. Meanwhile its contract for fifteen Short Type 184 floatplanes was running down and the twenty P.B.25s and the Night-Hawk were being completed. New work of a progressive nature was required and this was forthcoming from Air Department original designs, as well as Admiralty contracts for rebuilding aircraft returned from war service for repair.

These A.D. concepts had managed to escape the Government embargo placed on original design by the Royal Aircraft Factory. This curious anomaly of history has never been explained. The principle of what is sauce for the goose is sauce for the gander was overlooked and the matter was probably an instance of lack of co-ordination in the whole war effort at the time, until a new Prime Minister started to take things in hand as in the Second World War. In any event, the Admiralty had been far more successful in their procurement policy than the War Office. The Handley Page heavy bomber, the Rolls-Royce Eagle engine and the range of Sopwith combat aircraft were originally naval requirements, a telling point not missed by Pemberton Billing and C. G. Grey in their attacks on the official aviation policy.

So the Admiralty continued to foster its small but highly sophisticated Air Department which undoubtedly made a great impact on aircraft design, particularly in regard to structures. The mandatory manual Av.P. 970, entitled *Design Requirements for Service Aircraft*, owes its origin to the little booklet *Handbook of Strength Calculations* by Sutton Pippard and Laurence Pritchard on the basics first evaluated by Harris Booth and Harold Bolas and known as HB[2], which were mathematically clarified by Arthur Berry into the famous Berry Functions. All these notable people were on the Air Department staff at the time of this break-through in airframe stressing.

The concepts of the Air Department which were contracted to Supermarine consisted of the types known as the A.D.Boat, already in hand by Pemberton Billing Limited, the A.D.Navyplane and the N.1B Baby, the first British single-seat fighter flying-boat. After a shaky start to its career caused by hydrodynamic instability, the A.D.Boat was produced in small numbers, some of which were converted into civil passenger aircraft after the war. The Navyplane remained the sole example built at Woolston, largely because of engine supply shortages at the time, but the one Baby completed led to the Supermarine Schneider flying-boats.

An A.D. Boat with Hispano-Suiza engine.

The two A.D.Boat prototypes, 1412 and 1413, were already being flight tested at the time the new company was finally constituted. According to J. Lankester Parker, who flew the type at an early stage, it suffered from the same malaise that plagued other seaplane designs at the time, particularly those in the flying-boat class, its chronic porpoising on take-off. In addition, the A.D.Boat had marked yaw defects, so much so that at take-off the machine had to be pointed downwind and, as planing speed rose, edged crabwise round into the wind. One of the principal causes of directional instability was thought to be the small area of the fin and rudder which characterized the Booth/Bolas designs. Strangely enough, the Supermarine Schneider racing floatplanes of a later date had a similar take-off problem for an entirely different reason.

The overall designer of the A.D.Boat was Harris Booth, while Harold Bolas, Clifford Tinson and Harold Yandall were seconded from the Admiralty to Woolston Works to draft the details. Linton Hope was responsible for the lines and structure of the hull, the main attribute of which was its flexibility, enabling it to withstand the shocks and bumps of rough seas. On the circular hooped frames was a skin formed on a mould from double diagonal mahogany planking laid crosswise, with fabric sandwiched between the layers. The curved ribs of $\frac{1}{4}$ in rock elm were closely spaced as were the stiffened stringers.

23

This type of wooden construction stood the test of time until metal hulls were introduced by which time the hydrodynamic problems of planing bottoms had been largely solved. Those of the A.D.Boat were indicative of the search for knowledge on the subject, on which the experts could not agree, including G. S. Baker, who operated the Walter Froude model water-testing tank at the National Physical Laboratory. He had visited all the marine aircraft bases and was said to be the authority on matters like lift-off, hump speeds, angle of attack, shape and location of steps, and so on. The whole picture can be envisaged by a study of Linton Hope's own Paper on *Notes on Flying Boat Hulls* which appeared in the *Aeronautical Journal* of the Royal Aeronautical Society for August 1920. The controversies of the time were clearly brought out in the discussion which followed the presentation of the Paper.

So after juggling with the location of the main step and changing the rear step from a streamline shaped tail to square cut, the A.D.Boat finally became a practical proposition for sea patrol duties although its actual use seems limited. The first production machine, N1520, passed acceptance trials at the Isle of Grain on 5 September, 1917. As with other new aircraft types at the time, the A.D.Boat suffered the usual set-backs caused by the erratic supply of satisfactory engines. It was designed for the Sunbeam Nubian, which failed to reach requirements.

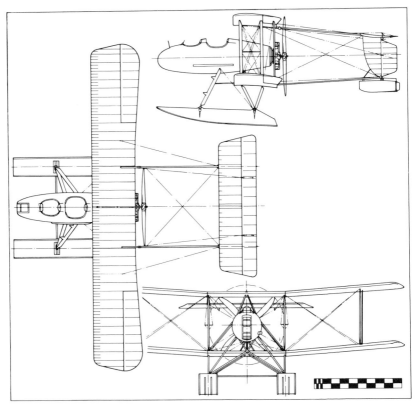

A.D.1 Navyplane

24

Hubert Scott-Paine and an Admiralty overseer with the Supermarine Navyplane.

Hispano-Suizas were fitted, both direct-drive and geared, the latter having trouble with its gearing as it did in the S.E.5a. Later on, the Wolseley Python and Viper and the Sunbeam Arab were fitted experimentally, apparently with better results but only when the useful employment of the type was past. Production aircraft totalled 27 but most went into store. N1712 and N1719 were sent to Isle of Grain naval air station for experimental use, the latter being fitted with hydro-vanes and flown in this form by Harry Busteed and Bentley Dacre. After the war N1529 was the first A.D.Boat to be converted by Supermarine as a civil passenger-carrying aircraft, and the further use of the new type, known as the Channel, is dealt with later.

The A.D.Navyplane was another initial Admiralty design by Harold Bolas given to Supermarine to complete detail design and construction. The machine, a single-engined pusher floatplane, was completed in eight weeks from the receipt of the master drawings, which led Murray Sueter, who in effect was the head of the Air Department, to send Supermarine a letter of commendation. The Navy-plane was intended for reconnaissance and bombing duties but in fact never reached the production stage, bedevilled again by the failure of its intended engine, the American Smith static radial (brought to Britain in January 1915 by John W. Smith). The high hopes for the Smith engine were not realized, as happened at a later date with the ABC Dragonfly. Air-cooled radials proved difficult to design despite their advantages in the saving of space and weight.

The Navyplane was a two-bay biplane with a high tailplane, to avoid the wash, and twin fins and rudders, and tail floats which were fitted with water rudders, all carried on four outriggers. It had a lightweight crew nacelle with a Lewis gun on a special mounting and carried W/T radio. A glazed nose which extended under-neath to the pilot's seat provided a good view forward and below, an essential feature for marine reconnaissance. The floats were of the pontoon type which, although much heavier than the sophisticated type designed by Linton Hope on his A.D.Boat principles, were more satisfactory in their operational use, the Linton Hope floats initially being hydrodynamically unstable.

25

Two prototypes, 9095 and 9096, were ordered but only 9095 was built and tested with the Smith engine in August 1916, by Commander John Seddon. It was tested again in May 1917, with the Bentley-designed A.R.1 rotary engine but performance is reported to have been poor. Later, an improved version of the Navyplane was schemed by Supermarine as the Submarine Patrol Seaplane as a possible replacement for the Short 184, which in fact was performing that duty quite adequately. The specification called for a pusher biplane with a 200 hp Sunbeam engine and a crew of two. It was to be capable of carrying four 100 lb bombs, type 52A wireless, signal gear, marker buoy and carrier pigeons. Performance specified was maximum speed 60 kt, minimum speed 35 kt and climb to 6,500 ft in less than 30 minutes. Contracts for six were placed with Shorts (N20—21), Phoenix (N22—23) and Supermarine (N24—25), the Supermarine contract being cancelled on 27 February, 1917, owing to pressure of other work on the N.1B Baby flying-boat and improvements on the A.D.Boat, but Phoenix and Shorts were asked to prepare detailed drawings although no actual aircraft materialized. Supermarine had prepared some working drawings but construction had hardly begun before cancellation.

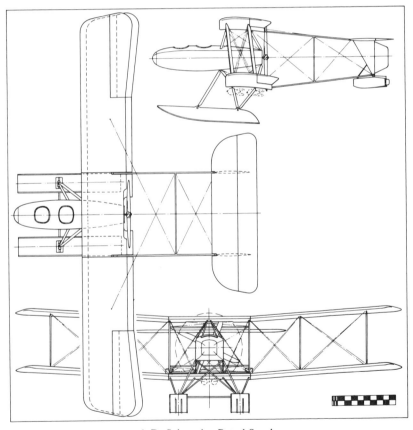

A.D. Submarine Patrol Seaplane

Supermarine Baby single-seat flying-boat. (*Imperial War Museum*)

Much activity was evident in naval circles to explore the possibilities of the single-seat fighter specially designed for naval requirements. Eastchurch and the Isle of Grain naval air stations had continued their evolution of new types in this field, mainly as improvements to the Sopwith Baby of Fairey or Parnall vintage. In this class specification N.1B was issued by the Air Department for a single-seat seaplane or flying-boat fighter, with a speed of 95 kt at 10,000 ft and a ceiling of at

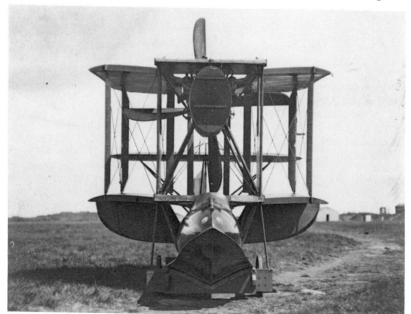

The Baby with wings folded for shipboard stowage. (*Imperial War Museum*)

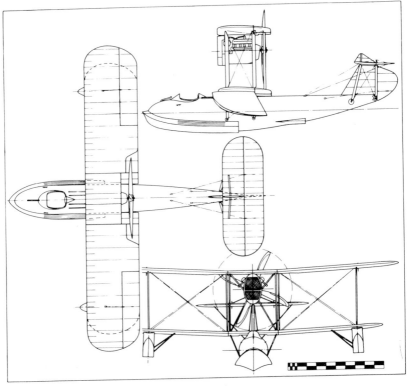

N.1B Baby

least 20,000 ft, no mean order in those days of dubious engine reliability. Tenders were submitted by Supermarine, Blackburn and Norman Thompson, and were all for flying-boat designs.

The Supermarine N.1B Baby was designed by F. J. Hargreaves on lines no doubt inspired by Bolas and also no doubt assisted by R. J. Mitchell, the promising young draughtsman who had participated in the detail design of the NightHawk and the Navyplane. It was a single-bay biplane with a pusher propeller driven by the geared Hispano engine. Other features were its Linton Hope hull, designed on the same principles as the A.D.Boat construction, and an inverted camber tailplane mounted on top of the single fin and small rudder with a small extra fin on top. Ailerons were first fitted to the upper wings only but later were embodied also in the lower wings. With the Hispano engine the N.1B Baby achieved 117 mph at sea level, and in August 1918, with a Sunbeam Arab engine, reached 111·5 mph at 10,000 ft.

Only one Baby was completed, N59, but its successors, the Sea King and the racing Sea Lions, achieved quite a measure of fame as related later. The second Baby, N60, would have differed from N59 in various aspects because a revised set of drawings had been raised before it was cancelled. The engine would have been the 200 hp Sunbeam Arab as tried on N59, but the third aircraft, N61, was not proceeded with although hull construction may have been started.

A.D.Boat—One 200 hp Hispano-Suiza. Pilot and observer.

Span 50 ft 4 in (15·34 m); span folded 14 ft (4·26 m); length 30 ft 7 in (9·32 m); length folded 42 ft 3 in (12·87 m); height 13 ft 1 in (3·98 m); wing area 455 sq ft (42·27 sq m).

Empty weight 2,508 lb (1,137 kg); loaded weight 3,567 lb (1,618 kg).

Maximum speed 100 mph (160·9 km/h); alighting speed 46 mph (74 km/h); duration 4½ hr.

Armament. One 0·303-in Lewis machine-gun in bow cockpit.

A.D.Navyplane—One A.R.1 rotary. Pilot and observer.

Span 36 ft (10·97 m); length 27 ft 9 in (8·45 m); height 12 ft 9 in (3·88 m); wing area 360 sq ft (33·44 sq m).

Empty weight 2,100 lb (952 kg); loaded weight 3,102 lb (1,407 kg).

Maximum speed 75 mph (120·7 km/h); alighting speed 36 mph (58 km/h); duration 6 hr.

Armament. One Lewis machine-gun and a torpedo.

N.1B Baby—One 200 hp Hispano-Suiza. Single seat.

Span 30 ft 6 in (9·29 m); length 26 ft 4 in (8·02 m); height 10 ft 7 in (3·22 m); wing area 309 sq ft (28·7 sq m).

Empty weight 1,699 lb (770 kg); loaded weight 2,326 lb (1,055 kg).

Maximum speed 116 mph (186·6 km/h); alighting speed 57 mph (91·7 km/h); duration 3 hr.

Figures as given in the 1919 Supermarine brochure.

The Channels

Early in 1919 Supermarine were contemplating converting some of the surplus A.D.Boats into civil passenger-carrying aircraft capable in a small way of starting an air service over short-haul sea routes. As early as May of that year they were in fact preparing ten A.D.Boats, purchased from the Admiralty, in the hope of completing arrangements for flying trips at Whitsun from Southampton to Ryde, Sandown, Shanklin and Ventnor, all seaside resorts in the Isle of Wight. The first works order for these conversions was raised in February 1919 and the first drawing for the modifications was issued on 25 February for the addition of a water rudder and another, dated 2 April, was for a new mounting for the 160 hp Beardmore, an engine in good supply. The first use of the name Channel in the Supermarine drawings register was on 14 February, 1920, when all drawings were changed from the Admiralty nomenclature to new schedules for the four-seat Channel type.

Of the ten aircraft being converted, five were to be used for the actual service with the other five in reserve for use alternately, thus giving ample opportunity for inspection and overhaul. A shortage of pilots was one of the factors telling against a regular service so the following officers were recruited from the former Royal Naval Air Service—J. Bird, B. D. Hobbs, F. J. Bailey, P. Brend, J. E. A. Hoare, H. G. Horsey and H. C. Biard. Some of these such as Sqn Cdr* James Bird and Sqn Cdr Hobbs together with Biard and Bailey figure quite prominently in subsequent Supermarine history.

*According to C. G. Grey in his unpublished manuscript 'Bats in my Belfry' James Bird and Noel Pemberton Billing were the only former officers of the RNAS to retain their rank of Squadron Commander in the postwar era, apparently by official dispensation.

The Channels were converted from the A.D.Boats by having an extra cockpit inserted just forward of the mainplanes and the 200 hp Hispano-Suiza engine replaced by the 160 hp Beardmore. With this additional cockpit the flying-boat could be used as a three-seat school machine or with the cockpits slightly modified as a four-seat passenger machine. The latter version was used for most of the passenger trips and a small water rudder was added to all the aircraft to improve the water-handling characteristics.

The ten that were re-purchased from the Admiralty and converted to civil use were registered as under:

Registration	RNAS No.	C of A issued	Constructor's No.
G-EAED	N1529	23/7/19	—
G-EAEE	N1710	23/7/19	—
G-EAEF	N2452	7/8/19	—
G-EAEG	N2451	28/5/20	975
G-EAEH	N1716	5/6/20	974
G-EAEI	N1715	28/5/20	973
G-EAEJ	N1714	14/8/19	972
G-EAEK	N1711	23/7/19	971
G-EAEL	N1528	28/5/20	970
G-EAEM	N1526	17/7/20	969

All had previously gone into store when completed and had no active service to record.

As soon as the certificate of airworthiness was issued Supermarine began using the Channels for joy flights and also started a passenger service from Southampton to Bournemouth from 23 July. On 30 July, a rare event for elderly people at that time, a woman of 72 and a man of 75 were taken on a flight, and during that same week several trips were made from Southampton to Cowes with passengers who had missed the ferry. Supermarine also applied for a service to the north east of France with stops at Cherbourg, Le Havre and St Malo. It is apparent from the above list that only three aircraft were available at this time, G-EAED, 'EE and 'EK, though these civil registrations were not worn but the Service serials retained. Embarkation took place at the pier at Bournemouth, and one of the pilots was Sqn Cdr B. D. Hobbs DSO, DSC, who had recently been recruited.

During the Cowes Regatta, one of the Channels was offering flights every day, and members of the Royal and other Yacht Clubs took advantage of this facility. Many members were enthusiastic and followed the yacht racing from the air. Col Wingfield chartered one on the evening of 7 August to fly him to Portsmouth and circle over HMS *Renown* as she sailed, carrying HRH the Prince of Wales on his journey to Canada.

On 16 August the flying-boat service to the Isle of Wight was inaugurated, with the two Channels taxi-ing from their Woolston base to the Royal Pier at Southampton, the service terminal. These aircraft were kept very busy, on occasion carrying prominent officials on flights over Southampton Water, among them the Mayor and Mayoress of Southampton, the Mayor of Winchester, the Sheriff and the Chief Constable of Hampshire, and some of the Councillors, including the only other lady, Mrs Welsh. Such civic patronage was a novelty then.

On 12 August the motor launch service run by Spencer Bros from Ventnor was immobilized through a shortage of petrol so one of the Channels flew over a sufficient supply of Shell motor spirit to enable service to be resumed. This was probably the first instance when fuel was delivered by air for another public service. On 27 August it was announced that the Channels had carried passengers from Southampton to Bournemouth and the Isle of Wight and Southsea and also that a service would soon be started from Southampton to Le Havre and the Channel Islands.

One of the Channels was used by Supermarine's managing director, Hubert Scott-Paine, during the 1919 Schneider Seaplane Contest at Bournemouth, to take him from the works and was also used on joy flights before the start of the contest on 10 September.

Venezuelan Channel on Woolston slipway.

The Supermarine flying-boat service operated from Bournemouth to the Isle of Wight only when weather permitted and during the first two weeks of September there were hardly any flights because of the rough seas and bad weather. On 12 September, one machine was flying Southampton–Bournemouth when the pilot spotted a mine about four miles off Hurst Castle and then half a mile further on saw a Government tug from Yarmouth. The pilot circled the tug and then flew low down pointing out to the captain the position of the mine. The captain of the tug altered course and put out a boat to the mine but neither pilot nor passengers of the Channel learned what happened because they had to continue to Bournemouth. For the rest of September, flights were made as and when the weather permitted, to Bournemouth, Southsea and the Isle of Wight, and on flights over and round warships lying at anchor in Bournemouth Bay.

The British railway strike of 1919 began on 27 September and this gave the Channels the opportunity of flying thousands of copies of the *Southern Daily Echo* from Southampton to Bournemouth. The proprietors of the *Echo* had the foresight to hire a Channel for this service which was undertaken quickly and smoothly and showed the possibilities of the flying-boat for commercial use. The newspapers were received by Supermarine at 6 pm and flown by Cdr Hobbs, arriving at Bournemouth at 6.43 pm and then taken ashore in several rowing boats.

It was Scott-Paine's idea to institute an air service over the English Channel to take over temporarily from the steam-packets which had ceased operations in sympathy with the railwaymen's strike. For this he chose Capt H. C. Biard to be responsible for the daily service irrespective of the state of the weather. This

31

flying-boat service from Woolston to Le Havre was inaugurated on 28 September when two machines left shortly after 5 pm each carrying a couple of passengers with luggage. On the way over they became separated in a storm but arrived at Le Havre safely. On the return journey one flew straight back to Woolston and the second alighted at Bembridge, Isle of Wight, to refuel and reached Woolston a little late but safe. From France, Biard had taken off safely and, expecting Hobbs up soon, flew around waiting for him. Hobbs, however, had trouble in getting airborne and at least half an hour was spent while he made some adjustments and could eventually take off. At last they set off together for England with Hobbs in the lead. Then Biard's engine suddenly spluttered and stopped for lack of fuel and he only just managed to glide to Bembridge and alight on the water near the town. It took him some time to get the necessary petrol because he was told 'it wasn't the season' but he eventually obtained some and managed to take off safely. Hobbs had not noticed Biard in difficulty but only missed him when he alighted at Woolston. An air search was begun for Biard so when he eventually arrived people were both exasperated and relieved.

On the following day two Channels again flew to Le Havre and this time they carried mail in addition to passengers. One of the letters was a message of greeting from the Mayor of Southampton to the Mayor of Le Havre, another from the President of the Southampton Chamber of Commerce and a third from the French Consul. The following day another Channel flew to Le Havre with two passengers and luggage. It was during this flight that the 'airline' had a very severe test. A howling gale developed, with sleet and hail getting worse as the time for departure approached. However, two passengers arrived for the cross-Channel service, one a naval officer and the other a Belgian millionaire financier, Monsieur Lowenstein, who seemed fed up with the English weather. Scott-Paine put a lifebelt round each of them before the start and the Belgian looked at it somewhat dubiously and queried its safety. Just before take-off Scott-Paine ran out and gave Lowenstein a pocket-flask of rum in case he felt cold on the flight. Biard took off safely into the teeth of the gale with the hail coming at them like machine-gun bullets, icicles grew on their gloves and coats and within half an hour the cold became intense. Biard could no longer feel his hands or feet at all and only moved the controls by instinct. The Belgian must have felt the cold too because he took out the flask of rum and took a good long drink, he then tried to pass it over his shoulder to the pilot but the flask tilted and the contents blew back straight into Biard's eyes. Biard said afterwards; 'It was more than a nuisance, one faulty touch on the controls would have ended our story, and worse still, all I got of that rum was the smell and it did smell so good!'

The rum however quietened the Belgian but after a time he must have found the hail really troublesome because he produced his gold-handled umbrella and tried with frozen hands to put it up, possibly in front of his face to keep the hail off, but Biard knew that it would blow back into the propeller so he grabbed the empty rum bottle and hit the Belgian smartly over the head. The Belgian and his umbrella disappeared into the bottom of the cockpit and thus was not troubled with the hail any more. The gale was so severe, at times the wind reached 100 mph, that it took Biard over five hours to reach Le Havre. The Belgian turned out to be a true sportsman, bearing Biard no malice for the assault and taking him to an hotel and treating him to the drink that he had missed during the flight. The price for that trip was £12.10s each, the standard rate. Whether or not they felt they had had their money's worth, certainly those two passengers would never forget it. During the 110 mile journey the airspeed read 55 kt but the 'ground'

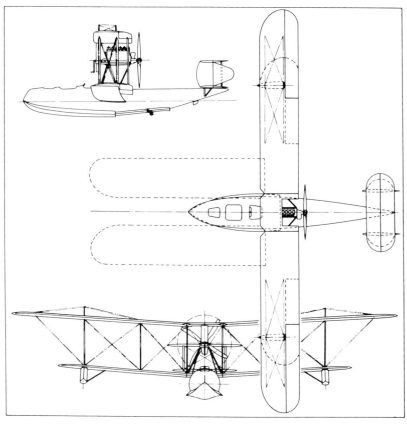

Channel I

speed was only 20 kt, and the steamer normally could cover the same distance in six hours, or about an hour more than the flying-boat that day.

Towards the end of the railwaymen's strike on 5 October, Biard and another Supermarine pilot, Capt F. J. Bailey, having no passengers to bring back from France, decided to make a race of it on the assumption that they had passengers and were behind schedule. They both took off together and flew neck and neck all the way until they sighted the Isle of Wight, when Biard turned off the course they had been following to head for Southampton. At this point Biard lost sight of the other machine but did not ease up until he was over Southampton Water when there was no sign of the other Channel at all. He alighted to pass the word and then took off to look for the wreckage. There on the far side of the Isle of Wight was the mass of floating wreckage which was the Channel G-EAEE. Biard flew slowly round and round looking for a body but could only see the aircraft, the wings broken, the hull smashed in two, and some canvas and twisted metal. A salvage ship arrived and slowly took the wreckage aboard, but no body. Biard turned his machine towards home when one more aircraft flew up, adding to the number already there to assist in the search for the body. It was a two-seater and in the observer's seat, none the worse for the accident except for scratches, was the 'body' itself. A fishing boat had seen Capt Bailey crash and had taken him to Southampton where he somehow managed to find someone to fly him back to the wreck to show the searchers that he was still very much alive.

When the strike of 1919 ended on 5 October, the service to France was discontinued, and it must be said here that it had never failed to operate. Unfortunately, no official encouragement was given to continue the service and thus the company decided to cease operations.

On 17 April, 1920, General Frederick Sykes, Controller-General of Civil Aviation, and Colonel Beatty paid an official visit to the Supermarine Works. Sykes was taken for a flight in one of the four-seat Channels over the Isle of Wight, Spithead, and the Solent, flown by Biard who alighted on the River Itchen amongst the normal shipping. Then followed demonstrations of the manoeuvre-ability of the Channel on the water, including taxi-ing at speeds of 20 to 40 kt, with turns among the river traffic. Another test was stalling from very low height on to the surface. The machine used for this demonstration was the school version with dual control (conversion from the passenger type took one hour) and it had been used daily for training pilots of the Royal Norwegian Naval Air Service.

Norway was interested in acquiring seaplanes both for naval use and for commercial air transport. A seaplane would obviously be much more suitable than a landplane at that time, considering the mountainous terrain of Norway with its deep inlets from the sea. In consequence a trial air route was planned along the west coast of Norway, to be opened in 1920 with Supermarine flying-boats. To fund their purchase the Norwegian public were invited to subscribe for shares in the Norwegian company.

Three Channels were bought in May 1920, G-EAEH, G-EAEI and G-EAEL. They received the Norwegian registrations N9, N10 and N11 in the name of the company, Det Norske Luftfartrederi A/S of Christiania (now Oslo). The trial service started on 9 August with the first two, and when N11 arrived on 16 August the route Bergen–Haugesund–Stavanger was officially inaugurated, the airline having received a Government contract for the carriage of mail between Bergen and Stavanger.

A Channel I moored at Bergen.

Originally it was thought that the three Channels would suffice for the service, keeping one in the air at any one time and one in reserve and one in maintenance, but the linking-up with the Bergen–Christiania railway needed two aircraft in the air at the same time, flying in opposite directions. As no more Channels were available at short notice, three German Friedrichshafen floatplanes were acquired, one on hire. In the inevitable comparison between them, the only case where the Channel was less efficient was that its engine, the 160 hp Beardmore, was less powerful than the 220 hp Benz of the German aircraft. Consequently, more overhauling was needed as the Beardmores had to be run full out in unfavourable weather because of lack of reserve power.

On all other counts such as stability and passenger comfort and the ability to operate in very bad weather, when the Friedrichshafens were unable to stay in the air, the Channels were judged superior. Despite considerable difficulties in operating regular air services during exceptionally bad weather, 93·5 per cent regularity up to 21 October was maintained and at the end of the season in December 1920, the figure achieved was 94·4 per cent. Of 212 flights scheduled 200 were completed, five being prevented by bad weather and seven by lack of aircraft. The number of scheduled deliveries of mail accepted by the postal authorities was 196.

The airline ceased operations in December 1920 from lack of public support, with the total number of passengers carried only 64, a load factor of 0·32 per flight. The failure was not caused by faulty organization or technical difficulties and had the company continued in the following summer season, given better weather it might have succeeded. Another factor in the airline's demise was the fact that the postal authorities put such a high surcharge on the air mail letters that a telegram was only slightly dearer. The amount of mail carried consequently was not as great as had been hoped. On the operating side, as far as the Channels were concerned, there was only one mishap when one of the engine struts on N11 broke, tilting the engine backwards and badly damaging the hull, causing a forced alighting on the sea. The passengers were taken off by boat but there is no record that the machine was repaired later.

On 20 June, 1919, the Norwegian Government issued, through its London representatives, a detailed specification inviting tenders for eight naval seaplanes with spares. Floats were called for, but in revised terms issued a month later a floatplane or flying-boat would be accepted, to be powered by the Rolls-Royce Eagle VIII engine. Vickers submitted their Viking amphibian first with the Wolseley Viper and then with the Rolls-Royce Falcon which was some 100 hp less powerful than the Eagle. Somewhat surprisingly, the Supermarine tender for Channels was accepted and four were ordered embodying the even lower-powered Beardmore engine of 160 hp. The fact that Channels were already operating reasonably successfully and the Viking was a new design from a landplane design team* may have influenced the decision.

The first two naval Channels for Norway went into service in May 1920, and the last was delivered in July. Their serial numbers were F-38, F-40, F-42 and F-44. Norwegian naval pilots had been through a six weeks familiarization course in March and April 1920 and so were able to take the aircraft over themselves for type approval. Little is known of the operational history of the aircraft. One of the first Channels delivered was a dual-control three-seater, used for training at the

---

*But R. K. Pierson, Vickers' chief designer, had sought the marine experience of S. E. Saunders and Co of Cowes, then a Vickers' subsidiary, in the Viking hull design.

Horten naval seaplane base. Another was used for a postal service between Christiania and Kristiansand from July 1920. Three were written off by crashes from unknown causes at various times, F-38 on 12 July, 1920, F-42 on 13 June, 1921, and F-44 on 15 May, 1923, while F-40 lasted until 1 March, 1928, when it was withdrawn from service. A replacement for F-38 was N10, acquired from the civil airline company and given the same number F-38 and rebuilt with a Siddeley Puma engine of 240 hp. N9 was probably acquired as well for cannabilizing for spares.

Before their demise, F-40 and F-44 were re-engined with Pumas which gave more power than the Beardmores. The Siddeley Puma installation had been studied by Supermarine early in 1920 to promote better performance especially for take off, and drawings had been raised in October 1920. Kits for conversion were supplied by Supermarine. The designation Channel Mark II was allotted later for the Puma version with additional modifications.

Three of the original batch of ten Channels were despatched to Bermuda in 1920, G-EAEG and G-EAEJ in April and the third one, G-EAEF, in November. These joined the aircraft of a company formed to promote flying in the Bermudas,

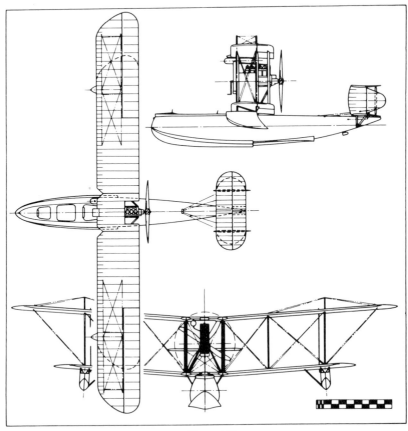

Channel II

An Orinoco Channel, showing camera access port for air survey.

Bermuda and West Atlantic Aviation Company combining the interests of A. V. Roe, Supermarine Aviation Works, and Beardmore Aero Engines. In *Flight* of 18 March, 1920, it was reported that Furness, Withy and Co of Bermuda were also associated with the enterprise but exactly how is not known, though the company was formed with the issue of 3,000 ordinary shares of £1 (sterling) each. In charge of the flying operations were Maj H. H. Kitchener and Maj H. Hemming, AFC, and the aircraft were used for pleasure or charter flights during the winter season of 1920. One letter in particular to Charles Pattison, the Supermarine representative, testified to the pleasure derived by passengers experiencing their first flights, and to the security felt when airborne in the Channel.

How successful the Channels were in establishing an inter-islands air service does not appear to be on record but they did pioneer the intensive area network of today. A service was planned from the Bahamas to Florida but was not followed up as the Channels were already suffering from lack of spares and one, G-EAEG, was sent to Trinidad in March 1921.

Two Channel Mark IIs with the Puma engine were sent to Trinidad for use in the British controlled oilfields and were used to survey the Orinoco delta in Venezuela and the river's 436 tributaries. The work was done by Bermuda and West Atlantic Aviation on behalf of the oil company and consisted of photographic air surveys to discover oil-bearing lands disclosed by partial destruction of the vegetation and to find suitable forest tracks and waterways leading to them. This original British air survey met with little initial success as far as can be ascertained but no doubt led to further air exploration in due course.*

These two Channel IIs (one was G-EAWC, the other's registration is not known) had some modifications, different wingtip float attachments and hull lines, with the bows adapted to take a special camera port-hole. The camera of the L.B. type was arranged to be lowered into position, and raised and the port-hole quickly closed by simple movements. The photographic plate racks were insulated against vibration and the photographers' compartment was separated from the main hull by a water-tight bulkhead in case the port-hole closing mechanism failed. The photographer was W. D. Wise and he had three assistants, not necessarily all airborne at one time. The camera and equipment cost about £1,300. The aircraft were flown at Woolston in March 1921, stripped down and shipped to Trinidad. In command of the expedition was Maj C. Gordon Patrick, DSO, MC, with Supermarine pilots C. E. Ward and F. J. Bailey accompanied by three technical assistants. The first flight was made over Port of Spain, the capital of the island, on 7 May, 1921, by Maj Patrick in the Channel named *Specialist*, after the name of the ship that took the aircraft from England. It seemed appropriate. The appearance of the machine over the town created quite a stir as many of its people had never seen an aeroplane in flight. For half-an-hour the business quarter came to a standstill as the streets became crowded with eager sightseers; tramcars slowed down to give a better view to their passengers and cars pulled up so that their occupants could watch. Even golfers on the town links ceased play to watch. At that time any airborne craft was a novelty, especially a flying-boat.

A few days later the Governor was taken for a flight around the island by Capt Bailey, who took off from Chaguaramas Dock over the assembly of boats, flew round the bay and over the *Specialist* at anchor in the harbour. The Governor was very favourably impressed. The same afternoon the Channel flew Major and Mrs Gordon Patrick on a test flight of one hour, passing over Chacachacars and south towards San Fernando. A height of 7,000 ft was reached over cloud cover, the highest reached during the trials. These details are by courtesy of the *Trinidad Guardian*.

From Trinidad the aircraft were flown to Venezuela where the party stayed in two steel barges moored in one of the main streams of the Orinoco delta, with the Channel flying-boats moored nearby. After the survey G-EAWC went on to Georgetown in British Guiana for further work of this nature but before completion of the task it was sunk by striking driftwood, the bane of flying-boats, in the river Essequibo. During its survey, however, its crew discovered a new mountain range. It is presumed that the two other Channels were left in Venezuela for further use but of this no record is available.

Early in 1921 a Channel I, with Beardmore engine, was delivered to Walsh Brothers and Dexter Ltd for use by the New Zealand Flying School. The flying-boat was registered G-NZAI, although this may not have actually been painted on, and during the period May–July shared with the Walsh flying-boat G-NZAS operation of an unscheduled daily passenger, mail and goods service between Auckland and Onerahi (for Whangarei).

The Right Rev Dr H. W. Cleary, Catholic Bishop of Auckland, is known to have used the Channel'boat to tour his diocese; and on 4 October, 1921, flown by George Bolt, with Leo A. Walsh and R. J. Johnson aboard, G-NZAI made the first flight from Auckland to Wellington.

*From this pioneering venture eventually came Hunting Aerosurveys of worldwide ramifications.

G-NZAI was the first aircraft of any kind to visit Fiji, and for about three weeks in July 1921 it made several tests, including flights round the two main islands of the Fiji group. A survey was made from the air of the whole coast line of Viti Levu. Had this exercise been followed by the establishment of a flying-boat air mail service, the long delay that existed in exchange of correspondence among the group would have been much reduced; but this did not happen, though the machine was used to a certain extent. It then returned to its base at Kohimarama, Auckland. At some time G-NZAI was fitted with a Puma engine.

In September 1924 the school was forced to close down, the Government taking over the New Zealand Flying School's assets, and G-NZAI was broken up when no buyer could be found for it in 1926 or 1927. Its hull was kept and used as a boat, surviving until as late as 1943 when it was disposed of by the simple expedient of burning, as it was of wooden construction.

Sometimes weather, though bad, can be an advantage as was the case when a Japanese delegation visited Southampton for a demonstration of the Channel flying-boat. The date was 14 March, 1921, a full gale was blowing and a strong spring tide was running, and even in the sheltered water in which the Woolston Works lay the sea was running in waves from four to five feet high. Into this a Channel was launched with the Japanese Naval Attaché and the chief of the Japanese Naval Air Service aboard. Capt Biard taxied out and then took off in just over five seconds after opening up the engine—a record for this type of flying-boat. The flight was round the Isle of Wight and then the return was made to Southampton Water where a good alighting was made in the very heavy seas, the wind blowing up to 50 mph. The Channel was then taxied for about a mile and a half against the ebb tide, demonstrating the manoeuvrability of the machine before it was taxied onto the slipway where the crew and passengers disembarked. The wind and tide were by then so strong that the landing crew consisted of the boatswain and no fewer than five hands because the wind was abeam of the

A Japanese Channel.

39

Chilean Channel with armament.

aircraft on the slipway. The amount of water taken aboard, including the 14½ minutes of the beaching, was only about 28 lb which was remarkable because the Channel had been taxied on the sea for 2¾ miles during the demonstration. This in such rough weather was so convincing that an order was placed for three Channels fitted with the Puma engine. These were taken to Japan by the British Aviation Mission to the Imperial Japanese Navy but little is known of their actual usage except that they were flown from the lake at Kasumigaura air base.

A Channel Mk II purchased for the Royal Swedish Navy in 1921 for an evaluation of the flying-boat type of aircraft for naval use had an unfortunate end for it crashed soon after delivery at Fjäderholmarna with fatal results for the pilot. Previously two Swedish naval officers, Cdr Werner and Capt Luback, had visited Vickers at Weybridge to examine the Viking amphibian but had chosen the Channel in preference because it had been designed for a convertible ski undercarriage.

The last Channel to be built was delivered to Chile in 1922 as a three-seat armed reconnaissance flying-boat. It carried Chilean markings but no registration, Service or civil. Its hull was completely different from its predecessors and seems to have been similar to the Seal/Seagull types which followed in the Supermarine line of succession. This hybrid was in fact listed as a Channel Mk II with the constructor's number 1167 and served with the Chilean Naval Air Service.

Channel I—One 160 hp Beardmore. Pilot and four passengers.
 Span (upper) 50 ft 5 in (15·36 m), (lower) 39 ft 7 in (12·6 m); length 30 ft (9·14 m); height 13 ft (3·96 m); wing area 453 sq ft (42·07 sq m).
 Empty weight 2,356 lb (1,068 kg); loaded weight 3,400 lb (1,542 kg).
 Maximum speed 80 mph (128·7 km/h) (Mk II 92 mph (148 km/h); alighting speed (Mk I and II) 53 mph (86·2 km/h); climb to 3,000 ft (914·4 m) 15 min; duration 3 hr.

40

Commercial Amphibian

To encourage the development of civil aircraft the Air Ministry announced in April 1920 that it would hold two competitions, one for landplanes and one for amphibian seaplanes, the former to start on 3 August and the latter on 1 September. The tests were to take place at the experimental air stations at Martlesham Heath and Felixstowe.

The contest for seaplanes was to ascertain 'the best type of Float Seaplanes or Boat Seaplanes which will be safe, comfortable and economical for air travel and capable of alighting on and rising from land as well as water. Each machine entered for the competition will be provided with seating accommodation for a minimum of two persons exclusive of crew. Machines and engines must have been designed and constructed within the British Empire. Machines are to fulfil all conditions required for a certificate of airworthiness and to carry life-belts for all persons for whom accommodation is provided, including the crew. With the machines fully loaded the boat or floats must be such that, if perforated in any one part, the boat or each float still retains positive buoyancy.'

The requirements continued—'Fuel load is to include petrol and oil sufficient to fly 350 nautical miles at 1,000 ft at a speed of not less than 70 kt and a load of 500 lb to include passengers, if carried, and life-belts but not including crew. Each machine should be capable of flying level at or above a speed of 80 kt with full load at sea level and should also be capable of flying level at or below 40 kt with full load at sea level'.

Other requirements included:

'A self-controlled flight of three minutes at 5,000 ft to check if the machine would fly itself at this height and with enough height to recover if the machine failed to do so.

'Formula W/G reliability and economy tests to be flown at a height of between 1,000 and 2,000 ft where W is the weight in pounds of useful load and G the

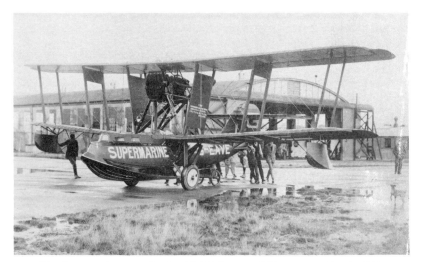

The Supermarine entry for the Air Ministry amphibian competition in 1920.

The Supermarine Commercial Amphibian clearing the balloons during the take-off tests at Martlesham.

number of gallons of petrol actually consumed during two $3\frac{1}{2}$ hr flights at 80 kt (recorded as percentage economy efficiency).

'Self-controlled glide in which the engine is to be throttled down or switched off at 5,000 ft and the pilot will remove hands and feet from the controls taking over again at 4,000 ft or below.

'Alighting tests—the machine to land over balloons at a height of 25 ft and in the take-off test it is allowed a run of 400 yds'.

The sea-going tests were to be conducted at Felixstowe marine base and included:

'Alighting and getting-off tests where the machines would start from a buoy and pass as high as possible between marker boats 75 yds apart 600 yds from the starting buoy. The machine then to fly to Martlesham Heath (some five miles) and land'.

Special marine tests were: Taxi-ing on the water including figure of eight, normal anchoring and mooring, and mooring out over 24 hours in both fair and moderate weather, and a getting-off and alighting test in rough water. Finally there was a towing test where the machine would be towed by a motor-boat supplied by the Judges Committee.

Three competitors arrived for the Seaplane section of the Air Ministry Competition; the Supermarine Commercial Amphibian G-EAVE flown by Capt J. E. A. Hoare, the Vickers Viking III Amphibian G-EAUK flown by Capt Stan Cockerell, AFC, and the Fairey III floatplane G-EALQ, with added wheel undercarriage, flown by Lt-Col Vincent Nicholl, DSO, DSC. The Beardmore W.B.IX and the Saunders Kittiwake failed to arrive, the latter having had trouble with its variable geometry wing on a test flight and crashing into rocks on alighting in the Solent, thus holing the hull.

The Supermarine Commercial Amphibian was designed and constructed in a hurry and was based on experience with the conversion of the A.D.Boat into the Channel. The hull followed the now well-established Linton Hope pattern, with two skins of mahogany, the inner laid diagonally and the outer longitudinally, and covered with fabric doped on. The complete hull was then finished in the immaculate boat-builders' varnish and polish. The wings were of unequal span with outwardly raked interplane struts and were non-folding, as the retractable undercarriage mechanism had to be accommodated in the structure. This undercarriage was made up of two steel tube structures hinged below the bottom inner planes and under the inner interplane struts. A rotatable tailskid was coupled to the air rudder and also served as a water rudder, and it had a special tiller, accessible to the pilot only when standing up, which gave him a clear view to steer accurately in narrow and crowded waters. He could also release a bolt holding the passengers' hinged cabin roof top in case of emergency.

The Supermarine machine was the last to arrive at Martlesham in the week ending 17 September with Capt Hoare supplying the marine touch by augmenting his Norfolk jacket and a tweed shooting hat with fisherman's rig of heavy jersey and grey trousers tucked into large sea boots. Reports suggest that most of the competitors treated the whole affair somewhat lightheartedly; nevertheless, the Competition was generally a success, particularly as a serious attempt to evaluate the basic requirements for civil aircraft capable of carrying passengers and freight.

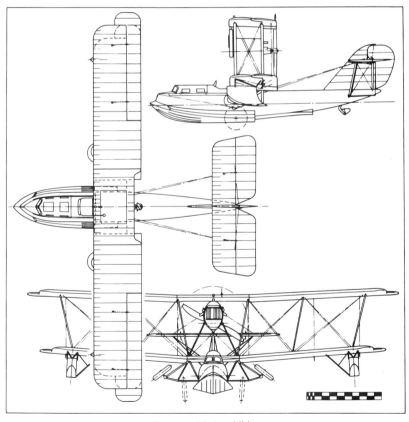

Commercial Amphibian

43

. The Supermarine entry was flown for the first time with full load as laid down in the requirements. At first it was thought that the propeller was unsuitable so Vickers kindly lent them one from the Viking. With it a short trial flight was made but the take-off run was still excessive and so the original was restored.

On 21 September the Commercial Amphibian undertook the reliability test and next day followed with the self-controlled flight, the take-off at sea, taxi-ing and figure-of-eight, towing, and the rough water take-off and alighting. The following day Capt Hoare flew the high and low speed tests at Martlesham and on the next day did the take-off land test then flying to Felixstowe for the anchoring and mooring pick-up, leaving the machine moored out for the 24 hr tests. The last test, the landing over the balloon screen, was done on 27 September. On the same day the Competition was concluded with the Viking completing the same test.

Throughout the whole of these exacting trials no adjustments or replacements were made to the Supermarine entry and it was the only one to complete all the tests called for in the programme. The efficiency of the undercarriage was proved by many landings and it was the only machine which suffered no failure of its amphibious gear and the only one to carry all the navigating instruments suitably grouped.

The winner of the Seaplane section was the Vickers Viking gaining the £10,000 first prize, and the second prize of £4,000 awarded to the Supermarine entry was doubled to £8,000 by the Air Ministry, because in their opinion it was such an excellent design and showed outstanding performance on its lower-powered Rolls-Royce Eagle engine, the other competitors having the 450 hp Napier Lion.

In their report on the Supermarine aircraft the judges made the following favourable comments: fittings for sea use very good and hanging steps, to facilitate work on the engine, light and serviceable; shape of hull and bows especially good in keeping spray off passengers; pilot's view was good and the stand-up position and tiller for taxi-ing especially good; the gearing of the magneto to the engine starting handle made starting considerably easier.

Criticisms included: cabin top should slide; cabin ventilator noise could be eliminated; unsatisfactory location of petrol pipes in cabin; too much cable in undercarriage gear classified as a maintenance risk and not clean mechanically; engine controls below standard of simplicity and convenience and wingtip floats too small and inadequately secured.

As regards control and performance the judges said that lateral control was not quick enough and may have been affected by the interplane side curtains but could be improved by simplifying the pulley system, using a larger control wheel with higher gearing with possibly a reduction in aileron size. They discovered no advantage in the device to lower all ailerons simultaneously to alter the wing camber, modern flap fashion. The long ground run on take-off was probably caused by the lower engine power and also by the fact that when the tailskid was down there was too little incidence on the wings.

The final comment of the judges was that the boat-type amphibian had the advantage of a large space for baggage and it practically abolished the risk of turning over on land in the event of undercarriage failure.

Only in one test did the Supermarine get zero marks and that was in the high- and low-speed section of the Competition. The judges based their score thus: for every knot over 80, one mark awarded; for every knot below, one mark forfeited; for every knot over 40, two marks forfeited; and for every knot under, two marks awarded. The Supermarine figure came to -14; but in each section the machine obtaining the highest number of marks was awarded the full percentage of marks obtainable. The percentages obtained by other machines were graded in proportion to the number of marks gained as compared to the highest machine, therefore no machine could be awarded negative marks.

It was solely in this part of the test (Speed and Getting Off) that the Supermarine machine fell down and so 20 per cent of the marks were not applicable. But for this it would have won comfortably; no wonder it was awarded the extra £4,000. With the Napier Lion engine it would certainly have been awarded more marks. In fact, immediately after the Competition the installation of the Napier Lion was considered, as was the adaptation of the machine to skis for snow work, to be interchangeable with the wheel undercarriage.

The career of the Commercial Amphibian was short lived because it crashed the following month, October, and was not rebuilt as such.

Commercial Amphibian—One 350 hp Rolls-Royce Eagle VIII. Pilot and two passengers.
Span (upper) 50 ft (15·24 m), (lower) 47 ft (14·3 m); length 32 ft 6 in (9·9 m); height 14 ft 6 in (4·4 m); wing area 600 sq ft (55·74 sq m).
Empty weight 3,996 lb (1,812 kg); loaded weight 5,700 lb (2,585 kg).
Maximum speed 94·4 mph (152 km/h); alighting speed 55 mph (88·5 km/h); maximum range 312 miles (502 km) at 80 mph (129 km/h).

Sea Eagle

A development of the Commercial Amphibian to carry as many passengers as possible with a single engine was studied by Supermarine in 1920. This was in response to a report that an official air link between Southampton and the Channel Islands was being considered in the Government policy of fostering civil aviation. This followed the pioneering operations with the Channel and the favourable result of the Air Ministry competition. Mitchell's first concept, dated 27 March, 1922, was in terms of an amphibian with folding wings and an enclosed cabin forward, and powered with a pusher Rolls-Royce engine.

It is difficult now to discover who actually was responsible for the idea of the regular Channel Islands service but two factors are known. One is that Major H. W. Rowlandson CBE conceived the notion of bringing fruit and flowers and other garden produce from the Channel Islands to Covent Garden by air and rail and the Air Ministry welcomed his suggestion. The other is that Commander James Bird, by then a director of Supermarine Aviation, had been appointed London representative to search for new business such as equipment for the new civil air routes being planned.

In the event, Air Ministry approval was given in June 1922 for an air service between Southampton, Cherbourg and Le Havre, with a subsequent service to the Channel Islands, in the name of the British Marine Air Navigation Company. *Flight* of 22 June, 1922, reported that the London and South Western Railway were interested and also that a Government subsidy would be granted to the new company for its operations.

Meanwhile Mitchell had developed his original concept into a machine to carry six passengers in the enclosed cabin, with the pilot and mechanic in a cockpit behind and above the cabin. The engine was a Rolls-Royce Eagle IX which drove

The first Sea Eagle, G-EBFK, with single overhead fuel tank.

a four-blade pusher propeller. The fuel was fed from a streamlined gravity service tank on the upper centre section. Constructional details follov ed normal Supermarine practice which by then had become standardized. The name of the new type, Sea Eagle, had been originally coined for an alternative variant projected for prospective round-the-world aviators, who at that time were looking for suitable aircraft of the amphibian type.

Supermarine had already started to build one passenger-carrying Sea Eagle when the Air Ministry agreed to pay the British Marine Air Navigation Company a subsidy of £10,000 and to pay for the aircraft and spares by a grant of £21,000. The objectives announced were the purchase of three Sea Eagle amphibians from the Supermarine company, a contract for petrol and oil from Shell-Mex and the establishment of an air service to Cherbourg, Le Havre and the Channel Islands. Hubert Scott-Paine and James Bird were nominated as directors with one share

Sea Eagle G-EBGR with twin fuel tanks.

46

each in the British Marine Air Navigation Company, registered on 23 March, 1923, as a private company. The major shareholders were the Supermarine Aviation Works and the Asiatic Petroleum Company (Shell-Mex) with 5,000 shares each.

Poor Major Rowlandson who had schemed the Channel Islands commercial service was ignored and lost all his money on the concept. Today air transport plays a great part in the marketing of Channel Islands vegetable produce, especially when the steamship service is out of action. Jersey and Guernsey are now among the busiest local airports in the United Kingdom.

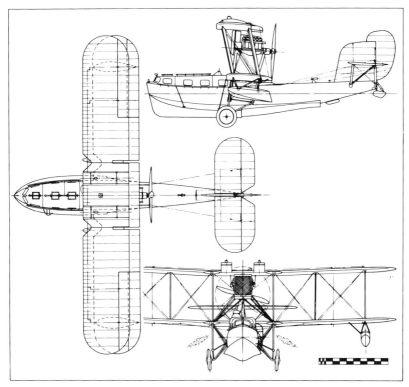

Sea Eagle

The order for three Sea Eagles was received and G-EBFK, G-EBGR and G-EBGS were built for the new air service, to carry six passengers and two crew. The first was flown by Biard at the beginning of June 1923. Major Wright of the Air Ministry said that in his opinion it was the finest sea-going machine he had ever flown. Pressure was indeed building up on the Air Ministry to encourage the development of seaplanes, as the following extract from *Flight* of 28 June, 1923, illustrates:

'Fortunately there are signs that the present Air Ministry is beginning to realize the vast possibilities of the seaplane but there is still a great deal of reorganization to be done in the Air Ministry departments before one can be certain that the seaplane will be given the attention it merits. It is no longer a secret that there are precious few, if any, officials left in the technical departments who have special knowledge of seaplanes and there are instances of technical men with specialist training in seaplane work who are now occupied in departments where their knowledge is of no use to them nor to the Air Ministry. Knowing this, one can better understand why units working with the Navy have to go to sea on land machines when, according to all common sense, they ought to be equipped with proper seaworthy seaplanes.'

A certificate of airworthiness was issued for the Sea Eagle on 11 July and the Air Ministry pilot who flew it on the trials expressed a high opinion of its flying qualities. In the 1923 King's Cup Air Race there were 17 entries, one of which was the Sea Eagle (with extra tankage) with Henri Biard as nominated pilot. He received the third highest time allowance from the scratch man Larry Carter on the Gloster Grebe. This was 1 hr 33 min 3 sec on Section I of the Race and 1 hr 31 min 28 sec on Section II, the race being over two days with three stages per day for a total distance of 793 miles. Start and finish were at Hendon and the staging posts were at Birmingham, Newcastle and Glasgow on the first day and Manchester and Bristol on the second.

On 13 July, the first day, Biard flew the Sea Eagle to Birmingham with four passengers, 91 miles in 53 min 23 sec, the fastest time for the leg from Hendon being 32 min 26 sec by the Siddeley Siskin flown by Frank Courtney. The next stage of 171 miles to Newcastle was flown by Biard in 1 hr 58 min 25 sec. While certain adjustments were being made during the one and a half hours compulsory stop, the port tyre burst, probably caused by heat from the sun, a phenomenon not unknown at the time on aircraft with wheels exposed to the elements during most of their active life. This mishap was particularly unfortunate because Biard had left his spare wheel with other spares at Birmingham to save weight and there was insufficient time left to effect a repair. He therefore decided to deflate the other tyre for a balanced take-off on the rims as he thought he still had a chance, with only eleven aircraft left in the race. His time to Glasgow, some 125 miles, was 1 hr 21 min 55 sec despite the line having to be crossed twice through pilot error, but he made a successful landing on his wheel rims although damaging them in the process. An attempt to replace his wheels with odd-sized ones from an outside agency led to Biard's disqualification. At that point he was lying seventh at an average speed of 91·4 mph—good going since the top speed of the Sea Eagle was only 93 mph. The winner of the race was Frank Courtney in the Siskin.

Biard's return to Hendon and then to base at Southampton was itself a little saga. With his undercarriage repaired he left for Manchester but low cloud forced him to follow the coast as far as Blackpool. After looking at Blackpool race-course* as a possible landing site to refuel, Biard decided that the ground was unsuitable and so alighted on the sea and taxied up the sandy beach on his wheeled undercarriage. Fortunately the long bows of the Sea Eagle prevented the machine from pitching forward and sinking in the soft sand. After refuelling he took off from the beach and flew to Manchester and Hendon. At both places he experienced further delays from official inspections to comply with the terms of the insurance policy. One interesting factor arose out of this adventure and that was a reduction of insurance premiums for amphibians flying over land, as it was considered that the risk of that type turning over on landing was much less than the normal landplane.

*No longer extant—now the site of Squire's Gate Airport.

On its return to base at Woolston, the Sea Eagle was examined and found to be fully serviceable with the exception of a wheel change. This was gratifying as the start of the new air service to the Channel Islands and France was imminent. Meanwhile, it transpired that the Air Ministry had amended the terms of the subsidy to £10,000 annually for a guarantee of 80,000 flying miles per annum and only 50 per cent of the cost of the aircraft up to £12,000. Treasury funds were difficult for civil aviation to get at that time and Government subsidies were needed, particularly for extension of British air services to the Continent.

On 5 August, Sir Sefton Brancker, Director of Civil Aviation in the Air Ministry, visited the Woolston works and was taken for a flight in the Sea Eagle, with five other passengers, for demonstrations of its seaworthiness including taxi-ing through lines of moored yachts assembled for Cowes Week, in Cowes Roads. The Sea Eagle then took off, circled the Royal Yacht and its guardship, HMS *Barham*, and returned to Woolston after about an hour. Sir Sefton was impressed by both the performance of the machine and its passenger comfort, which he compared with other passenger aircraft as the most comfortable, and also remarked on the reduced noise and absence of engine smells.

The first Sea Eagle at Seaview, Isle of Wight.

This flight was followed on 14 August by the first proving flight over the extended route of the new air service. On board were Sir Sefton with Lt-Col Sir Francis Shelmerdine, and other senior officers of Sir Sefton's staff, and Hubert Scott-Paine. A secondary purpose was to convey Sir Sefton to a glider and lightplane meeting at Vauville on the French coast. Flying time was about one hour compared with seven hours by steamship.

The opening of the regular service was being delayed until facilities were provided at Woolston to the satisfaction of the customs and immigration authorities. MARINE AIRPORT was painted in large letters on the roof of the Woolston hangars and this was certainly one of the first known public uses of the word airport so familiar today. Meanwhile, Sir Sefton could hardly suppress his enthusiasm

Sea Eagle G-EBGS at Woolston terminal, in Imperial Airways livery.

for his job of pioneering civil air transport and took Lord Apsley, Member of Parliament for Southampton, to Seaview in the Isle of Wight in the Sea Eagle to demonstrate its capabilities. Lord Apsley, although a member of the Lower House, made some noble remarks about the attributes of the machine including a prophesy that 'seaplane travel will be one of the first methods of aerial locomotion to gain popularity'—which of course came remarkably true until the maintenance of separate bases (with air traffic control) for landplanes and seaplanes put the latter out of business on economic grounds. Those survivors of the flying-boat era will remember with affection that leisurely and supremely comfortable mode of travel by air and water which pioneered so many world air routes.

Regular daily services began between Southampton and Guernsey on 25 September, 1923, and the schedule was—depart Woolston at 11.15, returning from St Peter Port at 15.30. The single fare was £3.18s and the normal flight time was $1\frac{1}{2}$ hr but could take up to $2\frac{1}{2}$ hr in adverse weather. Sea Eagle G-EBFK as flown in the King's Cup was used initially but G-EBGR and G-EBGS, with certificates of airworthiness both dated 2 October, also participated in the service until it ceased temporarily on 30 November. The two pilots employed were Capt H. C. Biard and Capt F. J. Bailey, both of Supermarine, and to them and the Supermarine company must be accorded the distinction of starting the first British flying-boat scheduled air service. Some 180 passengers had been carried to and from the Channel Islands but the service never was extended to the French coast because of Gallic objections and lack of aircraft.

The naming ceremony of the first two Sea Eagles took place on 13 October, when Biard and Bailey flew G-EBFK and G-EBGR respectively to Guernsey for the ritual, which was performed by Miss Edith Carey amid the cheers of the spectators. After the ceremony Biard left with three newsmen and his mechanic simultaneously with Bailey in the other machine carrying only his mechanic. The weather was very rough and to make matters worse Bailey's engine gave trouble and he had to alight in the sea off the Casquets.

50

G-EBFK, which had been named *Sea Eagle*, had an exciting time trying to fetch help for Bailey and finished up damaged in the harbour at Alderney, with one unconscious newsman and the cabin in a shambles. Meanwhile Bailey in G-EBGR *Sarnia* rode out the storm all night among the rocks, eventually drifting into sheltered water west of Alderney where he was located and picked up next morning with a disillusioned and disgruntled mechanic.

Thereafter, the service ran smoothly all the time fare-paying passengers were being carried, thus proving that an air service to the Channel Islands from the mainland was a viable proposition.

On 31 March, 1924, Imperial Airways, the ancestor of the present British Airways, was formed as the Government's 'chosen instrument' to develop British commercial air transport. It took over the assets and operations of Handley Page Transport, The Instone Air Line, Daimler Airway and the British Marine Air Navigation Company. Hubert Scott-Paine, managing director of Supermarine, who also had been chairman of BMAN, was one of the directors of the new airline consortium. At this point it is interesting to note that the actual Air Ministry subsidies paid out to BMAN had been for 1923–24, £3,846, and for 1924–25, only £178.

The two Sea Eagles G-EBGR and G-EBGS began Imperial Airways service from Southampton to Guernsey on 1 May, but the first Sea Eagle, G-EBFK, crashed on 21 May and so never came under the new control. The service was suspended in the summer of 1925 and a proposition to use one of the Sea Eagles for a service from London to Sweden came to nothing. Service was resumed in 1926 but G-EBGS was rammed and sunk by a ship in St Peter Port on 10 January, 1927, while at its moorings. G-EBGR continued the service, assisted during that year by the Supermarine Swan G-EBJY. On 26 July, 1928, the service was explored by the Short Calcutta G-EBVG and eventually the Calcutta G-EBVH took it over in October 1928.

The oldest major component of a British transport aeroplane of that time. The hull of G-EBGR, wrongly painted as G-EBGS, at Heston in 1954.

G-EBGR was now considered redundant and was withdrawn from use. The hull was preserved and exhibited alongside the Short Empire flying-boat *Capella* at the British Power Boat Company's display at Hythe, Hants, in February 1938. Finally, wrongly marked as G-EBGS, it was presented to John Brancker of BOAC in September 1949 by Victor Paine (half-brother of Hubert Scott-Paine) then publicity manager of Vickers (Aviation) who had acquired Supermarine in 1928. It was stored at Hythe base and then moved to Heston where problems of maintenance and storage caused it to be burnt on 13 February, 1954, a loss to aeronautical 'archaeology'.

The flying-boat service finally ceased on 28 February, 1929. Thus the pioneering efforts to establish a scheduled flying-boat air service, if not wholly realized were given practical form by Supermarine and made a significant contribution to air transport history.

Sea Eagle—One 360 hp Rolls-Royce Eagle IX. Pilot, mechanic and six passengers.

Span 46 ft (14·02 m); span folded 21 ft 1 in (6·42 m); length 37 ft 4 in (11·37 m); length folded 43 ft (13·1 m); height 15 ft 11 in (4·85 m); wing area 620 sq ft (57·6 sq m).

Empty weight 3,950 lb (1,791 kg); gross weight 6,050 lb (2,744 kg); overload weight 6,500 lb (2,948 kg).

Maximum speed 93 mph (149·6 km/h) at sea level; alighting speed 50 mph (80·4 km/h); climb to 5,000 ft (1,524 m) in 19 min; range 230 miles (370 km) at 84 mph (135·1 km/h).

Sea King

A project for a single-seat fighter flying-boat similar to the Baby was started on 29 October, 1919, under Supermarine job number 1169, when hull lines were drawn. With the cessation of hostilities the original N.1B requirement expired as did the use of the Baby. Supermarine decided to pursue the concept and various schemes were considered. Of these, in July 1919 a master drawing was finalized of a seaplane with a Napier Lion engine which became the Sea Lion I and was entered for the 1919 Schneider Trophy contest. After the race at Bournemouth, in which the Sea Lion sank, the fighter flying-boat concept was continued in an overall configuration similar to the Sea Lion. When this machine was completed it was named the Sea King I, powered with a 160 hp Beardmore engine. One modification was the deletion of the horn balances of the control surfaces. It was flown early in 1920 but there is no record of the exact date or the identity of the pilot.

How long the Sea King I remained in its original form is uncertain as so little was published and when it appeared at Olympia in July 1920, where it attracted much attention as the only single-seat seaplane fighter, the wing structure had been altered to that of an equal-span single-bay biplane. The hull and the T-type tail were the same but with the addition of a small triangular fin above the horizontal stabilizer. Another version is believed to have been flown with a Siddeley Puma engine which would have improved performance. This scheme also improved on the Baby's machine-gun mounting which had been right in the middle of the pilot's view, and was now moved to a lower position in the hull nose. Directional stability must have remained a problem as the rudder still appeared too small for adequate control.

Sea King I at the 1920 Olympia Aero Show.

Sea King II taxi-ing at Southampton.

Other schemes were considered at the same time as the Puma installation. One of these projects was for a two-seat fighter with a Lewis gun on a Scarff ring in the front cockpit giving more than 180 degrees of fire, and with provision for two parachutes and a fog horn, the latter introduced no doubt as a consequence of experience in the Schneider race in 1919 at Bournemouth, which had been fogbound. The deciding factor in choice of design was probably the issue by the Air Ministry in June 1921 of basic requirements for a D of R type 6 single-seat fighter for shipboard use, which could be satisfied by an amphibian but in the event was filled by the Fairey Flycatcher of conventional landplane fighter design. The scheme eventually chosen and constructed was that of 7 July which reverted to the single-seat amphibian layout with either a Lion or the larger Hispano engine. Meanwhile one design quite unlike any other at that time was for a tractor amphibian with either a Jaguar or a Jupiter air-cooled radial engine, shades of things to come in the Walrus and Sea Otter era.

The Sea King II was completed with the 300 hp Hispano-Suiza at the end of December 1921 and flew shortly afterwards, six months from design to first flight. Like the modified Mk I shown at Olympia, it was an equal-span single-bay biplane with a much modified tail reflecting the influence of Mitchell in the overall design. The horizontal stabilizer had been lowered in position and the enlarged fin and rudder consequently extended above, thus dropping the T form of the Mk II's

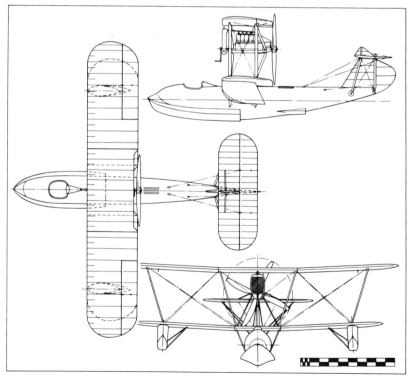

Sea King I

predecessors. The hull was developed on Linton Hope principles with mahogany planking attached to the rock elm timbers and frames by non-ferrous fixings and rivets with a covering of special pigmented doped fabric. The two steps were attached as separate components to the planing bottom and could be easily renewed in event of damage. An unusual feature was an attempt to avoid cavitation by inserting a tube running through the hull supplying ventilating air to the rear step. The idea was to facilitate 'unsticking' from the water by removing any vacuum behind the step during the acceleration build-up of speed for take off. No report exists of this system being used in any other Supermarine design so apparently the results were inconclusive.

Another innovation was that the pilot's back rest could be lowered to form a step for easy access to the starting magneto on one side of the engine and the filler cap of the petrol tank on the other. The undercarriage struts were so arranged that the landing shocks were not transmitted through the hull and were of the bent axle type with retraction upwards and outwards. The tailskid-cum-water rudder was substantial and was steerable from a wheel in the cockpit. The engine mounting structure was independent of the wing cellule enabling the outer planes to be removed without disturbing the power unit. In fact the whole wing structure plus the power unit could be removed by withdrawing eight bolts and the undercarriage by removing ten bolts. This facility was indicative of the ease of maintenance and interchangeability introduced into the design of the Sea King II.

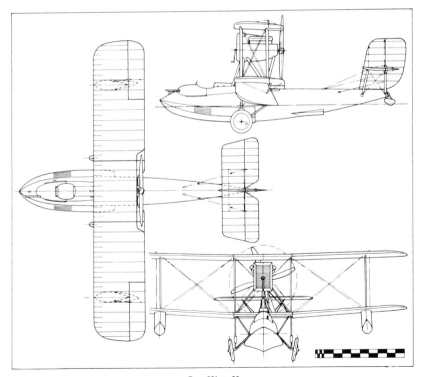

Sea King II

This latter characteristic was inspired largely by the policy of most aircraft firms of the time to make do and mend by using components and parts from other designs which had become obsolescent, such as the Supermarine-built Baby and the Sea Lion I.

Pilots who flew the Sea King II claimed that it had an unusual degree of manoeuvrability in that its aerobatic capability was the equal of any contemporary landplane fighter and was inherently stable. It was free from any change of trim, engine on or off, and could be flown hands off in reasonable weather conditions. There was no tendency to porpoise on the water as on some previous types. It was the first complete design over which Mitchell had full authority as chief designer and this extended to the modifications necessary when the Sea King was considered, largely on a suggestion by the editor of *Flight*, as an entry for the 1922 Schneider Trophy contest. It was renamed the Sea Lion II and achieved a notable success for Britain, although not a single customer could be found for it as the Sea King II amphibian fighter.

Sea King I—One 160 hp Beardmore or one 240 hp Siddeley Puma. Single seat.
Span (upper) 35 ft 6 in (10·82 m), (lower) 30 ft 5 in (9·27 m); length 27 ft 4 in (8·33 m); height 11 ft 7 in (3·53 m); wing area 339 sq ft (31·49 sq m).
Loaded weight (Beardmore) 2,500 lb (1,134 kg), (Puma) 2,646 lb (1,200 kg).
Maximum speed (Beardmore) 110·5 mph (177·8 km/h), (Puma) 121 mph (194·7 km/h).
Estimated speed with Napier Lion (as amphibian) 141 mph (226·9 km/h).

Sea King II—One 300 hp Hispano-Suiza. Single seat.
Span 32 ft (9·75 m); length 26 ft 9 in (8·15 m); height 11 ft 7 in (3·53 m).
Empty weight 2,115 lb (959 kg); loaded weight 2,850 lb (1,292 kg).
Maximum speed 125 mph (201·1 km/h) at sea level; climb to 10,000 ft (3,048 m) 12 min; duration 2 hr.

Schneider Sea Lions

One of the most influential competitions ever organized in aviation was that for the Jacques Schneider International Seaplane Trophy. In 1912, Jacques Schneider, a member of the family of French armament manufacturers, presented through the Aéro-Club de France, a striking bronze trophy displaying a sea nymph kissing a wave, for an international seaplane contest, with the express intention of fostering marine aviation which at that time had tended to lag behind landplane development. This far-seeing act started perhaps the most emotive series of air races ever held and led to more technical development of the fixed-wing aeroplane and piston engine than any other agency, it could be said, until the evolution of the jet engine. In the history of the successive contests for this coveted trophy, Supermarine played one of the most notable parts, a participation which eventually led to a vital involvement in a later and much more serious contest, the Second World War. The story of Supermarine's contribution to the history of the Schneider Trophy races starts here with the first of the racing Sea Lions.

The Sea Lion I entry for the 1919 Schneider Trophy event.

This was the Sea Lion I, developed from the Supermarine N.1B Baby. It took its name from the 450 hp Napier Lion engine which had replaced the Baby's much lower-powered Hispanos and Sunbeams and raised the speed from 117 mph to over 140 mph. The design work was directed by F. J. Hargreaves,* then in charge of the drawing and technical offices at Woolston. The wings of the Sea Lion I were of unequal span, with the interplane struts splayed outwards and with the engine on an independent pylon mounting. The engine was partly cowled with an oval car-type radiator mounted in the front. The T-tail resembled that of the Baby but the fin and rudder had been considerably increased in area. The hull was of the then familiar Linton Hope construction. The control surfaces all had aerodynamic horn-type balances.

Sea Lion I was one of the four British seaplanes which were available to compete in the 1919 Schneider Trophy Contest. This was to be held in Britain, a privilege gained by the sensational win of the Sopwith Tabloid in the 1914 contest held at Monaco. As the organizing body under the direction of the Fédération Aéronautique Internationale, the Royal Aero Club selected Bournemouth as the base for a triangular course of ten laps totalling 200 nautical miles, with Swanage and Hengistbury Head as the other turning points. A great contest was awaited in view of the vastly improved breed of aircraft generated during the 1914–18 War and their greatly improved performances. Indicative of this progress had been the direct flight of Alcock and Brown across the Atlantic in June 1919 in a Vickers Vimy.

The other British competitors were the Fairey and Sopwith floatplanes, the entries being limited to three aircraft from any one nation, with the Avro floatplane as standby reserve. France had entered two Nieuports and a Spad, all floatplanes, while Italy's one entry was a Savoia 13 flying-boat. In the event all had very mixed fortunes, some it must be admitted caused by bad organization which, with the choice of venue, came in for some severe criticism.

*Soon to be succeeded by Reginald J. Mitchell.

With the worst of bad luck, the Royal Aero Club were confronted on the day of the contest, 10 September, 1919, by fog, which delayed the start of the race until tea time. The subsequent fiasco has been told in detail elsewhere but here only the career of the Supermarine contestant is recorded.

The Sea Lion I arrived at one o'clock and tied up alongside the Supermarine launch *Tiddleywinks*, which was reputed to be the hull of one of Pemberton Billing's original designs for a slip-wing aeroplane, probably of the prewar German order for P.B.7s. By late afternoon conditions were considered to be clear enough for the race to start and the Fairey was the first away at ten minutes to five, followed by the Sea Lion, the Sopwith and the Savoia. The Sea Lion's engine was hand-started by Capt John Hoare for the pilot, Sqn Ldr Basil D. Hobbs, both Supermarine pilots. On ignition Hoare dived smartly overboard, being picked up by *Tiddleywinks*. The Sea Lion took off successfully and headed for the first turning point but ran into fog over Swanage Bay where the pilot lost his bearings, after having had a momentary sight of the Fairey machine and only just succeeding in avoiding a collision. Thinking that the visibility might be better lower down, he descended to near the surface where conditions were in fact just as bad.

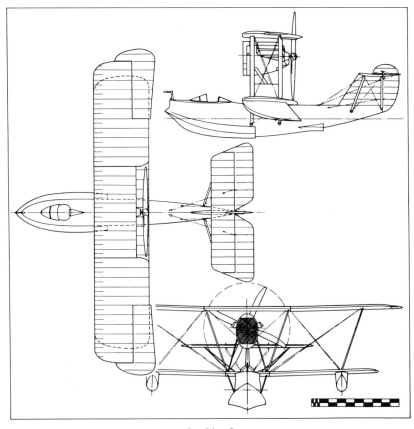

Sea Lion I

58

The Sea Lion I taxi-ing to the start of the 1919 race at Bournemouth.

Realizing that he must be in the vicinity of Swanage Bay and thus in danger of running into the cliffs, he alighted to work out his position. In this he failed but decided to take off in the direction of Bournemouth in order to get out of fog and then make a fresh attempt to find the Swanage marker boat. Unfortunately, on take off and just at the moment of leaving the water he felt a terrific bang, caused by hitting an unseen object. From a flying point of view the machine behaved perfectly and so he decided to continue the race at a greater height. This he did. He still did not see the Swanage marker but from the position of the Purbeck Hills was able to satisfy himself that he had at least gone round it.

Hobbs then flew to Hengistbury Head by compass course and found it clear of fog and rounded it safely to make his first alighting to the east of Boscombe Pier alongside the marker boat, as required by the rules. He made a perfect touchdown, but a hole in the bottom of the hull was so large that the boat almost immediately filled with water and there was no chance of beaching. The Sea Lion turned half over in an undignified position with the tail sticking up in the air. The motor launch picked up Hobbs, and when *Tiddleywinks* came up, Scott-Paine and Cdr James Bird of Supermarine secured the tail of the machine just before it sank and then towed it into shallow water where, with the help of rigging tackle, it was secured to Boscombe Pier and later salvaged and taken back to Woolston.

The only pilot to circumnavigate the course was the Italian naval pilot Janello in the Savoia. He completed the required number of laps but missed the correct Swanage turning point on each lap, by mistaking a yacht for the marker boat, and was disqualified. The race was then declared void. The Italians protested and the Royal Aero Club consented that, as a compliment to Janello's gallant effort, the 1920 contest would be held in Italy. The original decision that the race was void was upheld by the FAI.

The hull of the Sea Lion I was loaned to the Science Museum at South Kensington in 1921 for exhibition so it must have been patched up or repaired to some extent. In 1928 the Science Museum was short of space for their exhibits (as they always are) and so they wrote to Supermarine regarding its return. Supermarine replied on 3 November, 1928, stating that the hull was now obsolete and could be disposed of, which the Museum did by breaking it up.

The Sea Lion II, with enlarged fin, at Naples for the 1922 Schneider event.

Sea Lion II

The Schneider Trophy contest for 1920 was held at Venice where it was an uncontested fly-over for the Italians in a Savoia S.19 flying-boat, so notching up their first win. This meant that the Italians held the Trophy and so the 1921 contest was also held at Venice, which the Italians again won with a fly-over in a Macchi M.7 flying-boat. This was their second win. A third successive win would have meant that they could keep the Trophy. So for the 1922 contest held at Naples the entrants were three Italian aircraft, two French and one only from Great Britain, the Sea Lion II. Whereas by then the Italian and French teams had access to Government financial assistance, the Sea Lion was financed privately by Scott-Paine and Cdr James Bird of Supermarine, aided by the loan of a new 450 hp Napier Lion engine from Napiers. The British Government said that they could not afford to spend funds on this venture and pleaded the heavy financial burden caused by the 1914–18 War. The two French entries failed to put in an appearance and so the only challenger left was the Supermarine Sea Lion II.

This was a high-speed pusher flying-boat designed by R. J. Mitchell. The new Sea Lion was originally the single-seat Sea King II amphibian of 1921, but rebuilt as a racing flying-boat and fitted with the Napier Lion engine between the Sea King mainplanes, which were reduced in area by modifying them to a narrower chord. To offset the greater torque of the engine the fin area above the low-mounted tailplane was increased, as was the rudder area.

Scott-Paine, the managing director, took Biard aside one day in 1922 and asked him if he would like to fly in the Schneider Trophy race that year. He agreed and was then shown the actual aircraft almost completed in one of the building sheds. Before the race was completed Scott-Paine had spent over £6,000 so that Britain should have a worthy challenger. He also did wonderful work in getting together a real British team effort, for the loaned Napier engine would have cost £3,000 if purchased, another firm lent a high-speed propeller, the insurance company halved its rates to insure the machine, while Shell gave the petrol and Castrol the oil.

About a week after Biard had seen the new Sea Lion, still unfinished, the Italian authorities, without any warning, suddenly put forward the date of the race by fourteen days, which meant that much less time to get ready. Supermarine however were determined to be in and men worked day and night until the Sea Lion was completed, leaving very little time to give it the number of flight tests needed before it could be flown in the race. To make matters worse, the English weather turned against them and gales prevented it taking off on its first flight, with Biard kicking his heels and just looking at the aeroplane. Late that day the gales subsided and he ordered her out and the engine was started up. He taxied out and was very quickly airborne but when a couple of hundred feet above Southampton Docks the engine suddenly cut out completely and he was gliding towards a forest of funnels and ships, but by skilful flying managed to alight safely between them without damage. The aeroplane was towed back to the works with Biard very despondent, where it was again worked on that night.

The following day was again too windy for flying until just about sunset when Biard once more took the Sea Lion off. This time everything went according to plan and the pilot opened the engine flat out until the airspeed indicator was showing nearly 150 mph, which was faster than any flying-boat had ever flown before. Following this he turned and flew back again and did one or two sharp turns ready for the race itself with the machine answering sweetly to the controls every time. As it was getting dark, he alighted and taxied back to the slipway where at least a dozen eager operatives asked the same question, 'How fast?' Next

Napier Lion ready for installation in the Sea Lion II in the background. Left to right—Hubert Scott-Paine, R. J. Mitchell and W. T. Elliott.

61

day was reasonable at last and the Sea Lion was put through her paces, followed by more testing with only one or two final adjustments.

With all that behind them Supermarine came upon another snag, for no continental railway would guarantee either the safety of the machine or that it would be delivered at Naples in time to take part in the race. At the critical moment the General Steam Navigation Company came with the offer of the loan of a steamship complete with crew. ss *Philomel*, Captain Field, was sailed into Southampton Water where the mechanics and sailors together packed the Sea Lion aboard as if it were made of glass. Scott-Paine also journeyed with the ship to Naples where the aircraft was just as gently unpacked, swung outboard and lowered on to the calm blue water accompanied by three rousing cheers for luck by the crew of the *Philomel*.

As soon as everything was doubly checked Biard took off and immediately discovered that the cool breezes which came off the mountains surrounding the Bay of Naples created some surprising eddies of wind at about 3,000–4,000 ft where they met the hot air of the bay. From his boyhood he had always wanted to see Vesuvius so he decided to fly over it. He went steady at only 130 mph in order to have a good view but as he reached the volcano the hot-air blast from below promptly bumped him up 2,000 ft, going vertically upwards like a sailplane in a thermal, so that his view of the crater was distracted in jostling with the controls to avoid falling into it. By the time he had the aircraft again under control he was several miles from Vesuvius and wisely decided that the best way to see it was on foot, so flew back to Naples.

Every time Biard flew the Sea Lion, the Italian pilots, Passaleva, Zanetti and Gorgolino, with their experts and many other onlookers, watched every movement he made, timed her over every stretch and studied her on the corners, and formulated their plans for the race. Whereas the Sea Lion was on view to all, the French aircraft, two CAMS, were wrapped in mystery. Biard was careful not to open the Sea Lion up too much and on the final trials over the actual course he even cornered rather widely round the pylons, partly from ordinary caution and partly because he wanted to keep something up his sleeve for the race itself.

Before the main contest the participating aircraft had to pass strict navigation tests, including taxi-ing across the starting line, ascending, alighting, taxi-ing round buoys over two marked distances each of about half a mile at a minimum speed of 12 mph, covering the actual course in the air, alighting and finally taxi-ing across the finishing line. There was also a six hours' mooring-out test where the machines were just left at their moorings unattended, whatever the weather. This was to prove that the machines taking part were fully seaworthy and airworthy and capable of participating in the actual race. The two French CAMS entries did not turn up for these tests and so could not take part in the actual contest. This left three Italian and one British contestant only. The British machine stood up perfectly to all the tests but the fastest Italian machine, Passaleva's Savoia S.51, capsized at her moorings and later split her propeller plus other parts. This could and should have meant her disqualification but the Italians all showed up on the day and the British said nothing.

The day was 12 August, 1922, and Biard, wanting to keep as cool as possible, turned out in shirt sleeves and a pair of old grey flannel trousers. At the start of the race he was so busy with the controls, and the fact that he had to taxi over the starting line before taking off, that the Italians were all ahead of him. The engine ran perfectly and he almost hit the marker balloon on the first turning point in chasing the Italians but succeeded in missing it and then let the engine full out

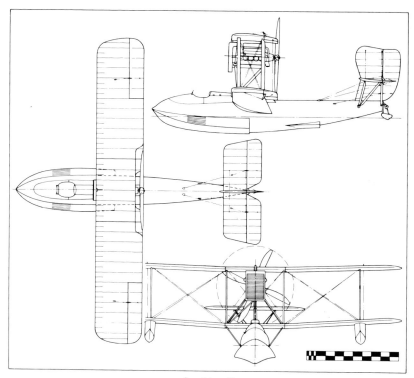

Sea Lion II

until he was doing 160 mph indicated airspeed, faster than he or the Sea Lion had ever travelled before. This surprise was the result of the Napier mechanics' tuning of the engine to absolutely top performance. After two circuits he had closed up on the Italians and they must have been watching him, because they teamed up closer to try to prevent him passing. Biard decided that he could not go round the outside of them because of the extra distance he would have to fly. Also he could not fly inside them in case he missed the line and be disqualified. This left him two choices, either to fly under them or over them and he decided on the latter course on one of the corners where they were not so bunched up. He waited for a quarter of an hour, holding the Sea Lion back before he decided to overtake, he got closer and closer with the wake from the machines in front threatening to turn him over, then he opened the throttle fully and pulled the nose up and over them. On looking down he could see the goggled faces of the Italian pilots below staring up over their shoulders, startled, grabbing at their controls, trying to urge their machines to greater efforts but to no avail. Biard was past and diving down in front of them at about 200 mph, wondering if the machine would hold together, and then round the balloon ahead of the Italians with them now rocking in his wake.

He got well ahead and so could afford to ease off the engine somewhat, with the result that the Italians gradually caught him up but not close enough to worry him. After he had completed twelve laps he decided on what he described as a bit of fun and opened the throttle wide open so that on rounding the last marker and diving down to level off he was once again almost touching 200 mph, and so down the final straight, over the finishing line at probably the world's fastest speed—certainly for seaplanes—and he had won for Britain. He did another couple of laps and then touched down where he could hear the tremendous yelling of the crowds.

His time of 1 hr 34 min 51 sec over the 200·2 nautical miles (370·5 km) course gave him an average speed of 145·7 mph (234·5 km/h), and Passaleva, who was second, flew the course in 1 hr 36 min 22 sec at 143·5 mph in the Savoia S.51, Zanetti in the Macchi M.17 was third at 133 mph, and Gorgolino was fourth at 123·7 mph.

The FAI granted the Sea Lion II the first World's Records in the marine aircraft class in January 1923 as follows:

1. Duration of 1 hr 34 min 51·6 sec
2. Longest distance accomplished 230 miles
3. Fastest time for 100 km—(62 miles) in 28 min 41·4 sec at 130 mph
4. Fastest time for 200 km—(124 miles) in 57 min 37·4 sec at 129·4 mph

Before Biard left Naples, he visited Vesuvius with Scott-Paine as promised, accompanied by some Italian friends and found it even more active than when he had flown over it. On the triumphant return to Southampton the team was met by a tremendous reception from the crowds, ringing handbells, beating shovels, whistling, ships' sirens and so on, and it was obvious that everybody appreciated what Biard, and the Supermarine and Napier companies, had so recently accomplished. Even the Mayor and Corporation turned out in full ceremonial dress.

The Sea Lion II on its return was purchased by the Air Ministry and allocated the serial number N157 and flown to Felixstowe where it was used for high-speed research on seaplanes.

The Sea Lion hull was of the standard Linton Hope circular section, with built-on steps and was divided into watertight compartments. The engine was mounted in a faired nacelle which contained the oil-tank and frontal radiator, and was very accessible and easily replaced when required. The complete wing structure with power unit could be removed from the hull by withdrawing just eight bolts. The amphibian gear was attached by only ten bolts but was not carried during the contest. The main differences from the Sea Lion I were a redesigned bow and fin and rudder, reduced wing area and the undercarriage (when fitted) retracted under the wings instead of up the side of the hull, as on previous aircraft. The fin area had been further increased at Naples to improve directional control.

Sea Lion III

For the 1923 Schneider Trophy race held at Cowes, Supermarine were not going to enter a machine. When Scott-Paine realized that the two British competitors, the Sopwith and the Blackburn Pellet, were inferior by his standards, and also influenced by the surprise entry of the US Navy Curtiss CR-3s, sponsored by the United States Government, he had second thoughts. The American floatplanes, powered by the new 465 hp Curtiss D-12 engines, were really lovely little machines and were amazingly streamlined. So at the last minute and under pressure because he did not feel able to spend £6,000 building another aircraft, he took over the old Sea Lion II. He knew it was not fast enough to beat the Americans in its existing form. He consequently decided to redesign and re-engine it to get at least another 15 mph over the previous year's winner, and recovered it from the Air Ministry for this purpose. This gave R. J. Mitchell the worst job of his career, to get more speed out of an aeroplane that had originally been redesigned for high-speed racing and indeed was the fastest seaplane in the world only twelve months before, but one which possibly would be outclassed.

Mitchell increased the wing area to cater for 400 lb weight increase, altered the lines of the bottom of the hull so as to offer less frontal air resistance with a slight increase in hull length. The wingtip floats were mounted on streamlined struts and once more there was a modified rudder with increased area. Napiers again supplied an engine, this time a Series III Lion of 525 hp, which was encased in a streamline cowling behind a circular nose radiator, in a much cleaner installation than those of the earlier Sea Lions.

The Sea Lion III as flown in the 1923 Schneider event at Cowes.

Naturally Henri Biard was selected as pilot. When he saw Sea Lion III for the first time he said, 'She is going to be a bit playful to get off the water', and he was proved right shortly after. He climbed into the cockpit, started up the engine and almost instantly found himself in the air. The machine had wanted to hydroplane into the air before flying speed was reached and this was not to his liking because, unless the pilot was careful, the aircraft would bump up and down on to the water at high speed and anything could happen. This no doubt was the old porpoising trouble again. The only thing as far as Biard was concerned was to open up the engine flat out from the start, take a phenomenally short run on the water and jump straight into the air with speed enough to climb straight away rapidly. This he considered was an asset for the race as long as he could manage the take off properly. After several flights he got the measure of the take off and the general handling characteristics in the air were really good, so that when he managed to get up to 160 mph he considered there seemed a chance against the Americans, however slim.

For the 1923 race there were eleven entries but as the race date approached most of them began to develop trouble of one sort or another. Kenworthy in the Blackburn Pellet (a converted N.1B design contemporary with the Supermarine Baby) had two amazing escapes from drowning when the machine finished up

65

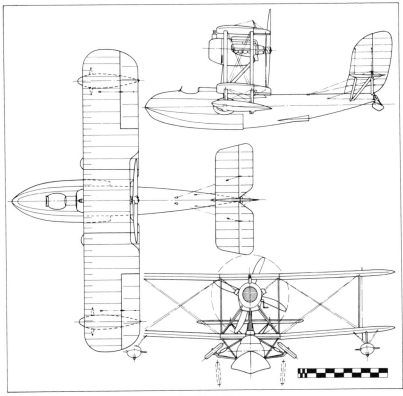

Sea Lion III

under the water. The second time it was too late to do anything about reconstruction because the mishap occurred during the navigation tests of the contest. The Sopwith-Hawker entry had crashed previously so that this once again meant that the Supermarine entry was the only one competing for Great Britain, and the two Italian entries were withdrawn before the start. The third American entry, the Navy Wright biplane, also was in difficulties on test off Selsey Bill, when its high-power Wright T-2 engine of reputed 700 hp disintegrated after only 20 minutes flying. This led to the breaking up of the three-blade metal propeller, the puncturing of the floats and the capsizing of the machine, without harming the pilot. But the showing of the Curtiss CR-3s in practice was ominous. Thus, this seventh Contest, held 27–28 September, 1923, at Cowes over a five-lap course totalling 186 nautical miles, had only four competitors for the race itself on the second day of the contest, two American, the British Sea Lion III and one French CAMS 38.

The two Americans took off first and the moment Biard saw them flying he doubted if the poor old Sea Lion could match them. He took off after them, the Sea Lion getting up so sharply off the starting line that the judges disqualified it but, on protests from General Brancker aboard the judges' barge, the disqualification was quashed. However, Biard knew nothing at all about this and was trying to persuade the last ounce of speed out of the Sea Lion in chasing the

Americans, with the lone Frenchman on his tail. On each turn at Selsey he cut his engine to get round more sharply and on the one leg with the wind behind him he could get up to over 170 mph, but to no avail. The Frenchman in the CAMS had engine failure on the first lap and so that left only three competitors. All finished the race, Lt D. Rittenhouse, US Navy, was the winner at an average speed of 177·38 mph, a new World Air Speed Record, Irvine, the second American did 173·47 mph, Biard coming in third at 157·17 mph. Just to give the crowd some consolation and the Americans a salute, as soon as Biard had crossed the line he zoomed to 5,000 ft over Cowes and descended round and round in a fast spiral to alight on the water. The aircraft was tied up and Biard went off to shake hands with Rittenhouse.

Scott-Paine was very disappointed at the failure of the Sea Lion to win the race but under the conditions of a limited budget out of his own and the company's funds, and the fact that the hull was originally built in about 1916, the aircraft had put up a good show against the Government-backed $2m high-speed flight of the Americans.

After the race the Air Ministry once again wanted the aircraft back and Biard had to fly it to the Isle of Grain air station from Southampton, which he accomplished in less than an hour, and said goodbye to it there. Sqn Ldr Rea then flew it from there to the Marine Aircraft Experimental Establishment at Felixstowe after being warned by Biard about the take-off, of how it wanted to rise before sufficient flying speed had been reached. Rea managed to deliver it safely.

The Sea Lion was then given over to Flg Off E. E. Paull-Smith for tests. He too was warned about the quick take-off characteristic but he insisted that the danger was greater if the aircraft was taken off at full throttle from the start. He said he would rather try it at first more slowly, though once again being warned. On 5 July, 1924, Smith went out for a trial flight, started up the engine, taxied beautifully on the water, found himself rising without sufficient speed to climb, rose only a few feet and the machine came down on its nose, bounced up again to about forty feet, stalled and dived straight in.

The Sea Lion III at Felixstowe Marine Aircraft Experimental Establishment.

The Sea Lion was smashed into a mass of twisted metal and splintered wood and Flg Off Smith was killed instantly, the whole mass being taken to the sea bed with him pinned in it. The wreckage was salvaged but was not worth putting together again. A sad end to a fine aeroplane and a splendid pilot.

For good reasons, this seventh Contest for the Schneider Trophy saw the end of the flying-boat as a contender in future races, however gallant the efforts of the Supermarine Sea Lions had been. The American combination of the outstanding Curtiss D-12 engine, with the highly streamlined Curtiss CR-3 airframe on floats, of low overall frontal area, was the deciding factor in the 1923 Schneider race. With the high-speed light alloy thin-bladed Reed propeller and the flush-mounted corrugated wing radiators, this sophisticated concept set a new pattern for high-speed flight in the next decade. In this context the single-seat flying-boat was out and floatplanes were the only answer from then on, and Supermarine were not behind in these ultimate developments.

Sea Lion I—One 450 hp Napier Lion IA. Single seat.
Span (upper) 35 ft (10·66 m), (lower) 28 ft 3 in (8·61 m); length 26 ft 4 in (8·02 m); wing area 380 sq ft (35·3 sq m).
Empty weight 2,000 lb (907 kg); loaded weight 2,900 lb (1,315 kg).
Maximum speed 147 mph (236·5 km/h); duration 2½ hr.

Sea Lion II—One 450 hp Napier Lion II. Single seat.
Span 32 ft (9·75 m); length 24 ft 9 in (7·54 m); wing area 384 sq ft (35·67 sq m).
Empty weight 2,115 lb (959 kg); loaded weight (less undercarriage) 2,850 lb (1,292 kg).
Maximum speed 160 mph (257·4 km/h); duration 3 hr.

Sea Lion III—One 525 hp Napier Lion III. Single seat.
Span 28 ft (8·53 m); length 28 ft (8·53 m); wing area 360 sq ft (33·44 sq m).
Empty weight 2,400 lb (1,088 kg); loaded weight 3,275 lb (1,485 kg).
Maximum speed 175 mph (281·6 km/h); alighting speed 55 mph (88·5 km/h); duration 3 hr.
Figures quoted are for aircraft in racing trim.

Seal and Seagulls

Following the successful Commercial Aircraft competition in 1920, the Air Ministry bought the winning Vickers Viking III for £8,000 and ordered from Supermarine a development of their Commercial Amphibian, which had won an augmented second prize. The two types of amphibian were allocated the serials N146 and N147 respectively. The first drawings for the Supermarine development aircraft were dated 25 November, 1920, and were labelled Seal Mk II so it must be assumed that the short-lived Supermarine Commercial Amphibian was regarded as Seal Mk I. Design and construction of the aircraft went ahead until May 1921, when it flew and, after contractor's flight trials, it was handed over officially at Woolston on 2 June, 1921. It was then flown by an RAF pilot direct to the Isle of Grain for Service trials.

Launching the Seal at Woolston.

The Seal was designed by Mitchell to incorporate the improvements suggested by the competition report on the Commercial Amphibian. The basic requirement was for a three-seat deck-landing amphibian intended as a fleet spotter and to be operated by Royal Air Force units aboard the Royal Navy's aircraft carriers, which was the operational pattern of that time. To facilitate deck landing, the Seal was to have the lowest possible landing speed and to have a high degree of control at low speed. First-class seaworthiness was essential when used as a seaplane.

Mitchell chose a tractor layout for his Seal II for no obvious reason other than that of balance. The liquid-cooled Napier Lion engine and the disposition of the crew combined with the requirement for rearward folding wings demanded by the minimal storage space in warships necessitated mounting the wings further forward

The Seal with a Sea King (left) contrasting tractor and pusher configurations.

69

than those of the Commercial Amphibian, which was a non-folder. The pilot was located forward in the nose and had a machine-gun on a retractable mounting for stowage, with a cover to keep water out of the cockpit. The fuel tanks were inside the hull behind the pilot thus isolating him from the rest of the crew, the wireless operator being just behind the wings and the rear gunner still further aft.

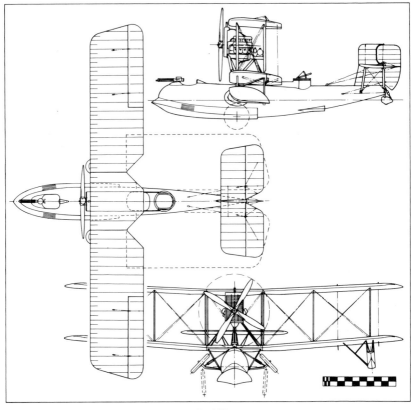

Seal II

The Seal was a wooden aeroplane following the established practice of detail design by Supermarine, with a Linton Hope type hull comprising an oval cross-section shell with the planing bottom and the two steps built on externally. The intervening space formed watertight compartments and minimized the effect of damage from flotsam. The dual-purpose tailskid cum water-rudder was located at the sternpost, forward of its position on the Commercial Amphibian, with an easily detachable shoe fitted to the heel of the rudder. Wingtip floats were carried on struts below the wings to give water clearance and gain maximum effect from their buoyancy.

Difficulties arose once more over yaw characteristics. The rudder design went through several permutations of shape, as three versions were drawn before the outline was arrived at on N146 as first flown. Obviously, directional control still needed attention because a fin extension was added and this final outline survived

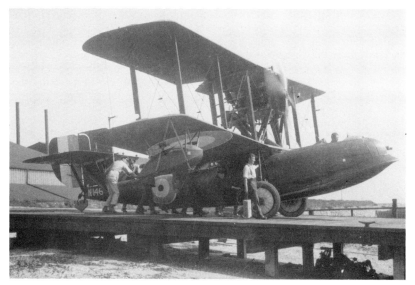

Seal N146 with modified balanced rudder.

into later versions of Seagull—as the Seal was renamed on 4 July, 1922, when all drawings were re-titled.

During the building of the Seal a design study was made under Air Ministry development contract 198793/20 for a fleet gunnery spotting amphibian. Nothing came of this but the project is of interest because its pusher layout foreshadowed the last of the Seagulls, the Mk V.

One Seal was exported to Japan in 1922 under the agreements reached between the Japanese Admiralty and Col the Master of Sempill, leader of the British aviation mission to Japan. This Seal kept company with the Channel IIs and a

A Seagull I at Tokyo naval base, with a Supermarine Channel in the background.

Seagull I in the naval base at Tokyo with other British aircraft intended to show the advanced designs available from Britain's industry.

Elsewhere in this book reference is made to the privations of the British aircraft industry after the First World War. Many of the smaller firms went out of business—small recompense for their valiant effort in producing the great air fleets with the aid of which the Allies achieved victory. With great fortitude Supermarine had kept afloat but in 1922 things had come almost to an impasse for them despite their minor successes. In consequence of the straits in which Woolston Works found themselves, with a rapidly dwindling order book, Commander Bird as London director went to see Air Vice-Marshal Sir Geoffrey Salmond who was then Air Member for Supply and Research of the Air Council. The following letter was received in reply from Sir Geoffrey's private secretary:
'Dear Commander Bird,

With reference to your interview with Air Vice-Marshal Sir Geoffrey Salmond, he wishes me to say that a proposal for placing anticipatory orders is under consideration; although no promise can be made that the proposal will be approved, he thinks it might be inexpedient on your part to close down your works entirely.

Having regard to this, you may think it fit to retain the minimum plant required for carrying out an order, the exact amount of which cannot yet be stated, but which might approach 18 machines, spread over the period ending March 31st, 1924.'

This tacit promise related to orders for the single-engined Seagulls which enabled Supermarine to remain in business. No doubt the far sighted decisions made by Executive air officers like Sir Geoffrey himself and Sir Sefton Brancker as Director of Civil Aviation saved much of the adolescent aircraft industry. Despite the paucity of Treasury allocations for aviation anyone with his heart in the air business somehow managed to survive.

The Seal II N146 was converted to the Seagull I with the more powerful 480 hp Lion II engine, a modified engine mounting and redesigned radiator shutters, wingtip floats and ailerons. A pilot order was placed by the Air Ministry in

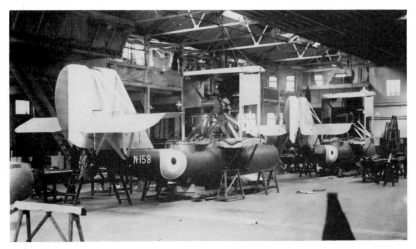

Seagull IIs under construction at Woolston.

Sir Warden Chilcott MP, Commander James Bird, General Bagnall-Wild (Director of Research), the Duke of Sutherland (Under Secretary of State for Air), Air Vice-Marshal Vyvyan and Hubert Scott-Paine, with Seagull II N9563 at Woolston in February 1923 on the occasion of a progress inspection of the Sea Eagle.

February 1922 for two Seagulls similar to N146 with further minor modifications and these were given the serials N158 and N159. These aircraft must have been under construction in anticipation of an order, for the Martlesham Heath report on type trials was dated March 1922. These trials were conducted with the Seagull in landplane form. Small-batch orders were later received by Supermarine which approximated to the eighteen aircraft promised. These kept the company afloat until its outstanding design for a twin-engined military flying-boat, which came after the Seagulls, brought stability at last.

Five Seagulls, N9562 to N9566, were completed in 1923. On 23 February the Under Secretary of State for Air, the Duke of Sutherland, with General Bagnall-Wild, Director of Research, and Air Vice-Marshal Vyvyan of the Air Ministry visited Woolston Works to inspect the aircraft under construction.

The Seagulls followed Supermarine detail design as already established, but the retractable undercarriage was a refinement of previous types in that the landing loads were carried by an almost vertical telescopic strut to the centre section front spar, with scarcely any load transmitted to the hull. By moving the upper end of the main telescopic strut in towards the centre of the aircraft, the wheels were lifted clear of the water.

Warning klaxons and dashboard indicators were not yet devised for these early amphibians nor indeed were many pilots accustomed to retractable under-carriages.* In May 1923 a Service pilot took off from the water in a Seagull at Cowes to fly to Gosport aerodrome and forgot to lower his undercarriage. The Seagull made a normal landing on its hull and the pilot only realised his mistake when the aircraft keeled over on one of its wingtip floats. No damage whatever resulted from this unpremeditated event and later the Seagull took off on its

---

*When claims are made for the first retracting undercarriages it is sometimes forgotten that Supermarine amphibians had standardized them years before but strangely never stowed them to reduce drag until the Seagull Mk V appeared.

73

Launching Seagull II N9607 at Woolston. (*Science Museum*)

wheels and alighted on the sea with the undercarriage properly raised. On record is at least one Short Sunderland flying-boat making a successful landing on an airfield during the Second World War.

The first production Seagulls were chosen to form 440 (RAF) Fleet Reconnaissance Flight in 1923 and in February of that year another batch of five was ordered, N9603 to N9607, to supplement the original five, and this was followed on 21 June by the largest order yet, for thirteen, N9642 to N9654. Six of these Mk II Seagulls were allocated as shipboard aircraft to HMS *Eagle*, a carrier converted from the former Chilean battleship *Almirante Cochrane*, first commissioned in 1920 but now to serve with the Royal Navy in the Mediterranean Fleet. After this tour of duty which included Malta, the Seagulls were assessed as having 'no potential naval use' which presumably meant as carrier-borne types. Aircraft such as the Fairey IIID which could operate either as floatplane or landplane had proved more tractable in service at sea so the Seagull's practical use was confined to coastal reconnaissance.

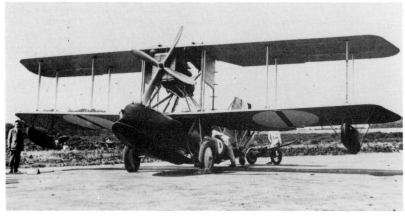

Seagull II as No.1 in the 1924 King's Cup Air Race. (*Science Museum*)

74

The single-engined Seagull was never an outstanding success but fortunately for Supermarine it was followed by a new highly promising twin-engined design—the Southampton. However Seagulls featured in public events such as the Royal Air Force Pageants of 1923 and 1924 and in the King's Cup Air Race of the latter year. The unique sight of a flying-boat taxi-ing past the enclosures at Hendon in the 1923 Pageant was indeed a novelty and in the 1924 event the Supermarine Seagull was 'fired' on by AA guns in the set-piece of the display but radioed for help by calling up a flight of Fairey Flycatcher naval fighters.

In the King's Cup Air Race of 1924 two Seagulls were entered by permission of the Air Ministry in the names of Cdr J. Bird (of Supermarine) and H. T. Vane (of Napier) under race number 1 and G. L. Wood and Capt L. Moseley as number 2. They were crewed by Henri Biard with Capt F. J. Bailey as navigator in one and by Col the Master of Sempill with Flt Lt C. G. Rea in the other. The Seagulls were flown in to Martlesham, the starting point, the previous day from neighbouring Felixstowe marine base and each received a handicap allowance of 3 hr 32 min from the two Siskin fighters on scratch. The refuelling stops were scheduled at Seaton Carew (West Hartlepool), Renfrew, Holyhead and Padstow, with the finishing line at Lee-on-Solent.

Supermarine experienced their usual run of ill fortune in this particular race which however should be regarded more as a sporting event than the international rivalries of the Schneider Trophy races which called for decidedly more serious effort in preparation of special aircraft. Both the Seagulls had exciting moments. Flying over Newcastle at 3,000 ft Biard heard a sharp metallic crack above the roar of his Lion engine and after passing a hasty warning note to Bailey was the recipient of a terrific crack on the top of his head. Later it transpired that a blade of the propeller had broken off and was found eventually in the bottom of the cockpit. Biard slumped over the controls and, with the aeroplane gyrating around the sky, pieces of metal were flying around the pilot and chunks were piercing the mainplanes. Biard recovered his senses and found the Seagull plunging down towards Newcastle. At the same moment the rest of the propeller came off, and sliced off the nose of the starboard petrol tank. There was a thumping roar and a blast of flame as the tank exploded. Fortunately the flames were carried aft by the airflow and nothing else caught fire. In its precipitate departure, the propeller smashed the radiator sending boiling water down Biard's back, luckily 'leathered'.

Biard was given to romancing but this near catastrophic experience disclosed how good a pilot he really was for, after making a steep turn over the Tyne, he quickly set about finding somewhere to land as his undercarriage was down; a water alighting was ruled out because one and a half minutes of valuable time was needed to raise it. He spotted the old Blaydon racecourse at Stella Houghs and put the Seagull down on a small slag heap with damage only resulting from the errant propeller; this, or what was left of it, was found two miles away where it had fallen into a backyard.

The Master of Sempill in the other Seagull was seriously delayed by a combination of minor troubles and arrived last of the six machines that finished, much to the relief of the awaiting crowd at Lee as he was over three hours late. His officially corrected time was 13 hr 48 sec, an average of 73·14 mph. At Renfrew he had to replace a broken wiring plate with one quickly made up by Beardmore's aircraft division and then was further delayed by a refractory engine which refused to start first time. A 30 mph headwind all the way to the South coast necessitated refuelling, both at Anglesey and at Padstow.

In April 1925 the Australian Minister of Defence announced that Supermarine Seagulls were to be acquired for the Royal Australian Air Force and these amphibians would be carrier-borne to avoid the necessity of building a seaplane base at Sydney. Six were ordered, serialled A9-1 to A9-6; they were classified as Mk IIIs with the Australian modifications from the British Mk IIs. The first of them was named by Lady Cook, wife of the High Commissioner for Australia, at Woolston in February 1926, in the usual nautical tradition with the words 'I name thee Australian *Seagull 1*' etc. Equally traditional in the air business was the acceptance flight with Henri Biard, Sir James Cook, and Sqn Ldr R. S. Brown, RAAF. All six Seagulls were delivered by sea and stationed at Point Cook, Victoria, where they were formed as 101 Fleet Co-operation Flight, RAAF, on 30 June, 1926.

Even before delivery specific tasks had been reserved for the Seagulls, and two had been allocated to make photographic reconnaissance surveys of various regions of Australasia. The first sortie was conducted on behalf of the Anglo-Persian Oil Company to cover an area of 10,000 square miles in Papua, investigating geological formations already located as oil bearing, and to locate suitable bases for future surveys after the monsoons had subsided. The Seagulls left Melbourne on 27 September, 1927, and arrived at Thursday Island on 13 Octo-

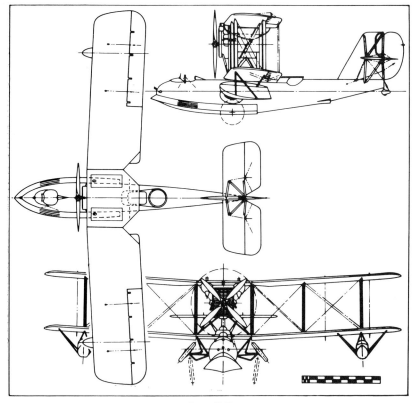

Seagull II

76

Royal Australian Air Force Seagull IIIs over Hobart, Tasmania, in 1930.

ber. The Papuans were disturbed by the sight of aircraft at first but later became accustomed to flying machines and actually travelled long distances to see them.

A great deal of survey was accomplished by the Australian Seagulls, covering 2,000 miles around the coast of Papua and adjoining Mandated Territories, the Great Barrier Reef and the Queensland coast, within range of Bowen, Mackay and Gladstone. The support ship HMAS *Moresby* acted throughout as seaplane tender. The distances flown on these tasks were remarkable for an aeroplane not designed specifically for long-range work. One flight made by Lt (later Air Vice-Marshal) E. C. Wackett from Melbourne covered 13,000 miles in easy stages. A naval pilot, Commander F. J. Crowther, reported that although the Seagull took over one hour to reach 8,000 ft, it was delightful to fly.

The first warship to be built in Australia (from parts supplied by the United Kingdom) was HMAS *Albatross*, an aircraft carrier commissioned on 23 January, 1929, from the Cockatoo dockyard* in Sydney. Its displacement was 6,000 tons and the Seagulls had to be hoisted aboard or lowered by ship's cranes. The carrier had a normal capacity for six at one time. The first Seagulls were embarked in February 1929 at Geelong and the Mk IIIs served for the next four years in *Albatross*, being transferred (those still serviceable) to the heavy cruisers *Australia* and *Canberra*, and they survived until replaced by the Seagull Mk Vs.

*Acquired by Vickers in 1947.

The curious situation whereby the Seagulls were deemed unsatisfactory as shipborne aircraft with the Royal Navy and yet seemed to have been so successful in Australian naval service is difficult to explain. But aircrew of 440 Flight on HMS *Eagle* reported that the Seagull Mk I suffered from lack of communication between pilot and observer caused by the interposition of the fuel tank in the hull and also that the stabilizing curtains which 'boxed' the engine installation made the machine very noisy. When the carrier reached the Mediterranean the Seagulls failed to cope with the sea conditions and with summer heat in Kalafrana Bay, Malta, and were not easy to deck land.

Seagull II N9605 with single fin. In the picture are R. J. Mitchell and Henri Biard (darker hat).

The Australian Seagull IIIs were identical to the RAF Mk II version with the exception of the radiators which were modified for tropical use and were oval in shape. Various experimental modifications were either planned or made on the Seagull II. One was to have been fitted with hydrovanes but apparently this idea was not pursued. During 1928 Handley Page slots and a new tail unit with twin fins and rudders were fitted to Seagull II N9605 and this individual aeroplane is usually regarded as Mark IV, although surviving Supermarine records contain no such classification. It received a civil certificate of airworthiness as G-AAIZ on 10 July, 1929, and this was issued to Tours and Travel Association Ltd of Brooklands who had leased the Woolston operating base from Imperial Airways with the purpose of reviving the Southampton–Channel Islands flying-boat service, dormant since soon after the Sea Eagles had been phased out.

High hopes were held that this enterprise would meet with greater success than previous attempts, judging from the advance publicity. G-AAIZ was converted to a six-seater with a Lion IIB engine and the cabin was advertized as 'luxuriously appointed'. With its Handley Page slotted wings the Seagull was claimed as 'the last word in air travel'. It was, but not in the sense intended, for after several brave

Seagull IV N9605 with Handley Page slots and twin fins and rudders.

attempts to keep to the schedule laid down in the published timetable, the service ended prematurely on Southsea Beach with engine trouble on 2 September. No other Seagull was converted for the Channel Islands service although a small fleet had been planned. The reason for fitting the twin vertical tail surfaces is not known but is assumed to have improved control in yaw and to have been borrowed from the triple fins and rudders of the contemporary Southampton, in which directional control was so good. On the other hand, they may have been introduced in connection with the airflow aft of the slotted upper wing.

Another factor under design review at that time and one which did not endear the Seagull to its pilots was its nasty habit of porpoising on take-off, the old bugbear of the flying-boat. Three Seagulls were subjected to tests in this matter at Felixstowe followed by comparative model tank tests by the National Physical Laboratory at Teddington. Various permutations of step position were tried out on N9606 and N9565. The tests must have convinced the authorities of the value

Seagull II G-EBXH was formerly N9653.

79

Seagull N9644 at Felixstowe in 1930 with Bristol Jupiter IX geared radial driving a pusher propeller. (*Ministry of Defence*)

of preliminary water-tank testing for after then no new seaplane design could be accepted without it. Action had been suggested after the fatal Sea Lion III accident to Flg Off Paull-Smith, a valuable pilot, as already recorded, but at long last C. S. Baker and the NPL had won their battle to make tank-testing for seaplanes mandatory.

Two other Seagulls received civil registrations, N9653 as G-EBXH and N9654 as G-EBXI, on 16 July, 1928, for operation by F. Tyllye and F. H. Winn as six-seaters for their Coastal Flying Boat Services at Shoreham. Both were fitted with the Napier Lion V. The intention was to provide a charter and joy-ride service, but again success proved elusive and the aircraft were scrapped in 1930 because of poor public response and the proposed air link with Dieppe failed to materialize. The three civil Seagulls were surplus to military requirements and had been sold by the Air Ministry when the type went out of service in 1928. Three more were sold at £100 each minus engines to the Australian authorities to add to their fleet, serialled A9-7 to A9-9, and obviously were a bargain, for spares.

In 1925 the Seagull was used to test the first British catapult for aeroplane launching at the Royal Aircraft Establishment at Jersey Brow, Farnborough. The pilot was Flt Lt R. A. de Haga Haig and the catapult trials were under the direction of P. Salmon assisted by J. D. H. Pritchard, S. Child, C. Crowfoot and A. R. Crossfield. Development of the catapult progressed from compressed air to cordite as energy source. As in pioneering work with the pilot ejection seat, the performance of the explosive charge was a criterion and after a successful initial launch by the Seagull on 19 May, 1926, and followed by a Parnall Peto on 6 July, the cordite-operated catapult finally went into service at sea on HMS *York* in May 1928. Later on, Seagull Vs made extensive use of the catapult system of deck launching from ships at sea.

The last experimental Seagull was to change the type's rather chequered story beyond expectation, particularly in naval and military circles. This exercise involved the fitting of a Bristol Jupiter IX geared air-cooled radial engine to Seagull II N9644 in a pusher layout, so reverting to the design philosophy of earlier years in the Commercial Amphibian and the Sea Lions. The reasons for this *volte-face* appear to have been a comparison of the tractor and pusher configurations or the possibility of reviving the single-seat fighter flying-boat, but its practical effect was to lead to the Seagull V, better known as the Walrus.

Seal II—One 450 hp Napier Lion. Pilot, wireless operator, gunner.
Span 46 ft (14·02 m); length 32 ft 10 in (10 m); height 14 ft 10 in (4·52 m); wing area 620 sq ft (57·6 sq m).
Empty weight 4,100 lb (1,859 kg); loaded weight 5,600 lb (2,540 kg).
Maximum speed 112 mph (180·2 km/h); minimum speed 55 mph (88·5 km/h); climb to 10,000 ft (3,048 m) 17 min; duration 4 hr.

Seagull I—One 480 hp Napier Lion II. Pilot, observer, wireless operator.
Span 45 ft 11 in (13·99 m); length 34 ft 6 in (10·51 m); height 13 ft 6 in (4·11 m); wing area 605 sq ft (56·2 sq m).
Empty weight 3,691 lb (1,674 kg); loaded weight 5,462 lb (2,477 kg).
Maximum speed 80 mph (129 km/h) at sea level; climb to 3,000 ft (914 m) 6·8 min, service ceiling 9,000 ft (2,743 m); duration 3½ hr.
Armament. One 0·303-in Lewis machine-gun aft of wings.
Report MM263C—March 1922.

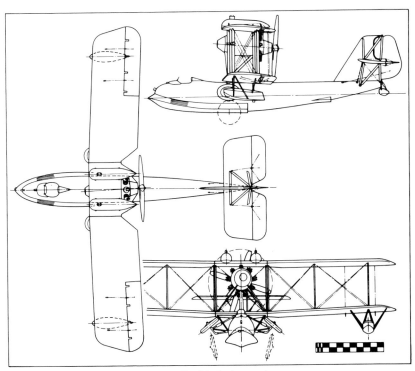

Seagull II with Jupiter engine

Seagull II—One 492 hp Napier Lion IIB. Pilot, observer, wireless operator.

Span 46 ft (14·02 m); length 37 ft 9 in (11·5 m); height 14 ft (4·26 m); wing area 593 sq ft (55·09 sq m).

Empty weight 3,820 lb (1,732 kg); loaded weight 5,691 lb (2,581 kg).

Maximum speed 85 kt (157·5 km/h) at 3,000 ft (914 m), 79·8 kt (147·8 km/h) at 6,500 ft (1,981 m); climb to 3,000 ft (914 m) 7 min 43 sec; service ceiling 9,150 ft (2,788 m); duration 4½ hr.

From report M327 of March, 1923.

Seagull III—One 492 hp Napier Lion V. Crew three.

Span 46 ft (14·02 m); length 37 ft 9 in (11·5 m); height 14 ft (4·27 m); wing area 593 sq ft (55 sq m).

Empty weight 3,820 lb (1,733 kg); loaded weight 5,691 lb (2,581 kg).

Maximum speed 85 mph (137 km/h) at sea level.

Climb to 3,000 ft (914 m) in 7·67 min; service ceiling 9,150 ft (2,789 m); endurance 4½ hr at 3,000 ft (914 m).

Armament. One 0·303-in Lewis machine-gun aft of wings.

Report MAEE M327 March 1923.

Scarab and Sheldrake

In February 1924 the Spanish Royal Naval Air Service placed an order with Supermarine for twelve Scarab amphibian flying-boats, based on the Sea Eagle, to be fitted with either the 360 hp Rolls-Royce Eagle IX or the 450 hp Napier Lion, and to be used for bombing and reconnaissance work, with a maximum bomb load of 1,000 lb.

The hull was built on standard Supermarine lines and was very seaworthy, and the cockpits remained consistently dry under all weather conditions. The machine handled easily and effectively on the water by means of its water rudder and could be turned in a radius of one span. It could also be towed in all conditions of wind and tide. All the crew were placed in front of the mainplanes, with good inter-communication. The pilot was seated right forward, with the gunner behind him. Furthest aft was the navigator/wireless operator, with his spacious wireless cabin in the hull immediately behind. This arrangement followed the original Channel layout, and dual control could be fitted in the middle cockpit. The retractable undercarriage was similar to that of the Seagull. Fuel supply was by direct gravity feed from the two petrol tanks situated on the top of the upper centre section as on the Seagull III. Twelve 50 lb bombs were carried on a revolving mounting in the interior of the hull in the area previously used for fuel in the Seagull. The bombs were discharged through a tunnel and aperture in the bottom of the hull, suitably closed when on the water, very similar to the arrangement fitted for air photography in the Venezuelan Channels. The underwing bombs were four 100 pounders.

The twelve aircraft were built during 1924 and bore the Spanish registrations M-NSAA to M-NSAL inclusive. These were special Government pseudo-civil registrations, where M stood for Spain, the second letter N for Naval, the third letter S for Ship, the fourth was A for Amphibian, and the last was the individual aircraft letter.

During April 1924 a special commission from the Spanish Navy visited Britain to inspect British aircraft construction and went to the Supermarine works to see

M-NSAA, the first Scarab for Spain, at Worthy Down for tests.

the progress of their order for the amphibian flying-boats. The party was led by the Marquis Soto Hermosa with Señor J. Franso and Admiral Don Pedro de Cardona, chief of the Spanish Naval Air Service.

M-NSAA, powered by the Eagle IX, was first flown by Biard on 21 May, 1924, in a short contractor's flight. This was followed by a flight a week later under full-load conditions, as required under the contract, before the Spanish officials concerned. After a quick all-round check, when nothing was found wrong, it was flown to Worthy Down near Winchester and landed before a group comprising the Spanish officials and RAF officers, including Flg Off E. E. Paull-Smith from Felixstowe, representing the airworthiness department of the Air Ministry. Also at Worthy Down were two members of a Greek Commission who had arrived

M-NSAL, the last Scarab for Spain, in the Woolston Works.

specially to witness the trials of the Scarab and to forward a report to their Government, but no Greek order resulted.

After a ground inspection, Flg Off Paull-Smith checked the loading sheet and essential details and then flew the aircraft back to Southampton, where he took it up for its official airworthiness test and declared it satisfactory. He stated however that 'with the present engine and full load this aircraft is not suitable as a Service type' which sounded rather critical about an aircraft which had not been ordered by his own Ministry. Other comments were that the Scarab's performance was similar to the Seagull but that it wallowed badly in turbulence. Biard then took off with two Spanish officers aboard, making test alightings in the rough waters near the Needles and also made maximum speed runs and a ceiling climb for their benefit. Back at Woolston this first Scarab was taken over by the Spanish Commission the same day.

Scarabs *en route* to Spain.

The Scarabs seemed rather unlucky for their future owners. For the official hand-over later, Admiral Cardona had come over to superintend the delivery of the machines and had brought with him a crack Spanish pilot to test fly them before they were finally accepted and shipped. He however was unused to aircraft of that size and had never handled anything like them before. He took one out into Southampton Water to test it and in trying to rise went nose first into the side of a Union Castle liner. This did the machine no good, though the liner was unscathed, but the pilot, who was not seriously hurt, mysteriously disappeared after the accident. The Scarabs were a little tricky to handle and after this incident Cardona insisted on being taken for a flight in one himself. The completed aircraft had been stored at Worthy Down and this is where the flight took place. The day the Admiral chose was a windy one and he, who was a heavy man, decided to sit in

84

The Sheldrake outside Supermarine Works.

the most forward cockpit. On take-off, a gust of wind nearly caused the machine to crash through a hedge at the end of the aerodrome, probably caused by the weight in the nose, but the flight was made successfully and Cardona said he had loved it!

For the shipment of the aircraft a newly-built 10,000 ton seaplane tender came from Spain. When Biard started landing the amphibians beside her it was discovered that, owing to some error in her construction, the lift, by which the aircraft could be lowered into the hold in the event of bad weather, was exactly four inches too small in one dimension. Try as they might the crew could not get them in the hold and in the end they had to be parked on deck under tarpaulin covers and lashed down, side by side, their wings folded back.

The Sheldrake at the Hamble Air Pageant in 1927.

85

On its way through the Bay of Biscay, a howling gale sent great waves over the ship's decks and seven of the machines were battered by the heavy seas before they even reached Spain. How many of the aircraft were delivered in one piece or were usable is not known but Spanish official sources have recently confirmed that several Scarabs were sent almost immediately on arrival in Spain to the Moroccan war and were in action against the Riff insurgents. In 1925 Scarabs took part in the Royal Review of the Spanish forces by King Alfonso at Barcelona.

In the foregoing account of the Scarab there is no precise placing of the type in the Supermarine design sequence. This is because of attempts made in the decade between 1920 and 1930 to improve designs by the simple and economical process of replacing major components by features borrowed from the constructor's other types. The Scarab was a good example of this practice. At the time Mitchell was experimenting with different hull configurations and there is little doubt that he

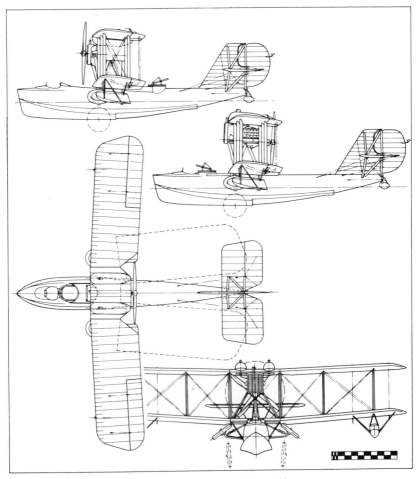

Scarab and Sheldrake

86

was not altogether satisfied with reports of the Seagull in service. Arising out of this, the Air Ministry placed an order in 1923 for what may be described as an improved Seagull, with most of that aircraft's superstructure and tail but with a hull like that of the Sea Eagle with upturned prow but with open cockpits. The serial allotted was N218.

The original Spanish enquiry for an amphibian bomber arrived about this time and in response Supermarine issued on 6 December, 1923, a specification written around the general-arrangement drawing for N218. This hybrid aircraft was called the Sheldrake and became on paper the prototype of the Scarab, although strangely the aircraft was not completed until 1927. Its only known public appearance was as number 17 in the fly-past of twenty different types in the Hampshire Air Pageant at Hamble on 12 May, 1927, an event organized by the Hampshire Aero Club. For comparison, the hull of the Sheldrake is included in side elevation with the drawing of the Scarab on the opposite page.

Scarab—One 360 hp Rolls-Royce Eagle IX. Crew three.
Span 46 ft (14 m); length 37 ft (11·3 m); height tail down 14 ft 8 in (4·47 m); width folded 17 ft 6 in (5·3 m); wing area 610 sq ft (56·7 sq m).
Empty weight 3,975 lb (1,805 kg); loaded weight 5,750 lb (2,610 kg).
Maximum speed 93 mph (149·7 km/h); landing speed 53 mph (85·2 km/h); estimated range 250 miles (402 km) at 80 mph (129 km/h).
Armament. One free-mounted 0·303-in Lewis machine-gun on Scarff ring in the rear cockpit. Bomb load up to 1,000 lb (454 kg).

Sheldrake—One 450 hp Napier Lion V. Crew three.
Span 46 ft (14 m); length 37 ft 4½ in (11·4 m); height tail up 16 ft 2½ in (4·94 m); wing area 593 sq ft (55 sq m).
Empty weight 4,125 lb (1,869·4 kg); loaded weight 6,100 lb (2,765 kg).
Maximum speed 103 mph (165·5 km/h) at sea level; landing speed 55 mph (88·5 km/h); estimated range 250 miles (402 km) at 85 mph (137 km/h).
Armament. One Vickers 0·303-in machine-gun in nose and one Lewis 0·303-in machine-gun in rear cockpit. Bomb load up to 1,000 lb (454 kg).

Scylla and Swan

Soon after the end of the First World War the Air Ministry were seeking improved designs for coastal-reconnaissance flying-boats to replace the Porte-Felixstowe F series, which had operated so successfully against enemy shipping and submarines in the confined seaways around the British Isles. Design work was started by Supermarine in 1919 on a twin-engined project known as the Shark torpedo carrier. Various schemes were explored and in 1921 a twin-engined amphibian was drawn with Rolls-Royce engines, one version of which was intended to interest the Instone Air Line.

Two separate contracts were placed with Supermarine, one in 1921 for a five-seat military boat seaplane and the other in 1922 for a commercial amphibian. The former was allocated the serial N174 and called Scylla and the latter, N175, named Swan. The Swan was ordered to specification 21/22 and this was the first twin-engined amphibian requirement in the world. While the Swan was completed and operated successfully for a time on the Channel Islands service as back-up aircraft for the Sea Eagles, the fate of the Scylla design is wrapped in mystery.

The first drawing of the Scylla entered in the Supermarine master drawing book is dated 22 March, 1922, and other drawings were prepared at intervals during 1922 of different items for the aircraft. Drawings for the twin-engine civil amphibian did not begin until October and then were produced for both types of aircraft in parallel, but after March 1923 work on the twin-engined civil amphibian was intensified and the Scylla drawings phased out. In May 1923 Rolls-Royce engines were first mentioned in the design of the Scylla and it must have been about that time that a decision had been reached as regards the two aircraft, because no drawings materialized of either the centre or upper planes for the proposed triplane Scylla and only drawings relating to taxi trials were produced. It is presumed that the first taxi trials were undertaken either in late February or early March 1924. The general-arrangement drawing of the Scylla as a taxi-ing machine was dated 1 December, 1923. It was for a flying-boat fitted with a bottom wing only, a tail unit, and two Eagle IX engines with an auxiliary engine, the 35 hp Green, in the hull driving a water propeller for slow-speed taxi-ing. This was basically going back to the time of Pemberton Billing whose original designs were for a slip-wing boat seaplane which did not materialize in any completed machines.

As can be seen from the photograph of Scylla N174 it was completed in its monoplane form and is believed to have taxied at Felixstowe but alas nothing else is known. From the drawing dated 19 December, 1923, it appears as a triplane flying-boat torpedo carrier fitted with two 550 hp Rolls-Royce Condor engines and thus it is assumed that this might have been the final design configuration but there is no other evidence in support.

Scylla nearing completion at Woolston Works. The water propeller can be seen beneath the N of the serial number.

The hull of the Scylla outside the Supermarine head office in Hazel Road, Woolston, before leaving for taxi-ing trials at Felixstowe.

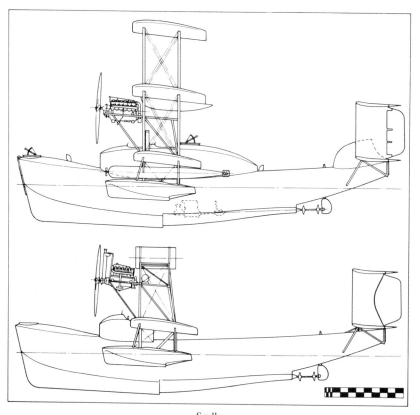

Scylla

The Swan, however, was completed as planned in 1924 but as a reconnaissance flying-boat fitted with two Rolls-Royce Eagle IX engines of 360 hp each. It was first flown by Biard on 25 March, 1924, and its equal-span two-bay wings were designed to fold forwards to minimize hangar storage although the width saved hardly justified the added complications and weight. In its original form of 1923 it was drawn as a twelve-passenger amphibian with the passengers seated in the hull and the crew of two in a separate raised cockpit on the top of the hull, above and behind the passengers, only protected from the elements by windscreens for the side-by-side pilot and navigator. For its first flight it had no windows for the passengers, no armament was fitted and it was used by the Air Ministry only as an experimental machine. It was sent to the MAEE at Felixstowe for tests and gained such excellent reports that an immediate order from the Air Ministry was received. A revised specification, R.18/24, was written up which eventually resulted in the Southampton flying-boat.

Even before the Swan's first flight R. J. Mitchell had converted its design to an armed reconnaissance machine fitted with two gun turrets on the upper main-planes, basically similar to those requested by the Air Ministry for the Vickers Virginia and flown as such later in 1924. In Mitchell's case he had the whole of the nacelle above the wing, with a position for the machine-gun on a front ring or a rear ring as required by the gunner. The aircraft also had a machine-gun in the bows and provision for two underwing bombs. This project was not pursued in the Swan but was taken up later on Southampton N9896.

The undercarriage retraction system of the Swan was an ingenious mechanism actuated by a fan mounted in the slipstream on a gearbox which, when faced forwards, retracted the undercarriage. When the gearbox was rotated about its vertical axis to face aft, the fan shaft thereby reversed and the undercarriage was

Swan N175 on slipway. The cut-outs in the top wing are to enable wing folding.

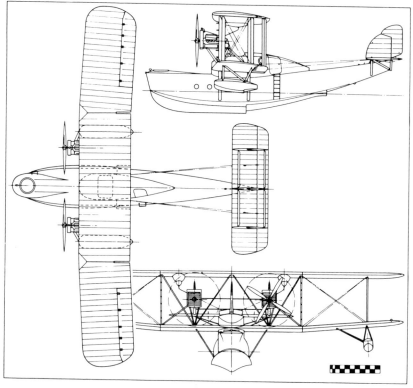

Swan

lowered. The control was operated by the pilot and the system took the manual labour out of the operation. With this new system, after one or two adjustments, the retraction could be made in about half a minute.

During these early trials it must have been found that performance was below requirements and so the Eagle engines were replaced by two Napier Lion IIBs of 450 hp and the Swan was first flown with these units on 25 June, 1924, for 1 hr 45 min. Two days later HRH Edward, Prince of Wales, visited Southampton to open a new floating dock and before doing so called at the Supermarine Aviation Works at Woolston. He was shown around by Squadron Commander Bird, the managing director, and Mr Leigh Mossley and visited almost all the workshops including No. 1 erecting shop. Then it was the turn of the Supermarine Seagulls to be inspected in No. 3 erecting shop, followed by the Swan on the slipway. Biard offered to show the Prince inside the cabins but he only smiled and said 'Not up that ladder—with this sword!'

At the time the engines were changed, the Swan was converted to a straight-forward flying-boat by the simple expedient of removing the undercarriage, the wing folding was dispensed with and the V-shaped slots in the leading edges of the wings were filled in. These modifications increased the top speed of the aircraft from 92 mph to 105 mph.

After contractor's trials, N175 was delivered to the MAEE at Felixstowe during August 1924 for further trials which again proved very successful. By 4 December, 1924, it had completed twenty hours of test flying, which by today's standards is little but in those days was considerable.

Mitchell must have realized that the large cockpit for the crew constituted a high drag component, as did the shape of the nose of the hull. In February 1926 he redesigned the Swan as the Mk II wherein he located the crew in the forebody of the hull in what had been the baggage compartment, streamlined the nose and completely eliminated wing folding, resulting in a shape very similar to the later Southamptons. He had also dispensed with the stagger so that the mainplanes were upright in side elevation, and the cabin windows were square in place of the original oval ones.

With trials completed the Swan returned to Southampton where it was further converted into the form and purpose originally envisaged for it, that of passenger carrying. For this configuration as a ten-seat passenger flying-boat, it was registered G-EBJY and first flew as such on 9 June, 1926. The pilot was Henri Biard, with F. J. Bailey, by that time manager of the Woolston airport, as passenger, eight young lady-employees of Supermarine, a representative of Imperial Airways (which was interested in the type for one of its seaplane services) and a

Visit by Edward, Prince of Wales, to the Supermarine Works in 1924. On the Prince's left is Sqn Cmdr James Bird (managing director) and next on the right is R. J. Mitchell. Others in the front row from left to right are Charles Grey (secretary), W. Elliott (works manager), G. L. Wood and Leigh Mossley (directors), and on the extreme right Victor Paine who for many years was publicity manager. Henri Biard is between Bird and Mitchell. The aircraft is the Swan amphibian.

The Swan, as G-EBJY, on Southampton Water.

The Swan at St Peter Port, Guernsey, in 1927 while operating Imperial Airways Southampton–Channel Islands services.

The cabin of the Swan. R. J. Mitchell is in the rear right seat.

pressman. On this flight the Swan took off with a comparatively short run, flew down Southampton Water to the Hamble river where it turned back towards the docks and made two trips to Lee-on-Solent during which two perfect alightings and take-offs were made. After approximately one hour's flying the aircraft returned to its base at Southampton.

The Swan in this form had its main cabin in the hull, modified to take ten passengers in wicker arm-chairs arranged five on either side of the cabin, with a small gangway and with a 'porthole' for each passenger. In front of the cabin was a compartment for passengers' baggage and mail, and aft of the cabin a lavatory.

A certificate of airworthiness for the carriage of passengers was issued for the Swan on 30 June, 1926, and it was loaned by the Air Ministry to Imperial Airways for civil operations. During its time with them it supplemented the Sea Eagles on the Channel Islands service in 1927 and during that year it also began a service to Deauville and Le Touquet plus an occasional flight to Cherbourg, but this was the last year of operations and the Swan was scrapped in the autumn. The real significance of the Swan experimental design was that it became the precursor of the Southampton, in its day the pride of the Royal Air Force.

Swan—Two 360 hp Rolls-Royce Eagle IX or two 450 hp Napier Lion IIB. Two crew and ten passengers.

Span 68 ft 8 in (20·9 m); length 48 ft 6 in (14·8 m); height 18 ft 3¼ in (5·6 m); folded dimensions—width 43 ft 9 in (13·33 m), length 56 ft (17·06 m), height 26 ft 1 in (7·95 m); wing area 1,264·8 sq ft (117·5 sq m).

Empty weight (Eagle) 7,800 lb (3,538 kg), (Lion) 9,170 lb (4,159 kg); loaded weight (Eagle) 11,900 lb (5,398 kg), (Lion) 12,832 lb (5,820 kg), later 13,710 lb (6,219 kg).

Maximum speed (Eagle) 92 mph (148 km/h), (Lion) 108·5 mph (175 km/h); cruising speed 83/87 mph (133·5/140 km/h); alighting speed 45/48 mph (72·4/93·3 km/h); climb (Eagle) to 5,000 ft (1,524 m) 12 min, (Lion) to 10,000 ft (3,048 m) 35 min 45 sec; service ceiling 10,200 ft (3,089 m).

A mixed flight of Southamptons flying past at an RAF Display at Hendon. The three nearest aircraft are Mk Is built in 1926 and others are Mk IIs delivered in 1927.
(*Vickers (Aviation) Ltd*)

Southampton

No doubt R. J. Mitchell will be chiefly remembered in history as the designer of the Spitfire. Before that, however, he had already made his mark as a great design engineer by the evolution of one of the most successful aircraft, in its class and in its time, ever to be operated by the Royal Air Force. This was the Southampton military flying-boat which embodied all the experience that the Supermarine organization had accumulated and set a new standard in marine aircraft. The exploration and surveys of overseas air communications by the RAF Southamptons proved to be of vital importance in the Second World War apart from their influence on the establishment of international air routes.

The emergence of a really efficient design in the large flying-boat class, after many disappointments since the phasing out of the F.5 and its variants, must have brought relief to the Air Ministry and to the marine reconnaissance squadrons of the Royal Air Force. The authorities were in fact on the point of giving up the requirement for a replacement of existing types of naval liaison and coastal patrol flying-boats. The first ray of hope came with the Felixstowe trials of the Supermarine Swan.

So the Swan virtually became the prototype of the Southampton and the Air Ministry took the then unusual step of ordering, in August 1924, six Southamptons straight 'off the drawing board', despite the fact that the Swan was originally supplied as an amphibian and its active service was limited to civil operations. Quite obviously this expeditious procurement was dictated by the technical appeal of the Swan concept as revealed by the Felixstowe trials at the MAEE, which had led to the writing of specification R.18/24. The contract was for six aircraft with serial numbers N9896 to N9901. In addition, a further contract was placed for an individual Southampton, N218, for experimental use by the Air Ministry.

The essence of the design of the Southampton was its simplicity. The Lion engines, leading British powerplants of the day, were mounted on pylons independent of the Warren-type centre section (with no wire cross-bracing), and maintenance or engine change could be undertaken with no disturbance whatever of the wing structure. Fuel supply to the engines was by gravity feed from the upper wing tanks so that no petrol lines were needed in the hull. A refuelling pump was later provided for pumping fuel up from a sump located amidships to the overhead tanks, while the aircraft was at anchor. Communication between members of the crew was easy. The rear gunners had a good field of fire, rearwards between the cantilever tail surfaces and downwards from either of the two offset gun positions, one on each side of the centre line of the aircraft.

The Mk I timber hull consisted basically of an inner body on which was built the planing bottom, steps and other appendages. This system comprised a complete double bottom running from the bows to the rear step, with the space between divided into ten watertight compartments. The inner body was free from obstruction and provided a clear passage from bows to tail as in previous Supermarine designs.

At variance from normal practice at the time, which was to build the lower wing roots into the hull, in the Southampton the main loads were carried by spar

The first Southampton hull under construction at Woolston with a Seagull III.

97

bracing tubes running down from the centre-section spars of the lower wing to reinforced stiff frames in the hull. The 'wireless' centre-section wing structures left the boat decking and the corresponding plywood-covered inner wing section entirely free for work by the crew and engineers. Leading edges of the wings were also ply-covered to smooth the aerodynamic entry.

The first of the batch of six Southamptons, N9896, was flown by Biard on 10 March, 1925, but on this first flight it sustained a damaged wingtip float. This design defect was temporarily adjusted by increasing the incidence of the floats and later they were redesigned. Contractor's trials were completed on 14 March and the Southampton was flown to Felixstowe for type trials, which it passed in good time with flying colours, including a test of its ability to maintain height on one engine.

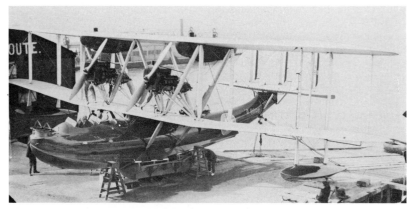

The first Southampton ready for launching at Woolston.

Delivery of Southamptons to the Royal Air Force began during the summer of 1925 to 480 Coastal Reconnaissance Flight at Calshot, a short distance from the manufacturer's works at Woolston. With a maximum range of the order of 500 miles and a cruising speed of 85/90 mph, it is not surprising that the Southampton was rapidly put into service.

When the six of the initial order had been completed further orders followed, and Supermarine had to look for more factory floor space and Commander Bird acquired a site on the sea front at Hythe on the other side of Southampton Water. There a large hangar, built during the 1914–18 War for aircraft assembly, was taken over for final erection of components made at the Woolston Works. Seagulls and Southamptons from then on were completed there and test flown from that base.

As soon as enough aircraft had been delivered to 480 (CR) Flight at Calshot, four Southamptons set out on a twenty-day cruise of 10,000 miles around the British Isles which included exercises with the Royal Navy in the Irish Sea and visits to coastal towns in Northern Ireland and southwest Scotland. In addition, a single Southampton flew from Felixstowe to Plymouth carrying Coastal Area commanding officers, thence to Carrickfergus, Belfast Lough, on to Oban and along the Great Glen to Cromarty, down to the Firth of Forth and back to Felixstowe.

The success of these cruises led the Air Ministry to issue a special communiqué on 8 October, 1925, ending with the following conclusions:

'Both cruises have shown that under conditions of weather which must throughout be considered distinctly bad, the Southampton flying-boats are capable of keeping the air and carrying out such observations as visibility will permit. What is more important, it demonstrates that a programme once having been drawn up, it can be adhered to practically independent of the weather. Refuelling at sea was carried out on all occasions without a hitch, and provided a certain amount of shelter is available when the flying-boats are not flying, it has been demonstrated that they can function successfully quite separately and independently of their land bases.' At that time the flying-boat had one great advantage over the landplane for this class of air communication, an unlimited expanse of aerodrome needing no preparation—the sea.

Starting on 2 July, 1926, two Southamptons, S1038 and S1039, flew under the command of Sqn Ldr G. E. Livock, DFC, to Egypt and back, from Plymouth via Bordeaux, Marseilles, Naples, Malta, Benghazi and Sollum to Aboukir, calling at Athens and Corfu on the return flight. Nearly 7,000 miles were covered, a lot in those days of limited overseas flying. A new feature of this long-distance flight was that the aircraft were in constant touch with land bases by W/T (wireless telegraphy).

A month after the return of the Southamptons from their Mediterranean flight, the Air Ministry decided to show the successful new flying-boats to the public. The Secretary of State for Air, Sir Samuel Hoare, welcomed four Southamptons of 480 (CR) Flight at Cromer and flew in one of them to Yarmouth. A demonstration tour was made to most of the East and South Coast towns from there round to Torquay, to the great interest of thousands of holiday-makers. Aircraft of any kind still attracted public attention in the 1920s and four flying-boats in a majestic

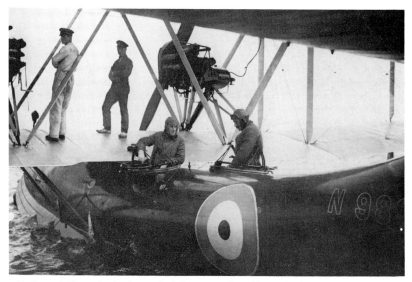

Sir Samuel Hoare in the forward of the gunners' positions aft of the wings during the prototype Southampton's East Coast cruise.

fly-past with eight roaring Lions was indeed a novelty. Later the fly-past became one of the regular features of the RAF Displays at Hendon.

While all this activity was going on with the Southampton wooden-hulled Mk Is in service, Supermarine were busy perfecting the light-alloy hull for N218. In this the Napier Lion V which powered the earlier Mk Is was replaced by the more powerful Lion Va which became the standard power unit of all Mk IIs. The twenty or so wooden-hulled RAF Mk Is were nearly all eventually converted to metal hulls and designated Mk II.

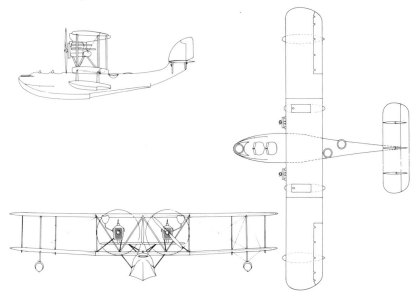

A Supermarine drawing of the Southampton II

With the adoption of the Mk II's metal hull came the saving of some 900 lb of structure weight, 500 lb in the weight of the much lighter duralumin hull and 400 lb of water soakage of the wooden hull. Range was increased by some 200 miles or alternately more stores or crew carried. The clean lines associated with the wooden hull were retained in the metal hull by a system of frames built up on a deep keel of duralumin plate, and suitably lightened by circular flanged holes and stiffened by riveted-on angles. Intercostal members were fitted between the frames and stringers to give longitudinal rigidity to the structure and the hull plating was fitted in rectangular sheeting with staggered joints arranged between the stringers and frames. Care was taken to ensure that the seaworthy qualities of the Southampton hull remained unimpaired with perfectly clean lines in the plating. The Mk II metal hull was single skinned unlike the Mk I with its double bottom and this provided more internal space and also more room for internal inspection. All light alloy components were anodized against corrosion, an important factor in marine aircraft. On reflection it seems today that here were all the elements of metal-skinned structures which could have been applied at the time to British designed civil landplanes and could possibly have predated comparative American developments.

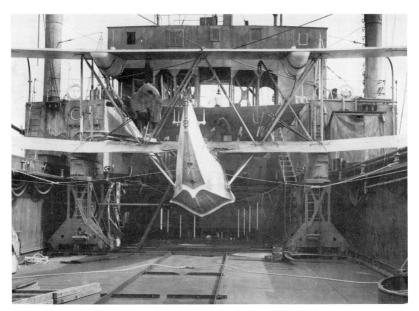

A Southampton II in floating dry dock at Milford Haven.

HRH The Duke of York (later HM King George VI) inspecting Southampton S1149.

101

The success of the metal-hulled Southampton was finally sealed by the Royal Air Force Far East Flight, undertaken by four Mk IIs, S1149, S1150, S1151 and S1152, in the latter part of 1927 and in early 1928, covering in all a total of 27,000 miles including the circumnavigation of Australia. This cruise was hailed at the time as one of the greatest achievements to date in the conquest of the air. Coming as it did just after the winning of the Schneider Trophy in September 1927 by the Supermarine S.5 racing floatplane, this put the Woolston company among the leading aircraft constructors of the day.

Metal-hulled Southampton II S1149 which acted as flagship of the RAF Far East Flight. Group Capt H. M. Cave-Brown-Cave is in the cockpit.

The objects of this challenging long-distance cruise with Southamptons were primarily to open up the Empire routes to the Far East and Australia and to collect information on potential seaplane bases, harbours and local conditions affecting aircraft operation, as up to that time (1927) only a few individual flights had reached Australia from Europe. It was also undertaken to give Service personnel experience of operating flying-boats away from land bases and supporting surface vessels and to exercise their initiative and resource under widely varying conditions.

There was no obligation to fly at high speed or to break records. Reliability was the keynote, and some of the figures quoted by Group Capt H. M. Cave-Brown-Cave, DFC, AFC., who commanded the Flight, in his paper before the Royal Aeronautical Society in 1929 are quoted here as testimony to the magnitude of the achievement. Including the extension of the tour around the South China Sea to Hong Kong and back via Indo-China and Burma to Singapore, the total distance flown excluding local flights was 27,000 miles (24,279 nautical miles), the flying time per aircraft was 351 hours 40 minutes and the average ground speed was 70 kt (80 mph). For the Hong Kong flight the spare machine S1127 replaced S1149 for experimental purposes, on Air Ministry orders.

102

The RAF Far East Flight at RAF Station Seletar, Singapore, where it formed No.205 Squadron on completion of the cruise.

Other technical points mentioned by Cave-Brown-Cave in his paper were modified fuel tanks of tinned steel instead of light alloy (to ease repair problems if needed), with capacity increased to 250 gallons each, and the oil tanks were increased to 18 gallons each. The radiator surface was increased to nearly 50 per cent more than standard in home waters to maintain a maximum coolant temperature of 76 deg C. No standard armament was carried. It should be emphasized that the aircraft of that time had no automatic pilots or blind-flying panels! Leitner-Watts metal propellers were eventually fitted to all aircraft *en route* and proved efficient. No great problems were encountered from shrinkage in the wooden members of the superstructure and little adjustment was needed.

Officers of the RAF Far East Flight 1927–28. Front row (left to right) Flt Lt C. G. Wigglesworth, Sqn Ldr G. E. Livock, Group Capt H. M. Cave-Brown-Cave, Flt Lt P. E. Maitland, Flg Off G. E. Nicholetts, Flt Lt S. T. Freeman. Back row (left to right) Flt Lt D. V. Carnegie, Flg Off B. Cheeseman, Flt Lt H. G. Sawyer, Flg Off S. D. Scott and Flg Off L. Harwood.

103

One problem that did arise in tropical waters was the rapid encrustation of barnacles and other marine growths on the hull bottoms. Paint on the upper parts of the boats and superstructures also deteriorated, particularly if black. This involved repainting during overhaul at Singapore on the outward leg and much replacement of light alloy rivets with stainless steel ones. Protection was then provided by final coats of a dope varnish known as V84 with a gum added for good adhesion. No doubt the special attention paid to the Far East Southamptons before and during the cruise amounted to the first fully tropicalized Service aircraft.

Some fourteen months had elapsed before the Far East Flight finally completed its mammoth assignment at Seletar air base, Singapore. There it was disbanded and re-formed as 205 Squadron, the first unit of the RAF in the Far East, under the command of Group Capt G. E. Livock, DFC, AFC.

During September 1930 four Southarapton Mk IIs, S1228, S1229, S1234 and S1058 of 201 Squadron, RAF, which had been formed from the original 480 (CR) Flight at Calshot, made an extended tour of the Baltic under the command of Grp Capt E. R. C. Nanson, CBE, DSC, AFC. Places visited were Esbjerg, Copenhagen, Stockholm, Helsinki, Tallin, Riga, Memel, Gothenburg and Oslo. Demonstrations were made to the various air forces and government representatives and much interest was created among the general public during fly-pasts and inspections at the moorings. The distance covered was 3,331 nautical miles and the total flying time for the four aircraft was 226 hours. The cruise was completed without any incident or mishap except when S1228 dragged its moorings in a severe gale at Copenhagen and was saved with some difficulty from drifting ashore.

The overseas cruises by the Royal Air Force put the Southampton in the forefront of marine aircraft. Its superior performance over those of comparative European flying-boats led to enquiries from other countries and in due course orders materialized from the Argentine, Japan, Turkey and the Royal Australian Air Force. In 1930 the United States Navy were quoted £7,000 for airframe less engines but no order was forthcoming, probably because of economic conditions then prevailing in the United States. The basic design of the Southampton was so attractive to the Air Ministry that some desire to 'stretch' the concept into even better developments was almost inevitable at that time of formative progress in military aircraft. N251 was rebuilt from a standard RAF Southampton with a Saunders-Roe A.14 experimental hull which it was claimed saved weight by using corrugated panels for the outer skin instead of the stringers and rivets of the normal Mk II smooth-skinned hull. This conversion was done by Saunders-Roe at Cowes and eventually resulted in the design of the Saro London flying-boat. N252 became quite a different aeroplane as the Southampton Mk X. N253 was powered experimentally with steam-cooled Rolls-Royce Kestrels and led to the Southampton Mk IV, serial S1648, prototype of the Scapa.

Other Southamptons were the subject of experiments. Sweepback of the outer wings was first introduced in 1927 in the seventh batch order and was obviously necessitated by alterations in the service loadings.

The original experimental Southampton, N218, having proved the light alloy hull for the Mk IIs, was further used to test sweepback under varying load conditions, then as a flying test-bed for the Bristol Jupiter IX air-cooled radial engine and its derivative the Jupiter XFBM, the prototype of the Bristol Pegasus. As far as can be ascertained it was the intention to re-engine the Southampton with geared air-cooled radials as Mk III, but in the tests with the Jupiters in N218 vibration was experienced which caused the project to be abandoned if in fact one

Southampton N251 with Saunders-Roe A.14 stainless steel hull.

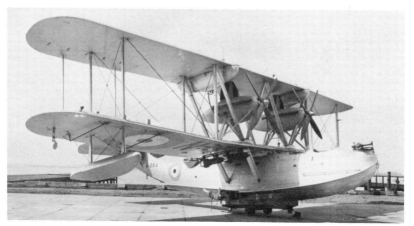

Southampton N253 with all-metal airframe and evaporative-cooled Rolls-Royce Kestrels.

Southampton N218 with Jupiter engines and Handley Page slots.

existed, although 'Mark III' was mentioned in several contracts. Subsequently Mk III was taken to refer to metal-winged Southamptons. N218 was also used to test the Handley Page leading-edge slots on the Southampton, again with no apparent advantage as they were not adopted on the Service aircraft of that type.

Another of the early Southamptons to have an adventurous career was the first, N9896, which was also used extensively for various experiments at Felixstowe, retaining its wooden hull throughout. As stated earlier, it was flown to the MAEE after only six hours' testing by Biard at Woolston. Known originally and officially as the 'Swan Conversion' to specification R.18/24, it joined the Felixstowe development flight on 2 May, 1925, and after 26 hours' test flying set off on a three-day cruise to Rosyth in the Firth of Forth and back, then a fourteen-day exercise flying from the Scilly Isles as base, and finally a week's cruise around coastal waters. According to a report, all or most of this flying was done by a junior officer, Flg Off H. G. Sawyer, which alone testifies to the confidence placed in the design by the authorities. They must have been strongly encouraged by Sawyer's report to engage in the series of long range and independent flights already described.

In 1926 N9896 was the subject of tests on alternative arrangements of the fuel tankage by placing the bulk in centre-section tanks and the remainder in the hull and eliminating the normal underwing tanks, presumably to reduce drag. With ballast to make up the weight to that of the unconverted machine, flight trials disclosed no difference in performance. Similarly, trials made in 1928 with twin fore-and-aft gun turrets mounted above the top wing of N9896 also proved abortive, as parallel trials with like installations on the top wing of the Vickers Virginia I also disclosed control problems, caused by the extra drag and weight above the centre of gravity. Apparently, N9896 was intended to be converted as the prototype Mk III on contractual evidence but on the inconclusive trials of N218 with radial engines this project was abandoned. One experiment with this

Southampton N9896 with fore and aft fighting tops.

Southampton N9900 being fitted with Mk VIII torpedo and having main fuel sump filled.

aeroplane that did have some success was the fitting of Leitner-Watts metal propellers in which pitch could be adjusted on the ground. With these metal propellers a gain of about 5 mph was made in maximum speed with a decrease in ceiling height, but a decided advantage was achieved in removing the irritating 'beat' of the engines on long flights. These Leitner-Watts metal propellers were used most of the time during the Far East Flight of Southamptons and contributed to the comfort of the crews during long hauls.

Another Southampton of the first full contract, N9900, was also used for experiments. In this case a Mk VIII torpedo was slung under each wing root for dropping trials, and N9900 also pioneered the installation of a refuelling sump in the hull, to eliminate the necessity for two of the handling crew to climb up on the top wing.

To gain experience of covered-in flight decks in flying-boats, a Mk I, S1059, was converted in 1929 with a canopy extending over the first and second pilots' cockpits. The official report on this innovation spoke of a marked improvement in crew comfort in the air and in spray protection during movements on the water, despite a small restriction to all-round visibility. The improved canopy, as shown in the picture of S1162, was fitted to variants of the Mk II known as the 'Persian Gulf' type, and used by 203 Squadron, RAF, in Iraq. Enclosed flight decks were adopted as standard on the Scapa and Stranraer, successors of the Southampton.

The basic Southampton airframe was used for experimental work in improved metallurgy and Mk II K2889 was given, in September 1933, a hull constructed from a new magnesium-aluminium alloy, for extended testing into its corrosion-resisting properties. Mitchell had pleaded for better stainless steels in his contributed reply to the Cave-Brown-Cave Paper already mentioned and the then new Firth-Staybrite steel was in fact used for the bottom part of the hull of the three-engined Southampton Mk X. Meanwhile, N253, powered with steam-cooled Rolls-Royce Kestrels, was constructed to Air Ministry contract as a metallized airframe. The wings had light alloy spars of double-channel section

107

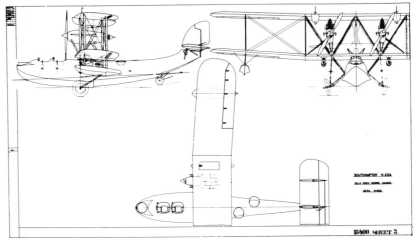

A Supermarine drawing of Southampton N253 with Kestrel engines.

with light alloy ribs, and the struts, designed and made by the Bristol Aeroplane Company, were of steel with light alloy fairings. From N253 emerged the prototype of the Scapa, S1648.

One of the most important discoveries of the Far East Flight of Southamptons was the need for more research into anti-corrosion materials and finishes in aircraft, particularly in relation to the effects of sea-going conditions. The new dope finish known as V84, as mentioned previously, was applied to the aircraft after major overhaul at Singapore on the outward leg of the cruise and was found especially effective.

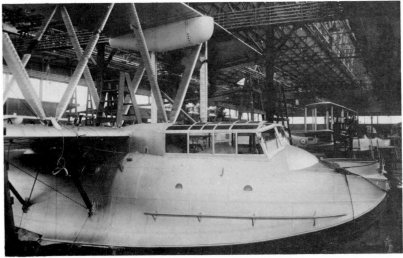

Southampton II S1162 with 'Persian Gulf' cabin top, seen in the hangar at Hythe on Southampton Water.

Official inspection of Turkish Southampton IIs at Izmir (Smyrna).

Advantage was taken when converting N253 to an all-metal structure in introducing Frise balanced ailerons (under licence from Bristol) which improved lateral control. By contrast, the fitting of Handley Page slots to N218 produced no improvement in the lateral control or stability at slow speeds, according ·) a report made to the Turkish naval authorities when they bought six metal-hulled Southampton Mk IIs in 1933. The Turkish aircraft were powered by 500 hp Hispano-Suiza 12Nbr engines and received the British B serials of N3 to N8. Although performance was improved with the higher-powered engines, irritating vibration was experienced with this variant and some strengthening of the rear part of the hull and of the tail surfaces was introduced in an attempt to cure the trouble, which was most evident in the front cockpits.

The Argentine Southamptons were completed in 1930 with 450 hp French Lorraine 12E engines, which, like the Napier Lions, were of the broad arrow type. The first five had wooden hulls and the sixth the Mk II type light alloy hull. Later the order was increased to eight aircraft with two more of the metal-hulled type. For the wooden-hulled variety the serial numbers were HB1 to HB5 and the metal-hulled variant carried the serials HB6 to HB8. The difference in external

One of the Argentine Navy's Southampton Is.

109

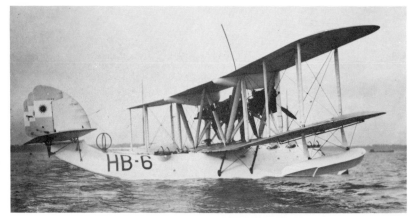

Argentine Navy Southampton II HB-6.

appearance between the two types can be seen in the accompanying pictures. The first Argentine Navy Southamptons were delivered to Puerto Belgrano in August 1930, and the type operated successfully for a number of years. On 21 March, 1931, Edward, Prince of Wales, accompanied by his brother, Prince George, flew in an Argentine Southampton from Buenos Aires to Montevideo in the course of an official visit to South America, in particular to attend the British Empire Exhibition at Buenos Aires.

Two wooden-hulled Southamptons were supplied to the Royal Australian Air Force and given the serials A11-1 and A11-2 and are now thought to have been former RAF Mk Is. The Japanese Southampton purchased from Supermarine in 1929 was a standard Mk II with metal hull and Lion engines. It was delivered to Oppama naval air depot and test flown over the Yokosuka naval base before

Wooden-hulled Southampton I A11-2 for Royal Australian Air Force No. 1 Training School.

The Japanese Southampton II.

being flown to its final destination at the Kure Arsenal operational headquarters. Subsequently it appears to have been converted to an 18-seat cabin airliner and used for regular services on Kyushu by Japan Air Transport. The commercial sale was handled by the Mitsubishi company.

The five flying-boat squadrons of the RAF equipped with Southampton Mk IIs were 201 at Calshot, 204 at Mount Batten (Plymouth), 210 at Felixstowe and Pembroke Dock, 203 in Iraq and 205 at Singapore. Mk IV and Mk V Southamptons became the Scapa and the Stranraer and are described separately, as is the three-engined Southampton X. A Southampton Mk II with Armstrong Siddeley Jaguar air-cooled radial engines was supplied to Denmark in 1930 and Mk II S1235 was loaned by the Air Ministry to Imperial Airways for carrying mail between Alexandria and Salonika for three months from 15 November, 1929. It

Southampton II S1235 as G-AASH when it was operated by Imperial Airways. (*RAF Museum*)

111

The civil Southampton II in Japanese airline service.

carried the civil registration G-AASH and was used to assist in maintenance of the trans-Mediterranean services after the loss of the Short Calcutta G-AADN *City of Rome* in the Gulf of Genoa on 26 October.

There was one other civil-registered Southampton. This was J-BAID operated by Nippon Kokuyuso Kenkyujo on regular passenger services over the Osaka-Takamatsu-Matsuyama-Beppu route during the mid-1930s. This was probably the Mk II aircraft delivered to Japan in 1928. It had eight seats on each side, windows in each side of the hull, and was initially a quite austere conversion although later the cabin was considerably improved.

Southampton II—Two 500 hp Napier Lion VA. Crew four.
Span 75 ft (22·86 m); length 49 ft 8½ in (15·15 m); height 20ft 5 in (6.2 m); wing area 1,448 sq ft (134·5 sq m).
Empty weight 9,696·5 lb (4,398 kg); loaded weight 15,200 lb (6,895 kg).
Maximum speed 95 mph (153 km/h) at sea level, 93 mph (150 km/h) at 2,000 ft (610 m); initial rate of climb 368 ft/min (112 m/min); climb to 6,000 ft (1,829 m) in 29 min 42 sec; service ceiling 5,950 ft (1,814 m); absolute ceiling 8,100 ft (2,469 m); range 544 miles (876 km) at 86 mph (139 km/h) at 2,000 ft (610 m); endurance 6·3 hr.
Report MAEE F.98.

Seamew

The idea of a small shipborne twin-engined amphibian was first mooted by Supermarine in 1924 when a project drawing was prepared for a new type, to be powered by two Siddeley Lynx engines, with a span of 46 ft, length 35 ft and height of 13 ft 1 in. This first drawing was dated 23 October, 1924, and it schemed an aircraft with twin fins and rudders, a crew of three, a gunner aft of the wings, a gunner just forward of the wings and the pilot in the bow cockpit. The hull was similar in construction to that of the wooden Southampton type as were the floats and their mountings. The wings were designed to fold backwards along the hull. A feature of the aeroplane was the use of a thick high-lift aerofoil section (Göttingen 387) in biplane form to retain a low stalling speed with increases in load and fuel but to remain within the restricted dimensions for shipborne aircraft. A modified version was drawn on 5 January, 1925, showing a slightly different rudder and undercarriage, the rear gunner being situated immediately aft of the mainplanes instead of several feet away and the tailskid located beneath the tailplane on the stern of the hull. Both designs specified four-blade propellers.

The Air Ministry must have seen one or other of these designs because contract 60044/25 was placed in 1925 for two aircraft of this type and the serial numbers allocated were N212 and N213. It is obvious that low priority was given to this contract because of Supermarine's work on the Southampton and also on the design of the S.4 racer, as little design progress was made until October 1925 and then only the odd drawing or two. The latter half of 1925 was occupied with the design and building of the Seagulls for Australia and also the conversion of the Seagull with Handley Page slotted wings. The detailed design of the Seamew therefore did not begin until the middle of March 1926 and then the S.5 floatplane and the Southampton with metal wings were going through the design office; consequently the Seamew was neglected again. With the 1926 Light Aeroplane Competition and the construction of the Sparrow II for it during July and August and the design of the Nanok during August and September, not until October 1926 was work resumed on the Seamew. Supermarine at that time were really working to capacity.

During this period the Seamew was redrawn, on 10 February, 1926. The tailskid was back in its original position on the second hull chine, the crew

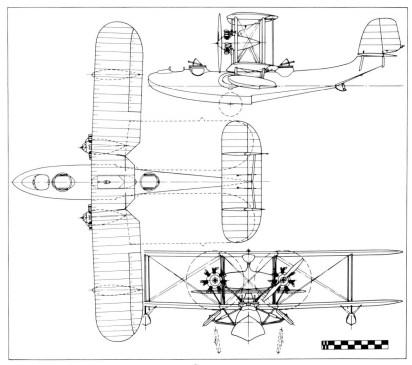

Seamew

113

Seamew N212 heading for open-sea trials.

positions were unaltered but a different shape of fin and rudder and slightly raised gunners' cockpits were shown. The next general arrangement drawing, of 2 September, 1926, was a proposal for a civil Seamew with seating for four passengers in the centre section of the hull and two in the forward gunner's cockpit. Both these designs planned an underslung fuel tank beneath the centre of the upper wing and also two-blade propellers.

The year 1927, however, introduced the Southampton Far East Cruise effort and included work on the other mentioned aircraft but time was found at last to finish off the design and construction of the first Seamew. This aircraft, N212, finally had its first engine runs on 5 January, 1928, and its first flight took place on 9 January in the hands of Henri Biard.

Details of the Seamew and of its proposed civil version were not released until May 1929 and the latter was offered as a private 'air yacht', probably to counter similar designs in this class being publicized by other manufacturers. In commenting on the Supermarine announcement, *Flight* of 23 May, 1929, remarked that the employment of reduction gearing had resulted in considerably increased performance especially in taking off and in reducing the length of run, as well as improving the climb. From this it appears that the Seamew was first flown with the direct-drive Lynx.

Following the initial flight trials several projects were drawn up of the basic Seamew fitted with more powerful engines, so that it seems evident that it could have been underpowered. The engines mentioned are Jupiters, Jaguars and geared Lynx, all three of these drawings being produced in March 1928. In parallel were two designs fitted with a single Napier Lion XI or a Bristol Jupiter VI. The Lion XI installation was a pusher, the wings had a small amount of sweepback, the aft gunner had been left out, and the radiator was an integral part of the engine nacelle so that it formed a well-streamlined body.

The Seamew had a wooden hull as mentioned but the mainplanes were of wood and metal composite construction with fabric covering. The engines fitted were two Armstrong Siddeley Lynx IVs (geared) and gave 238 hp at 2,100 rpm normal and 249 hp at 2,310 rpm maximum, driving two-blade 10 ft diameter wooden propellers.

The first Felixstowe report issued, dated 22 June, recorded the failure of the hand-starter gear on the Lynx engine. In a later report, dated September 1929, the following comments were made. During preliminary trials at a loaded weight of 6,304 lb it was found that the life of the brass-tipped wooden propellers was very short caused by their hitting water during the early stages of take-off, even in calm sea conditions. Only limited flight tests were possible. No reasons were given for this, but the report did mention that it was not possible to climb at the best climbing speed because the aircraft was so very nose heavy. It was returned to Supermarine for modification, where the range of adjustment of the tailplane was altered to give a more negative angle, and balanced rudders were fitted in place of the original unbalanced ones. Tests were also to be made at a reduced military load of 500 lb in order to increase the life of the propellers.

After its return to Felixstowe it resumed test flying but failure of the mainplane fitting on N212 was discovered whilst in flight after a flying time of only 65 hr 50 min and this report was dated 8 February, 1930. Trouble had been experienced by Supermarine with the stainless steel used for fittings (not spars) as indicated by Mitchell in his comments on the Far East Flight of the Southampton. It had become necessary to replace a large number of the fittings on operational Southamptons under a special contract unofficially called 'de-staining'. The Seamew had been built throughout with this suspect material and to conduct a similar exercise with it would have entailed considerable expense in making new fittings and rebuilding the airframe. In consequence, as the type did not show sufficient promise to justify this course, both N212 and N213 were scrapped after a limited life, a decision probably accelerated either by fatigue or by corrosion. The Seamew was in fact Supermarine's first attempt in metal construction to any extent.

Seamew N212 with Armstrong Siddeley Lynx engines and two-blade propellers. (*Ministry of Defence*)

Seamew N213 with smaller-diameter four-blade propellers. (*Ministry of Defence*)

The second Seamew built, N213, was fitted with four-blade propellers some two feet less in diameter than the two-blade types, in an obvious attempt to solve the problem of water ingestion. This was a matter that affected the larger Southampton to a lesser degree but its two-blade propellers were so much more efficient than four-bladers that the RAF accepted a high replacement rate. On the other hand the small diameter four-blade propellers of Seamew N213 inevitably meant a loss in rate of climb. These factors were responsible for Supermarine reverting to their classic layout of one engine with a single propeller, protected from 'solid' water by the hull, when they came to evolve the Walrus and the Sea Otter. From that point of view the Seamew experiment could be deemed a useful exercise. It also gave Mitchell much food for thought in thickness ratio of aerofoils as was to be seen later when he came to design the Spitfire wing.

Seamew—Two 238 hp Armstrong Siddeley Lynx IV. Crew two.
    Span 45 ft 11½ in (14 m); length 36 ft 5⅝ in (11·12 m); height 15 ft 1 in (4·6 m); wing area 610 sq ft (56·7 sq m); sweepback 2 degrees.
    Empty weight 4,675 lb (2,120 kg); loaded weight 5,800 lb (2,631 kg).
    Maximum speed 95 mph (153·35 km/h) at 2,000 ft (610 m); maximum rate of climb 523 ft/min (159·4 m/min); climb to 9,000 ft (2,743 m) 22 min; service ceiling 10,950 ft (3,337 m).
    Armament. Two 0·303-in Lewis machine-guns on mountings fore and aft of mainplanes.
    Report MAEE F/46.

Nanok, Solent and Southampton X

Among the various enquiries resulting from the success of the Southampton was one from Denmark for a three-engined version for the Navy, to carry torpedoes slung under the inner lower mainplanes, similar to the arrangement experimented with on Southampton N9900. The order for one aeroplane was received by Supermarine on 17 June, 1926, for delivery in one year at a contract price of £10,000 less engines, which were to be 430 hp Armstrong Siddeley Jaguar IVAs. The type was named Nanok, Danish for polar bear, and was designed and constructed on well-established lines closely following previous Supermarine practice.

The Nanok was first flown by Henri Biard on 21 June, 1927, but was found to be nose heavy, particularly at low speeds. This was caused by the slipstream missing the horizontal tailplane and was cured by fitting an auxiliary elevator of the all-flying type between the upper part of the vertical fins. Some time later, in April 1928, the Nanok performance was checked again at Felixstowe after the type had undergone some modification but although some improvement was recorded it was still some three mph down on the contracted speed. This was one of the reasons given for its cancellation.

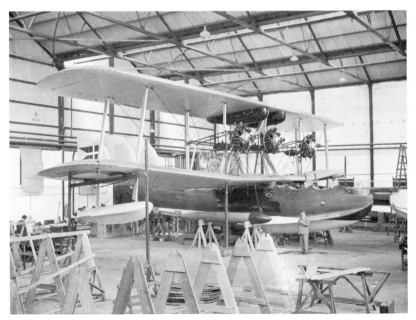

The Nanok for Denmark nearing completion.

The Nanok during its flight trials.

The Solent G-AAAB after conversion from the Nanok. The all-flying elevators can be seen.

The Solent casting off for trials.

This left Supermarine with an unwanted aircraft but eventually they contracted with the Hon A. E. Guinness to convert it into an 'air yacht' for his private use. Beyond the replacement of the Danish Service number 99 by the British civil registration G-AAAB there was little change externally, but internally, the Solent, as the aeroplane was renamed, was luxuriously fitted out with comfortable cabins to carry up to 12 passengers. The Solent became well-known for its flights from Hythe seaplane base on Southampton Water to Dún Laoghaire harbour, County Dublin, and thence across Ireland to Lough Corrib near the owner's home in County Galway. A profusion of stretches of water and soft bogs probably made the flying-boat as safe as or safer than a conventional landplane in the event of forced landing during the trans-Ireland flights.

The success of the Southampton as a reconnaissance flying-boat led the Air Ministry to consider larger and more powerful types to cover probable Service and civil demands for greater lifting capacity and longer range. At the end of 1929 Supermarine had five project flying-boat designs under examination—a Southampton replacement, with a civil version called the Sea Hawk, and the Air Yacht, all with three engines; a four-engined civil type; and the civil 'Giant', as it was unofficially called, with six engines. Of all these projects, two only were completed and flown, the Air Yacht and the Southampton replacement known as Mk X. The only reason for the latter designation was to link the design with its namesake by way of reflected glory. In the event the Southampton X was not a success but it had the effect of causing much rethinking about Supermarine design policy, as related later in connection with the Scapa and Stranraer.

Typical Vickers all-metal structure detail can be seen in this Weybridge picture of the Southampton X superstructure.

The Southampton X was allocated the serial N252 reserved originally for development aircraft along with N251 and N253 as mentioned earlier. It was quite unlike its namesake and appeared as a three-engined sesquiplane, that is, with a much wider-span upper wing. While the hull was the responsibility of Supermarine, the wing superstructure including the engine mountings was entrusted to Vickers Weybridge, which had become associated with Woolston in the Vickers (Aviation) merger of 1928. The curious thing about these two major parts of the aeroplane was that they both came out considerably overweight on design esti-

119

View of the Southampton X with Armstrong Siddeley Jaguar engines.

mates with the cumulative result that the flight performance of the Southampton X was well below specification requirements.

There could be no mistaking the performance recorded during the initial trials of the Southampton X which took place at the end of March 1930 from Southampton Water, for it was flown by Capt J. 'Mutt' Summers, who was rapidly becoming one of the most experienced test pilots in the country. Official tests made later by Felixstowe marine experimental base confirmed the poor performance with the Armstrong Siddeley Jaguar VIC engines, and subsequent changes to the Armstrong Siddeley Panthers and Bristol Jupiter XFBMs of greater power failed to make up the leeway. An attempt to lighten the superstructure by reducing the size of the wingtip floats and modifying the outer strut bracing and float supports also was insufficient to reduce the structure weight by a significant margin. The specified empty weight was to be 10,090 lb but at Felixstowe, in November 1930, with the original Jaguar engines, the actual machine weighed 13,427 lb, while the all-up weight was 21,117 lb as against the normal specified 17,580 lb.

In practical terms this meant that the speed of the Southampton X was some 15 mph below that required, the climb was woefully slower than the six minutes to 5,000 ft predicted, and the ultimate specified ceiling of some 15,000 ft was hopelessly over-estimated as the greatest height reached at Felixstowe was 6,400 ft. With the Jupiter XFBM engines, these figures were bettered by a fair margin, top speed being raised to 130 mph at 4,920 ft, still five mph below specification, and the service ceiling to 11,800 ft. On the other hand, this performance was still

This view of the Southampton X, with Bristol Jupiter engines, shows the external hull stringers of Saunders-Roe design practice. (*Supermarine Aviation Works*)

120

better than that of the Saunders-Roe A.7 Severn, which was of a similar weight and configuration and had three Jupiter XIF engines, a top speed of 124·3 mph and a ceiling of 8,930 ft with slightly less Service load. Neither the Southampton X nor the Severn obtained a production order but a derivative of the latter, the A.27 London, did achieve that status. As will be seen in the description of the Scapa and Stranraer, Supermarine dropped the three-engined concept and reverted to the well-proven twin-engined layout and abandoned the policy of cutting airframe costs through the use of angular members and longitudinal planking in hull construction. The stainless steel planing bottom of the hull of the Southampton X was not repeated in later designs and Supermarine wing structures were subsequently based on the metal wings of the experimental N253 with the Kestrel engines.

Interior of the Southampton X, showing the engineer's station and the closely-spaced frames which were part of the then current Supermarine design philosophy.

While it has not been possible to obtain incontrovertible evidence on the order of engine installation, available information, including photographic evidence, appears to indicate that the Southampton X first flew with Armstrong Siddeley engines—first the Jaguar and then the higher-powered Panther. While still in its original configuration it was fitted with the Bristol Jupiter XFBM as Type 185 and then at Felixstowe as Type 188 with Jupiter XIFs and an enclosed flight deck. Finally major modifications were made when the Panther engines were re-installed in Townend rings with the outer interplane struts moved outboard and smaller floats fitted, with underwing tanks compensating for the loss of reserve fuel space in the larger floats of the original design. Although this may sound complicated, the permutations are made clearer by reference to the illustrations and captions although it is still difficult to distinguish between the Jaguars and the Panthers as first fitted, as the chief difference was larger bore cylinders on the latter type of engine.

Nanok—Three 430 hp Armstrong Siddeley Jaguar IV. Crew five.
   Span 75 ft (22·86 m); length 50 ft 6 in (15·4 m); height 19 ft 6 in (5·94 m); wing area 1,571·8 sq ft (146 sq m).
   Empty weight 10,619 lb (4,817 kg); loaded weight 16,311 lb (7,399 kg).
   Maximum speed 113·5 mph (182·7 km/h) at sea level, 101·2 mph (162·9 km/h) at 10,000 ft

Southampton X N252 with three Bristol Jupiter XFA engines and stainless steel hull.

The Panther-engined Southampton X with horn-balanced rudders.

The Southampton X at Hythe, with Armstrong Siddeley Panther engines and Townend drag-reducing ring cowlings.

(3,048 m); stalling speed 64 mph (103 km/h); range 240 miles (386 km) [640 miles (1,030 km) as reconnaissance] at 80 mph (129 km/h).

Maximum rate of climb 607 ft/min (185 m/min); climb to 5,000 ft (1,524 m) in 10 min 20 sec, 10,000 ft (3,048 m) in 31 min; service ceiling 10,920 ft (3,328 m).

Armament. Two 0·303-in machine-guns, one in bow and one amidship. Two 1,534 lb (700 kg) torpedoes, one under each bottom mainplane.

Report MAEE F/29.

Performance figures with 10 ft (3·05 m) diameter airscrews in place of original 9·625 ft (2·93 m) units.

Solent—Three 400 hp Armstrong Siddeley Jaguar IVA. Crew five.

Span 75 ft (22·85 m); length 50 ft 2 in (15·3 m); height 19 ft (5·78 m); wing area 1,576 sq ft (146·6 sq m).

Empty weight 9,840 lb (4,469 kg); loaded weight 16,500 lb (7,485 kg).

Maximum speed 111 mph (178·5 km/h) at sea level; alighting speed 54 mph (87 km/h); climb to 5,000 ft (1,524 m) 10 min; service ceiling 11,000 ft (3,353 m).

Southampton X—Three 570 hp Bristol Jupiter XFBM. Crew five.

Span 79 ft (24·1 m); length 55 ft 6 in (16·9 m); height 21 ft (6·4 m); wing area 1,235 sq ft (114·7 sq m).

Empty weight 13,975 lb (6,339 kg); loaded weight 23,000 lb (10,433 kg).

Maximum speed 130 mph (209 km/h) at 4,920 ft (1,500 m); normal range 1,000 miles (1,609 km) at 100 mph (161 km/h); maximum rate of climb 500 ft/min (152·4 m/min); climb to 9,840 ft (3,000 m) 18 min; service ceiling 11,800 ft (3,597 m).

Armament. Three 0·303-in Lewis machine-guns in bow and amidships. Bomb load 1,000 lb (453·6 kg) carried beneath the lower mainplanes.

Air Yacht

A design out of character for Supermarine, but one which has always created interest among air historians, appeared in 1930 as the Air Yacht. Completed in some secrecy as a luxury air yacht, as its name implies, for a private customer, it bore the imprint of Dornier Wal influence, one of which had been under test at the nearby Calshot air station. Since the early days there had always been a great deal of contact between Woolston and Calshot; indeed when Supermarine were in need of a spare pilot for a test flight they borrowed one from Calshot, a practice that had qualified official approval. In fact, the Air Yacht started life as a project reconnaissance flying-boat and finished up as a most luxuriously equipped civil aeroplane. Its short career had at least the distinction of creating plenty of excitement for its owners and crew and columns of copy for the more sensational newspapers, and the aeroplane even became mixed up with high-level diplomacy, as related later.

The Air Yacht was the first multi-engined monoplane designed and built by Supermarine, their only experience with monoplanes being limited to the experimental Sparrow II and to the Schneider S.4 and S.5 racers. The Air Yacht originated in a project design for a three-engined flying-boat to meet Air Ministry specification 4/27 for armed reconnaissance. The first drawings dated 7 November, 1927, showed a biplane with machine-guns in the bows, amidships, and in the stern firing rearwards and downwards, with bombs carried on inner stations under

The Air Yacht, with Jaguar engines, at Hythe.

the lower mainplanes. The wings were attached to the top of the hull, and the drawings also showed pylon mounted engines similar to those on the Southampton. The hull, like that of the Southampton Mk X, was a development of the Saunders-Roe A.14 corrugated-panel type as experimented with on Southampton N251. Angular triple fins and rudders were drawn and these were retained as well as the hull in the alternative monoplane version of the design, which eventually materialized as the Air Yacht.

Flotation sponsons sprouting from the lower part of the hull in place of wingtip floats accentuated the Continental aspect of the Air Yacht outlines. These highly streamlined sponsons later embodied the refinement of a step to aid hydrodynamic lift-off, but this feature increased drag considerably. Sloping V struts braced the high wing to the sponsons and the wing was mounted above the hull on a cabane of struts high enough to give propeller clearance. The engines were Armstrong Siddeley geared Jaguar VIs of 490 hp each and fitted with drag-reducing Townend rings in faired installations, with long exhaust pipes and two-blade wooden propellers. The airframe was constructed in duralumin with stainless steel fittings. All flying surfaces were fabric covered.

The Air Yacht was ordered by the Hon A. E. Guinness to supersede his Supermarine Solent as a flying yacht for cruises to and around the Mediterranean, much in the same way as a sea-going yacht would operate. Consequently, it was fitted out with all the luxury equipment of the period and more, such as temperature regulation in the cabins by a hot and cold air system. Most of the furnishing familiar today in custom-built privately-owned airliners was in evidence, including the owner's cabin complete with bed, a small bath and a private toilet. Electric light was fitted throughout the interior and the galley had complete cooking facilities. The section of the flying-boat devoted to the owner's guests also included wash basins, a toilet and a pantry, and between the latter and the owner's cabin was a comfortable lounge with settees, sideboards and a folding table in the middle.

Crew quarters were forward of the domestic service area and cabins and were arranged for a crew of four with two berths immediately below the open cockpits. The two pilots were seated on each side of a gangway, with adjustable controls to suit any pilot and with a let-down seat between them for a mechanic. Behind were two open cockpits for occasional use by the passengers or crew.

The Air Yacht was first flown in February 1930 by Biard. It was named *Flying Oma*, which the workmen on the job twisted into *Flying Amo* which was Service slang for 'ammunition'. During the following year little was done by way of flying so the assumption is that this was the time taken in leisurely scheming and fitting out the aircraft with its sumptuous interior. This is more or less proved by the fact that the contract price was originally some £35,000 but by 17 June, 1931, the actual cost incurred was nearly £52,000!

On 8 May, 1931, the Air Yacht was flown to Felixstowe for certificate of airworthiness trials but by July it had flown only nine times and had spent 570 hours at its moorings. It was flown at an all-up weight of 24,900 lb but in the Felixstowe report of the following October the corrected weight was quoted as 23,348 lb with an engine type change from Jaguars to Panthers of 525 hp each, which meant an increase of total power of 105 hp. Despite the power increase, it was found impossible to maintain height with any practical payload on two engines, with the third throttled right back. The flying qualities of the aeroplane were considered good, with controls reasonably light and responsive, but rudder control was slightly over-balanced at all speeds. Manoeuvrability was good but the turning circle was large as was to be expected from the machine's large moments of inertia inherent in the design.

During these lengthy trials damage occurred to the stub sponsons, the starboard one failing in waves three to four feet high. Repairs and replacements were paid for by the Air Ministry, which indicates that they still had an interest in the progress of this novel flying-boat design. In the meantime the registration G-AASE had been allocated and the certificate of airworthiness was finally granted on 22 December, 1931.

In the end the Air Yacht was rejected by Guinness in favour of a Saro Cloud and it was put away in the hangars at Hythe. Then one day in October 1932 a

The Air Yacht under construction at Hythe, with Southampton production in progress.

125

The Air Yacht, with Panther IIA engines, at Felixstowe in 1931. (*MAEE*)

wealthy American lady, Mrs June Jewell James, who was living in the Southampton area, was shown over the Air Yacht by the Hythe base caretaker and she bought it from Supermarine, intending to use it for cruises in the Mediterranean and elsewhere.

Under its new owner the Air Yacht was renamed *Windward III* and it was

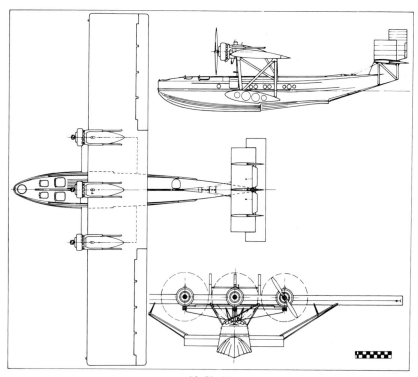

Air Yacht

126

powered with Armstrong Siddeley geared Panther IIAs. Biard was seconded from Supermarine to act as the first pilot and he soon found out that the new owner was not only imperious and impulsive, but also showed courage under operational conditions which would have terrified most people. So it was that she arrived suddenly at Woolston one day and fully expected to fly to far-away places on the nod, despite the fact that the tide would be out for several hours and a complete engine overhaul was in progress. As can be imagined, this Canute-like attitude was ineffective but eventually, on 11 October 1932, the Air Yacht sailed off down Southampton Water into the wide blue yonder—to adventures that defy adequate description.

Reaching Cherbourg on the first leg of the cruise after two hours flying, Biard saw with some trepidation the blue skies rapidly turning to black, with wind rising and storm clouds gathering. He wanted to fly on to a more sheltered anchorage but Mrs James was determined that her party, comprising seven persons, should sleep aboard. The barometer was visibly dropping, with Biard getting more and more worried. Then, at about 10 pm a launch came alongside the Air Yacht with a message from the Admiral of the Port saying that their position in the exposed Roads was dangerous and he could not be held responsible if the passengers did not come ashore at once. Mrs James replied that she and her guests were going to stay aboard for, as Biard remarks in his biography, 'she cared no more for danger than she cared for Admirals'. Of course Biard, with his long experience of marine aviation, was right, for in the night a frightening tempest arose which tossed the Air Yacht around on its moorings like a cork, but fortunately these held fast. After three hours of torture for everyone aboard the pilot tug came alongside and took them off, after some exciting moments which ended in Biard bundling owner, owner's dog and himself into the boat as the last in.

That was not quite the end of the story as told by Biard. The redoubtable Mrs James got herself mixed up in a further argument with the Admiral over the peremptory refusal of a Navy Lieutenant to take her out to the Air Yacht in a naval cutter. This led to what Biard describes as the longest telegram ever to the President of the French Republic resulting in the Admiral receiving supreme orders to go to Mrs James with an apology, which he asked Biard to do for him as he was afraid of women!

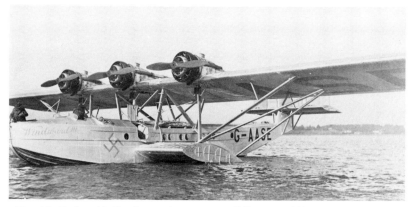

The Air Yacht with Panther engines, seen at Felixstowe while carrying the name *Windward III* and swastika motif.

127

However, all was finally cleared up in another lengthy telegram, this time to the directors of Supermarine from Mrs James. She contradicted much of the exaggerated news reports of the storm incident, testified to the stout construction of the aircraft and praised pilot-boat and naval air station rescuers. After that, Biard took off for St Nazaire to pick up Mrs James, who had gone to Paris, only to be forced back into Cherbourg by more bad weather. The flight, when resumed, reached Naples without further incident but more misfortunes were to come.

While in Naples awaiting further orders from Mrs James, Biard had to undergo medical attention for an old injury and the Air Yacht was taken over by Tommy Rose, the well-known test pilot. On the evening of 25 January, 1933, he was flying Mrs James and party near Capri when the machine went into a flat stall and fell into the sea, breaking a wing. Accounts of the event differ considerably but undoubtedly Mrs James acted with her usual fortitude in attracting the aid of local fishermen, who rescued the party and beached the Air Yacht. It was impounded against payment of salvage claims under marine law and the only parts of it probably brought back to England were the engines, according to Supermarine employees still surviving.

Air Yacht—Three 525 hp Armstrong Siddeley Panther IIA. Four crew and six passengers.
  Span 92 ft (28 m); length 66 ft 6 in (20·3 m); height 19 ft (5·8); wing area 1,472 sq ft (136·7 sq m).
  Empty weight 16,808 lb (7,624 kg); loaded weight 23,348 lb (10,590 kg).
  Maximum speed 102 kt (189 km/h) at 2,000 ft (610 m); maximum rate of climb 380 ft/min (116 m/min) at 2,000 ft (610 m); service ceiling 6,500 ft (1,981 m).
  Report MAEE F/86

Scapa and Stranraer

When the time came for Supermarine to offer a successor to the Southampton Mk II, in place of the abortive three-engined Southampton X, advantage was taken of Vickers' and other technical facilities, aerodynamic and hydrodynamic, to improve hull design and to introduce a more refined superstructure of better drag characteristics. The influence of the Schneider high-speed experience on Supermarine design was also evident. With the improved performance promised from the new Rolls-Royce Kestrel engines as indicated by their installation in the experimental Southampton N253, a new design was prepared by Mitchell called at first the Southampton Mk IV and later the Scapa. A further development of this concept with wider span two-bay wings came still later as the Stranraer, the last of the Supermarine twin-engined flying-boats.

The prototype of the Scapa, Southampton Mk IV S1648, was offered to the Air Ministry by Supermarine, backed by Sir Robert McLean, chairman of Vickers (Aviation), at no extra cost, in place of the last Southampton of the final contract. This proposal was accepted despite the Air Ministry's attempt to redeem the disappointing results of the three-engined flying-boats by writing a new specification. The comprehensive reports on S1648 issued by the technical office of Supermarine at the time testified to the progress being made then by Mitchell and his team in sophisticated aircraft design methods. The following extract from the report on the hull design for the Scapa, written by Arthur Shirvall, Mitchell's hydrodynamic specialist, is indicative of this trend.

The prototype Scapa, S1648, on test.

'A change of policy in 1931, favouring twin-engined flying-boats in place of the somewhat unsuccessful three-engined boats recently produced, rendered it obvious that our best course was to revert to the Southampton Mk II—a type that had proved itself during years of service in the RAF to be a really sound and reliable job with a good general performance—and use it for the development of a new design.

'With reference to the hull of the aircraft, this course had been strongly urged five years previously but a policy of economy with a resultant tendency towards rectangular sections, flat plates and square corners caused the proposal to be disregarded.

'Since no tank testing was conducted on models of the Mk II until after the machine was built the success of the hull must be attributed to pure chance.

Converted Southampton Mk II S1122 with evaporative-cooled Kestrel engines.

129

The metal-structured Scapa under construction.

Compared with its predecessors and certain also of its successors, its lines were good and it is generally recognized in marine work that a pretty boat is likely to prove a good boat. . . . The performance of this hull (Southampton Mk II), as demonstrated subsequently full scale and also in the tank, was sufficiently remarkable to justify its use as a basis upon which to shape a new improved form.'

The first Mk IV hull therefore closely resembled the Mk II, the main differences being a lengthened bow with the forefoot deepened, this having the effect of making the bow sections below the chine less full and the waterlines finer. On the planing bottom, the beam over the chines was increased at the aft step to clean up the water performance of the hull at large incidences when taking off, to avoid wash over the tail surfaces. The topsides of the Mk IV hull were modified to give more spacious accommodation and to make the amidships gun turrets less obtrusive. Water-tank testing proved that the new hull in model form for Mk IV was better than a tank model to the same scale of the Mk II, especially at lower speeds, but in practice the wider beam proved unsatisfactory as it resulted in an unpleasant pitch forward when the rear step contacted the water. Part of the hull bottom of S1648 was removed and replaced by a Southampton II after-portion in a continuous round-the-clock 'crash' programme occupying a whole week.

Technical progress was also evident in the aerodynamic and structural reports on the Southampton Mk IV design disclosing improved methods in wind-tunnel testing, weight analyses of structure and close adherence to the requirements of the specification, R.20/31, which was received by Supermarine on 5 November,

1931. The superstructure was a cleaner design than that of the earlier Southamptons and dispensed with interplane strutting to a large extent, relying on wire bracing for structural rigidity. The engine pylons disappeared and the Kestrels were mounted in a nacelle forward and under the top wings which saved much drag but introduced trim corrections because of the higher thrust line above the centre of gravity. One of the main reasons for lifting the engines on the Mk IV was to avoid water ingestion by two-blade propellers as experienced with the standard Southamptons which, as mentioned in connection with the Seamew, led to the RAF accepting their high redundancy as they were so effective for quick take-off, some 14 seconds with full load. The radiators of the engine coolant were located, unusually, at the rear of the nacelles.

The Southampton IV was an all-metal aeroplane with fabric-covered flying surfaces and the materials used were light alloys of aluminium with stainless steel fittings. The main wing spars were fabricated by rolling sheet into a corrugated cross-section somewhat like the Greek letter epsilon. No doubt much was learned by the Supermarine technicians from the extensive programme of research and development put into this Scapa prototype and even more from the contemporary Schneider racing experience. Beverley Shenstone, a Canadian who had joined Supermarine from Junkers, presented a report on small drag losses caused by out-of-date detail design practice in fittings, gaps and so on exposed to the air flow.

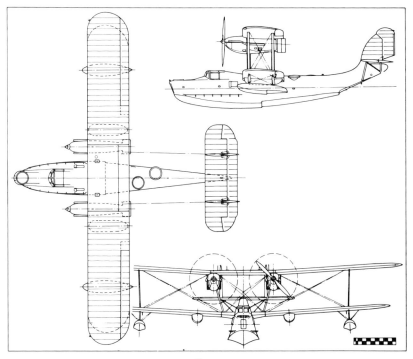

Scapa

131

Roll-out at Woolston of the prototype Scapa. 'Mutt' Summers and R. J. Mitchell (with hat) are in bottom right corner.

The experimental Southampton N253 with its steam-cooled Rolls-Royce Kestrel IIIMS engines gave better performance figures than the Southampton N218 with unsupercharged Napier Lion Vs, according to Felixstowe reports. It had a better sea-level speed by some 10 mph and had a better climb to 10,000 ft by about 10 min. The Kestrel had been evolved as the British answer to the Curtiss D-12 and its derivatives, the type that had carried all before it in the Schneider Trophy races and had been imported to power the Fairey Fox day bomber, which was faster than contemporary British fighters. So the favoured choice for the Southampton replacement was the liquid-cooled 525 hp Kestrel IIIA, and the Scapa's performance in service rose to 143 mph at 2,000 ft.

K4191, the first production Scapa at Felixstowe. (*MAEE*)

'Mutt' Summers first flew the Southampton IV S1648 for 10 min from Woolston on 8 July, 1932, and followed up with some forty test flights before it was collected by Flt Lt Pickering on 29 October for delivery to MAEE, Felixstowe. There it underwent further trials including a 10 hr nonstop flight over the North Sea. Type approval was given to S1648, still named Southampton IV, on 1 April, 1933. A month later Pickering flew it to Malta, where it was attached with its pilot to 202 (FB) Squadron at Kalafrana base. Various checks and flights were made in accordance with requirements for overseas acceptance, and these included the trials of an autopilot and a long-distance flight to Gibraltar and back to check range and fuel consumption. At the end of June, Pickering took the aircraft on a cruise to Port Sudan via Sollum, Aboukir, Lake Timsah and back, an exercise which took a month. During his stay in Malta he demonstrated the new type in flight to the Governor of Malta, Sir Harry Luke, and its Prime Minister, Sir Ugo Mifsud, as well as to the Commander-in-Chief, Mediterranean Fleet, and the Air Officer Commanding, Mediterranean.

The prototype Scapa with 18-in torpedo amidship.

On the conclusion of the proving flights and the return of S1648 to Felixstowe, the Air Ministry ordered twelve of the newly-named Scapas, K4191—K4202, to production specification 19/33 to equip certain flying-boat squadrons. The first was 202 in Malta which in 1935 received its Scapas to replace Fairey IIID and IIIF floatplanes it had been operating since 1929. The Scapa followed the tradition established by the Southamptons and undertook some long-distance cruises, notably one around the Aegean and another by two Scapas to Calabar, Nigeria, via Algiers, Gibraltar, Gambia, Gold Coast (now Ghana) and Lagos, with an out and home distance of 9,000 miles. The AOC Mediterranean, Air Commodore P. G. Maltby, took part in this flight. In 1937 Scapas of 202 Squadron participated in anti-submarine patrols during the Spanish Civil War to protect neutral shipping before returning to the United Kingdom for re-equipment. No. 204 Squadron at Mount Batten received its Scapas in August 1935 and shortly after moved to

Scapa K4200 taking off from Kalafrana seaplane base in Malta.

Egypt during the Italo-Abyssinian confrontation. On returning to the United Kingdom it continued to fly its Scapas until early in 1937. No. 240 Squadron was re-formed at Calshot in 1937 from the Seaplane Training Squadron C Flight and took over some of 202's Scapas. The solitary Scapa of 228 Squadron at Pembroke Dock, K7306, had quite a chequered career which ended in its crashing off Felixstowe in August 1938 while engaged in early radar trials with Bawdsey Manor experimental station. Most of the remaining Scapas were taken out of regular service in 1939 and replaced by more powerful aircraft such as the four-engined Short Singapore III.

At about the same time as the specification R.20/31 was being written around the cleaned-up version of the Southampton which became the Scapa, another requirement was issued by the Air Ministry for a general purpose coastal patrol flying-boat capable of carrying 1,000 lb more military load for 1,000 miles and maintaining flight on one engine, carrying 60 per cent fuel. This the Scapa was unable to do with the extra load nor indeed could it meet the performance required by the new specification, R.24/31, with that load. So Supermarine submitted for R.24/31 a larger aircraft than the Scapa. The Stranraer, as this new type was eventually named, was therefore a 'restricted' development of the Scapa.

There were two competing tenders, by Supermarine and Saunders-Roe, for this specification and the latter was accepted. Mitchell however went on with his improved Scapa design to such purpose that a contract was eventually placed with Supermarine. He had considered three projects, an enlarged Scapa, a sesquiplane similar to the Southampton X, and a thin-wing version with a two-bay structure. With a maximum speed of 163 mph, a stalling speed of 51 mph, (a speed range of 3·2 to one) and a single-engine capability, combined with an ultimate ceiling of 20,000 ft, the third alternative, which became the Stranraer, outbid all contemporary British flying-boats in its class.

The wing span, area and weight of the Stranraer were twelve per cent greater than those of the Scapa, and while the rudders had the same area, the elevator was seven per cent larger with much bigger aerodynamic balances. The trim tabs fitted

134

to the rudders were sufficient to hold the aircraft straight with one engine shut down. Although the Kestrel engine was considered for the Stranraer, the type ultimately chosen was the moderately supercharged Bristol Pegasus IIIM. These engines were mounted under the top wings on the same thrust axis as the Kestrels on the Scapa but, as radial air-cooled types, dispensed with radiators and their plumbing. Long-chord Townend drag-reducing rings were fitted around them in conjunction with streamlined nacelles. Fuel was carried in the centre section of the top wings with the oil tanks and integral oil coolers in its leading edge. The wings were ten feet wider span, and two-bay interplane struts on each side were introduced for structural reasons.

Although the hull of the Stranraer was larger than the Scapa's, with an increased cross-section of eighteen per cent, the hydrodynamic drag of the bare hull was the same as measured in tank tests at St Albans. The front gun was made retractable and the cabin top had no dip behind it as on the older design. The middle gunner was lowered somewhat and a tail gunner was added in a neatly faired position behind the control surfaces. The tail gunner's hooded windshield actually increased speed by over two knots.

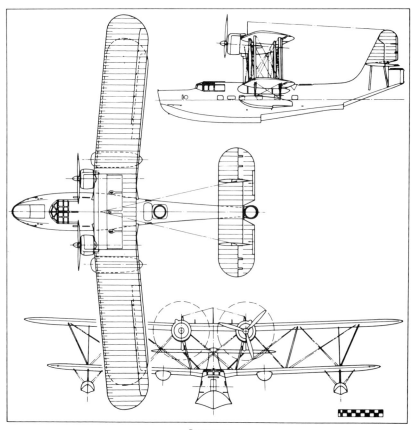

Stranraer

The airframe of the Stranraer followed much the same pattern as that of the Scapa, with detail improvements and cleaning up as dictated by the experience and exhaustive analysis of the earlier machine. Even more extensive use was made of the composite metal known as Alclad—which was duralumin plate rolled in the hot mills, with a coating of pure aluminium on each side for corrosion protection. Indeed much of the airframe, including the hull skin, was fabricated from components of Alclad. Detail fittings were of stainless steel. Anodic treatment was also extensively employed to counter corrosion. The fact that Stranraers lasted so long in Canadian service and that one now stands proudly in the RAF Museum at Hendon testifies to the efficiency of this extensive treatment against corrosion, the bugbear of marine aircraft.

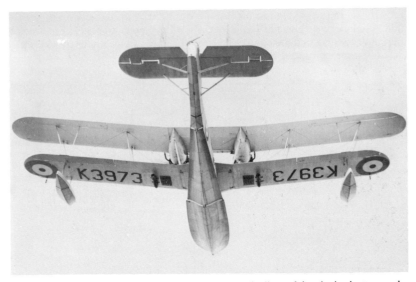

This view of the Stranraer prototype, K3973, shows the lines of the planing bottom and the elevator cut-out aerodynamic balances.

Most of the Stranraer's increased load was made up by two 250 lb bombs carried under the lower inner mainplanes, by universal carriers for those bombs or for overload fuel tanks for ferrying purposes, and by rations for the normal crew of six and other small items, none of which inventory was mandatory on the Scapa. The usual adjuncts to long-distance cruises as initiated by the Southamptons were carried as standard, such as sleeping and cooking equipment, collapsible engine-servicing ladders and staging, sun awnings, sea anchors, in fact all the paraphernalia which became familiar to Coastal Command aircrew in the Second World War. The Stranraer had a lower centre section free from obstructions, like the Southampton, which could be used for the stowage in flight of a spare engine or to transport a torpedo. This clear space was made feasible because the wing stubs were built integrally with the hull, following Scapa design detail.

The first flight of the R.24/31 Stranraer was made by 'Mutt' Summers from Southampton Water on 27 July, 1934, for 15 minutes. He was accompanied by flight observer Radcliffe, mechanic Hastings, Trevor Westbrook, the factory superintendent, and Alan Clifton of the design staff. Another flight of 30 min was made in the afternoon in which George Pickering was second pilot and Ernest Mansbridge represented the design office. Pickering had left the RAF to join Supermarine at the invitation of Mitchell, who had been impressed with his previous flying of the Southampton IV and the Seagull V prototypes.

After an intensive flight-test programme similar to that undergone by the Scapa, Pickering delivered the prototype Stranraer R.24/31, serial K3973, to MAEE at Felixstowe on 24 October, 1934, and remained there to participate in the official trials. K3973 was powered by 820 hp Bristol Pegasus IIIM engines driving two-blade wooden propellers. Later, production Stranraers had 920 hp Pegasus X engines driving three-blade Fairey-Reed metal propellers of fixed pitch. With the more powerful Pegasus, the maximum speed of the Stranraer was increased to 165 mph and the climb to a thousand feet a minute up to 10,000 ft, a performance unmatched anywhere at the time in the flying-boat class.

The initial order for seventeen Stranraers was to production specification 17/35 and they were allocated serials K7287 to K7303. Although Stranraers were used only in home-based Coastal Command Squadrons 209, 210, 228 and 240 and by B Flying-Boat Training Squadron and 4 OTU, they had quite an adventurous time as their individual careers testify. A coincidental task of K7287, the first production aircraft, was to fly from Pembroke Dock in July 1937 to survey the possibility of establishing a flying-boat base at Wig Bay, Stranraer. Later on, Stranraers were used with Londons and Singapores for instructional training at the Stranraer base, named 4 OTU in 1941.

In June 1938, Stranraers of 228 Squadron pioneered the use of another wartime flying-boat base when they engaged in exercises at Oban and then went on to the fleet base at Invergordon. Five Stranraers of 228 went on a cruise of over 4,000 miles out and back in September 1938 to Lisbon, Gibraltar and Malta, for exercises with the Mediterranean Fleet. During the Munich crisis the squadron flew its Stranraers to their planned war location at Invergordon but on return to base started to replace its Stranraers with Sunderlands.

Some of the discarded boats of 228 were passed on to 209 Squadron which was re-equipping with Stranraers in place of Singapore IIIs. This conversion was completed in March 1939. The squadron was placed on a war footing on 3 September, 1939, and its Stranraers participated in patrols between Scotland and Norway from Invergordon to intercept enemy shipping. In this duty the aircraft were fitted with an overload tank under one wing and bombs under the other. They were withdrawn from 209 Squadron in April 1941 and the last operational patrol of RAF Stranraers was made on 17 March by 240 Squadron when the Supermarine type was succeeded by the Catalina. The last Stranraer in British service was K7303 at Felixstowe until 30 October, 1942.

In Canada, however, the forty Stranraers built by Canadian Vickers at St Hubert, Montreal, served with the Royal Canadian Air Force bomber reconnaissance squadrons 4, 5, 6, 7, 9, 117 and 120 off the eastern and western seaboards of Canada on anti-submarine patrols, accompanied after 1943 by Consolidated Catalinas and their Canadian-built versions, the Cansos. The RCAF Stranraers were powered by either 960 hp Bristol Pegasus Xs driving four-blade wooden propellers or by 1,010 hp Pegasus XXIIs with three-blade de Havilland two-position propellers. The first order for the RCAF Stranraers was placed on 31 March, 1937, for five, and the first delivery, serial number 907, was made on 9 November, 1937, to 7(BR) Squadron. This aeroplane flew continually until

RCAF Stranraer 910, QN-H of No. 5 (BR) Squadron, Dartmouth, Nova Scotia, in June 1940. (*Public Archives of Canada*)

7 February, 1945, and the last Stranraer in the RCAF was 949, retired on 20 January, 1946.

Harry Tate, who joined 6(BR) Squadron of the RCAF at Aliford, Queen Charlotte Islands, British Columbia, in December 1941 as an aero-engine mechanic, said in the *Journal of the Canadian Aviation Historical Society*, 'The Stranraer was an extremely rugged aircraft and could be landed and taken off on open ocean if the swells were reasonable. It was much more seaworthy than the Catalina and Canso and could absorb considerably more punishment without staving in the hull.' It was one of those aeroplanes that attracted affectionate nicknames and in Canada was known variously as the 'Stranny' or 'Strainer' and according to Tate as 'The Whistling Bird Cage', a reference to the in-flight sound emanating from its many bracing wires.

An ex-RCAF Stranraer in service with Queen Charlotte Airlines of Vancouver as CF-BXO.

One remarkable feature of the building of the RCAF Stranraers by Canadian Vickers from Supermarine technological information was that only one additional drawing was ever requested from the design company 3,000 miles away and that was for a propeller. This must have been an all-time record. The Stranraer represented the optimum design in twin-engined biplane flying-boats. 'It had sufficiency of control and stability about all three axes,' so said its final technical report.

Fourteen of the RCAF Stranraers came onto the Canadian civil register. One, CF-BYL, owned by Spilsbury and Hepburn was lost on 31 August, 1946, but the company's successor, Queen Charlotte Airlines, operated four as 20-passenger aircraft on routes from Vancouver—CF-BYI (c/n CV184), CF-BYJ (c/n CV205), CF-BXO *Alaska Queen* (c/n CV209) and CF-BYM *Tahsis Queen* (c/n CV228). Some of these were re-engined with 1,000 hp Wright R-1820 Cyclones driving three-blade Hamilton Standard propellers. CF-BXO was sold to Stranraer Aerial

Enterprises in June 1962 and in 1963 passed to Pacific Western Airlines. Restored as RCAF 920 of No. 5 Squadron this aircraft is now in the RAF Museum at Hendon.

That it survived in airline service so long in British Columbia, in fact until 1958, was hardly surprising for it was ideally suited to its environment, although after 20 years unbroken operation it could hardly be described as youthful.

Scapa—Two 525 hp Rolls-Royce Kestrel IIIMS. Crew five.

Span 75 ft (22·85 m); length (on chassis) 53 ft (16·2 m); height (on chassis) 21 ft (6·4 m); wing area 1,300 sq ft (121 sq m).

Empty weight 10,030 lb (4,500 kg); loaded weight 16,080 lb (7,290 kg).

Maximum speed 142 mph (228·5 km/h) at 3,280 ft (1,000 m); alighting speed 64 mph (103 km/h); maximum range 1,000 miles (1,610 km) with 2,650 lb (1,200 kg) military load at 100 mph (161 km/h) at 5,000 ft (1,524 m); maximum rate of climb 625 ft/min (195 m/min); climb to 9,840 ft (3,000 m) 20 min; service ceiling 15,500 ft (4,720 m).

Armament. Three 0·303-in Lewis machine-guns, one in bow and two amidships. Bomb load 1,000 lb (453 kg) carried beneath lower mainplanes.

Stranraer—Two 920 hp Bristol Pegasus X. Crew five.

Span 85 ft (25·9 m); length (on chassis) 54 ft 10 in (16·7 m); height (on chassis) 21 ft 9 in (6·64 m); wing area 1,457 sq ft (135 sq m).

Empty weight 11,250 lb (5,110 kg); loaded weight 19,000 lb (8,625 kg).

Maximum speed 165 mph (265·5 km/h) at 6,000 ft (1,830 m); alighting speed 58·5 mph (94 km/h); range 1,000 miles (1,610 km) at 105 mph (169 km/h) at 5,000 ft (1,524 m); initial rate of climb 1,350 ft/min (411·5 m/min); climb to 10,000 ft (3,048 m) 10 min; service ceiling 18,500 ft (5,645 m).

Armament. Three 0·303-in Lewis machine-guns in bow, amidships and tail. Bomb load 1,000 lb (453·6 kg) carried beneath lower mainplanes and eight 20 lb (9 kg) bombs in bays in underside of lower mainplanes.

Supermarine specification 437/2/a.

Stranraer CF-BYM of Pacific Western Airlines, with Wright Cyclone engines and de Havilland three-blade two-position propellers.

140

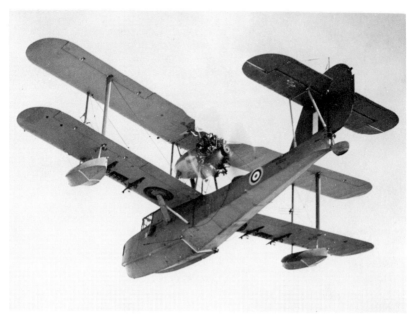

A particularly fine view of the Walrus, or 'Shagbat' as it was widely known.

Seagull V and Walrus

The origins of the Seagull V have already been outlined in the genesis of the Seagulls and in particular of the Mk III with a pusher Jupiter IX engine. In 1930 there was still a requirement for a naval single-engined reconnaissance amphibian flying-boat and drawings were produced for Supermarine Type 181. One version was for a pusher aeroplane and another for a tractor, aimed at an Australian requirement. Nothing materialized from these projects but after the Schneider Trophy activity had subsided, in 1932 Mitchell started work on a similar design under Type 223, model tests having been continued in Vickers' St Albans water tank to try to improve the hydrodynamics of the earlier amphibians. The Royal Navy had shown little interest in the Seagull III so another private venture was started and its specification was sent to the Royal Australian Air Force, which had made such good use of the earlier Seagulls. From such tentative beginnings came the Walrus. It served the Royal and Commonwealth navies as the foremost fleet gunnery-spotting and observation 'platform' during crucial times, being shot-off by catapult from cruisers and recovered by crane from the sea. When its work was done in naval operations, the Walrus came to the aid of the Allied air forces as the prime air-sea rescue vehicle, operated from land bases by the Royal Air Force. Thus after many years the amphibian aeroplane had proved that its conception way back in aviation history was not misplaced.

141

The prototype Seagull V under construction at Hythe early in 1933.

Wing characteristics were examined in June 1932 and in August data were provided for wind-tunnel tests. The following month the Bristol Pegasus was being considered as power unit and a need was envisaged for a catapulting capability from warships at sea. The first reference to the designation Seagull Mk V was in November 1932 indicating that Mitchell was basing the concept on the previous Seagulls but involving a complete redesign including, for the first time for Supermarine, a one-step hull.* There were two versions—Type 223 naval co-operation amphibian in a Rolls-Royce Kestrel pusher layout and Type 225 as a civil flying-boat, with a similar engine arrangement. Only Type 223 was proceeded with and by March 1933 such progress had been made that the hull had reached the stage shown in the photograph, with the engine mounting and nacelle fitted ready for a Pegasus air-cooled radial. At this time an Australian specification was received which corresponded closely to that of the Seagull V, except that the Supermarine strength factors were higher and their aircraft weight estimates lower. With various modifications or additions as required in the specification the all-up weight would be exactly the same.

The Seagull V was flown by 'Mutt' Summers on 21 June, 1933, as Type 228, from Southampton Water. Most of the drawings prepared for Type 223 were used so there could have been little difference between the two. After satisfactory take offs and 'landings' on both water and land, the latter at Eastleigh aerodrome,

*The design of the Seagull V/Walrus was influenced by the experience of Monro, a design draughtsman who had joined Supermarine from Canadian Vickers. He was familiar with Canadian flying-boat design including the original Vedette.

Summers issued a confident test report on the flying and handling characteristics but criticized the rigidity of the undercarriage and the lack of steering capacity on the ground. Despite this the Seagull V, bearing the marking N-1, appeared at the second SBAC Show at Hendon on 26 June, 1933, where Summers put up a fine exhibition of its manoeuvrability. He had made quiet enquiries about the strength of the Seagull and to the surprise of all—including Mitchell, who had no inkling of what was to happen—proceeded to 'loop-the-loop', a flying-boat aerobatic not seen since the days of the Supermarine Baby. Four days later on its return to Woolston, the Seagull V was put through an extended test flight of 1 hr 12 min at what amounted to an overload weight of 6,650 lb. Take-off time was nine seconds, the top speed about 125 mph with corrections and the height reached was 13,000 ft.

Further flights exposed the deficiencies of the undercarriage, and after rectification of these and other adjustments the aeroplane was flown to Felixstowe on 29 July, 1933, for Air Ministry trials, bearing the identification N-2 instead of N-1, as worn previously, to avoid confusion with a Southampton also listed as N-1. The MAEE report on the Seagull V was not flattering and the Supermarine rejoinder was that it criticized an unusual type of aircraft, being an amphibian with a drag-reducing retractable undercarriage, in fact the first British *military* aeroplane with one.* The MAEE pilots, C. H. Mapp and A. G. Pickering, produced performance figures which matched Supermarine's own, all of which interested Air Marshal Sir Richard Williams, Chief of the Australian Air Staff, when he visited Woolston in November 1933. Before he could take action he considered it necessary for the type to show a catapulting capability.

On 19 January, 1934, the Seagull was flown to Farnborough for catapulting trials and later in the month live launches were made by Flt Lt S. R. Ubee of the experimental flying staff of the Royal Aircraft Establishment. By the middle of

*The Air Ministry conducted the trials on behalf of the Australian authorities to the RAAF specification, which contained requirements not included in British official requirements.

The prototype Seagull V N-1 on which 'Mutt' Summers did aerobatics at the SBAC Show at Hendon in 1933.

February the empty weight of the aircraft had gone up to 5,016 lb and the loaded weight to 7,049 lb, a large proportion of the increases being accounted for by greater military load and the catapulting attachments. This increase necessitated structural alterations. At the end of these trials Mitchell was dissatisfied with the aircraft's general aerodynamic 'dirtiness' which had lost it some seven mph of airspeed and ordered a clean up of parasitic drag much on the lines of Beverley Shenstone's report mentioned earlier.

The prototype Seagull V, as N-2, on the catapult at the RAE, Farnborough, in January 1934.

The structure of the Seagull V is best described as 'mixed', the wings being built on stainless steel front and rear spars with tubular flanges and corrugated webs and with spruce and plywood secondary members. The leading edge was plywood-covered to promote strength and smooth airflow entry, otherwise the wings were fabric covered. The horizontal stabilizer was similarly constructed with a stainless steel primary structure, including the supporting struts to the rear fuselage, and wooden secondary members, but the fin was built integrally with the hull, the rudder being wooden framed.

The one-step hull was of light alloy throughout, the frames being fabricated from straight angles and plates, and the skinning was of flat plates, which facilitated rapid production and repair. The engine was mounted between the mainplanes above the hull in a streamline nacelle and the various types of Bristol Pegasus engines fitted all drove four-blade propellers. For the initial tests the machine had the Pegasus Mk IIL2P. The pusher propeller slipstream, impinging on one side only of the vertical fin, set up a yawing moment and this was countered by angling the engine mounting by three degrees to starboard, a feature retained throughout the career of the type, including the Walrus production. The fuel tanks were located in the upper wings just outboard of the centre section, and capacity was 122 gal, later increased to 155 gal. The normal crew of the Seagull and of the later Walrus was three, a pilot, a navigator and a wireless telegraphist. There was provision for a retractable forward gun to be mounted on a Scarff ring in the bows and an aft gun position.

Despite the unfavourable terms of both Felixstowe and Martlesham reports on the Seagull's landplane performance, the Air Ministry framed specification 6/34 for a single-engine biplane amphibian and to this the Australian Government ordered 24 aircraft in August 1934, allocated Australian serials A2-1 to A2-24.

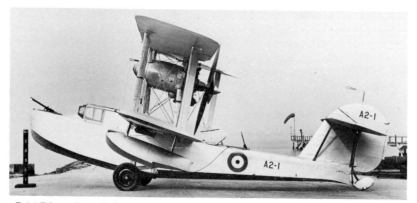

RAAF Seagull V at Felixstowe in 1935 for trials with Bristol Pegasus IIM2 and auto-slots on the upper wings. (*MAEE*)

This order had a somewhat irregular course for it was interrupted by Air Ministry orders which started to materialize in 1935, although British interest had been so lukewarm up to that point. In fact in the presence of Alan Clifton, the Director of Technical Development was heard to say, on viewing the Seagull V prototype, 'Very interesting—but of course we have no requirement for anything like this'. Almost famous last words.

The first Australian Seagull, A2-1, was flown by George Pickering on 25 June, 1935, with Trevor Westbrook and 'Digger' Pickett, the flight engineer, for only 10 minutes because the elevator trim-tab controls had been crossed. The following day it was flown again for 30 minutes with Westbrook as observer. On 1 July it flew to Hendon for the Royal Air Force Display carrying a large number 11 in white on both sides of its hull. There it was demonstrated on the ground and in the air with Major H. J. Payn as passenger. Major Payn had been seconded to Supermarine from Vickers at Weybridge and was not only a capable design technologist but also a fine test pilot. Pickering had virtually taken over Supermarine test flying at that time and handled nearly all the Australian Seagulls on their constructor's trials.

The first Australian Seagull V on the Woolston slipway.

145

Australian Seagull Vs A2-2 and A2-12.

Various teething troubles were ironed out and A2-1 passed acceptance trials at Felixstowe and Martlesham, where it was flown throughout by Flt Lt Tony Ragg. Pickering delivered it direct to HMAS *Australia* at Spithead on 9 September. The second Seagull, A2-2, was delivered by Pickering to Lee-on-Solent on 18 October and was then embarked on HMAS *Sydney*. The rest of the Australian Seagulls were shipped for service with No. 1 Seaplane Training Flight at Point Cook, Victoria, and later with 101 Flight, RAAF, at Richmond, New South Wales.

Meanwhile the prototype N-2 was taken aboard the aircraft carrier *Courageous* for shipborne trials with the Home Fleet off Gibraltar in 444 Flight, then equipped with Fairey IIIFs and Fairey Seal floatplanes. The amphibian was a novelty to the ship and its aircrews but two experienced officers, Lt Cmdrs Caspar John and W. T. Couchman, had been chosen to conduct a comprehensive programme of flying including fleet co-operation. Both these officers later became Admirals, the former becoming Admiral of the Fleet. N-2 was returned in *Renown* for trials to be continued at Sheerness and in the Solent. Recommendations made in the Navy report included increased-buoyancy wingtip floats, removal of wheel brakes to save weight, and alteration of the wireless set position. After further trials on other naval ships and catapult launches from *Ark Royal*, the Air Ministry purchased N-2 under contract 362547/34 with serial K4797 and it was flown to Lee-on-Solent on 1 January, 1935, for use by the Royal Navy.

Allocated to 444 Flight aboard *Nelson* as Admiral's 'barge', the Seagull V was used during cruises to the British West Indies and then in home waters. On 4 October, 1935, Lt Jago had to fly the new commander-in-chief, Admiral Sir

Roger Backhouse, in the Seagull from Hendon to *Nelson* but in alighting along-side forgot to retract his undercarriage. The machine turned turtle and its occupants had to be rescued. The Seagull was salvaged to be returned to Woolston for repair. There, an undercarriage position indicator was fitted, probably one of the first ever, as retraction was still a novelty. K4797 was also fitted with a Pegasus IIM2 engine which gave a brake horse power of 625 hp at 6,500 ft compared with 2,500 ft of the similarly powered IIL2P.

After re-fit K4797 was delivered to Lee-on-Solent by Pickering on 22 January, 1936, from where Lt Jago flew it aboard *Furious* for transport to Gibraltar. In order 'to strike the aircraft below' the tyres had to be deflated and the hydraulic oleos let down to get the machine into the hangar. A similar procedure had to be adopted with the Australian Seagulls aboard HMAS *Albatross*. On arrival at Gibraltar, K4797 was hoisted outboard but in taking off, Lt D. C. V. Pelly, the pilot, had the misfortune to collide with an anti-submarine boom and crashed. All the crew were rescued but the machine sank and was not recovered. So ended the colourful career of the prototype, labelled variously as N-1, N-2, and K4797, and named respectively Seagull V and Walrus, but its counterparts produced in some hundreds certainly lived to justify all the labours put into its lineage from the original Commercial Amphibian of 1920.

Before the first Australian Seagull had flown, Supermarine had supplied tenders to the Air Ministry and on 4 April, 1935, specification 2/35 was issued, followed by contract 391700/35/c4 (c) for twelve Seagulls, serialled K5772 to K5783. Under Corrigendum 1 to specification 2/35 the name was changed from Seagull to Walrus. Later, the engine specified was the Bristol Pegasus IIM2 as with it Supermarine had promised a four mph speed increase and an extra 500 ft in ceiling from the production aircraft. These twelve of the first Air Ministry order for the Walrus were built immediately after the first twelve Seagulls for Australia. K5772 was flown by Pickering on 18 March, 1936, from Woolston, landing at Eastleigh and then proceeding to undergo oil cooling tests and measurement of service ceiling and level speeds before returning to Woolston the following day.

First production Walrus, K5772, during trials.

147

A production Walrus I at Felixstowe for performance trials. (*MAEE*)

K5773 was first flown on 3 April and after a further test flight on 7 April was re-engined with a Pegasus VI which gave 125 hp more than its previous Mk IIM2 and this type was adopted for the main production of the Type 236 Walrus. The second batch, K8338 to K8345, was ordered in 1936, and the last twelve Australian Seagulls were completed along with this series. By the time the last had been delivered, the RAF had received 40 Walruses, a considerable number in view of the original attitude of the Air Ministry towards the type.

Although the belated acceptance of a requirement for a shipborne amphibian aircraft was gratifying to Supermarine, once British orders started to flow, and thus delaying the later Australian deliveries, complications arose in production. The arrival of the first order for 310 Spitfires on 3 June, 1936, followed by an additional contract on 10 July for 168 Walrus, the largest received to date, meant

Production Walrus I hulls at the Itchen Works in 1939.

that production facilities were stretched to the limit. A new factory, built on reclaimed land a short distance up the River Itchen from the Woolston works, was opened in February 1939 and there Walrus hulls were constructed and towed over to Hythe for erection and flight test. Even this additional production capacity was inadequate when Spitfire orders began to assume massive proportions later in 1939, and Walrus production was transferred to Saunders-Roe at Cowes, complete with jigs and tools, which were shipped across the Solent to the Isle of Wight. Saunders-Roe eventually produced 461 Walrus of which 190 were of Mk II variant with a wooden hull.

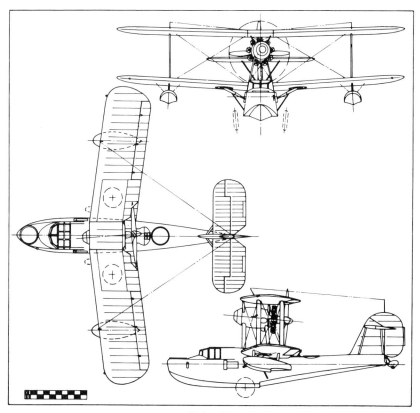

Walrus II

The Mk II Walrus was much used for training aircrews, as the wooden hull, although heavier, was easier to repair. Its production enabled a pool of skilled woodworkers to be drawn on for war work and avoided the extensive use of priority light alloys. The prototype Mk II hull was constructed by Saunders-Roe's factory in Anglesey, North Wales, and the completed aeroplane, X1045, was flown by George Pickering and Sqn Ldr L. Ash on 2 May, 1940. Pickering found the Mk II Walrus with the wooden hull 'smoother and much quieter'. One modification introduced by Saunders-Roe was the substitution of a rubber-tyred tailwheel for the all-metal wheel of the Supermarine-built Walruses and aircrew reported that it reduced the noise when landing on hard runways.*

There had been little change in the original design apart from minor improvements dictated by largescale production, but aircraft were altered in service according to their particular mission, so reverting to the practice first introduced in the 1914–18 War and since continued through various general purpose types. At times the Walrus was fitted with two machine-guns, with bombs or depth charges, with air-sea rescue containers and rings around the bows for picking up survivors from the sea and, after 1942, with air-to-surface vessel (ASV) radar for reconnaissance.

The Walrus served on most of the capital ships of the Royal Navy, the Royal Australian Navy and the Royal New Zealand Navy, and in most of the 1939–1945 war theatres throughout the world, including the African deserts. In the

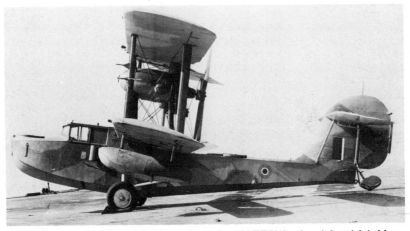

The first production Walrus II with wooden hull at MAEE Helensburgh for trials in May 1942. (*MAEE*)

Norwegian campaigns it fought off Messerschmitts, in the Pacific it was used for photographic reconnaissance of atolls, and was the first aircraft ever to be seen by the inhabitants of Pitcairn Island, descendants of the Bounty mutineers. It was catapulted from ships, flown off heavy seas and from jungle strips, landed on ice floes, carried secret agents, and rescued many survivors of sunken ships and aircrews down in the 'drink'. It was even asked, when still in the air, to accept the white flag surrender of a town in Madagascar, when that island was wrested by amphibious forces from Vichy French control. In fact the operational history of the Walrus was so far-reaching and colourful that it prompted Lt-Cmdr Nicholl, a naval officer, to write a complete book on the subject.** Here it is possible only to highlight some of the more outstanding exploits.

The first real action was on 12 February, 1940, when the Walrus from HMS *Dorsetshire* sighted the German merchant ship *Waikama* out of Rio de Janeiro which, when intercepted, was scuttled. Walrus took part in the short and abortive Norwegian campaign of 1940 and two of them from HMS *Suffolk*, after

*Supermarine retained the design authority for all Walrus production as later with all Spitfire contracts.
**The Supermarine Walrus*—G. W. R. Nicholl—G. T. Foulis, London.

New Zealand Walrus I NZ151 off HMS *Leander*.

Retrieving a naval Walrus at sea.

151

Walrus I L2180 being returned to its hangar on HMS *Sheffield*.

reconnaissance 'spotting' at Stavanger, flew back to Aberdeen 'landfall'. One of them, L2284, had been airborne for five hours, a record for a fully-equipped Walrus. They also participated effectively in the East African campaign against Italian forces, which included the first known dropping of an 'agent', and also against Vichy French outposts.

With German surface raiders at sea attacking British and other shipping, Walrus from Commonwealth ships were early in action to assist in their destruction. In 1941, nearly all of the twenty-one enemy raiders or their supply ships sunk or captured were spotted or attacked by Walrus aircraft. In the same year, when the war in the Mediterranean had reached its peak, seven Walrus attached to 201 Naval Co-operation Group at Aboukir flew local patrols off Alexandria and also stores into Tobruk at night, bringing out casualties on return. As 701 Squadron, seven Walrus (three with ASV radar) operated out of Egyptian harbours on night search and escort missions and from Turkey on air-sea rescue for a year, until August 1943 when the unit was disbanded. Shipborne Walrus also took part in some of the North Cape convoys to Russia, notably the notorious PQ17, when P5706, after being towed for three days by an anti-aircraft ship, had to be dumped on a quay near Archangel and left there, having run out of fuel.

Advances in radar technique rendered the Walrus too slow for spotting by 1943 so the Royal Navy started to phase them out. The last to go were those on the battleships *Duke of York* and *Rodney* and the cruiser *Belfast* so that by March 1944 all catapult flights had been disbanded.

As the role of shipborne reconnaissance ended so the duty of air-sea rescue began in earnest by the Royal Air Force. The Navy had used the Walrus for this purpose on occasion so its utility had been proved. With the increasing tempo of raids by Allied air forces on enemy-held Europe air-sea rescue operations had to be intensified. One RAF Squadron, No.277, saved 598 personnel from the 1,000 who were rescued around the British Isles, and the first ASR squadron—No.700—formed as such by the Royal Navy, saved 19 lives in the first six weeks of operation. In New Guinea a Walrus rescued Lt J. Carter from behind the Japanese lines on 7 July, 1944, and many others owed their continued existence to the ubiquitous 'Shagbat', the favoured Service nickname of the Walrus. Though no actual number has been recorded, the rescues must have run into thousands.

With the cessation of hostilities and the run-down of Walrus-equipped units forty were sold for civil use including some to the parent company of the constructors, Vickers-Armstrongs. Six were acquired by United Whalers for their 1946/47 whaling season and three of these, registered G-AHFL, G-AHFM and G-AHFN, were used from the factory ship *Balaena* which had been fitted with the catapult and recovery crane from HMS *Pegasus*. The aircraft proved only moderately successful, flying without undercarriages in the Antarctic regions, and they were not used again. G-AHFN had won the Folkestone Aero Trophy at Lympne on 31 August, 1946, flown by John Grierson, who later was appointed to manage United Whalers air fleet in the Antarctic. Two Walrus were embarked on the Dutch whaling factory ship *Wilhelm Barendsz* but were not used. Others sold but not used are listed in the Appendices.

Following acquisition of Southamptons and their satisfactory operation, Turkey ordered six Seagull Vs with Pegasus engines and they were delivered in 1938. Eight Walrus, flown as N33 to N40 by Supermarine, were exported to the Argentine in 1947 under serials 2-0-25 to 2-0-32 and some were used by the Argentinian Antarctic Expedition which surveyed Deception Island and Discovery Bay. Another Walrus, HD874, was taken on a similar exercise by an

Walrus G-AJNO operated by Scottish Aviation.

Australian Expedition in 1947 but made only one sortie, to photograph the volcano Big Ben, before being wrecked in a gale. The one Walrus in existence today is in the Fleet Air Arm Museum at Yeovilton, having been painstakingly rebuilt by apprentices at RNAS Arbroath with the hull of L2302 as a basis; and a Seagull V is being restored by the Royal Air Force Museum. These two examples will be the only reminders of a specialist type of aeroplane that, after many vacillations of official policy, proved its point.

The first Argentine Walrus I, M-O-9.

RAAF Seagull V A2-4 reconditioned as VH-ALB. (*Courtesy Neville Parnell*)

At one and the same time Supermarine earned the distinction of supplying the Royal Air Force with its slowest front-line type, the Walrus, and with its fastest, the Spitfire.

Seagull V—One 625 hp Bristol Pegasus IIM2. Crew three.
Span 46 ft (14·02 m); length (on chassis) 38 ft (11·6 m); height (on chassis) 15 ft (4·57 m); wing area 610 sq ft (56·67 sq m).
Empty weight 4,640 lb (2,105 kg); loaded weight 6,847 lb (3,106 kg).
Maximum speed 125 mph (201·2 km/h) at 3,280 ft (1,000 m); alighting speed 54 mph (87 km/h); range 634 miles (1,020 km) at 95 mph (153 km/h); maximum rate of climb 900 ft/min (274 m/min); climb to 10,000 ft (3,048 m) 17·25 min; service ceiling 15,500 ft (4,724·4 m).
Armament. Two Vickers K machine-guns in bow and amidships.

Walrus I—One 750 hp Bristol Pegasus VI. Crew four.
Span 45 ft 10 in (13·97 m); length (on chassis) 37 ft 7 in (11·45 m); height (on chassis) 15 ft 3 in (4·65 m); wing area 610 sq ft (56·67 sq m).
Empty weight 4,900 lb (2,233 kg); loaded weight 7,200 lb (3,266 kg).
Maximum speed 135 mph (217·3 km/h) at 4,750 ft (1,448 m); alighting speed 57 mph (91·7 km/h); range 600 miles (965·6 km) at 92 mph (148 km/h); maximum rate of climb 1,050 ft/min (320 m/min); climb to 10,000 ft (3,048 m) 12·5 min; service ceiling 18,500 (5,639 m).
Armament. Two Vickers K machine-guns, one in the bow and one amidships.

The prototype Sea Otter K8854, showing Alan Clifton's 'scissors' solution to the conflicting claims of propeller thrust and aircraft stowage height.

Sea Otter

Even before the flight test of the first production Walrus, Mitchell was working on an improved version powered by one or other of the Bristol sleeve-valve engines, the Aquila or the Perseus. In February 1936 he met the Air Ministry's Director of Technical Development to discuss a Walrus development, from which meeting certain requirements emerged. The more important included an increase in loaded weight; equipment and internal layout to be the same for either cruiser or carrier operation; the new type to be suitable for the carrier *Furious* as was the original Seagull V N-2; a dive-bombing capability; a longer range, and finally, a limited wing span of 46 ft. On that basis Supermarine submitted costing figures, detailed drawings and technical data to which the Air Ministry issued 'Instructions to Proceed' on 17 April, 1936, allocating serials K8854 and K8855 for two prototypes.

In the Supermarine report of 28 May, 1936, the improved Walrus was fully defined as Type 309, with a loaded weight of 8,500 lb and fitted with a Bristol Perseus VI air-cooled radial engine developing 796 hp at 4,000 ft. When the official specification 5/36 was received it required the construction method to be the same as the Walrus and the overall dimensions to be similar. Cruising speed was to be 100 kt for 920 miles range and stalling speed under 48 kt.

Work on the two prototypes proceeded slowly, influenced by the build-up of Walrus and Spitfire production in 1938, but in August investigations were initiated into the possibilities of fitting three-blade constant-speed propellers for production aircraft. Here it should be emphasized that the main difference between the Walrus and its development Type 309 as yet unnamed was that the latter was a tractor aeroplane, thus giving yet another tilt to the Supermarine single-engined 'see-saw' already described in these pages. The visible evidence in

156

the illustrations shows an aeroplane externally cleaner than the Walrus, particularly in its tractor propeller and engine installation. The 'off-set' engine of the older type was eliminated; instead the vertical stabilizing surface was of aerofoil section to counteract torque.

The criterion of the early test flights of the new type, known at first as the Stingray, was the choice of propeller. George Pickering took K8854 for its first trials on 23 September, 1938, with a Perseus XI and a two-blade wooden airscrew and after a run of about a mile he managed to get the machine onto its single step. The propeller, two-bladed because of height restrictions and limited in diameter to clear the hull, gave insufficient thrust to get the machine through the hump speed. For further trials on 29 September a two-position three-blade de Havilland propeller was used but again the take-off time of 30 seconds and a very slow climb were disappointing. A solution was found by increasing the solidity characteristics of the propeller by introducing a four-blade type consisting of the two-bladers set at 35 degrees instead of the usual 90 degrees. This unusual arrangement was made to comply with the height restrictions of cruiser hangars; a normal two-blade propeller can be 'parked' horizontally. Known as the 'scissors' propeller it proved as satisfactory as a normal 90-degree type. On the third test flight of the aeroplane, renamed Sea Otter—the name Stingray being deemed unsuitable—George Pickering reported that its take-off with the 'scissors' propeller was much quicker and its behaviour, including taxi-ing, very similar to that of the Walrus.

Then followed the normal pattern of test flights and modifications to rectify minor defects, such as slight porpoising before take-off, until on 11 January, 1939, Pickering was able to report favourably on the Sea Otter's performance, particularly in rudder control and in a diving speed of 155 kt with a stalling speed of 54 kt. In February, sea recovery trials were started by Pickering from HMS *Pegasus* and these consisted of lowering the machine over the side with the engine running, casting off the crane hoist and then hooking back on with the ship under way at seven knots. Some modification of Walrus recovery techniques was indicated as a result of these trials. In March the Admiralty requested an alteration in the shape

The prototype Sea Otter K8854 with ASV radar aerials on the interplane struts.

of the nose of the hull to counter water-spray tendencies and the fitting of a three-blade Rotol hydraulic constant-speed propeller. This was fitted to K8854 after its return from catapult trials at the RAE and an improvement in take off from water and land was recorded. Shipboard catapult trials were made from *Pegasus* in two stages during July, the second involving some 15 launches. Ministry seaworthiness trials were due in September 1939 and because of the outbreak of war these were made by Flt Lt Dennis of the MAEE from Southampton Water as Felixstowe was considered too vulnerable.

A high-level technical delegation visited Supermarine on 26 January, 1940, to announce that it had been decided to put the Sea Otter into production. One of its requirements was a reduction of landing speed to the level obtained from the first prototype fitted with 50-ft span wings taken from K8855, the second prototype, after bomb-damage at Woolston. Reversion was to be made to the originally specified 46-ft span wings, fitted with flaps to obtain the desired effect. Other required improvements included more headroom on the flight deck and a Vickers K gun in the nose. During 1940, contract specification I/P2 was issued to Blackburn Aircraft for 190 Sea Otters in all but the company was unable to accept it as it was already loaded with work on other types and the contract was cancelled in

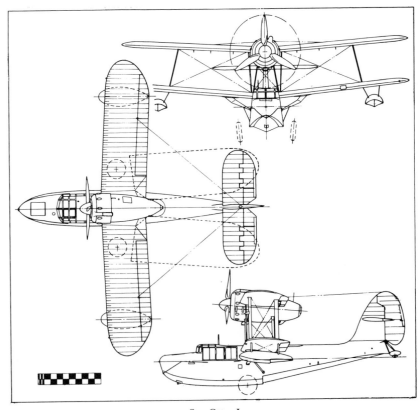

Sea Otter I

158

A Sea Otter and a Seagull ASR.I on the slipway in front of the restored Itchen Works at Southampton in 1947.

1941. These Sea Otters would have had the Perseus but cooling troubles with that engine had persisted, evidenced by high lubricating oil temperatures.

Consequently, an engine change was made on the prototype to the Bristol Mercury XX poppet-valve type of 920 hp, and a test flight on 2 May, 1941, by Jeffrey Quill from Worthy Down to Eastleigh and back with climbs to 10,000 ft disclosed no problems with oil temperatures. The heavier-duty 965 hp Mercury XXX, as fitted and flown in January 1941, was specified for production aircraft. Not until January 1942 was an order placed for 250 Sea Otters, with Saunders-Roe of Cowes, who were already in production with Walruses. Some were completed at their Weybridge works* as were some Walrus, alongside Walrus reconditioning and repair work. Several changes had been made in the specification requirements as the design progressed through its development stages. The re-writings of the original 5/36 were respectively S.7/38 and S.14/39, and the official designation became Sea Otter ABR Mk I, the initials meaning 'amphibian boat reconnaissance'.

The first production Sea Otter, JM 738, was flown by Jeffrey Quill from Cowes in January 1943, as George Pickering was recovering from the effects of the disintegration of a Spitfire in a dive. Only a day or so after being cleared medically for flying he was tragically killed on 2 June, 1943, in a land accident to a military vehicle. Quill thereupon took over as Supermarine chief test pilot.

Initial flight trials were continued from Worthy Down airfield and for water performance from Southampton Water. In these trials the time for take off from water was found excessive, the machine was sensitive to changes of crew position and height was lost when the engine was throttled back below zero boost. These details and Service loading weights received attention before the second production aircraft, JM739, was flown to the RAE in April for catapult trials at an overload weight of 10,250 lb. After that JM739 was delivered to MAEE, then located at Helensburgh in Scotland, for further water handling trials, and thence

*Located in the industrial estate near Addlestone.

to *Pegasus* for on-board catapult trials. At this point some doubts were expressed as to the need for an improved type as the Walrus was doing so well. This led to comparative trials between the two aircraft but no conclusions were made known. The Sea Otter definitely had a longer range and could accept overload, an important factor in picking up 'ditched' bomber crews. There had been occasions when a Walrus, having picked up more than its complement of survivors, had been unable to take off and had to taxi all the way back to base with its load. In common with the Walrus, the Sea Otter, besides being used in its primary task of naval reconnaissance, was also intended for air-sea rescue. JM977 was converted for this role by removing the armament and other Service items and given the designation ASR Mk II (Naval) on 23 May, 1945. The first fully-equipped ASR.II was JN249, and it is believed all aircraft produced later were Mk IIs including the last batch, RD869 to RD922. Meanwhile JM738 had been delivered to AAEE Boscombe Down for the final type acceptance.

Further improvements made as development flying continued included a larger water rudder to improve manoeuvrability on the surface, and this was eventually made retractable, with an indicator dashboard lamp showing whether it was up or down. A sting-type arrester hook was added so that the Sea Otter could be operated from escort carriers under all conditions, including from American ships with their shorter flight decks. The pilot's rearward view was improved by adding blisters to the Perspex cockpit canopy. The arrester hook was first fitted to RD876 which was tested at the AAEE, Boscombe Down, during June 1946, presumably with land-based arrester gear. The first production aircraft to be fully equipped for deck landings was RD920, one of the last batch of Sea Otters built and of the

The Qantas Sea Otter VH-AJO at the Rose Bay flying-boat base near Sydney.
(*Australasian Petroleum via Qantas*)

The four-seat Type 503 Civil Sea Otter G-AIDM used for demonstration to potential customers.

ASR Mk II (Naval) variant. Experiments in rocket-assisted take off were conducted by the MAEE at Felixstowe on a Mk I, JM909, by fitting RATOG.

The Sea Otter came into operational service late in the war, the first naval squadron, 1700, being formed at Lee-on-Solent in November 1944 and the second, 1701, also at Lee in February 1945, followed by 1702 in June. Its career therefore had little chance to emulate that of its predecessor, the Walrus, and by the time the fourth squadron, 1703, was formed in August 1945 the war was over. Some units however had been attached individually to the Pacific Fleet in readiness for the final assault on Japan, pre-empted by the dropping of the atomic bomb. On 'VJ' day most of 1700's Sea Otters were shore-based at Trincomalee in Ceylon.

Meanwhile Sea Otters continued in air-sea rescue duties with 18 and 19 Groups RAF and at naval air bases. The total on charge in April 1949 at Service stations was 30, with seven on HM ships and a further 48 in store or under repair, with an unspecified number still serving overseas. In preparation for Service use of the variable-incidence monoplane Seagull ASR Mk I, rapidly approaching completion, JM909 was used at Itchen for pilot training in water handling, manoeuvring in crowded shipping lanes, taxi-ing up and down slipways and coming up to moorings, as well as providing practice for coxwains and other waterborne personnel.

With the cessation of the war all firms were searching for means of buying their aircraft back from the Government for re-sale for civil or military use. Eight Sea Otters were acquired by the Royal Danish Air Force and allocated serials 801 to 806, the intended 807 which was ex-JM807 being damaged beyond repair before wearing its new number, while the eighth was used for spares. The Danish Sea Otters were used for search, rescue and training. Another eight were bought by the Dutch Naval Air Arm during 1949–50 and bore serials 18-1 to 18-8 and were used mainly for air-sea rescue duties. One Sea Otter was converted into a four-seat passenger aircraft as Type 503 with registration G-AIDM, and six were

161

purchased by the French colonial authority in Indo-China as Type 497 and exported by ship to Saïgon. A possible sale to Chile of three Sea Otters was rendered abortive by the refusal of the Chilean Council of Foreign Trade to grant an import licence. Details of other Sea Otters ordered or registered are given in the Appendices.

The Sea Otter was the last of the Supermarine biplane flying-boats to reach production. Surprisingly for such a pioneering firm, it bore a close resemblance in layout to the first, the P.B.1 of 1914, in that it was a single-engined biplane with a three-blade tractor propeller, despite all the waverings between tractor or pusher layouts during the long history of this interesting type of specialized aeroplane.

Sea Otter—One 965 hp Bristol Mercury XXX. Crew four.
Span 46 ft (14 m); length 39 ft 10¾ in (12·2 m); height (on ground) 15 ft 1½ in (4·61 m); wing area 610 sq ft (56·7 sq m).
Empty weight 6,805 lb (3,086 kg); loaded weight 10,000 lb (4,536 kg).
Maximum speed 163 mph (262·3 km/h) at 4,500 ft (1,371 m); alighting speed (without power) 65 mph (104·6 km/h); normal range 690 miles (1,110 km); maximum range 920 miles (1,480 km) with overload tank; initial rate of climb 870 ft/min (265 m/min); climb to 5,000 ft (1,524 m) 7 min; service ceiling 17,000 ft (5,181 m).
Armament. One Vickers GO free gun forward with 200 rounds and twin Vickers K machine-guns aft with 600 rounds. Bomb load four 250 lb (113 kg) bombs beneath the lower wings.

Type 322 S.24/37 Dumbo

A requirement for a shipborne torpedo dive-bomber reconnaissance aeroplane to replace the Fairey Albacore was made known in 1937 when on 9 November the Air Ministry issued specification S.24/37. Tenders were received from seven aircraft constructors and from these Supermarine and Fairey were awarded contracts for one prototype each. The Fairey submission materialized into the Barracuda, which was produced in some quantity, but the Supermarine design was of more advanced concept which took some time to develop and resulted in only two completed aircraft. An important factor in awarding Fairey the contract was Supermarine's preoccupation with the production and development of the Spitfire. The Supermarine S.24/37, nicknamed Dumbo because of its elephantine shape, was an interesting experiment as it embodied a variable-incidence wing, one of the rare examples in aeronautical design practice.

The specification required a monoplane of robust construction to withstand deck landings and take offs, with improved speed and range over the Albacore. The engine was to be air-cooled, of British manufacture and having passed the 100 hours type test, and drive a variable-pitch propeller. The aeroplane was to be capable of being catapulted in land or seaplane form, in the former case to be fitted with arresting gear. All-up weight, with 1,500 lb of bombs or a Mk XII torpedo weighing 1,550 lb, was not to exceed 10,500 lb in landplane form. Operational criteria which dictated the final configuration were the limiting dimensions for ship stowage and a dive-bombing angle of 70 degrees to the horizontal. At a meeting in the Air Ministry on 25 January, 1938, between official

Type 322 Dumbo in high-speed configuration. (*Vickers*)

representatives and Vickers-Supermarine design executives it was decided that the best solution to the problem posed by the limiting dimensions was a variable-incidence wing. In view of the mechanical complications involved, a fixed under-carriage was proposed if the performance specified could be achieved without retraction. The air-brakes or special flaps thought to be necessary to fulfil the dive-bombing requirement were not, in fact, fitted—to avoid extra complication and weight. After some discussion the cruising height of the aeroplane was fixed at 10,000 ft.

Engine choice for the two S.24/37 prototypes originally fell on the new Rolls-Royce Exe, a 24-cylinder air-cooled type with sleeve valves and of X configuration, which was being developed by Harry Cantrill, one of the chief design engineers at Derby. It was installed in Fairey Battle K9222 at Hucknall but engine development was curtailed in September 1938 so that Rolls-Royce could concentrate on the development and production of the Merlin. The alternative air-cooled type was the Bristol Taurus still undergoing development and all available engines were being used in the Fairey Albacores. The final choice for the Super-marine S.24/37 was the Rolls-Royce Merlin; although a liquid-cooled type, at least it was in full production.

The specification's exacting requirements placed a premium on a small wing area and for this reason a fully-slotted and extensively flapped wing was chosen to develop maximum lift. Large incidence at low speeds enabled full advantage to be taken of these aids to lift, and at such a coarse setting the fuselage remained at a reasonable incidence, ensuring normal flow over the tail. This adjustable correlation of wing and fuselage incidence also promoted aerodynamic efficiency at cruising and higher speeds, provided the pilot with a better view of the deck in three-point landings, enabled the nose of the aeroplane to be depressed on the approach or when dive-bombing to the pilot's advantage in sighting, with the same bonus to the bomb aimer in level flight. The high wing gave the observer an excellent view for spotting and observation, and the cantilever tail unit offered minimum obstruction to the rear gunner's view and field of fire.

163

The S.24/37 Dumbo in high-speed configuration with zero wing incidence.

Joseph Smith, who had succeeded R. J. Mitchell as chief designer of Supermarine, favoured the variable-incidence wing principle since it provided such an excellent view for the pilot, a feature so lacking in many designs. With slots open and flaps down a maximum lift coefficient of 2·6 was aimed at. Full-span slots and part-span slotted-flaps were deemed necessary to achieve this figure, but with the added introduction of slotted-ailerons a maximum lift coefficient of 3·9 was registered with engine on and a corresponding 57 mph stalling speed. Very few aeroplanes had reached such a high figure; even the maximum lift coefficient of the Lysander was only 2·38.

Although at first it was considered that a variable-incidence tailplane might be needed, calculations showed and subsequent flight trials confirmed that adequate

Supermarine S.24/37 Dumbo R1810. The wing with full-span slats and flaps is seen in the high-lift position.

164

trimming could be provided by the variable-incidence gear of the mainplane. The leading-edge slots operated automatically while the landing flaps were linked to the incidence-change mechanism, which was driven by an electric motor. To prepare for landing all the pilot did was to press a button—not more than lowering the landing flaps on a conventional aeroplane. The difference was that, as the wing incidence-change mechanism operated and the airspeed was allowed to fall, the fuselage attitude remained virtually constant. This novel feature was used from the outset on the two Supermarine prototypes and no modifications whatever were made, apart from the electric operating-motor replacing the initial manual control, a system that proved very slow in operation and consequently unpopular.

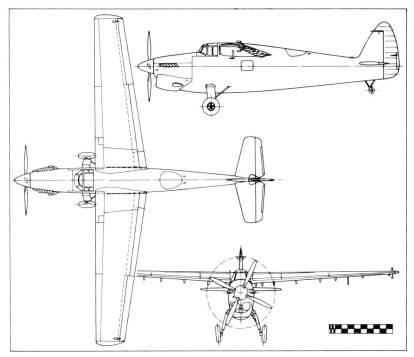

Type 322 (S.24/37) Dumbo

To reduce construction work in what was primarily an experimental type, a decision was made to use wood wherever possible, particularly as light alloys were in short supply. The fuselage aft of the firewall was constructed from diagonal-grain plywood glued to a primary structure of solid spruce longerons and wooden frames reminiscent of the S.4 racer. The tailplane was also covered with diagonal ply with spanwise stringers in quantity and spar-type reinforcement only for the attachment fittings. The wing of composite construction was in three portions, the centre section and two outer planes. To comply with naval requirements, a folding joint was provided on a raked spar, so that when the aircraft was folded the main spar flanges were unbroken. This main spar had duralumin flanges and webs with steel fittings while the rear spar and the wing ribs were of wood. The wing covering on the first prototype was diagonal plywood but on the second the skinning was of Alclad sheeting (aluminium-coated duralumin) introduced to increase torsional rigidity. The slats on the leading edge were similarly Alclad covered on wooden frames. Where the wing passed through the cabin, steel tubing was used to provide drag and torsion bracing aft of the main spar, which was attached to the fuselage by two hinges consisting of plain phosphor-bronze bearings. This spar-hinge unit took nearly all the flight loads as it was close to the centre of pressure. The coupled operating screw-jacks were attached to the rear spar and all loads were vertical with no possibility of inadvertent incidence reversal. The flying controls were led out into the wing at a point where the movement of the wing did not affect the tautness of the system.

Before the first prototype was completed a Rolls-Royce Merlin 30 was installed. It flew in February 1943 as R1810, followed by the second, R1815, shortly afterwards with a Merlin 32. After protracted contractor's trials and modifications R1810 was delivered to the RAE in November 1944. There it was regarded purely as an experimental aeroplane as the time for its production had long passed, with the Barracuda fulfilling the role. However its usefulness in probing one aspect of variable geometry must have been considerable and incidence-changing gear has been used on other aircraft, notably the Chance Vought Crusader fighter. The principle was applied to the last of the Seagull line of amphibian flying-boats, the S.12/40 ASR type, with considerable success but again too late as helicopters had already started to replace such fixed-wing aircraft. In 1947, R1815 was used as a 'chase plane' at Chilbolton test base by Supermarine for the Attacker initial low-speed trials.

Type 322—One 1,300 hp Rolls-Royce Merlin 30 (in R1810) and one 1,645 hp Merlin 32 (in R1815). Crew three.

Span 50 ft (15·2 m); length 40 ft (12·1 m); height 14 ft 2 in (4·2 m); wing area 319·5 sq ft (29·7 sq m).

Empty weight 9,175 lb (4,170 kg); loaded weight 12,000 lb (5,454 kg).

Maximum speed 279 mph (446 km/h) at 4,000 ft (1,216 m); stalling speed approx 58 mph (92·8 km/h); maximum range 825 miles (1,328 km) at 160 mph (257·5 km/h) at 2,000 ft (610 m) with 30 gal reserve fuel.

Armament—One 18-in Mk XII torpedo of 1,500 lb (680 kg) or six 250 lb (113 kg) bombs or six 500 lb (226 kg) bombs. One 0·303-in Browning machine-gun in wing and one 0·303-in Vickers K or Browning machine-gun in the rear cockpit (never fitted).

Weights, performance and armanent for R1815.

The prototype Seagull ASR.I with original tail arrangement. Note the shadowgraph of the contra-rotating propellers.

Seagull ASR.I

Last of the Supermarine flying-boats was the Seagull ASR Mk I, first considered in 1940 in response to Air Ministry specification S.12/40 for an advanced fleet reconnaissance amphibian, capable of ship stowage. After the success of the Walrus, and its derivative the Sea Otter, further development of this specialized class was at that time considered desirable. Advantage was taken of Supermarine's considerable research on the variable-incidence wing for its Type 322 Dumbo high-wing monoplane in introducing this feature in its submission to the requirement.

The tender design was being prepared at the time of the enemy bombing of Woolston in September 1940, but interruption of design work was slight and the drawings and files were transferred almost intact to the hutments of the University College of Southampton. The Supermarine brochure was duly submitted to the Ministry in October and it covered monoplane and biplane versions, both with either the Rolls-Royce Merlin 30 or the Bristol Taurus. These projects were considered at an advanced design conference in April 1941.

Meanwhile more work was being done on the aerodynamics of the high-lift wing as explored in the S.24/37 Dumbo, mostly at RAE Farnborough, who in this connection were conducting tests on a scale model of the Miles M.18 with a wing with full-span flaps and inset ailerons but no variable incidence. More wind-tunnel tests at Farnborough were made during 1942 and 1943 on a one-sixteenth scale model of the new Type 347 to determine stability characteristics associated

167

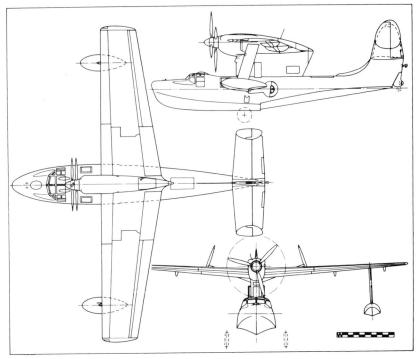

Seagull ASR.I

with the changing wing incidence settings, as well as tail effectiveness and other aspects of the complete aeroplane. The variable-incidence wing was fitted with full-span 40 per cent chord slotted flaps with inset ailerons and full-span leading-edge slats.

This highly specialized wing was mounted parasol fashion above the hull on a single pylon or 'trunk' which was in structural principle similar to a two-spar wing placed vertically. The aerodynamic loads on the wing, and conversely the weight of the hull and the thrust loads, were all transmitted through the pivots of the front-spar root joints (which were provided with plain phosphor-bronze bearings) and the two incidence-operating screw jacks operating on an auxiliary rear spar, very similar to the Dumbo arrangement. The motive power for the incidence-changing gear was a 1·5 hp electric motor and this and other high-lift devices were worked from an engine-driven alternator of 8·5 KVA output.*

The hull structure comprised two longerons and the chines, with a series of light alloy frames closely spaced, all covered in flush-riveted Alclad sheet. The main spar of the wing had rhomboidal flanges with an eight-gauge Alclad web. The pressed light alloy ribs were spaced along the wing, which was covered in flush-riveted Alclad skin. Forward of the wing junction the light alloy engine mounting

*This was one of the first uses of alternating current in aircraft, the object being to synchronize electrically the motors which operated the wing flaps and slats, to avoid mechanical complexity.

was supported by the pylon structure which also housed the oil and coolant radiators of the Merlin-engined version. Cooling air entered through the leading edge of the pylon, flowed upwards to the rear of the engine, and forwards past the cylinders to its exit behind the large propeller spinner. This feature was retained in the Taurus-engined design project and also when the later Griffon-engined version came to be built. Behind the rear spar of the pylon 'trunk' was a standing-observation position with a good view rearwards and downwards through two transparent panels. Above this position the tail end of the engine nacelle housed a modified Nash and Thomson turret with four 0·303 Browning guns. A good field of fire was obtained rearwards 'through' the novel 'butterfly' tail with its large dihedral. The light alloy wingtip floats were attached to the front spar by a cantilever strut. Each housed a telescopic jury strut for bracing the wing, when folded, to the hull.

In the original submission a biplane version had been offered with a lower top speed and a higher ceiling, but the Supermarine brochure stated 'the preferred design is the monoplane which represents the modern conception of a naval amphibian, a combination of Walrus and Spitfire experience; seaworthiness plus performance'—in other words mating of the slowest and fastest aircraft. 'Instructions to Proceed' were received by Supermarine from the Air Ministry on 9 April, 1943, for the production of three monoplane aircraft to specification S.12/40, serials PA143, PA147 and PA152.

After several conferences the Admiralty decided that the aircraft need not be considered for below-deck stowage on the earlier carriers and so allowed a welcome relaxation in span, folded dimensions, height and weight, factors hitherto determined by considerations of the ships' lift capacity and height between decks. It was this decision that enabled the larger and more powerful Griffon engine to be used in the Seagull ASR, as detailed later in connection with the change of specification. All three aircraft were to be assembled in the experimental department at Hursley Park. The hulls were constructed there, the wings at Castle Road, Salisbury (one of the Spitfire dispersal centres), and the tails sub-contracted to and made by Folland Aircraft of Hamble. The first aeroplane was to have manually-folding wings but the other two were to have hydraulic operation for the same function.

As the Sea Otter was now in full production and satisfying its roles the urgency for its replacement had diminished, so work continued at a slow pace. Most of the theoretical research concerned the optimum configuration of the 'butterfly' tail. Further wind-tunnel tests in May 1944 at the RAE covered a proposed conventional T-tail layout and on others with 35 and 40 degree dihedral. The 40-degree dihedral tail gave better stability; in the conventional type turbulence was caused partly by the wake from the large wing-supporting pylon impinging on the vertical fin and so reducing its efficiency. This problem became progressively worse with increase in wing incidence and most serious in the landing regime with a possibility of buffeting on the full-scale aircraft. The efficiency of the conventional tail was estimated at only 75 per cent but the dihedral types showed up to 85 per cent of the theoretical optimum. To try to increase this figure, one dihedral tailplane was investigated at 20 degrees, with end fins for directional stability and rudder power. This combination was good but stability in yaw was too high, indicating that the area of the end fins could be reduced by 40 per cent. Further tests were made later in that configuration as adopted for the prototype construction. For ease of manufacture the fins were set at 90 degrees to the tailplane in front elevation.

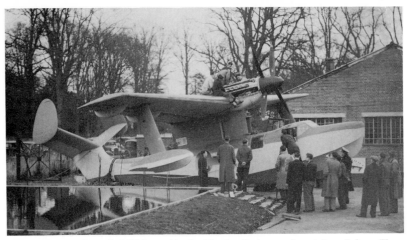

The prototype Seagull ASR.I outside the Hursley Park experimental workshop. The pool was for civil defence firefighting only!

On 27 November, 1944, the specification was changed to S.14/44 to cover an air-sea rescue and reconnaissance flying-boat with the original's gun turret omitted and the Rolls-Royce Griffon RG14SM engine (in effect a modified Griffon 8) being substituted for the Merlin 30. With these changes the Seagull became the Supermarine Type 381, with the official designation ASR Mk I. Some difficulty was experienced in finding a propeller to match the thrust requirements of 6,000 lb at 40 fps airspeed. Close co-operation between Supermarine and Rotol, the propeller company, then ensued and various cropped variants of existing models were tried, including some from the Supermarine Seafang fighter. Rolls-Royce also assisted by modifying the front cover of the Griffon and altering the reduction gear ratio to suit the combination. The propeller diameter was limited to an extent by the Seagull being required originally to occupy roughly the same shipboard space as the Sea Otter, hence the exercise of cropping existing types of propeller. The six-blade contra-rotating type selected assisted this diameter reduction and eliminated torque on take-off, so avoiding the need for aileron or rudder trim controls.

The first Seagull ASR.I, PA143, flew on 14 July, 1948, from the water at Itchen in the hands of Lt Cdr Mike Lithgow, who had joined Supermarine from the Fleet Air Arm. Taxi-ing trials had been started there with Jeffrey Quill, Mike Lithgow and Basil Brown (the fitter) aboard, from 21 June onwards, when pronounced rolling from side to side was experienced at slow speeds and there was difficulty in keeping the 'boat straight. During deceleration there was also a tendency for the starboard float to bury itself in the water so setting up hydrodynamic drag and a swinging moment. Longer float struts cured that problem. The combination of tides and slipway conditions at Itchen restricted the test flying, so after brief ground-handling tests at Lee-on-Solent the Seagull was flown on 7 August to Chilbolton to continue its test-flying programme, flying back to Southampton for any water testing needed. It appeared at the ninth SBAC Display at Farnborough on 11 September, 1948, where it created a favourable impression, piloted by Mike Lithgow.

170

Preliminary flight-test reports contained criticisms of the airflow over the aeroplane, indicating buffeting in several forms. Investigations of this phenomenon on a one-sixteenth scale model in the low-speed wind tunnel at University College of Southampton discovered the main causes of disturbance as leakage of air between the nacelle and the wing at the leading edge, retarded flow from the radiator ducts when its flaps were open, and breakaway of flow at the junction of the pylon and wing undersurfaces near the trailing edge at fine incidences, this last item having the effect of reducing the airflow over the tailplane with consequent loss of directional stability. These defects were cured by sealing the wing-to-fuselage joint with rubber strips, the fitting of shrouds or louvres over the radiator flaps and duct exits and, in the case of the yawing problem, by providing a central vertical fin and rudder.

These modifications were embodied on PA143 and subsequent flight tests in the first eight months of 1949 confirmed the effectiveness of the improvements in suppressing the buffet trouble. The fore and aft oscillation of the control column which had been particularly noticeable at high speeds was very much reduced, and diving the aeroplane to 268 knots ASI induced only a small but acceptable oscillation. The stalling speed with flaps up and zero incidence was reduced by six to seven knots and the Seagull could then be flown with the radiator flaps fully open.

Throughout the first test flights and the preliminary trials, the Seagull prototypes, PA143 and PA147, were powered by the Rolls-Royce Griffon 29 which developed 1,815 hp and was fitted with a two-speed single-stage supercharger and a fuel injection pump. The Rotol hydraulic propeller finally chosen was 10 ft in diameter and had duralumin blades. Production aircraft were to be fitted with the Griffon RG30SM, which was basically a Griffon 57, and would have had water-methanol injection.

Seagull ASR.I PA147 with modified 'trunk', lengthened float struts and partially modified vertical tail surface. (*Charles W. Cain*)

171

The second prototype, PA147, was first flown on 2 September, 1949, by Mike Lithgow, who also flew it at the SBAC Display at Farnborough on 15 September. Shortly after, it was subjected to proving trials at the RAE into the *Ark Royal* Mk 10 deck-arresting gear at an all-up weight of 15,430 lb, including air-sea-rescue equipment carried under the port wing. This was followed by deck-landing trials on HMS *Illustrious* in October to investigate its suitability for arrested landing, to prove the arrester gear and to check the deck handling, securing and slinging gear. Fifty-four landings were made in wind speeds of 16 to 22 knots with the wing incidence varying from five degrees to eight and a half. Three pilots, Mike Lithgow, Lt Cdr Richmond and Lt Parker conducted the trials, which concluded with a satisfactory report. Two Service pilots, from the AAEE at Boscombe Down, could have been even more impressed with the handling of the aeroplane given more practice. Two abortive landing attempts by the AAEE pilots, caused by missing the pick-up wires completely, led to 'overshoot' take-offs with no difficulty, as the Seagull could be airborne from rest in 300 yards, thanks to its high-lift wing. A sidelight on the proceedings was that the Seagull had to be flown ashore after each day's trials because the lifts on *Illustrious* were too narrow to accept it for hangar stowage. Advantage was taken of this to ferry five people ashore, with all their baggage, on each flight, thus presaging the ship-to-shore service eventually adopted with naval helicopters, although personnel at the time were flown ashore singly in the back seat of Fairey Fireflies.

Further development of the type resulted from the testing of the first prototype, PA143, by the MAEE at Felixstowe in December 1949. Various recommended improvements, such as the modified fins and rudders in conjunction with water-

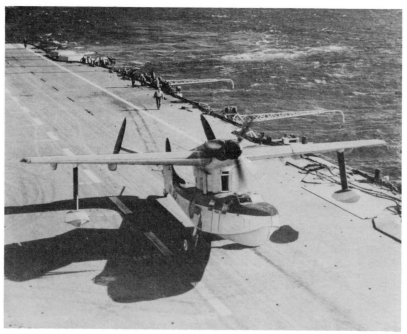

A Seagull ASR.I on HMS *Illustrious* in 1949. (*Fleet Air Arm Museum*)

Seagull ASR.I PA143 with fully modified central fin and rear nacelle.

rudder alterations, produced a big improvement in the Seagull's manoeuvrability on the water. General handling in the air was also better, particularly using flaps and ailerons at slow speed. Mike Lithgow used to fly along the Basingstoke—Andover railway line Bradshaw-fashion watching the trains go by! In fact he could get the Seagull to fly as slow as 35 mph, a speed more associated with lightplanes in the Supermarine Sparrow class than with a military aeroplane of amphibian capability, weighing in the region of 15,000 lb. Leslie R. Colquhoun, who had joined Supermarine as a test pilot from the RAF, and had flight-tested the Seagull with most of the modifications referred to above, gained the World's Air Speed Record for amphibians over 100 kilometres when participating in the Air League Cup Race at Sherburn-in-Elmet on 22 July, 1950, at 241·9 mph, in PA147.

Experiments continued with the two Seagulls, such as with light alloy radiators and rocket-assisted take-off, but they were eventually sold as scrap in 1952, with the third airframe, PA152, only partly completed. So ended the Supermarine contribution to the development of a unique class of fixed-wing aeroplane—the amphibian—capable of flying from land or water, off ships or airfields, in a great variety of operating conditions.

Seagull ASR.I—One 1,815 hp Rolls-Royce Griffon 29. Crew three.
    Span 52 ft 6 in (16 m); maximum width wing folded 23 ft 6 in (7·17 m); length 44 ft 1½ in (13·46 m); height (tail down) 15 ft 10½ in (4·84 m); wing area 432 sq ft (40·13 sq m).
    Empty weight 10,510 lb (4,770 kg); loaded weight 14,500 lb (6,583 kg).
    Maximum speed 260 mph (418 km/h) at 11,800 ft (3,599 m); normal range 875 miles (1,408 km) at 131 mph (211 km/h); maximum rate of climb 1,430 ft/min (436 m/min) at 7,000 ft (2,133 m) in MS gear; service ceiling 23,700 ft (7,229 m); take off run from deck 312 ft (96·7 m) in 31 mph (50 km/h) wind.
    Performance figures are estimates for production aircraft with Griffon 57.

The first S.5 on its launching trolley at Calshot in 1927 before its first test flight.

Schneider S Series

Although the American Curtiss CR-3 floatplanes had run away with the 1923 Schneider Trophy race at Cowes and, as previously suggested, the race had probably seen the end of the flying-boat as a racing type, Mitchell and Supermarine were still unconvinced. So a new design was started for a single-seat high-speed flying-boat with unconventional features. From the alternative layouts proposed, that reproduced here shows the most promising. This project was given Air Ministry support and was called the Sea Urchin, an obscure link in the Supermarine line of succession.

From the general arrangement drawing by Frank Holroyd as approved by Mitchell, dated 10 December, 1923, and redrawn here, it can be seen that the keynote of the Sea Urchin was reduction of frontal area and careful streamlining, following the pattern of the Curtiss racers. The bulky Rolls-Royce Condor engine of 600 hp was installed in the hull, driving the pusher propeller through bevel-geared shafts. This arrangement in itself would have been quite an innovation in a small aeroplane of under 24 ft span. The superstructure was of sesquiplane form, that is with the lower wing only one third the area of the top wing. The tail surfaces were also smaller and of better aerodynamic shape than those of the Sea Lion III. The thrust axis of the propeller was located along the datum chord of the top wing, and single interplane struts of I form were reminiscent of the design refinement originated by Harry Folland in the S.E.4 of 1914.

A top speed of 200 mph was predicted by Mitchell but the Sea Urchin was never completed. This was mainly because the Condor engine never quite fulfilled its early promise as a more powerful version of the proven Rolls-Royce Eagle and because the engineers still had not satisfactorily solved the problems involved in bevel-geared shafting to transmit high power in a small lightweight installation.

So the Sea Urchin project was stillborn which was a pity because a comparison between it and Supermarine's next effort in the high-speed seaplane class would have been exciting. This new project was the revolutionary S.4 cantilever monoplane which set a pattern in specific aircraft design that persisted through the next two decades. It was classified as S.4 by Mitchell as he no doubt regarded the Sea Lions I, II and III as S.1, S.2 and S.3 respectively, the S simply indicating Schneider. The decision to go ahead with the new design was taken jointly by the Supermarine and Napier companies on 18 March, 1925, and the British Government supported the construction by agreeing to purchase the aeroplane if the venture was successful and the original cost was divided between the engine and airframe makers. In fact the S.4 was designed and built in five months and first flew in the hands of Henri Biard on 24 August, 1925.

The one-piece monoplane wing with normal front and rear spars of spruce flanges and plywood webs had a number of spanwise stringers rebated into wing ribs, which had spruce flanges and ply webs. This structure was then covered top and bottom with plywood sheeting gradually increasing in thickness from the tips to the centre line of the wing. A trough was built on the undersurface of the wing to carry the water coolant pipe from the engine to the Lamblin-type radiators. These underslung radiators were the only protuberances on the whole machine. An interconnected flap and aileron system was introduced, the ailerons being able

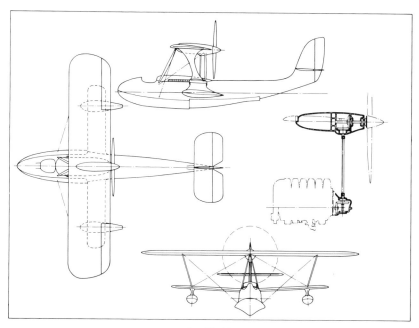

Sea Urchin

175

The semi-monocoque wooden rear fuselage of the S.4 under construction at Woolston in June 1925.

to act either independently or in conjunction with the flaps. Oddly enough, flaps were not used by Mitchell on any of his succeeding Schneider racers.

The fuselage was built in three sections; the engine mounting, the centre and the rear monocoque. Apart from steel fittings and the two A frames of steel tubing, which comprised the backbones of the centre body, the S.4 was constructed entirely in wood. It was interesting to note the resurrection of the monocoque fuselage after a lengthy gap in time, for the Deperdussin winner of

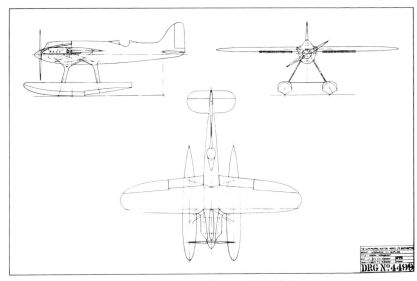

A Supermarine drawing of the S.4

This view of the S.4 shows the low-drag frontal area with cantilever wing and Lamblin underwing radiators, foreshadowing the Spitfire design.

1913 had used that type of streamlined body. The floats were attached to the bottom of the two sloping A frames, the one-piece wing passing between the frames and attached to them, while the engine mounting was attached to the forward frame.

A special version of the Napier Lion twelve-cylinder, water-cooled engine of the broad arrow configuration was developed to produce 700 hp for the short period of the race. This brief engine life was a general characteristic of Schneider engines, particularly of those that came later. The Lion had direct-drive to the propeller, and starting was by a Bristol gas starter unit. The propeller was an all-metal Fairey-Reed type.

The S.4 at Calshot in August 1925.

177

The S.4 at Woolston.

The floats, of the single-step type, were of wooden construction broadly following the detail design of the Supermarine flying-boats, that is, a fore-and-aft keel member along the bottom centre-line, with port and starboard chines, the three members forming the pronounced Vee underside of the floats. Double watertight bulkheads were provided and the whole structure was flexible enough to absorb a considerable amount of punishment in rough water.

The fuel and oil systems were conventional except that the petrol had to be carried in several tanks, there being insufficient room for a single unit. The oil cooler was located on the underside of the fuselage, only the cooling fins being exposed to the airstream.

Biard was never really happy with the S.4, in particular with the position of the wings in relation to his eyeline from the cockpit, set so far back in the fuselage. Taking-off and alighting were hazardous because of this blind spot and on the first take-off he nearly hit the liner *Majestic* simply because he just did not see it, hard as that may be to believe. He soon realized he was flying a very fast machine and he also disliked the 'unstayed' wings as he described them. On alighting from this first flight he glided gracefully between two marker posts, blissfully ignorant of dredging operations ahead, a traumatic experience for the Supermarine executives watching.

Film taken at the time of the flight trials, which were made from the RAF base at Calshot, disclosed the long run needed to reach 'hump' speed and take-off which characterized all the Schneider contenders. This factor emphasized the value of the seaplane contests in developing high-speed aircraft from an unlimited runway in the expanse of sea, in the absence then of variable-pitch propellers and auxiliary lift devices. In the actual 1925 Schneider race at Baltimore, the British contenders proved to have better water behaviour than the American or Italian entries. Before leaving for the United States, the S.4 flown by Biard captured the World Speed Record for Seaplanes and the British Speed Record at 226·75 mph. Curiously, this achievement, which had received assistance from the RAF, was not released for publication for a month, until an announcement, issued presumably by Fairey Aviation, said that the feat had been accomplished with a Fairey-

178

Reed duralumin propeller. A new propeller was made for the race but was not ready in time for testing before the British entrants and the teams set out for Baltimore in the Atlantic transport ship *Minnewaska*. During the voyage Biard slipped on the deck and hurt his wrist and this proved only the first of a run of disasters that befell the S.4 enterprise.

On arrival at Bay Shore, Baltimore, the British team led by Capt C. B. Wilson, appointed by the Royal Aero Club, found the accommodation for machines and crews much below accepted standards and reminiscent of the 1919 Schneider fiasco at Bournemouth. The aircraft were housed in tents and bad weather added to the difficulties. Little practice flying was possible, especially for the Gloster entrants, but Biard did manage to test the S.4 with the new propeller, which proved an advantage. The weather was terribly cold and, through working on the aircraft in a tent in such conditions, Biard caught influenza. The weather worsened into a gale and his crew came to tell him, while he was in bed in his hotel, that the tent had collapsed and a broken tent pole had fallen across the rear end of the S.4 causing damage. Although it was the eve of the mandatory navigability and mooring tests, in which the competitors had to appear on the starting line, the essential repairs were completed in time.

The pre-race tests involved take-off and alighting. So on 23 October, Biard, having recovered from his ills including the injured wrist, took the S.4 for the take-off and then proposed to do some straight runs over the course in the process of qualifying. The machine behaved perfectly with the Lion engine running well and he rounded the judges' boat moored out in Chesapeake Bay. He then flew back at high speed towards the pierhead with the intention of doing another straight run but on coming out of the turn the control column suddenly set up such violent side-to-side oscillations that he lost control, and according to his own

Henri Biard in the S.4 ready for take off at Baltimore on 23 October, 1925, on the only Schneider test made with the aircraft.

179

words written at the time, and later in his book, Biard said that the phenomenon was an amplified repetition of the tremor of the wings he had experienced during the flight trials at Calshot. S.4 and Biard ended up at the bottom of Chesapeake Bay. By some miraculous means he managed to cling on to some buoyant wreckage and after floating for some time Hubert Broad appeared alongside in the Gloster III and threw him a lifebelt. One rescue boat broke down and a second appeared after Biard had been some 40 minutes in the very cold sea. After a medical examination it was announced that he had again damaged his wrist, and he had a pain in the chest. Later in England he was found to have two broken ribs and damage to some stomach muscles which gave him continuous trouble until operated on in Naples in 1931, as mentioned in connection with the Supermarine Air Yacht.

In the Paper on the 1925 Race given before the Royal Aeronautical Society in 1926, Major (later Sir John) Buchanan of the Air Ministry made no reference to the incident and little was said in the ensuing discussion, apart from a reference by Biard to the effect that he wished he had known that there was no need to dive on to the course as was the practice in other high-speed events. This seems to suggest that he thought diving to build up speed was a contributory cause of the loss of control.

Not until the phenomenon of flutter was better understood did the probable cause of the S.4 trouble emerge, as with other high-speed aircraft of the time, especially fighters. In the case of the 1925 Schneider race and the failure of the cantilever-wing S.4 to appear at the starting line, it was significant that the winners of the succeeding Schneider contests were all wire-braced monoplanes.

As it was, the 1925 Schneider race was won by Lt Jimmy Doolittle of the US Army flying the Curtiss R3C2 biplane at 234·4 mph, with Hubert Broad second on the Gloster III biplane at 199 mph. On 27 October, the day after the contest, Doolittle with the Curtiss took the World Seaplane Speed Record from the S.4 at 246 mph. One of the lessons learned from the 1925 race was Doolittle's precise cornering, which lost him only 11 mph compared with his speed on the straight legs of the course. From this and the technical superiority of their winning aircraft, it was obvious that the Americans had left little to chance and had completed a rigorous programme of pilot training and aircraft and engine development testing. It became clear that in future races similar methods would have to be adopted for Britain to have any hope of success, a point made by Mitchell before the Royal Aeronautical Society in a lecture in 1927.

In this he said: 'After the failure of the British team to win the race in America in 1925 it was brought home to all interested that our machines were a long way inferior to the American machines and that if we wished to hold our own again in this important field of aviation we should have to treat the matter much more seriously. Furthermore, it became obvious to all that machines could no longer be entered for these races by private enterprise. It is true that the Air Ministry had loaned the machines for the race* but very little opportunity had been given for research and experimental work and the engine designers had been working independently.'

In consequence, the Air Ministry at the end of 1925 had decided to expand their programme for the development of high-speed aircraft and ordered wind-tunnel tests on quarter-scale models of all high-speed seaplanes. This policy was ex-

*This appears to indicate that the S.4 was eventually purchased by the Air Ministry, although written-off. Its allocated serial number, N197, was never worn.

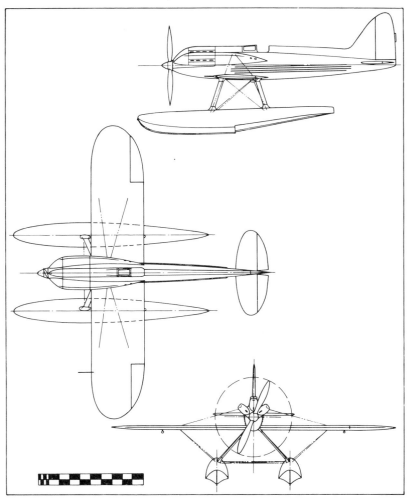

S.5

tended when they placed orders for three racing aircraft each from Gloster
Aircraft and Supermarine Aviation.

Specially-developed engines were also ordered from the Napier company, and
later a further back-up aircraft was ordered through Col W. A. Bristow, of the
Royal Aero Club, to be built by Short Brothers and powered by a Bristol Mercury
radial air-cooled engine, with George Carter (later of Gloster Aircraft) as con-
sultant designer. The specification 6/26 issued on 19 March, 1926, included the
following requirements: speed not less than 265 mph at 1,000 ft; controllability at
high speeds; power unit to be the ungeared Napier Lion VIIA of 750 hp at 3,000
rpm; alighting speed with engine off not more than 90 mph. Service serial
numbers issued were N219, N220 and N221 to Supermarine, N222, N223 and
N224 to Glosters, and N226 to Col Bristow for his Short Crusader. Another

promising design by S. E. Saunders and P. Beadle, which was a low-wing monoplane similar to the Supermarine S.5 design and with a predicted speed of 285 mph, was not accepted by the Royal Aero Club, which was responsible for the British entries.

The original intention was to enter these machines for the 1926 race. Various delays in their completion and testing led to the target being altered to the 1927 contest, as the Air Ministry were now determined that the finished products and the teams should be the finest in the world.

The Schneider Trophy contest had become by then a matter of intense international rivalry and of great national prestige. This was particularly so in the case of Italy which had won the 1926 race from the Americans when Major Mario de Bernardi came home at 246·496 mph on the Macchi M.39 monoplane, which looked not unlike a braced-wing S.4. This latest Italian victory at Hampton Roads prevented the Trophy being won for the third time running by the United States (which would have ended the series for good) and this was another incentive for renewed British effort.

In the case of Supermarine, the problems Mitchell had to face in any new design were reduction in aerodynamic drag and overall weight and satisfactory performance on the water. He had been working on these factors even before the specification was issued, and one general arrangement drawing dated 17 November, 1925, showed a similar planform to the S.4 but with a low wing. Comprehensive wind-tunnel tests were made at the National Physical Laboratory on models of all the British entrants. Three variants of the proposed configuration for the Supermarine S.5 were submitted. One was a gull-wing design; a second had a low wing braced by W formation struts with a tie strut between the floats; and in the third the strutting was replaced by wire bracing and this was the form eventually adopted. Ten different float designs of the three distinct models were tested, as described fully in Reports and Memoranda 1300 of the Aeronautical Research Committee. The results obtained, summed up as resistance in lb/sq ft at 100 ft per sec, were fuselage S.4—9.3; S.5—6.6; float S.4—5.0; S.5—4.43. The cross-sectional area of the fuselage was reduced by some 35 per cent in the S.5 by tailoring the Lion engine to the aircraft designer's requirements as far as possible, with a very closely-fitting fuselage around the pilots—larger ones had difficulty in getting in and out, such were the lengths to which Mitchell went in his attempt to achieve perfection.

This streamlining of the fuselage meant that there was insufficient room for the fuel and the starboard float was used for this purpose, with the dual advantage of providing an offset load to counter engine torque, particularly when accelerating for take-off. This unconventional fuel tank also lowered the centre of gravity, which aided stability in the air. The structure weight of the S.5 was 36 per cent of the aircraft in racing trim compared with 45 per cent for the S.4, attributable in great part to the use of bracing wires between wings, floats and chassis, to promote a lighter and more rigid airframe. The elimination of the two struts between the floats and the reduction in frontal area of the S.4's four main chassis struts gave an estimated speed increase of five mph, while the bonus from streamlining was approximately eleven mph. Reduction in frontal area of the floats by 14 per cent, by giving them a lower reserve buoyancy of some 15 per cent compared with that of the S.4 floats, produced a further speed increase of four mph. The greatest gain was made by the adoption of wing-surface radiators in place of the S.4 Lamblin type and the estimated increase in speed from this source was approximately 24 mph.

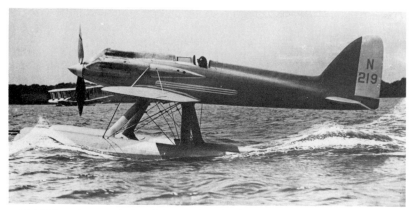

S.5 N219 under tow during Solent trials. The flying-boat in the background is a Southampton.

While the Schneider aircraft for the 1927 race were under construction, a Service High Speed Flight was formed at Felixstowe where the selected RAF pilots started training to a rigorous programme comparative with that undergone by Olympic athletes. This time nothing was to be left to chance.

The S.5 fuselage was of duralumin monocoque construction, that is as far as a metal structure could be said to be one-piece. The skin was light alloy plate while the rear fuselage and tail were similar to those of the S.4. The wooden wings, of Raf 30 aerofoil section, were of the two-spar type with plywood covering, and carried built-in radiators covering almost the whole of the upper and lower surfaces. These water radiators were fabricated from 30 gauge copper sheet in

An engine test with the direct-drive Napier Lion in S.5 N219, with an apparently satisfied Mitchell walking away.

183

sections, each eight and a half inches wide, rolled to the wing contour and with upper and lower surfaces sweated together, leaving the water channels as corrugations on the inner surface. This was quite an ingenious solution to the elimination of drag caused by exposed corrugations as on the Curtiss and the Lamblin type radiators. The outer surface exposed to the airflow therefore offered no additional air resistance. The tail unit was constructed in wood, with the tailplane spars built into the rear fuselage and the whole covered with plywood. All control rods and levers were enclosed except the aileron control, and extreme care was taken to avoid protuberances.

The floats of the S.5 were of the Vee bottom, single-step, type as on S.4 but were made in duralumin and steel, the shell being 18 gauge on the bottom and 20 gauge on the topsides. The starboard floats on all the S.5s were offset eight inches from the aircraft centreline and carried the 55 gal fuel tank, but N219's was slightly longer.

First of the British 1927 Schneider contenders to fly was the Short Crusader with the uprated 810 hp Bristol Mercury engine. This was flown by Bert Hinkler from Felixstowe on 4 May, 1927. The first S.5, N219, was flown by Flt Lt O. E. Worsley on 7 June, also from Felixstowe, powered by the Napier Lion VIIA with direct-drive propeller. No major modifications were needed to the S.5s, which showed the benefit of the wind-tunnel and other research that had preceded the flight trials. The critical choice of suitable propellers was made from 24 manufactured, 19 for the S.5s by Fairey Aviation to the metal Fairey-Reed design, and the others by Gloster.

Difficulties with the racing versions of the Napier Lion engine were experienced mainly through the very high (ten-to-one) compression ratio. Burnt pistons and valves resulted despite the use of 'light cut' petrol with anti-knock tetraethyl lead additive. With the help of F. Rodwell Banks, a pioneer in the introduction of leaded fuels into Britain, these problems were overcome in time for the Lion to be ready for the 1927 race in two versions, the direct drive VIIA of

The S.5 N220 and Gloster IVB and the 1927 RAF Schneider team at Calshot. Left to right: Flt Lts Schofield, Worsley, Webster, Kinkead and Sqn Ldr Slatter.

184

The 1927 Schneider Trophy race at Venice. Flt Lt Kinkead in the Gloster IVB is seen diving under the direct-drive Supermarine S.5 flown by Flt Lt Worsley in front of the crowds on the Lido.

900 hp in N219, as stated above, and the geared VIIB of 875 hp, turning a slower revolving propeller in the S.5s N220 and N221. No supercharging was used. Lubricating oil cooling was provided by corrugated tinned steel coolers mounted along the sides of the fuselage, the oil passing from the engine into one cooler, thence through a filter into the tank behind the pilot's position and back through the other cooler to the engine. The water coolant circulation system was interesting, the hot water passing from the engine into the header tank behind the central cylinder block of the Napier engine, thence through piping to troughs along the trailing edges, across the wing through the corrugations to troughs along the leading edges, whence return piping took the cooled water back to the engine.

The race was scheduled for the end of September at Venice, Italy being the host country by having won the previous contest. S.5 N219, Gloster IVA N222 and Crusader N226 arrived at San Andrae, the British base on the Venice Lido, on 31 August aboard the collier *Eworth*, while S.5 N220 and the Gloster IVB N223 arrived on 13 September aboard the aircraft carrier *Eagle*. Two days before that, Flg Off H. M. Schofield (not to be confused with 'Tiny' Scholefield of Vickers) had crashed the Crusader into the lagoon on a practice flight, an accident caused by the classic error of crossed controls, in this case the aileron cables. Schofield was rescued badly bruised, which put him out of selection for the team of three actually allowed to participate.

No other misfortunes befell the British team and the following took the starting gun on 26 September—Flt Lt S. M. Kinkead in the Gloster IVB N223 with geared Lion VIIB engine; Flt Lt S. N. Webster in the S.5 N220 also with a geared Lion and Flt Lt O. E. Worsley in the direct-drive S.5 N219. This was indeed a brave show justifying all the efforts made in the new deal of advanced technology

185

and practice prompted by the Air Ministry after the previous debacles attributable largely to lukewarm official support.

In the spectacular race, watched by a huge crowd strung along the beaches of the Lido, the Italian machines dropped out one by one, mostly through engine trouble, leaving the British contestants to lap consistently until the seventh and last lap, when Kinkead lost his propeller boss through engine vibration, thought to be due to loose propeller shaft splines, and had to retire. Webster was the winner at 281·65 mph with Worsley second at 273·01 mph. The best lap speed of the Italian Macchi M.52s was seven mph slower than the average speed of Worsley and of Kinkead's completed laps and the result must have been a bitter disappointment to Mussolini, who attended the contest and congratulated the winners. It was indeed a famous victory and reflected great credit on the designers and the engineers of the aircraft and engines and upon the Royal Air Force team of pilots and mechanics, under the command of Sqn Ldr L. H. Slatter.

After the event the British Press woke up to the fact of a national triumph somewhat tardily, for one of the authors of this book had to ring up his local RAF station after vainly looking for the result in the London evening papers on the day of the race. He was rewarded with a rather surprised 'thank you' from the lady switchboard operator for his enquiry and congratulations. This little story illustrates how fickle is public interest and memory, as became evident in the succeeding races.

On return from Venice, Mitchell was fêted by the Corporation of Southampton and the RAF High Speed Flight disbanded! The Schneider aircraft were taken over by the MAEE at Felixstowe, the winning S.5 being displayed to Londoners on Horse Guards Parade on 30 November. The Italians atoned for their Schneider failure to a certain extent when later in 1927 Major de Bernardi raised the World Absolute Air Speed Record to 416·62 km/hr on a Macchi M.52, which was well below the Schneider Trophy winning speed of 453·282 km/hr. Consequently the Air Ministry planned to raise it still further with the S.5s and on 12 March, 1928, Flt Lt S. M. Kinkead made an attempt over the Solent off Calshot with the third S.5, N221. The conditions were unfavourable, with a glassy calm sea, and Kinkead was unwell at the time. In approaching the three kilometre marker he flew straight into the sea and was killed, a loss to the RAF of a very fine pilot. The accident was thought to have been caused by bad visibility attributed to the mirror-like surface of the sea, which Grp Cap L. S. Snaith, a pilot of the 1931 British team, later said was one of the hazards of flying Schneider aircraft.

In June 1928 Flt Lt D'Arcy Greig took over the re-formed High Speed Flight, testing propellers for S.5s N219 and N220 to find the most suitable type for the highest speed. An attempt by him to beat de Bernardi's figures for the World Record succeeded by an insufficient margin to justify a claim to the FAI. The S.5s were used for the preparation of the team for the succeeding races, in fact N219 came third in the 1929 race as related later.

After the 1927 contest, interest in the series waned and further British Government support for continuing a high-speed programme seemed problematical. In view of the difficulties in providing time for developing new types of higher performance in one year, the Royal Aero Club was able to persuade the international body, the FAI, to give a two-year breathing space between races. The 1929 race was therefore fixed for early September at Spithead on a quadrilateral course of seven laps of a 50-km circuit, with two acute corners of 150 degrees. For Britain to maintain the success gained with so much effort at Venice renewed vigour was required. A team of the best pilots was needed from the RAF, and on the technological side it was necessary, in view of the inevitable strong Italian challenge, to produce better aircraft of greater power.

The Napier Lion, which had stood the brunt of the foreign competition for so long, was by 1928 reaching the end of its possible development, short of super-charging. A contract was awarded for such a development but the Napier company were under the impression that the Lion could go on for ever in existing form and did not accept this task with alacrity. Mitchell, and others in more official places, could see that a new power unit was needed for the 1929 race. It needed a change in the top management of Rolls-Royce, in which A. F. Sidgreaves suc-ceeded Basil Johnson as managing director, before that company, through Henry Royce himself, accepted an Air Ministry invitation to design a new engine of high power, specifically for the Schneider contest aircraft to be built by Supermarine. This late-hour decision was to have far-reaching consequences.

So the design of the R engine, as it was named, was begun by Royce and A. G. Elliott in their office at West Wittering in November 1928, which left little enough time to produce a winner. Time was undoubtedly saved by adopting an existing engine, albeit only partially developed at that time, the H type or Buzzard of 36·7 litres, as compared with the Napier Lion of 24-litre capacity. The 825 hp Buzzard was intended for large multi-engined flying-boats, such as the Supermarine 'Giant' and the Short Sarafand, and was virtually a scaled-up version of the successful Rolls-Royce Kestrel. The main changes were a new supercharger designed by Royce and J. E. Ellor, a specialist on supercharging who had joined Rolls-Royce from the Royal Aircraft Establishment, and a general strengthening of highly stressed engine parts and cleaning up the externals to fit the highly streamlined Supermarine S.6 which Mitchell was rapidly evolving. This practical engineering was being done at Derby by A. J. Rowledge, who already had the design of the Napier Lion and Rolls-Royce Kestrel to his credit, and it involved the design of a new crankcase to suit the greater stress demands and to match the streamlined shape of the S.6 forebody.

Installing a Rolls-Royce R engine in an S.6. Mitchell is facing the camera.

187

This view of an S.6B at Woolston shows the close spacing of the formers.

The power output of an atmospheric internal combustion engine is dependent upon the mass airflow through the engine and this was achieved in the Rolls-Royce R by the new supercharger of Royce and Ellor and by increased engine speeds facilitated by Rowledge's work at Derby. In technical terms a convergent-divergent airflow into the carburetter facilitated a reduction in kinetic energy which produced a gain in the pressure energy of the mass airflow into the engine. All this technological advance resulted in a racing engine of 1,900 brake horse-power at 2,900 rpm for a weight of 1,530 lb, which was far better than any other figure to date at 0·8 lb/hp, but for one hour's operation only.

However, the attainment of these figures was not without its problems. In the first place, the impeller of the supercharger had to be double-sided to produce the required airflow within the dimensional limits set by the aircraft designer in his fuselage cross-sectional areas, a criterion already mentioned in regard to the S.5. Then, when the endurance tests of the first R engine were started at Derby in 1929, power started falling off at 1,800 hp after a 20 minutes' run—which resulted in a hot engine with distorted and burnt exhaust valves and sooted-up sparking plugs. This is where Rodwell Banks again came to the rescue. He attributed the trouble to the use of pure benzole as a fuel. As there was only a month to go before the contest he cured the matter simply by recommending the dilution of the benzole with a 'light cut' leaded gasoline.*

Meanwhile Mitchell had been busy tailoring his S.6 design to the new engine, his call for a minimum of 1,500 hp being exceeded to his delight by some 400 hp. He could now envisage speeds approaching the 400 mph mark and some of his design assumptions around the S.6 concept were a striking proof of the proverb that coming events cast their shadows before them. He estimated a level speed of 350 mph, a diving speed of 523 mph and a rate of climb of 5,000 ft/min, figures not reached by fighters until seven years later. These estimates were in fact to reappear as the design characteristics for the Spitfire. The increased weight estimate of 4,500 lb for the S.6 fully loaded, compared with the 3,250 lb of the S.5, was to cater for the much heavier engine and the consequently larger aeroplane.

*A specimen formula for the R engine was 78 per cent benzole, 22 per cent naphthalene-based Romanian gasoline with a small lead additive.

Structurally the S.6 was designed much on the same lines as the S.5 except as regards material which was wholly of light alloy and steel fittings, in tune with the official mandate of the time for the metallization of airframes. The wings retained the conventional two-spar construction, with ribs comprised of diaphragm webs with large lightening holes and flanges of extruded angle section. The wing surface radiators for the engine coolant were made from 24-gauge continuous duralumin sheets, rather than copper strips as used in the S.5. They were riveted together with spacers 1/16th inch thick to provide the water cavity. These radiators were screwed to the top and bottom of the wing structure and formed the entire wing surface less ailerons. The fuselage was of the semi-monocoque type like the S.5 and consisted of 46 hoop frames either six or seven inches apart with only one longitudinal member running along each side as extensions of the engine bearers. The whole of the fuselage including the integrally-built fin was skinned with duralumin sheet, the fin incorporating the oil tank. In the S.6 the forward float struts had to be repositioned from those on the S.5 to support the larger and longer engine. The engine cowling also had to be tailored to suit the R engine.

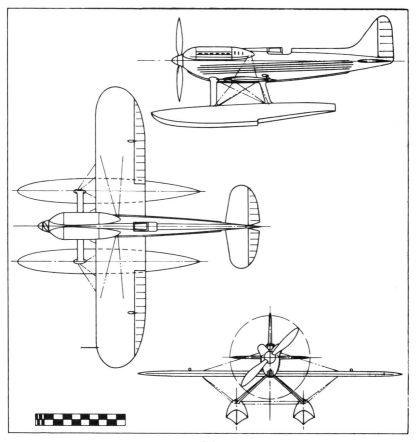

S.6

189

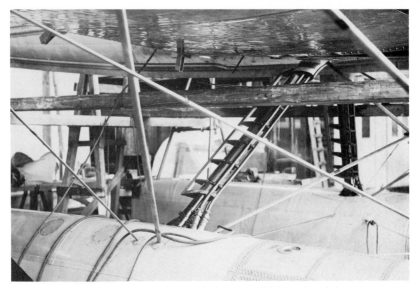

Fuel and coolant lines inside float strut fairings of an S.6.

Otherwise, detail design including the coolant system followed much the same pattern as had proved successful on the S.5 but, for the thirsty and powerful R engines on both the S.6 and its successor the S.6B, fresh thought had to be devoted not only to the fuel tankage problem but also to the oil cooling system.

In the S.6 the centre portions of both floats were used as fuel tanks, and in the S.6B, with its even more powerful engine, considerably more fuel was carried in the starboard float to balance the enormous engine torque, as defined later. With the R engines, operating temperature was indeed critical. In fact, in the 1931 race the S.6Bs were flown on throttle settings dictated solely by the coolant water temperature gauge. Because of this critical temperature, a special oil cooling system had to be devised. Hot oil from the engine passed along the fuselage side coolers (similar to the S.5) to the top of the fin whence it ran down the insides of the fin skin via ribs and gutters to an integral tank with a filter, thence by the return coolers under the fuselage back to the engine. Small vanes placed in the cooler oilways kept the oil in contact with the outer surfaces, and this innovation, arrived at after much experiment, increased the efficiency of the cooling system by 40 per cent.

Four aircraft were ordered by the Air Ministry early in 1929 to specification 8/28, two S.6s from Supermarine on contract S27042, and two Gloster VI monoplanes with, for the first time, a supercharged Napier Lion—the VIID. The monoplane concept was also an innovation for Harry Folland, Gloster's experienced designer, who had been responsible for a series of single-seat high-speed biplanes since 1914. To universal regret, the Golden Arrow, as the Gloster VI was named from its glittering bronze finish, failed to compete in the race through fuel system malfunctioning, for it was a beautiful aeroplane with streamlining carried to perfection in the Folland manner. The S.6s were given serials N247 and N248 and the Gloster VIs N249 and N250.

The two S.6s were built together but so much progress was made that the first fuselage was already partially finished by 20 April and the first skin panel fitted by 10 May, with the job virtually completed by 10 June. By 21 June the R engine was installed for load tests, still using, as part of the exercise, the time-honoured bags of sand. The floats, which were basically of the same structural design as those of the S.5, were completed by 3 July. When weighed, the figures obtained were empty 3,976 lb and loaded, including fuel and oil, 5,120 lb, some 700 lb over designed weight, evenly spread among major components, including the engine. The first S.6 was brought out from the erecting shop for engine runs on 30 July. No serious snags arose and the aeroplane was delivered to Calshot on 5 August.

An S.6 nearing completion at the Woolston Works.

N247 was first flown from Calshot on 10 August and N248 on 25 August, both by Sqn Ldr A. H. Orlebar, commanding the re-formed High Speed Flight. Before the flights there was consternation at Supermarine because the S.6 would turn in circles when the engine was opened up, a gyration caused by the enormous engine torque. Take-off was possible only when most of the fuel had been transferred to the starboard float. Although the race was less than a month away Mitchell decided to improve the water handling by lengthening this float and increasing its fuel capacity to 90 gallons, with the port float carrying 25 gallons. This increased the loaded weight to 5,250 lb, and advantage was taken at the same time to move the centre of gravity forward by one inch to counteract some tail heaviness experienced in flight trials at top speed. During these trials the radiator area was found to be inadequate and had to be extended by adding float radiators on N247 on the sides and on N248 on the top. This again increased the loaded weight, to 5,500 lb, and the stalling speed went up to 110 mph. Small wingtip air scoops were added at this time to take ram air into the wing to assist in cooling the upper and lower surface radiators internally. With these modifications the full power of the R engine could at last be utilized. The float radiators on N248 were later modified to the side type as fitted to N247. The floats of the S.6 had been the subject of exhaustive water-tank tests on models of different shapes by the National Physical Laboratory, and the type finally adopted represented about the optimum design possible in the time available for experiment.

Four countries had submitted entries for the 1929 contest, Great Britain, Italy, France and the United States. France withdrew early because she could not get three aircraft ready in time, despite the two-year concession by the FAI. The Americans were able to offer one aeroplane, the Mercury, which was more or less a private venture powered with a liquid-cooled Packard engine. This class of engine was in a decline in the US at the time because of the rapid development of the air-cooled radial type, one of the chief architects of which was Sam Heron, who had emigrated to the United States from the Royal Aircraft Establishment at Farnborough. Lt Alford Williams' Mercury was however withdrawn because of engine installation problems. This left only the Italians to contest at Ryde, the starting and finishing point for 1929.

Both the British and Italians also had their share of problems in the hectic days preceding the contest. As expected, the Italian efforts had received the full support of their Government and no fewer than four new types of racing aircraft using three new engines had been designed for 1929, the Fiat C.29, the Macchi M.67, the Savoia Marchetti S.65 and the revolutionary Piaggio P.7, which rose up out of the water on hydrovanes for take-off, initially propelled by a water screw. Five of these machines were wrecked in trials and two pilots were killed on Lake Garda, the Italian Schneider test area. So they arrived at the start with two M.67s and one M.52, while the British team relied on the two S.6s with S.5 N219 standing in for the Gloster VI, still not raceworthy.

The perambulations of the S.6s between Calshot and Woolston, for engine changes and the minor repairs and adjustments needed during the run up period preceding the race, were made by carrying the aircraft on pontoons towed by motor launches. During this time, as was to be expected, the aircraft sustained various small bumps and dents. The most serious setback occurred on the very eve of the actual race after the seaworthiness tests had been completed and the racing engines finally fitted in place of the practice ones and ground tested. A. C. Lovesey, Rolls-Royce engineer in charge, noticed some aluminium specks on the electrode of one of the sparking plugs which he had extracted after the engine run, indicating a damaged piston. A further engine change was prohibited by the rules but officials of the Royal Aero Club decided that a cylinder block could be removed and changed. A spare block was hurriedly driven down from Derby in Ernest Hive's famous 'hack' Rolls-Royce. A number of Rolls-Royce engineers who had come down by coach on an outing to see the race and who were distributed in various hotels around Southampton were located and worked all through the night to effect the change.

As the day fixed for the race approached, 7 September, it became clear that although the British aircraft and pilots were in a state of readiness, except for the Gloster VI fuel troubles, the Italians, despite their great efforts to redress the balance created by the British victory at Venice in 1927, had not made the technical progress needed to ensure victory. They were still relying on direct-drive engines with no supercharging boost and were still getting exhaust fumes in the pilots' cockpits from the centre cylinder block of their Isotta Fraschini 'broad arrow' engines, although Napier in 1929 had put the centre block exhaust ports on the opposite side to carry the black smoke in the propeller slipstream away from the windscreen and pilot. The Italian request for a postponement of the contest to

The men involved in winning the 1929 Schneider Trophy event. Left to right: Clark (RAE), Ransome (AID), Buchanan, later Sir John (DTD Air Ministry), Holroyd (Supermarine chief draughtsman), Lovesey and Lappin (Rolls-Royce), Robertson (Supermarine liaison officer) and R. J. Mitchell.

a later date was not acceded to, mainly on grounds of expediency of organization and expense, but they sportingly turned up to compete with five pilots and six aircraft, three of them new types.

In the nine days remaining before the race the Italian team were given full facilities at Calshot for engine tuning and runs and trial flights and just managed to get their new Macchi M.67s through the race preliminaries of take-off, alighting and mooring, in time. Their third competitor was the converted 1972 Macchi M.52, current holder of the World Speed Record. This machine actually came second in 1929 at 284·52 mph piloted by Warrant Officer T. Dal Molin, with Flt Lt D'Arcy Greig third at 282·11 mph on the S.5 N219 with a geared engine, which had been second at Venice with a direct-drive Lion. The winner was Flg Off H. R. D. Waghorn flying S.6 N247 at 328·63 mph. Flg Off R. L. R. Atcherley on the other S.6, N248, completed the course at 325·54 mph but was disqualified for turning inside a marker on his first circuit, an error probably caused by losing his goggles. Atcherley, however, had the satisfaction of capturing the World's Closed Circuit Speed Records over 50 km and 100 km at 332·49 and 331·75 mph respectively, on his sixth and seventh laps. Both M.67s retired on their second laps—Lt G. Monti with a broken oil pipe from which he sustained burns to arms and shoulders, and Lt F. R. Cadringher, who was overcome by engine fumes, entailing a forced alighting off Ryde.

The 1929 race was blessed with perfect weather and was watched by crowds conservatively estimated at around one million people—including Edward, Prince of Wales, and the Prime Minister, Ramsay Macdonald. The Press was really alert this time and spread eulogistic columns and pictures all over their pages. Similar extensive coverage was given to the world speed record attempts made after the contest by the Gloster VI and the S.6s. The existing record was held by de Bernardi on the same M.52 flown by Dal Molin in the race and stood at 318·62 mph. This was exceeded on 10 September by Flt Lt G. H. Stainforth on Gloster VI N249 at 336·3 mph, showing that the fuel supply faults had been cleared for straight runs. Sqn Ldr A. H. Orlebar, commander of the High Speed Flight, thereupon took out S.6 N247 and achieved 355·8 mph but on 12 September, also with N247, reached 357·7 mph, which was eventually accepted by the FAI as a new World Absolute Air Speed Record.

At the victory ceremony and dinner held on the liner *Orford* on the evening of the 1929 Schneider Trophy race, Ramsay Macdonald pledged Britain to accept any challenge for 1931 that might be forthcoming, while General Balbo, the Italian Air Minister, said that Italy's task would begin 'tomorrow', meaning that they would go on with their high-speed aircraft, which they did, eventually regaining the world speed record. Less than two months later the British Government reversed its decision when the Air Ministry announced that there would be no official support or RAF team for the 1931 contest.

The full text of the official announcement ran as follows:

'The Government have had under review the future policy in regard to the

Presentation of the Schneider Trophy to the British team on board ss *Orford* in 1929. Prime Minister Ramsay Macdonald is making his promise that Britain would defend the Trophy. On his left is the Italian Air Minister, General Balbo. Mervyn O'Gorman, chairman of the Royal Aero Club, is seen hand on chin.

194

Schneider Trophy contest in 1931 and subsequent years. After careful consideration, it has been decided that a Royal Air Force team will not again be entered,
thus leaving British participation to private enterprise under the auspices of the
Royal Aero Club.

'Two main considerations influenced the decision:

(1) That, owing to Government participation in recent years, the contest has
assumed a character not in accordance with the intentions of M. Jacques
Schneider, its originator and donor of the trophy.

(2) That, although the entry of a Royal Air Force team was calculated to give a
much needed impetus to the development of high speed aircraft—and did so
notably in the two latest contests—sufficient data have now been collected for
practical development in this direction and the large expenditure of public money
involved by Government participation is therefore no longer justifiable.

'This decision should not, of course, affect the entry of British machines in
future contests. Convincing proof has now been furnished of what the British
aircraft industry can do, and the wide public interest displayed should make it
possible for our pilots and machines to compete in what is intended to be a
sporting international event on a basis of private enterprise.'

This naive decision by a socialist administration was weak in several respects. In
the first place Jacques Schneider donated the trophy to encourage the development of seaplanes, as stated in the previous story of the Sea Lions, and not
necessarily for a 'sporting' contest comparative with events like the King's Cup
Air Race or the American Pulitzer speed races, although even these had a
practical value in aircraft development. Secondly, the implied suggestion that
high-speed aircraft had reached their potential development was an extraordinary
statement to come from a Ministry that was already planning high-performance
fighters to specifications similar to Mitchell's design assumptions as defined
earlier. The real truth of the matter was probably that neither the Air Ministry nor
the Royal Air Force were wholly in accord with the announcement which was
obviously politically inspired.* Britain, with other countries, was experiencing a
severe economic depression and large Government expenditure had been committed to the Empire airship scheme with R 100 and R 101, a policy that had still to
prove its futility at the time of the Schneider announcement.

As *The Times* pointed out in reviewing the announcement, the day for private
enterprise involvement in a contest of such high technological demands had
passed in 1923 with the United States Government-sponsored team, and the USA
had since relinquished its chance of winning the trophy outright when this official
support was withdrawn after the 1926 race, won by Italy. It went on to say that the
effort was not just the work of two companies in making the aircraft and engines
but embracing the valuable contributions of numerous public and private research facilities, oil and fuel companies, accessory firms, and of course the
organization of the race itself involving many other authorities, marine and
otherwise. *The Times* considered that the supply of pilots was problematical as no
civilian could be expected to lay aside his normal vocation to undergo the
specialist training needed, even if he was a skilled test pilot.

---

*On 7 December, 1935, the Air Ministry issued specification 35/35 for a high-speed aero-
plane in the requirements for which was this statement—'Since the time of the Schneider
Trophy Race the problem of producing an aircraft in which all other qualities are to some
extent sacrificed for speed has always been a matter of great importance.'

However neither the Royal Aero Club nor the Society of British Aircraft Constructors was prepared to take the matter lying down and on 17 December, 1930, a meeting was convened by the latter body to discuss the expense of staging the 1931 contest. These deliberations evaluated the costing under three headings—the re-conditioning of existing and the supply of additional machines and engines, the acquisition of pilots and personnel, and the organization of the race and facilities, including foreign entertainment. A small committee was set up with Col Bristow, Commander James Bird, Air Commodore Holt and Mr B. E. Holloway as members. It assessed the race organization expenses alone at £12,000 and guarantees were obtained from the Royal Aero Club (£10,500) and from ten leading aircraft firms in various increments of £500. It should be emphasised that the aircraft industry was quite small at the time and no company was rich. These estimates took no account of the cost of the aircraft or of operating personnel, and finally it was considered that the expense of entering a British team in 1931 was too high.

What followed is shrouded in the mists of the past but circumstantial evidence seems to indicate that Col the Master of Sempill, at that time one of the leading figures in British aviation, went to Jersey in August 1930 presumably to interest Lady Houston in sponsoring his forthcoming attempt to fly over Everest, the world's highest peak, for the first time. The further assumption is that he mentioned Britain's predicament over the Schneider contest, an issue that later was the subject of Press agitation. What is certain is that Lady Houston, a noted eccentric and philanthropist, who had inherited a large fortune from her late husband, a shipping magnate, gave £100,000 to sponsor Britain's 1931 entry. She had made no secret of her detestation of Ramsay Macdonald and all his works. The story of how the first intimation of this sponsorship came to London is also based on circumstantial evidence but the legend is that the gallant Lady sent her diminutive retainer by boat and train from the Channel Islands to deliver an important letter to Commander Harold Perrin, secretary of the Royal Aero Club. He had no appointment and at first had difficulty in gaining admittance to the presence. What reaction Harold Perrin had when he opened the envelope containing the offer he never recorded but the red carpet certainly went down for the somewhat bemused retainer. If the story is not true, it deserves to be!

By whatever method this welcome message was delivered in January 1931, it left little enough time for resurrecting the British Schneider high-speed programme, abandoned after the 1929 triumph except for experimental work at Felixstowe with some of the aircraft. Although quite naturally the Air Ministry did not advertize the fact, they were inwardly pleased that British participation in 1931 was now possible and the RAF obviously welcomed the opportunity to compete for the third time. It was also obvious that the only possible British contender would have to be a modified S.6 with a Rolls-Royce R engine of increased power. Mitchell decided to make as few changes as possible to achieve a higher performance in redesigning the basic S.6. Essential improvements included provision for greater loads of fuel and oil, a more efficient oil cooling system, more engine coolant surface, redistribution of fuel in the floats to counteract increased engine torque, improved float design, statically balanced control surfaces, a new design of propeller, together with slightly increased aircraft dimensions except fuselage and a general strengthening of the airframe and bracing to cater for the increased weight.

Full use was made of research and development facilities, in particular the wind tunnel of the NPL at Teddington and the duplex water tank of Vickers at St

N247, the reserve S.6A, and S.6B S1595, the winner of the 1931 Schneider Trophy event.

Final engine test of the S.6B S1595 before winning the Schneider Trophy outright for Britain in 1931.

Albans. This work continued from February until a few days before the contest in September. It entailed tests on the drag of floats, oil coolers and anti-flutter devices, internal cooling of wing radiators, on the complete model aeroplane with and without propeller, on different forms of propeller and on the yawing problems experienced with the S.6 during taxi-ing.

Of special interest at the time was the investigation into flutter then proceeding, a phenomenon that had become increasingly evident as airspeeds rose. NACA* aircraft circular 154 reports 'On the S.5s slight aileron flutter was experienced if the controls were allowed to get slack. Calculations showed that with the increased speed of the S.6Bs there was a possibility of trouble in this respect and mass balances were therefore fitted as a precautionary measure. When travelling at maximum speed, the ordinary inaccuracies of construction make themselves felt by producing air loads upon the fin and stabilizer which necessitate loads upon the control column to correct. Since the tail unit is built into the fuselage no change in rigging is possible. The elevators and rudder were therefore provided with small flaps on their trailing edges which were adjusted to the angle necessary to trim hands and feet off at top speed. These flaps were only a few inches in area but proved extremely effective in use.'

No sign of this trouble had been experienced with the S.6s but later it was believed that they had been dangerously close to the limit of both wing and tail flutter. During the first flight of the reconditioned N247, the 1929 winner, on 2 June by Sqn Ldr Orlebar, violent tail flutter occurred when nearing maximum speed and continued for some time even with the engine throttled back, probably the result of weakening of the rear fuselage from the initial oscillations. It was impossible to redesign the aeroplane in the time available so the rudder surface was mass-balanced by means of streamlined bob weights fixed on brackets on

*National Advisory Committee for Aeronautics—the American contemporary of the British Aeronautical Research Committee.

198

both sides of the surface. To preclude the possibility of wing flutter the ailerons were similarly mass-balanced. Wind-tunnel tests showed negligible increase of drag from these excrescences.

The two new aircraft ordered for the 1931 contest were given the serials S1595 and S1596 and classified as S.6Bs while the two reconditioned 1929 S.6s N247 and N248 were re-classified as S.6As and modified to the same standard. This was important because the new regulations issued for 1931 required the navigability and seaworthiness tests and the race itself all to form part of a continuous contest on the same day. These new conditions meant that the competing aircraft would have to carry more fuel, and hence increased weight, and Supermarine's problem was to improve take-off performance, needing an improved design of float and demanding some 20 per cent increase in horse power from the engine.

The floats of the S.6Bs had to take the additional weight of the more powerful Rolls-Royce R engine developed for the 1931 race as well as the increased weight of fuel. Considerable research was made to improve their form as well as increasing their volume. To improve fore-and-aft stability they were increased in length from the S.6 type and made narrower. Drag was reduced by a fair margin, compared with that of the S.6 type, by carefully planned wind-tunnel testing of six

Dame Fanny Lucy Houston whose generosity made possible Britain's outright win of the Schneider Trophy, and Flt Lt J. N. Boothman AFC who flew the S.6B to victory in 1931. (*BBC Hulton Picture Library and Supermarine Aviation Works*)

different models. In addition the whole surfaces of both floats except the planing bottoms had to be brought into service to carry more radiator area in addition to the whole of the wing surfaces, so critical had the dissipation of engine-generated heat become in the S.6B.* Mitchell rightly called it a flying radiator for, of the total 'wetted' surface area of the S.6B of 948 sq ft, no less than 470 sq ft was radiator surface, including the oil cooling. The system of passing ram air from air scoops in the wingtips through the interior of the wings for cooling the undersides of the radiator surfaces as used in S.6 was the subject of much experiment by the RAE at Farnborough to improve its efficiency in heat transfer and drag reduction.

*40,000 British Thermal Units per minute.

No doubt the most difficult problem set by the S.6Bs was in control and handling, particularly at take-off. This was due to the effect of the low air speed of a coarse fixed-pitch propeller at large throttle openings. When the first S.6B, S1595, was delivered, it was found impossible to take off because of its continual yawing on the water. The propeller had been specially designed for the S.6B and was 8 ft 6 in in diameter. Eventually, after interchange with the S.6A propeller and further experiments, one of 9 ft 1½ in diameter was found to be the most efficient and was used in the contest.

S1595 was flown successfully on 29 July, 1931, by Sqn Ldr Orlebar, who had again been chosen to lead the High Speed Flight. No doubt one of the greatest contributions the Schneider Trophy made to the advance of aeronautical science was to hasten the perfection of the variable-pitch propeller and the development of variable-geometry devices such as landing and take-off flaps and slots. This necessity was emphasised in a lecture in 1968 to the Historical Group of the Royal Aeronautical Society by Grp Capt L. S. Snaith, one of the 1931 Schneider team, on 'Schneider Trophy Flying'. In this he said 'The effect of torque was our main concern. As engine power increased the left float was forced deeper into the water and this, coupled with the forward movement, dragged the aircraft to the left. With these two opposing forces to contend with, the start of the take-off had to be at least 45 degrees out of wind and full right rudder had to be applied—and held on.' He went on to say that directional control could be attained only when the aeroplane had accelerated sufficiently and was pulled round into the wind. The pilot was not out of the wood even then. There was a porpoising tendency which needed the control column to be held right back throughout take-off, the most critical part of the whole operation. When the aircraft eventually unstuck it did so quite suddenly. 'It leapt off the water and into the air at a pronounced angle and in

The 1931 RAF High Speed Flight. Left to right: Flt Lt E. J. Linton Hope, Lt G. L. Brinton RN, Flt Lts F. W. Long and G. H. Stainforth, Sqn Ldr A. H. Orlebar, Flt Lt J. N. Boothman (winner), Flg Off L. S. Snaith and Flt Lt Dry (engineer).

a partially stalled condition, virtually hanging on its propeller', he continued. 'It was the hardest thing to resist an impulse to let the control column go forward. If we failed we ran into serious trouble. The whole manoeuvre was complicated because many a time we had to take off blind, our goggles being misted up or covered in water.' Grp Capt Snaith further described the alighting regime as dictated by the fact that the aeroplane was exceptionally 'clean' and deceleration very slow. The cushioning effect between the wing and water was largely responsible and the view ahead was impeded by the nose more and more as the speed dropped and the angle of attack increased. Considerable wash on the surface of the sea was also a hazard when alighting, and Flt Lt E. J. Linton Hope's S.6A cartwheeled and sank from this cause and he was withdrawn from the team with a burst ear-drum. He was replaced by Lt G. L. Brinton, seconded from the Royal Navy, who on his first take-off on an S.6A probably let the control column go forward to correct the acute attitude of the aircraft, bounced to an irrecoverable height and dived straight in. This was the second fatality sustained by British pilots in the Schneider aircraft, the other being Flt Lt Kinkead in 1928 on the S.5 speed record attempt. These fatal accidents and those of the other national teams regrettably revealed the danger accepted by the pilots and testified to their exceptional skill and courage in probing what was at the time the threshold of knowledge of high air speed.

A parallel dedication was displayed by the Rolls-Royce test engineers who took considerable risk from burst engines on the test-beds, not only for the 1929 contest but also when raising the output of the R type to 2,300 hp, the figure Mitchell was asking for in order to beat the Italians in 1931. Only a week before the race did the uprated R engine pass its one-hour type test. Modifications from 1929 comprised an increase of engine speed by 300 rpm, a higher supercharger gear ratio, a larger air intake to the carburettor, articulated connecting rods in place of the blade and fork type, and the introduction of sodium-cooled exhaust valves as then recently developed in the United States at McCook Field.

In the event only one national team appeared on the starting line, that of Britain. Both the Italians and the French had suffered setbacks to their contenders and both had lost a pilot. The Americans were still trying to sort out problems with high-powered engines suitable for contention. The contest was delayed by one day through bad weather until 13 September, when Flt Lt John Boothman completed the course at an average speed of 340·08 mph in S.6B S1595. This meant that Britain had won the Schneider Trophy outright and it became the property of the Royal Aero Club. It only remained to go for the World Absolute Air Speed Record which Flt Lt George Stainforth captured in S.6B S1596 on the same day at 379·05 mph. A point of interest in the 'fly-over' by Boothman in the Race was that he had to throttle back to avoid exceeding his water temperature limit, which in fact decided the winning speed.

After the 1931 and last contest came the inevitable decision by the Air Ministry to close down the High Speed Flight and to restore the Calshot base to its flying-boat squadron. Only an intercession by Sir Henry Royce (knighted in 1930 for his services to the aircraft industry) saved the day for an attempt to be made to raise the record to over 400 mph with the S.6Bs, an achievement earnestly desired by Ernest Hives, experimental manager of Rolls-Royce and later Baron Hives of Duffield, and of course by Supermarine's Mitchell. So with R engine number 27 installed in S1595 and fed by a special fuel prescribed by Rodwell Banks and consisting of 30 per cent benzole, 60 per cent methanol, 10 per cent acetone and one part per thousand tetraethyl lead, George Stainforth achieved the world

Vice-Admiral Sir Richard Smeeton, representing the Royal Aero Club, handing over the Schneider Trophy for safe keeping to Dame Margaret Weston, Director of the Science Museum. (*British Aerospace*)

record of 407·5 mph on 29 September, which figure was duly homologated by the FAI. Rodwell Banks, whose doctored fuels had caused so much havoc to the paint finish of the Schneider aircraft by their 'stripping' properties, went on to help the Italians recover the world record with his fuel technology. Perhaps the last word on the Schneider series must be left to him.

He said, 'Probably the most important series of events in aviation between the wars occurred in 1927, 1929 and 1931 with the Schneider Trophy contests of those years resulting in three consecutive wins by the Royal Air Force High Speed Flight teams and the Trophy being won outright for Great Britain. These particular contests were to be significant landmarks, where the importance of the fuel in permitting greatly improved engine performance was fully demonstrated and where subsequent military engine and fuel developments were to go hand in hand.'* He could have added that these powerplant advances could not have been fully exploited except through the genius of aeroplane designers like Reginald Mitchell, who disclosed his true worth in the Spitfire, his supreme creation, in the design of which so much Schneider experience was used later.

Fifty Years of Engineering Learning—F. R. Banks—*The Aeronautical Journal*, March 1968.

Schneider S Series

	S.4	S.5	S.6	S.6B
Engine	Napier Lion VII	Napier Lion VIIA	Rolls-Royce R	Rolls-Royce R
HP at rpm	680/2,600	900/3,300	1,900/2,900	2,350/3,200
Serial/Racing Number	4	N219 6 N220 4 (Winner) N221 None	N247 2 (Winner) N248 8	S1595 1 (Winner) S1596
Span	30 ft 7½ in (9·33 m)	26 ft 9 in (8·15 m)	30 ft 0 in (9·14 m)	30 ft 0 in (9·14 m)
Length (overall)	26 ft 7¾ in (8·12 m)	24 ft 3½ in (7·32 m)	25 ft 10 in (8·18 m)	28 ft 10 in (8·79 m)
Length (fuselage)	25 ft 0 in (7·62 m)	22 ft 0½ in (6·71 m)	25 ft 3 in (7·7 m)	25 ft 3 in (7·7 m)
Height	11 ft 8½ in (3·57 m)	11 ft 1 in (3·38 m)	12 ft 3 in (3·73 m)	12 ft 3 in (3·73 m)
Wing area	139 sq ft (12·9 sq m)	115 sq ft (10·68 sq m)	145 sq ft (13·47 sq m)	145 sq ft (13·47 sq m)
Empty weight	2,600 lb (1,179 kg)	2,680 lb (1,215 kg) N220	4,471 lb (2,028 kg) S.6A	4,590 lb (2,082 kg) S1595
Loaded weight	3,191 lb (1,447 kg)	3,242 lb (1,470 kg) N220	5,771 lb (2,617 kg) S.6A	6,086 lb (2,760 kg) S1595
Maximum speed	226·75 mph (365 km/h) World Seaplane Record	319·57 mph (514·3 km/h)	357·7 mph (575·7 km/h) World Speed Record	407·5 mph (655·8 km/h) World Speed Record 390 mph (627·6 km/h) in level flight
Alighting speed	85 mph (136·8 km/h)	85 mph (136·8 km/h)	95 mph (152·9 km/h)	95 mph (152·9 km/h)

The Supermarine Type 224 and specification F.7/30, with cranked gull wing and fixed undercarriage, was known as the Spitfire, but was completely redesigned by R. J. Mitchell to produce what became one of the world's outstanding aircraft.

Type 224 F.7/30

In 1930 the Air Ministry issued specification F.7/30 for a single-seat day and night fighter with a speed of 195 mph. It was to have exceptional manoeuvrability, a longer endurance than any previous fighter, a low landing speed and a steep initial climb for night interception, and an excellent all-round view. The armament specified was four Vickers guns, and two-way radio telephone equipment was to be fitted. To meet these requirements a new outlook was needed in fighter design, which had tended to stagnate since the end of the First World War. The appearance in 1925 of the Fairey Fox two-seat bomber with its 400 hp Curtiss D-12 liquid-cooled engine and its superfine streamlining had exposed the shortcomings in performance of contemporary biplane fighters. The Supermarine answer to specification F.7/30 introduced 'many novel features regarding which, at the time of design, there was little or no information'—to quote their wind-tunnel report, but it said that their tender embodied the experience gained by the firm in high-speed aeroplanes and other monoplane types.

It had an all-metal structure, and thick gull-wing and short cantilever undercarriage were arrived at after much comparative wind-tunnel testing by Vickers at Weybridge, although straight wings and a retractable undercarriage were examined in this programme. The design incorporated one of the first attempts to reduce weight of coolant and radiators for liquid-cooled engines.

Its lack of success was not attributable to the weakness of the specification, as has been said, but more to the groping for design progress in Mitchell's first attempt to apply knowledge gained from the Schneider racers and the flying-boats

to a practical landplane fighter, a different proposition. How quickly he reacted to
this initial failure is now well known but in the event none of the F.7/30 submissions gained favour, including Bristol's Type 133 gull-wing monoplane with
cantilever undercarriage, so similar to the Supermarine F.7/30. The order in fact
was captured by the Gloster SS.37 Gladiator to production specification 14/35, so
reverting to the proven biplane configuration with air-cooled radial engine to
fulfil the requirement for the time being.

A preference had been expressed by the Air Staff for the Rolls-Royce Kestrel
IV engine with evaporative cooling, a development subsequently known as the
Goshawk. The theory of this system in a liquid-cooled engine was that by letting
the water boil and condensing the steam, instead of cooling the water before it
boiled as in a conventional honeycomb radiator, much weight of water would be
saved. The system worked well in certain aircraft but indifferently in others,
efficiency largely depending on the relative positions of the condenser and header
tank. In the case of the Supermarine F.7/30, a further saving was made in drag by
using the leading edges of the wing as condensers, an idea obviously inherited
from the S series racers with their surface radiators and developed for the
six-engined Type 179 monoplane flying-boat project. To improve the efficiency of

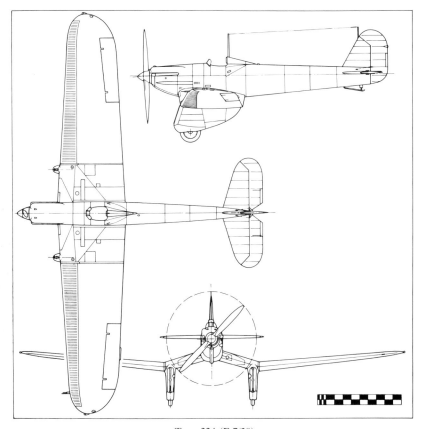

Type 224 (F.7/30)

the condensers, corrugations were introduced chordwise, but in Mitchell's improved design which led ultimately to the Spitfire proper, these were abandoned as drag-inducing. The name Spitfire had been proposed* and indeed adopted for the machine but according to reports at the time Mitchell was not impressed with it. Later on of course the name acquired a legendary significance.

The 'bent' wing design introduced problems of lateral stability, and several combinations of centre-section anhedrals and outer-plane dihedrals were wind-tunnel tested before a satisfactory arrangement was reached. Tests on directional stability with the tunnel model indicated that the fin and rudder originally proposed were insufficient and their size was therefore increased. Other features which Supermarine embodied in their F.7/30 were the air-brake (a panel swung out from the underside of the fuselage) and small fillets between the wing and fuselage. Somewhat unusually for the time, a full-size model of the cockpit was made and tested in Vickers' large wind tunnel to establish the effect of various windscreens on cockpit draught.

From the time the first proposals were submitted by Supermarine to F.7/30 on 20 February, 1932, there were several returns to the drawing board for revised dimensions and estimated figures. By July the shape had changed, with the following modifications: a general increase of dimensions consequent upon an increase of wing area with only a slight weight increase, in order to reduce the wing loading; the cockpit enlarged and the tailplane lowered; finally, the exhaust and steam condenser systems modified and the wheel-track decreased. At this stage the design under Type 224 had a span of 46 ft, a wing area of 300 sq ft, an estimated weight of 4,000 lb, and an estimated speed of 240 mph.

By November detail design was in progress with the condenser forming the leading edge of the outer planes back to the light alloy single spar at one third of the chord, with a fabric-covered rear portion. When hot, the condenser expanded causing the wing to curve in a slight arc in plan and the ailerons to lose end-clearance and nearly jam in flight. The rear fuselage was of the semi-monocoque form of closely-spaced frames and flush-riveted panels with longitudinal stringers following Schneider practice. The armament was four 0·303 machine-guns, two mounted conventionally in the front fuselage and two in the undercarriage fairings inboard. The diameter of the exhaust collector was reduced to allow the bullets clearance when the synchronized fuselage guns were fired. No attempt was made to retract the wheels of the undercarriage as on the Bristol 133 to the same specification, despite Supermarine's long experience with retractable undercarriages on their amphibians.

Some twenty months elapsed between the official 'Instructions to Proceed' with the Type 224 and its first flight by 'Mutt' Summers on 19 February, 1934, but in the interim Mitchell was involved in studies of alternative configurations in an investigation of the theoretical high-altitude performance and ceiling, based on the calculations of his technical office. The general conclusions were that a low wing loading was more advantageous than a small size of aeroplane for high-altitude performance; a monoplane of about seven to one aspect ratio would have a better altitude performance than a normal biplane; high wing loading could lead to high-altitude performance if the aspect ratio was high enough and there was an optimum wing loading for maximum top speed.

---

*According to J. D. Scott in *Vickers—A History* by Sir Robert McLean, the Company Chairman.

Although the Rolls-Royce Kestrel had been successful as the British answer to the American Curtiss D-12, its derivative with steam cooling, the Goshawk, was not a success and only a few were built. Consequently none of the aircraft designed around it achieved any significant order. However, aero-engine design was on the threshold of the Merlin project, started by Rolls-Royce as a private venture, the Air Ministry pleading no funds. In the meantime Trevor Westbrook and Beverley Shenstone of Supermarine visited the United States on a fact-finding mission in regard to American aircraft and production methods in comparison with their British equivalents; one of these being the Supermarine F.7/30, first of its type as a monoplane fighter, and having better structure weight percentage than comparative American machines with the possible exception of the Northrop Gamma with its revolutionary wing structure eventually adopted by Douglas. Westbrook and Shenstone thought that in flying qualities and combat effectiveness, British aircraft were better at that time. The Americans on the other hand designed and built more quickly, although the F.7/30 entries were completed within times as good as those of comparative American civil aircraft unencumbered by Air Ministry procedure and regulations.

The Supermarine F.7/30 K2890 appeared at the RAF Display at Hendon as No. 2 in the New Types Park on 30 June, 1934. Most of the test flying was done by 'Mutt' Summers, with H. W. R. Banting of Vickers, Weybridge, Major H. J. Payn, and George Pickering, Supermarine's own test pilot, assisting at times. Its performance was disappointing, the top speed recorded being 228 mph, some 17 mph below wind-tunnel estimates, while the climb to 15,000 ft was 9·5 minutes, considerably exceeding the wind-tunnel estimate of 6·6 minutes. Here it should be said that the Air Ministry had requested an increase in overall dimensions after the tender had been submitted because they considered Supermarine's proposed wing loading of 15 lb/sq ft too high. This was probably the factor that led to the later assertion that the Air Ministry had bungled the F.7/30 specification which, to the contrary, was quite advanced for its time and was followed shortly after by F.5/34 and a further step forward to the Spitfire/Hurricane era of greatly improved performances.

Supermarine Type 224 F.7/30 at the RAF Display at Hendon in 1934. (*Courtesy Philip Jarrett*)

The Type 224 with cowlings removed and showing the header tank behind the steam-cooled Rolls-Royce Goshawk engine. (*B. Shenstone*)

As mentioned before, none of the entries for the F.7/30 competition succeeded in official trials at Martlesham, and Mitchell continued his investigation into improvements of the basic Supermarine design. By increasing the wing loading to 18·4 lb/sq ft, employing straight and thinner wings and a retractable undercarriage, he was able to offer an estimated top speed of 265 mph, much nearer his original target, following his memorandum dated 2 May, 1934. In this he indicated various improvements needed to bring the F.7/30 design up to his own high standard.

For example, he suggested trials of different gear ratios for the engine-performance trials, and tests with four different propellers of varying pitch and diameter, as well as tests with three different exhaust systems on silencing and flame damping and effect on performance. Two shapes of wing root fillets were to be examined for their effect on control and to the same end Mitchell proposed a modified tailplane to study stability and control effects. The corrugated leading-edge coolers for the Goshawk engine were to be replaced by smooth skin surfaces, and modifications were drawn up to replace the Rolls-Royce ejectors in the cooling system, which were deemed inefficient. He also proposed split trailing-edge flaps, and for the first time a cabin for the pilot, to study effects on his view and on general performance gain by reduction of drag. Of course, a retractable undercarriage came into his calculations, preferably with the wheels stowed into wells in the underside of the wings; as well as introducing a tricky mechanical problem, the undercarriage geometry greatly affected the ultimate shape of the wing, as will be seen later.

All these proposed improvements to Type 224 were costed at about £3,000 but by the end of 1934 only some £390 had been expended since so little progress had been made towards any positive development of the original F.7/30 K2890 airframe. Two Goshawk engines were tried during its career during which it acquired some indignity by being towed backwards around Eastleigh in airfield runway tests on both grass and tarmac with its tailskid on a truck to measure the towing force on a spring balance and the coefficients of friction. George Pickering flew it to the RAE at Farnborough on 24 July, 1935, where it became popular as the officers' 'hack', being in fact a very good flying machine. On 25 May, 1937, it went to AAEE, Martlesham Heath, and eventually to Orfordness for use as a gunnery target.

Meanwhile Mitchell and the Supermarine design team had concentrated their forward thinking on two main developments of Type 224. The first was schemed with a cabin and retractable undercarriage and thin straight wings and embodied a number of the improvements, as already detailed. The second project had a more refined outline, with the cabin merged into the top decking of the fuselage. These schemes were merely steps to the Spitfire proper, the advent of which had to await the availability of the new Rolls-Royce engine.

Type 224—One 600 hp Rolls-Royce Goshawk II. Single-seat fighter.
Span 45 ft 10 in (13·97 m); length (tail up) 29 ft 5¼ in (8·97 m); height (tail up) 11 ft 11 in (3·63 m); wing area 295 sq ft (27·4 sq m).
Empty weight 3,422 lb (1,552 kg); loaded weight 4,743 lb (2,151·4 kg).
Maximum speed 228 mph (367 km/h) at 15,000 ft (4,573 m); landing speed 60 mph (96·6 km/h); climb to 15,000 ft (4,573 m) 9·5 min; absolute ceiling 38,800 ft (11,826 m).
Armament. Four 0·303-in machine-guns, two in the fuselage and two in the wing roots, all synchronized to fire through the propeller arc.

Spitfire

'Always the Spitfire and its family will be regarded as a classic example of British aeronautical achievement, proved and tested over eleven years of production and Service use. Originally designed by the late R. J. Mitchell in 1935, the prototype Spitfire first flew in 1936; since then over 22,000 have been manufactured in 33 different types. This remarkable aircraft remained a front line fighter throughout the whole period of the War . . .' With these words Joseph Smith, who had succeeded Mitchell as Supermarine's chief designer in 1936, opened his classic lecture on the famous fighter to the Royal Aeronautical Society on 19 December, 1946. He went on to say that one of the main achievements in the development of the machine was the enormous increase in power, accommodated without material alteration in the size of the aircraft '. . . due to the whole-hearted co-operation of the Rolls-Royce design team, without which the development life of the Spitfire and Seafire might have been seriously curtailed.' At an earlier date, in March 1943, Smith had stated to a US Army Air Force mission from Wright Field that Supermarine's engineering philosophy was to retain the basic airframe design and to make only such modifications and changes as would improve performance or were necessitated by a step-up in the powerplant ratings. The prime factors that determined the continued success of the Spitfire in service were the genius of its designer, Mitchell, the achievement of the Rolls-Royce engineers in keeping the performance of the Merlin and Griffon engines ahead of the comparative performance of the German engines, and the faith that 'Joe' Smith placed in his predecessor's masterpiece.

Beyond all doubt R. J. Mitchell did a great deal of thinking before he committed himself to the final configuration of the prototype Spitfire, K5054. Most of his sculpturing of the lines appears to have been done on the drawing board and the wooden mock-up, one photograph of which survives as reproduced. He had become sceptical of wind-tunnel results after his experience with those produced for the F.7/30, and he rejected, much against the current trend of aerodynamic thought at the time, the thick wing high-lift philosophy, which was being pro-

Jeffrey Quill flying the prototype Spitfire modified to Mk I standard with full armament and camouflage finish.

pounded among others by Vickers' own Weybridge and Supermarine joint design committee. In fact, R. K. Pierson and Barnes Wallis exploited the space provided inside the Wellington's geodetic thick wing by one of the first installations of wing fuel tanks; the Supermarine designers, on the other hand, displayed great ingenuity by installing not only a retractable undercarriage but also an eight-gun battery in the then revolutionary thin wings of the Spitfire. This was one of the advantages, apart from aerodynamic, deriving from the adoption of elliptical wing geometry, for which some credit must be accorded to Beverley Shenstone, Supermarine's aerodynamicist.

All the forethought of Mitchell and the ambition of his design team to exploit their Schneider successes by evolving a number-one fighter would have been fruitless if a corresponding advance had not been made in powerplant design. While the Kestrel had restored the balance of favour for the liquid-cooled engine in British fighters with the Hawker Fury, Rolls-Royce came to the conclusion in 1932 that a more powerful type was needed for future requirements, as the Buzzard, which had sired the Schneider R engine, was deemed too large and heavy, much in the same way as the Rolls-Royce Condor had been rejected previously for interceptor fighters. The Merlin, when it appeared in 1933 as a private venture, was a scaled-up Kestrel with only two major differences, the cylinder block with the crankcase top half as a one-piece casting, and a steam-cooling system modified from that used for the Goshawk. Flight testing of one of the so-designated PV12 prototype engines confirmed the shortcomings of the water evaporative cooling system, previously exposed in the F.7/30, so pure ethylene glycol was introduced as the coolant. In due course, the Merlin emerged as an advanced powerplant of over 1,000 hp, suitable for installation in the new breed of eight-gun fighters being designed by Hawker and Supermarine.

Although an improved F.7/30 design with the Goshawk had been approved by the Air Ministry, the advent of the Merlin made all the difference to the scheme. It is a matter of history that there emerged from the ungainly angular Super-marine Type 224, like a butterfly from its chrysalis, one of the most beautiful aeroplanes ever designed, and possessing, for its time, heavy fire power which was so soon to be put to the test.

At meetings of the Board of the Supermarine Aviation Works (Vickers) Limited in October and November 1934 the whole subject of the Supermarine fighter was considered. A proposal by the Air Ministry that the F.7/30 should be re-engined with a Napier Dagger was rejected and Mitchell was authorized by the Board to design a completely new fighter free from official specifications. The background to this decision was the work already done by Mitchell and his team on improvements to the F.7/30. Sir Robert McLean, Supermarine's chairman who was also chairman of Vickers Aviation, had great faith in Mitchell and had collaborated closely with A. F. (later Sir Arthur) Sidgreaves, managing director of Rolls-Royce Limited, since the winning of the Schneider Trophy by the Supermarine S.6B with the Rolls-Royce R engine. From this association, and Hawker's engine requirement for its Hurricane, came Rolls-Royce's crucial decision to design a new engine of a size and power between the smaller Kestrel and the larger R engine, embodying all current technological advances. High

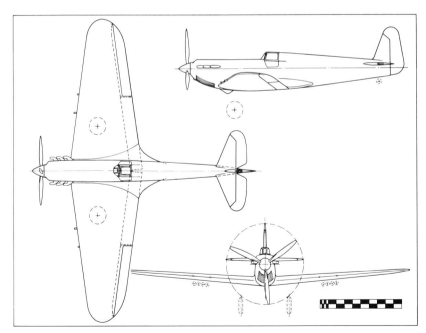

F.7/30 development

211

The mock-up of the Type 300 Spitfire in the hangar roof at Hythe. The last Stranraers can be seen under construction. (*A. Fitz-Hugh*)

hopes were held in official places for the two new monoplane fighters to be designed around the new Rolls-Royce engine, eventually to become famous as the Merlin. Rolls-Royce however had to bear much of the initial development costs themselves and even contributed £7,500 toward the cost of the Spitfire prototype.

A contract for this improved version of the F.7/30 was placed by the Air Ministry on 1 December, 1934, and an advanced copy of the covering specification F.37/34 was received by Supermarine on 28 December. This accepted the main proposals contained in Supermarine's own specification 425a and their general arrangement scheme under Type 300. From the brief requirements of F.37/34 it was evident that its purpose was to sanction what was initiated as a private venture.*

A similar procedure was adopted with the contemporary design which became the Hawker Hurricane. For both projects the new Rolls-Royce engine was specified. It was clear that the Air Staff were intent on acquiring much more

---

*The correct assessment of the private venture/official specification controversy is unequivocally defined in the official histories of the Second World War – *Design and Development of Weapons*—Postan, Hay and Scott—HMSO and Longmans Green.

advanced aircraft irrespective of rigid procurement mandates. At the final mock-up conference at Woolston held in May 1935, representatives of the Air Ministry operations branch pressed for the wing-mounted eight-gun armament already specified for the F.5/34 submissions and indeed first installed in the Vickers Venom radial-engined fighter prototype. This requirement was readily accepted by Mitchell on 29 April, 1935, under enabling specification 10/35, the conditions of which had been circulated but never issued for tender. This policy of anticipating requirements characterized the subsequent career of the Spitfire design, with *ad hoc* decisions preceding official confirmations. Each major development was engineered usually ahead of changing operational demands. It is a matter of history that the successful British aircraft of the Second World War were planned or designed before the war while some later designs never quite reached fruition in time to make a significant contribution in service, at least in their primary duty.

The four development stages of the basic Spitfire airframe were evaluated by Postan as: the original conception by Mitchell in the prototype K5054 and the Marks I and II powered by the early Merlins; the Mark III with the Merlin XX and the Mark Vs with the Merlin 45; the group first represented by the Mark IX with the two-stage Merlin 61 series; and finally the Mark 20 series engineered to take the larger and more powerful Rolls-Royce Griffon. Postan credits Joseph Smith and Alan Clifton with this remarkable feat of structural adaptation, but the whole Supermarine organization was of recognized merit and great experience, aided in no small measure by the Rolls-Royce experimental flight establishment at Hucknall, especially in regard to the engine installations.

Despite the Spitfire's legendary reputation, there was in fact no mystique about Mitchell's design. It was a straightforward merger of all the technical knowledge of the time into one composite piece of machinery, including its powerplant which, with the airframe, had embodied all the experience of high-speed flight gathered from the Schneider Trophy races. Mitchell was in fact much more practical than is commonly supposed and has been described by his closest technical collaborators as more an aeroplane enthusiast than a theoretician. The same could be said about other designers at that time, when so much of their creative thought had to be checked by the time-honoured method of trial and error. In the case of the Merlin Spitfire everything came right at the psychological moment—a rare event in aircraft and engine design.

Spitfire Mk I K9793, with Merlin II and two-position de Havilland metal propeller, at Martlesham in July 1939. (*Ministry of Defence*)

213

As Postan says 'the Spitfire was probably the only highly successful aircraft to incorporate certain features such as the thin wings, which at the time of its inception may have been considered well in advance of existing practice'. At the time of its arrival in operational service, the Spitfire was faster at its designed altitude than its German adversary, the Messerschmitt Bf 109, although perhaps inferior in climb and speed above that altitude. This deficiency soon received the attention of the Rolls-Royce engine designers and the fuel scientists, and one of the factors which influenced forthcoming events was the introduction of 100-octane fuel at the outbreak of war in September 1939, enabling a power increase in the Merlin II through higher boost pressure. In addition, a new pressurized coolant system was introduced at the same time, with a mixture of water and glycol (as anti-freeze) replacing the pure glycol system at atmospheric pressure, steam-cooling having been abandoned. Lower cylinder-head temperatures and therefore prolonged engine life were obtained with this system.

The Messerschmitt had had the advantage of battle experience in the Spanish Civil War. It also had a lighter airframe mounting a larger engine than the Merlin in the Spitfire. Although such factors promoted better climb and higher altitude performance, the more robust construction of the Spitfire airframe and Merlin engine facilitated greater development as operational demands increased later on. Initially, too, the Spitfire was at some disadvantage in combat against the German fighter whose fuel injection system permitted inverted flight and negative g, while the Merlin's carburettor cut out momentarily under these conditions. This shortcoming was partially solved by Miss Shilling of the RAE who devised a simple washer with a restricted orifice in the pipeline so that sufficient fuel could be retained for completion of the manoeuvres.

The basic structure of the Spitfire remained largely unaltered throughout many changes of operational duties and increases of power and weight. Some local strengthening was made from time to time, but not until the appearance of the Mk XII with the larger Rolls-Royce Griffon engine was any major change needed, when a girder type mounting replaced the Merlin's tubular engine mounting.

When the Spitfire 20 series was introduced, with much increased weight and higher performance, the wings were completely redesigned to higher strength factors. Even in this major change the elliptical planform was retained since experience had proved that this shape had an unsuspected bonus in its low induced drag at great altitudes. This had become evident in high-altitude operation, particularly by the unarmed photographic reconnaissance versions, in which manoeuvrability and efficient control were of paramount importance.

The following structural description is primarily of the Spitfire I but may be taken as representative of all later versions. The fuselage was of stressed skin construction of oval cross-section and tapered towards the rear. It had four main longerons and 15 channel-section frames numbered 5 to 19. The Alclad skin was riveted to the frames and stiffened between them by Z-section intercostals which were riveted in place before the skin panels were attached to the frames. The fin was integral with the tail end of the fuselage, which was detachable and bolted to the main portion by 52 bolts and four studs round a double frame.

The five forward frames had the tops cut off and were thus of U-shape, the tops being joined by the top longerons. This portion of the fuselage housed the fuel tanks and, behind the tanks, the cockpit. Lateral members braced the fuselage at frame 5, which carried the fire-proof bulkhead, and at frame 8. There was further bracing between these frames in the form of two detachable, diagonal members

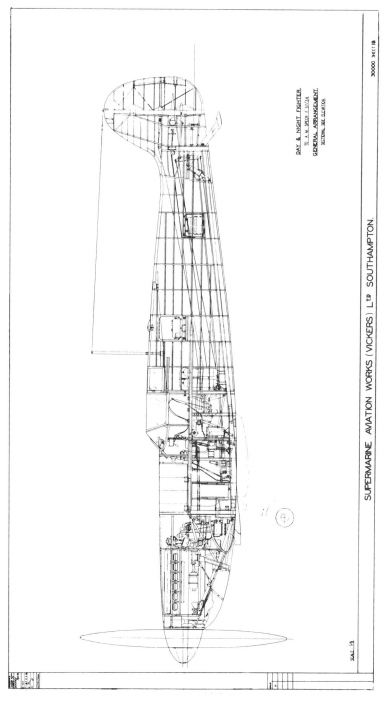

SUPERMARINE AVIATION WORKS (VICKERS) L^TD SOUTHAMPTON.

DAY & NIGHT FIGHTER.
TO A.M. SPECIF. F.37/34
GENERAL ARRANGEMENT
SECTIONAL SEE ELEVATION

30000 SHEET 1B

SCALE 1/8

Supermarine drawing of the Spitfire Mk I, showing fuselage structure, engine installation and controls

extending across the tank bay and fitted after the bottom tank was in position. Frame 11 braced the structure behind the cockpit seat and was the foremost of the complete frames shaping the fuselage.

Each wing was a separate, stressed-skin, elliptical structure. It was, essentially, a single-spar wing, but had an auxiliary spar. The main spar and leading edge were constructed as a separate unit torsion box to which the main portion of the wing was afterwards assembled in a jig. The main spar construction consisted of two square-section booms and a plate web. The booms were built up of square-section laminations, making the root ends practically solid, but tapering towards the tip first to channel-section and finally to angle-section. The root end of this spar carried the pintle on which the retractable mainwheel unit pivoted.

The wings were attached to the fuselage by their main spars at the fire-proof bulkhead, and by the auxiliary spars at frame 10. The auxiliary spar attachment used only one bolt, but the main spar attachment used three bolts in the top boom and four bolts in the bottom boom. The control surfaces were of metal, but initially were fabric covered.

The mainwheel units were cantilever structures and retracted outwards, into the undersurface of the wings. The retraction was effected hydraulically, in the first few aircraft by hand pump but later by an engine-driven pump. Initially, the tailwheel was non-retractable.

The Spitfire prototype, K5054, was hand-built and so differed from production aircraft, notably in the wing covering. Aft of the main spar this was of narrow strips of light alloy to facilitate the double curvature as designed into the wing geometry. The Spitfire wing was an example of the generalization that a good wing makes a good aeroplane. Its aerodynamic characteristics were—aerofoil section NACA 2200, thickness chord ratio 13 per cent at the root, tapering to 6 per cent at the tip, while the angle of incidence varied from 2 deg at the root to minus half a deg at the tip. This geometry induced a twist to the wing to which can be ascribed its undoubted efficiency. All this was achieved without any major wind-tunnel testing of Mitchell's final configuration, except for small alterations to tail settings following spinning tunnel-tests at RAE in 1934.

The fuselage of the prototype only was built as a one-piece structure with an integral fin. The engine cowling was fabricated from a multiplicity of hand-formed

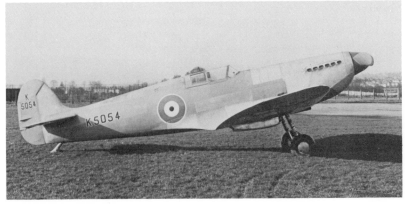

Spitfire prototype K5054 at Eastleigh in the cerulean-blue finish in which it visited a number of air stations on Empire Air Day in May 1938. (*Ministry of Defence*)

216

panels to the streamline shape needed for a high-speed aeroplane, and each cylinder had its own exhaust pipe, later replaced by an ejector type exhaust stack said to promote the conversion of exhaust heat into thrust. A similar claim was made for the RAE/Meredith type ducted radiator located beneath the starboard wing, with the oil cooler similarly placed beneath the port wing. The carburettor intake was initially inset into the underside of the engine cowling with a bleed-off for the boundary layer but later was redesigned to be flush-fitting. No doors were fitted to the undercarriage wheel wells. K5054 originally had a tailskid.

For the first flight on 5 March, 1936, the undercarriage was locked down and a fine-pitch propeller was fitted to give the pilot more rpm and so more power on take-off. Apart from a slight swing on take-off, the prototype and early Spitfires were comparatively easy to handle, allowing 'Mutt' Summers, Vickers' chief test pilot, to make his historic remark after landing from the first flight, 'Don't touch anything.' The deficiencies of the aeroplane in its rolling characteristics came to light later when replacement of the fabric-covered Frise-type ailerons by metal-covered versions enabled later versions with clipped wings to match the roll efficiency of German adversaries, notably the Focke-Wulf Fw 190. Some idea of the potential of the Spitfire was gained during early tests when George Pickering, Supermarine's own test pilot, reached a speed of 430 mph in a dive. The only change made before the machine was delivered to the AAEE at Martlesham Heath for its first official trials was the elimination of the triangular balance horn on the rudder.

The trials on 8 and 9 June, 1936, were attended by Mitchell himself. Although then in declining health, he had the satisfaction of realizing that the magical figures for an advanced fighter, dreamt up in 1929 when he was designing the Schneider S.6 to take the Rolls-Royce R engine of nearly 2,000 hp, had been achieved, with a speed of 350 mph and a climb to nearly 10,000 ft in three and a half minutes. This technical success was all the more remarkable in that it more than matched the initial performance of its contemporary, the Hawker Hurricane, for the latter had had the advantage of a better fighter pedigree from its forebears, notably the Kestrel-engined Fury. Mitchell had never designed a fighter before the F.7/30 and Supermarine had long left the scene since the days of the Baby, the Sea King and their flying-boat Schneider derivatives, all single-seat aeroplanes. However, the Hurricane and Spitfire were soon to become immortal brothers-in-arms.

Various plans for the expansion of the Royal Air Force had come and gone but under the Government Scheme F, which heralded the greatest growth in the aircraft industry since 1918, Supermarine received their order for 310 Spitfires on 3 June, 1936, to a value of one and a quarter million pounds sterling. This, with an order for 168 Walruses to follow, must have sounded to the tiny Southampton firm, although a subsidiary of the mighty Vickers-Armstrongs combine, as something beyond their wildest dreams.

The hand-built Spitfire prototype had proved such an efficient aeroplane that the production of the type in quantity posed problems which at that time were completely alien to an aircraft industry highly specialized but emaciated between the wars. The mass-production methods of the motor car industry exemplified by Morris and Austin were a world apart from the batch construction pattern followed by the aircraft manufacturers, and obviously a different approach was needed if the required output of aircraft was to be achieved. The breakdown system of major component manufacturers was adopted by the Air Ministry, in which the various parts of the aeroplane—wings, fuselage, tail, undercarriage and

Spitfire fuselages awaiting sub-contracted wings, at the Itchen Works in 1939. Stranraer and Walrus production can be seen in the background.

numerous other parts were made separately, often by different constructors, and married into the complete aircraft at a central erecting establishment.

In consequence of the official requirement that three-quarters of the Spitfire components were to be sub-contracted, some inevitable 'bottlenecks' were encountered, particularly in the supply of wings. The result was that at the end of 1937 six Spitfires were complete but for their wings. This problem was resolved eventually by the parent firm making sets of wings themselves in addition to fuselages and other parts. With passage of time the sub-contractors gained experience in stressed-skin construction of which they had little knowledge hitherto. Whether the Air Ministry, at that time the procurement authority, was right in applying the split-assembly system to such a thoroughbred as the Spitfire, with its delicate curves and fine angles, can only be a matter of opinion.

The first production Spitfire, K9787, had flown at Eastleigh on 14 May, 1938, and was delivered to the AAEE at Martlesham Heath on 27 July for official handling trials. Two days later K9792 was delivered to No.19 Squadron at Duxford, Cambridgeshire, and thus became the first Spitfire in the Royal Air Force, and No.19 Squadron was destined to become the 'guinea pig' unit for Service modifications, and the Air Fighting Development Unit at Duxford worked closely with the Rolls-Royce flight test centre at Hucknall, Notts.

In March 1938 the Government Scheme F was replaced by Scheme L, under which 12,000 military aircraft were to be produced by early 1940, and under this revised requirement Supermarine received an additional order for another 200 Spitfires. At that time only four sets of wings had been delivered although 35 fuselages had been completed at Woolston and 25 transferred to Eastleigh awaiting final assembly, nevertheless, by the end of 1938, by producing wings from its own jigs Supermarine had delivered 49 Spitfires. On the outbreak of war on 3 September, 1939, nine squadrons of the RAF had been equipped, 19, 41, 54, 65, 66, 72, 74, 602 and 611, completion of the first order for 310 having been accomplished, despite the early problems, in the preceding month. From then on there was a steady if slow increase in the supply of operational Spitfires right up to the time of the type's acid test in the early brushes with enemy aircraft over the northeast coast of Britain towards the end of 1939 and in the skirmishes over the English Channel leading to the Dunkirk evacuation—and thereafter in the decisive Battle of Britain.

Completed Spitfire Is at Eastleigh early in 1939.

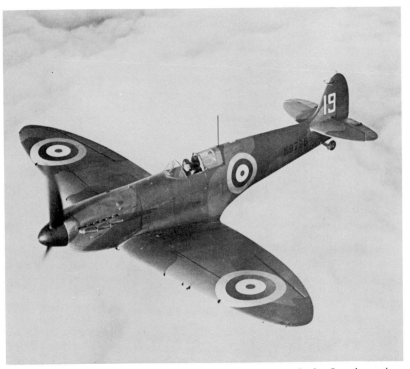

Spitfire I K9795 with No. 19 Squadron in October 1938. This was the first Squadron to be equipped with Spitfires. (*Imperial War Museum*)

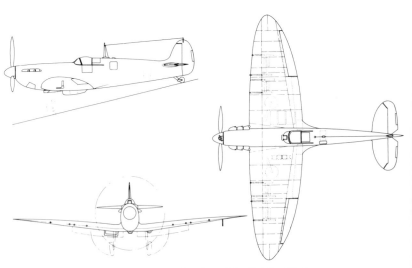

A Supermarine drawing of the Spitfire Mk I

The first Spitfire Mk Is were delivered to 19 Squadron with the Merlin II engine driving a wooden two-blade fixed-pitch propeller. The sub-types, Mks IA and IB, followed with the de Havilland two-position three-blade propeller, from the 78th production aircraft onwards, and, with the Merlin III fitted from the 175th production aeroplane, the Spitfire could take de Havilland or Rotol propellers on a standardized driving shaft, which enabled constant-speed types of either make to be fitted. These high-efficiency propellers, enabling full power to be achieved through the engine crankshaft at operational heights, had a marked influence on performance so vital in the forthcoming Battle of Britain. When that opened in all its ferocity in July and August 1940, a mobile unit of the de Havilland propeller division went round with conversion units for constant-speed to all the RAF squadrons still using the two-position type.

Martlesham's report on the first Spitfire handling trials said 'The aeroplane is simple and easy to fly with no vices. All controls are entirely satisfactory for this type and no modification to them is required except the elevator control might be improved by reducing the gear ratio between stick and elevator. In general the handling of this aeroplane is such that it can be flown without risk by the average fully trained fighter pilot'. At that time the importance of lateral manoeuvrability at high speeds in combat had not been appreciated and the heaviness of fabric-covered ailerons in those conditions had not been fully realized. In the case of the Spitfire this problem was not completely solved for a considerable time although various later expedients such as metal skinning the ailerons and cropping the wing tips improved rate of roll, as already mentioned.

In his lecture in 1948 to the Southampton and Weybridge branches of the Royal Aeronautical Society, Jeffrey Quill, chief test pilot of Supermarine throughout the Second World War with a vast experience of flying all versions of Spitfire and Seafire and of combat flying with 65 Squadron in the Battle of Britain, said, 'Fighting performance is the over-riding consideration. Most air combats between fighter and fighter are virtually won and lost before the actual engagement.

Simulated scramble of No.65 Squadron in May 1939. The aircraft are Spitfire Mk Is with fixed-pitch wooden propellers.

There is a phase when the contestants become aware of each other's proximity (either visually or by ground control) during which both sides make every effort to place themselves in a favourable position to attack. This usually involved a period of full throttle, steep climbing and sharp turning, probably at an unfavourable indicated air speed and possibly at a height well away from the maximum power altitude of the engine. The aeroplane with the more lively performance under such conditions has the advantage'.

Spitfire squadrons were used to attack the German fighter escorts in the Battle of Britain because of their superior fighting performance, notably in capacity to out-turn the enemy. The Spitfire was docile in the stall and the diving speed limit of the early aircraft had been raised to 450 mph EAS. The wing's elliptical planform gave a very low lift-dependent drag. The power available was thus not wasted and could be used fully to maintain speed and height in tight turns. Additionally, the low aspect ratio reduced the various stress loads on the wing structure which could be correspondingly lighter. On balance, in 1940 the Spitfire had the edge on contemporary fighters, notably the Messerschmitts Bf 109 and Bf 110 (when used as fighter bombers) and the American Curtiss Mohawk with which the French air forces were mostly equipped before the collapse of France in June 1940. The Curtiss however had much lighter ailerons at high speed and was so much better in rate of roll than the British fighters that much attention was directed to aileron response from then on. Fortunately the Focke-Wulf Fw 190 with its superior rate of roll did not appear until after the decisive Battle of Britain. The one factor on the British side which undoubtedly strongly influenced the result was the constant-speed propeller, which enabled the pilots automatically to use the optimum engine power under prevailing operational conditions and to fly their aircraft with the greatest efficiency.

Other detail improvements made in the production aircraft included an improved cockpit hood of curved form to replace the original flat type, a bullet-proof windscreen which could be cleared by a de-icing fluid system, armour plating behind the rear engine bulkhead and the pilot's seat, and an engine-driven pump for undercarriage operation. Most of the development of the Mks I and II however concerned the armament, on which the Air Staff placed much emphasis, to obtain even greater fire power despite the success of the eight-gun wing-mounted battery and the Browning machine-gun, the British version of the American Colt.

After the initial trials and acceptance of the Spitfire as a front-line fighter for the Royal Air Force and the making of the few modifications as outlined above, the only major requirement left was the increase of weight of fire power. Consequent upon the failure of the Westland Whirlwind four-cannon twin-engined fighter to meet performance and delivery expectations and the designation of the Bristol Beaufighter as its replacement—a process which took time—it became necessary to consider improving still further the eight machine-gun armament in the single-engined fighters. The rapid introduction of armour in enemy aircraft had to be countered by more fire power particularly when it became apparent during the night raids which followed the Battle of Britain that enemy bombers were being equipped with 20 mm cannon.*

The suffixes added to the Mark numbers of certain Spitfire variants referred to the armament fitted to the wings: A meant eight 0·303 Browning machine-guns;

*A Heinkel He 111 which crashed in October 1940 near the Gordon Boys' Home, Woking, was found to have belly-mounted cannon.

B, two 20 mm British Hispano cannon plus four 0·303s; C, the universal wing facilitating the fitting of differential combinations of cannon and machine-guns, as originally designed for the Mk III development, which was intended to embody all the improvements to the basic design as dictated by operational experience, particularly in action.

One of the more remarkable features of subsequent Spitfire developments was the ingenuity with which so many operational adaptations were made to meet requirements unforeseen at the time of the original thin-wing design. The contemporary Hurricane of more conventional structure was able to carry even heavier military stores at a later date but this did not detract from the dexterity displayed by the Supermarine designers, aided in no small measure by their official advisers. Lord Beaverbrook, in 1940, the newly appointed Minister of Aircraft Production, authorized the building of 30 Mk IB cannon-only wings. The completed Spitfire IBs assembled and tested at RAF Brize Norton were delivered to 19 Squadron to do their 'guinea pig' act once again, without much success at first.

A Spitfire VB during tests at Wright Field in 1943. (*USAF*)

At this point it is interesting to note that Mitchell was fully aware of the extreme importance of fire power in action, and several late notes in his diary testify to his interest in the F.37/35 specification for a cannon fighter. Against this, Supermarine specification 451 was issued by him on 29 March, 1936, for a version of the F.37/34 Spitfire design equipped with four 20 mm cannon. F.37/35 was eventually met by the Whirlwind. Later on Supermarine evolved a highly promising design for a twin-engined Spitfire as described elsewhere but stillborn because of preoccupation with developments of the Spitfire proper, and abandoned like the Supermarine B.12/36 bomber project. Mitchell's inspiration and that of his design team knew no bounds, nor did that of the Air Ministry who were preoccupied in devising a multiplicity of fresh specifications. Despite this burst of inventive technology, Supermarine's design resources had to be harnessed to the evolution of the Spitfire into its many variants with which story the rest of this section is devoted, except for that of the Seafire which is accorded special treatment.

223

As the war progressed, so the Spitfire was required to fly faster and higher. The aim was always to have the advantage of height. The Merlin XII gave a higher rate of climb and ceiling, as installed in the Spitfire Mk IIA, fitted with the standard eight 0·303 guns. With two cannon replacing the four inboard guns the type was designated IIB, a blister in the top skin of the wing provided clearance for the ammunition drum of the cannon.

Development of the Merlin engine by Rolls-Royce led to the introduction of a two-speed supercharger in the Merlin XX of 1,240 bhp, installed in the experimental Spitfire III intended as a major advance on the Mks I and II by embodying all the service experience gained so far. Top speed approached 400 mph but only two aircraft N3297 and W3237 were completed. New features, notably the clipped wings, retractable tailwheel, internal bullet-proof windscreen, strengthened undercarriage with wheel cover flaps when retracted, were incorporated in later Marks, which justified the 90,000 man hours spent in its design. Similarly the Mk IV was the first attempt to adapt the larger Griffon engine to the Spitfire airframe. This project became the prototype of the Mk XII.

The next stage, after fire power had been increased, was to improve the Spitfire's performance, especially at height, as the air battles were tending to take place at greater altitudes.* In addition, the massive formations known as fighter sweeps were being planned to carry the offensive over enemy-occupied territory, with Britain still fighting alone at that time. These fighter formations were largely composed of Spitfire Vs, which Mark had arrived through the evolution of the more powerful Merlin 45 with a greatly improved supercharger and induction system permitting much higher boost pressures. Much attention had been given to centrifugal supercharger development by A. C. Lovesey and S. G. (later Sir Stanley) Hooker of Rolls-Royce following the original work of J. E. Ellor, and the new Merlin 45, rated at 1,315 maximum hp at 16,000 ft, gave the Spitfire VA marked superiority over the latest Messerschmitt, the Bf 109F, which had appeared in May 1941.

The mass air flow philosophy of the Schneider R engines had been superseded by a quest for higher intake manifold pressures to increase power, almost a parallel situation to that of the Schneider Trophy races when the Italian engine designers mostly sought more power by increasing cubic capacity whereas Rolls-Royce went in for supercharging. The Daimler-Benz 601 series engines fitted in the Bf 109s had a 25 per cent greater displacement than the Merlin; consequently, Rolls-Royce were obliged to accelerate their development programme by introducing higher manifold pressures, to match the Daimler-Benz power, in aircraft fitted with Merlins. At the same time a lot of engineering had to be done to fit the basic airframe to take a quart in a pint pot! This was particularly true of the further developments involving the larger two-stage Merlin 61 and Griffon engines.

A Spitfire Mk I, X4334, was adapted at Hucknall with a Merlin 45, under the supervision of Ray Dorey who initiated a small batch of Hucknall conversions of Mk I/II airframes to Mk V standard, Supermarine then taking over the main production. A similar procedure was adopted when the Merlin 61 appeared as the fighter version of the Merlin 60 two-stage engine already being test flown in the Vickers Wellington VI high-altitude bomber under development. An immediate answer was needed to the Focke-Wulf Fw 190A-1 which had appeared suddenly during a fighter sweep over Northern France in September 1941.

*The highest recorded air combat of the Second World War was between a Spitfire VB (modified) and a Junkers Ju 86P.

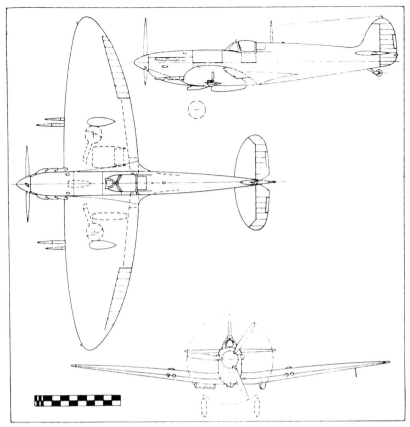

Spitfire Mk VB

It soon became clear that this new enemy type with its air-cooled radial engine, much larger than the Merlin and closely cowled to reduce drag, and with a superlative rate of roll, was decidedly superior to the Spitfire V. Conversion was in fact already in hand at Hucknall of two Spitfires to take the new Merlins 60 and 61, the former the existing Mk III N3297 and the latter a Mk I, R6700. Again Ray Dorey set up a conversion line for Mk IXs, as the Mk Vs with the Merlin 61 were designated. The new type which went into service late in 1942 was more than a match for the Fw 190. The two-speed two-stage supercharger of the 60 series, which embodied an aftercooler to permit even higher boosts, had provided the large increase of power required throughout the whole range of altitude.

Comparative trials were made by the Air Fighting Development Unit at Duxford between the Spitfire IX and a captured Focke-Wulf 190. The impression of the pilots involved was that provided the Spitfire had the initiative it had a good chance of victory. It had a slight advantage in speed except below 2,000 ft and between 18,000 and 20,000 ft. Because of better acceleration, the 190 had a slight advantage in initial climb, was faster in the dive and was more manoeuvrable, although the Spitfire could easily out-turn the German fighter. The 190 had a

225

superior rate of roll and if attacked by the Spitfire in a turn could flick over and dive in the opposite direction, which both the Mk V and Mk IX found difficult to follow. The manoeuvre was like the 'Immelmann' turn of the 1914–18 War brought up to date! To improve the Spitfire's roll characteristics, Middle East squadrons adopted the clipped wingtips and aileron gap shrouding suggested by Duxford but it took some time for Fighter Command to introduce similar modifications. This delay arose apparently from a difference of opinion between the AAEE and the AFDU as to the value of such modifications.

The final stage in development of the Spitfire as a fighting machine was the installation of the Rolls-Royce Griffon engine and the consequent redesign necessary to strengthen the airframe. However well the Merlin had done by way of increased power over a wide range of altitude performance, it was inevitable that sooner or later it would be overtaken by its larger relation which had a 36 per cent greater displacement. But it was not until the end of April 1944 that Spitfire XIVs became operational with the two-stage Griffon 61, the first to be superior to the Merlin at altitude. The adaptation of the Griffon, whose direct ancestors were the Buzzard and the Schneider R engine and was of a size at one time thought impossible for a Spitfire, was a remarkable feat of aircraft engineering. The installation of a Griffon III in a Spitfire VC airframe was undertaken at Hursley Park experimental workshop. Several major differences had to be accepted from Merlin installations, notably left-hand instead of right-hand propeller rotation; a girder-type engine mounting as distinct from the tubular-type then going out of fashion; and the provision of a separate accessory gearbox mounted on the fireproof bulkhead, driven through a shaft and coupling from the engine and dispensing with the festoon of accessories on and around the engine as previously practised.

Another factor that helped to squeeze the larger Griffon into the Spitfire airframe was the resiting of the camshaft and supercharger gear drives at the front of the engine instead of at the rear as on the Merlin. The drive-shaft for the rear-mounted supercharger and accessory gearbox was carried on bearings through the lower crankcase to save engine length. Even so, the Spitfire XII with the Griffon III was two feet longer than the original Mk I and this was mainly attributable to the five-blade propeller's very long spinner and the enlarged rudder to compensate for the added side area forward. When the time came to install the Griffon two-stage 60 range the intercooler was placed on top of the supercharger between the cylinder banks and so did not affect the length of powerplant installation. Cooling the high pressure airflow into the engine from two-stage supercharging was essential because of the very high temperatures generated thereby.

Early flight tests disclosed some roughness in handling the prototype Spitfire XII and this was later improved. The rate of roll of the Spitfire had already proved inadequate in the Battle of Britain days, according to Jeffrey Quill, who had flown with 65 Squadron during those hectic times. Later, metal-covered ailerons improved rate of roll and reduced stick forces at up to 350 mph. Further experiments by the RAE involved the fitting of balance tabs and reduction or elimination of the wing-aileron gap as first suggested by AFDU at Duxford.

So much development of the basic Spitfire design had been made by the end of 1943 to meet the ever increasing tempo of operational requirements and the widening band of differential usage, that a radical redesign was planned to bring together all the improvements to date into a Spitfire that was to be the last word in refinement and performance. Such a project had been planned long before with

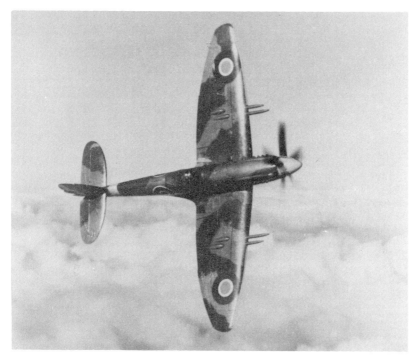

The end of the line. A Spitfire F.24 with slightly different planform but essentially the same structural concept as the original K5054.

the Griffon engine installed in the advanced Mk III airframe and classified as Mk IV, to become eventually the prototype of the Mk XII. To avoid confusion with previous variants already well tried, the newly designed airframe was classified as Mk 20, Roman numerals having officially given way to Arabic. One Mk 20 was built but its production version, Mk 21, was manufactured in quantity.

The main difference between the Mk 20 and previous types was the completely redesigned wings, of stronger construction and of slightly increased area, to accept increased weight and to improve performance at even greater heights. The original elliptical planform was retained to a large degree but in production aircraft the tips were rounded off so that the span was only an inch greater than that of the Mk XIV. All the experience gained from the many versions of earlier wings was embodied. The main load-bearing structure of the original Spitfire wing was the torsion box formed by the built-up spar at 25 per cent chord and the 14-gauge duralumin leading edge. In the new wing load-bearing was extended behind the spar with a series of torque boxes with rigid reinforcement at all openings for inspection panels. Armament was standardized at four 20 mm cannon.

Much attention was paid in the new wing design to solving the lateral control shortcomings of earlier Marks, especially the provision of maximum rate of roll. It was at this point that the collaboration between the Supermarine designers and Ministry and Service technicians came closest, despite claims of earlier official influence during the initial design stage which were only true in part.

In the new wing the ailerons were positioned further outboard, with piano-type hinges instead of the bearing type as on earlier Marks. The aerodynamics were the subject of much investigation at this time, ultimately resulting in the laminar-flow wing, with straight leading and trailing edges, which distinguished the Spiteful development as related later. For the Spitfire 21 and its derivatives the original conception of an elliptical wing form was retained.

Performance was also enhanced by the adoption of hydraulically-operated doors for the lower half of the wheels when retracted, thus presenting for the first time an unbroken underwing surface to the airflow, save for the blisters needed for the larger wheels. The undercarriage legs were strengthened and lengthened, partly to cope with the increased weight but mainly to allow the Griffon propeller to return to the same diameter as that of the Merlin-powered Spitfires, as earlier Griffon conversions had to use smaller propellers. Also for the first time the Mk 20 series embodied a larger wheel than all the predecessors from the original prototype, the Dunlop Company having been previously forced to increase tyre pressures and strengths to accommodate increased weights. The improved wing had design factors as follow: a theoretical aileron reversal speed of 850 mph compared with the 580 mph for earlier Marks; overall wing stiffness improved by 47 per cent; rate of roll 120 degrees per second at 300 mph. The speed of the Mk 21 was 450 mph, almost exactly 100 mph faster than that of the prototype Spitfire, with similar advances in figures for climb, ceiling and payload. Over the whole range of Spitfire and Seafire variants, of which 48 were identifiable, all-up weight had increased from 5,800 lb to over 11,000, engine power from 1,020 hp to 2,050 and maximum speed from the 364 mph of the Mk I to the 452 mph of the Seafire 47. A résumé of all the officially recognized variants follows.

Spitfires or Seafires were in action throughout the war in the front line of most theatres of operations. Their exploits have already provided aviation historians with a wealth of material, and stories of what they were and what they did will never end.

Type 300 F.I

Completed as day and night fighter with full navigational and lighting equipment, oxygen supply and two-way radio. Parachute flares for emergency landing, and CO_2 emergency system for lowering mainwheels. Fitted with reflector sight for eight 0·303 Browning guns and camera gun or cine camera. Bullet-proof windscreen and armour plate behind pilot seat (both fitted retrospectively); with cockpit heating and warm air to guns to prevent freezing. De-icing fluid spray for windscreen. Rear-view car-type mirror fitted retrospectively. Classification amended to distinguish between eight machine-guns as IA and IB with two 20 mm cannon displacing four of the 0·303 guns. Under Type 323 the 48th airframe of the Mk I production at Southampton was converted to a purely high-speed aeroplane for an attack on the World Air Speed Record and in accord with specification 35/35 for a high-speed type. Bearing the SBAC class B marking N17 this Spitfire, K9834, recorded 410 mph with a special Merlin IIIM engine of 2,160 hp. As German specially-designed types had already raised the record to nearly 470 mph, the attempt was abandoned. The all-up weight of the Spitfire I was quoted officially as 5,800 lb and its Merlin II or III of 1,030 hp gave it a speed of 364 mph, with an initial climb of 2,530 ft/min and a ceiling of 31,500 ft.

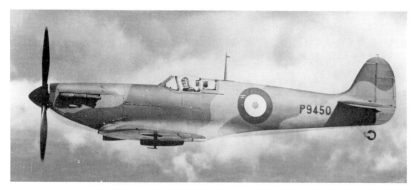

A Southampton-built Spitfire I with Merlin XII engine.

Type 329 F.IIA/B

With the Merlin XII of 1,150 hp to promote higher rate of climb and ceiling, the Mk II was the first type to be produced by the Castle Bromwich aircraft factory of Vickers-Armstrongs. Detail equipment was as for Mk I, with again a sub-division into IIA and IIB according to armament fitted as above. Originally designated IIC, some 50 Spitfire IIs were allocated to non-combatant duties for air-sea rescue, equipped with a dinghy and other survival gear stowed in the parachute flare chutes. In 1942 they were reclassified as Spitfires ASR.II to avoid confusion with the C universal wing. All-up weight of the standard Mk II was 6,150 lb, speed was 370 mph, climb was 2,600 ft/min and ceiling 32,800 ft.

Type 330 F.III

As already stated, the Mk III was to be the refined successor to the Mks I and II to enhance the already high reputation of the Spitfire. The engine was the two-speed Merlin XX of 1,240 hp. Clipped wings which reduced the span from the original 36 ft 10 in to 32 ft 7 in and a retractable tailwheel were other improvements, which

A Spitfire Mk III with Merlin XX, clipped wings and retractable tailwheel.

also included the moving of the bullet-proof portion of the windscreen to the inside to reduce drag. This Mark saw the introduction of the C universal armament wing later used on a number of other variants. Speed had increased to 385 mph but the Mk III did not go into production although its improved features were adopted in later Marks.

Type 337 F.IV

First attempt to install the larger Griffon in a Spitfire airframe led to the redesigned Type 356 Mk 20 series and the interim Type 366 F.XII, pressed into service to counter low-level raids by the Focke-Wulf Fw 190. (Not to be confused with PR Mk IV—see later.)

Type 349 F.VA/VB/VC and LF.VA/VB/VC

Most prolific production of all Marks, the V had six variants in high- and low-altitude roles, also with conversions to the early Seafires. To accept this differential use the high boost Merlin 45 was adapted in nine versions. With the universal wing adopted from the Mk III and the A and B wings already in use, a wide selection of armament was available. Armour protection increased and additional heating for outboard gun bays to permit high-altitude operation in VB and VC. Fuel supply improved with pressurized tanks over 25,000 ft. Landing lamps deleted and metal-covered ailerons introduced. For operation in Middle East, air intake filters provided in tropical versions. To increase range jettisonable fuel tanks could be fitted. For ground attack a 250 lb or 500 lb bomb could be carried in normal bomb cradle with adaptor to fuselage. Used for patrolling and fighting at all heights in temperate and tropical zones and adapted to many other operational requirements, the Mk V could be called the 'workhorse' of all the Spitfires. Speed (VA) 376 mph; weight (VC) 6,785 lb.

A Spitfire Mk VB tropicalized for the Western Desert. The intake duct housed a Vokes Millevee dust filter.

230

A high-altitude Spitfire Mk VI with extended wingtips, pressure cabin and four-blade propeller. Its Merlin 47 carried an accessory drive for the Marshall blower.

Type 350 F.VI

Pressure-cabin version of Mk VB to relieve pilot lassitude at 40,000 ft by providing atmosphere as at 30,000 ft under cabin pressure of 2 psi. Development of pressure-tight bulkhead, sealing of structural joints and pressure-tight glands for piping and control runs aided by previous experience on high-altitude Vickers Wellington V and VI. The Merlin 47 of 1,415 hp had an extra accessory drive for Marshall blower. Automatic cabin pressure-control valve later evolved to replace manual control. Ground detachable non-sliding cockpit hood with emergency jettison. Extended wingtips increasing wing area from standard 242 sq ft to 248·5 sq ft. Four-blade propeller for greater efficiency at height. All-up weight was 6,700 lb.

Types 351 and 360 F.VII and HF.VII

These Marks had the two-speed two-stage Merlin 60 and 70 series which brought new life to the Spitfire basic airframe, as first exploited fully by the Mk IX (an extemporization) by converting earlier airframes. The extended wingtips of the previous Mark were retained and the retractable tailwheel from the experimental Mk III was adopted. For the first time each wing leading edge carried a small fuel tank. The larger protuberances of the engine forward needed balancing by a larger rudder and trim tab at the rear as characterized subsequent Marks. The HF.VII had the Merlin 71 with a Bendix injection carburettor, an innovation for a British engine. Weight with the new Merlin had risen to 7,875 lb and speed of the HF.VII was 416 mph. Both types had the pressure cabin as developed on Mk VI.

231

Spitfire Mk VII MD124. This was the first variant with the two-speed two-stage 60 series Merlin.

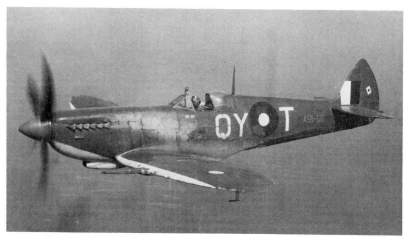

Spitfire HF.VIII A58-516 of the Royal Australian Air Force. (*RAAF*)

Type 359 F.VIII, LF.VIII and HF.VIII

Mk VIII was an unpressurized VII fitted with versions of the Merlin 60 and 70 series according to intended role. In high-level duties the extended tips remained, for low-level the standard Spitfire wingtips were clipped, and for normal duties the familiar Spitfire planform was retained. Most Mk VIIIs went to Italy and the Middle East and to the Far East where they replaced the Royal Australian Air Force's Spitfire Vs. Vokes Microvee air filters were standard fitments, to prevent ingestion of dust in desert and jungle warfare. This was an ancillary service never properly recognized.

Type 361 F.IX, LF.IX and HF.IX

Exigencies of war demanded immediate use of the Merlin two-stage engine of the 60/70 series to raise the performance of the Spitfire to match the Fw 190 and the Bf 109. Production of the Mk VIIIs could not catch up so conversion of Mk IIs and Vs to take the new engines was instigated by Rolls-Royce at Hucknall. Production facilities at the Castle Bromwich factory were switched from Mk Vs to IXs aided by common airframe components. The IXs mixed with Vs in operational sweeps confused opposing fighters because of the superior performance of the IXs, indistinguishable in the air. The addition of the intercooler radiator led to the symmetrical disposition of the underwing ducting for the first time. Mk IX introduced the 0·5 Browning gun to the universal wing which had two 20mm cannon outboard and two 0·5 guns inboard, this armament being signified by the suffix (e) to the nomenclature. It also used the gyro gunsight for the first time. Supercharger gear change was effected automatically by barometric pressure aneroid and a new 'universal' air intake system embodying the air filter with a shut-off control abolished need for tropicalization. Provision was made for carrying two 250 lb bombs at the cannon wing stations in addition to that made for a drop tank or 500 lb bomb centrally mounted as on Mk V. Normal all-up weight 7,500 lb. Maximum speed 416 mph.

233

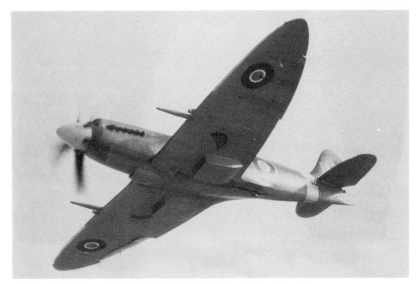

Spitfire Mk XIV RB140 with Griffon 65 engine.

Type 366 F.XII

The first Spitfire to enter service with the Griffon engine has already been discussed above as a milestone in the Mk IV development of the basic design. The engine, a Mk III, was larger and longer than the Merlin 61 although only fitted with a single-stage supercharger with no intercooler. With the very large spinner of the four-blade propeller and the large rudder to balance its increased side area, the overall length of the XII became 31 ft 10 in. It had improved speed at low

DP845, the prototype Spitfire F.XII seen with mock-up installation of six 20 mm cannon and modified single slotted flap.

234

Spitfire F.XII MB882 of No.41 Squadron. This was the first version to go into service with the Griffon engine.

altitude and to improve manoeuvreability the wings were clipped as on the experimental Mk III. The lengthening of the nose with the larger engine caused a deterioration of the pilot's view forward and the top cowling was 'tailored' by blisters over the cylinder banks to fit snugly and so improve his view between the vee so formed. Another change necessitated by the new engine was the removal of the oil tank from under the larger crankcase, to a position behind the fireproof bulkhead in front of the top main fuel tank and the hollow girder engine bearers carried the residue oil. The retractable tailwheel, as on Mk III, was also fitted after the first few of the one hundred XIIs produced.

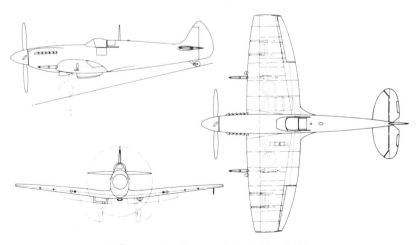

A Supermarine drawing of the Spitfire F.XII

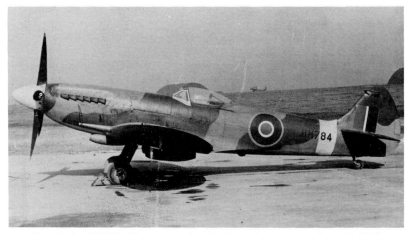

The Spitfire F.XIV with rear-view hood and cut-down rear fuselage. (*AAEE*)

Type 379 F.XIV, FR.XIV/XIV(e)

While the Mk XII was introduced into service as an interim type to take immediate advantage of the higher power of the Griffon at low level, the first Spitfire with this engine to be put into largescale production was the Mk XIV with the two-speed two-stage Griffon 65—so flexible in performance that no low-or high-altitude variants were necessary. Its mounting, designed by Supermarine, was assembled with the engine to form a complete powerplant. The first six XIVs were assembled at Hucknall with this power unit and airframes from Mk VIII production. Various figures have been quoted for the XIV but its low-level performance was good enough for it to be used to chase the V1 flying bombs, aided by a plus 21 lb/sq in boost from a special fuel. The FR.XIV and FR.XIV(e) were used for low-level sorties especially on photographic missions and incorporated for the first time a 'tear drop' cockpit hood giving rearward vision with the top line of the fuselage lowered.

Production Spitfire F.XIV RB140 with conventional cockpit.

236

Air Chief Marshal Sir James Robb's personal Spitfire XVI, presented to him for rapid transport by Supermarine. It was later put on display at the Montague Motor Museum, reclaimed as Government property and eventually sold for £150!

Type 361 LF.XVI

This was a version of the final LF.IX(e) using the same maker's Type number but powered with the Merlin 266 built by Packard of Detroit. Improvements in this Mark included increased tankage for longer range and the modified 'rear view' fuselage. Clipped wings were standardized when the type was largely used for ground attack.

Type 394 F.XVIII/FR.XVIII

The classic elliptical wing outline of the Spitfire had its final appearance with the PR.XIX, which actually was delivered a year earlier than the XVIII with the same wing shape. With strengthened wings and undercarriage the XVIII was the last stage in the chain of airframe development through the VII, VIII and XIV to the 'idealized' Spitfire in the 20 series. To facilitate its use for photographic as well as fighter reconnaissance, it had increased tankage.

A Spitfire FR.XVIII of No.31 Squadron over the Suez Canal in 1948.

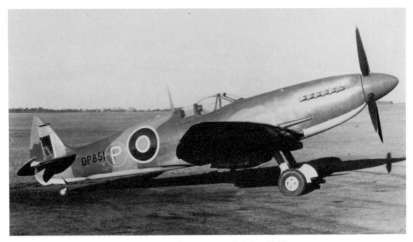

The second prototype Spitfire F.20.

Type 356 F.21, 22, 23 and 24

As the type number discloses, the 20 series had been long in materializing as the ultimate Spitfire development. The lateral control had at last been perfected and the main characteristics of the Mk 21 have been dealt with earlier. In the 22 and 24 the rear-view fuselage was embodied with enlarged tail surfaces as on the Seafire 46. A 24-volt electrical system was standardized. The Mk 23 was a proposed variant which did not materialize but was to have had a lifted leading edge giving improved aerodynamic performance.

Prototype Spitfire F.21, PP139. (*Vickers-Armstrongs*)

238

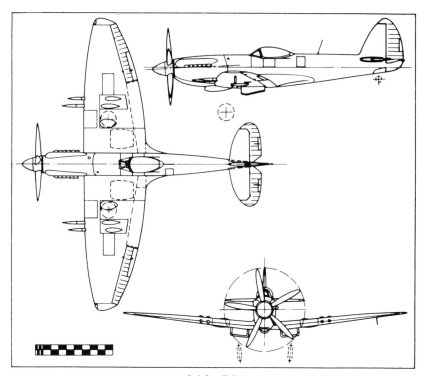

Spitfire F.24

Spitfire F.24 VN479. (*Vickers-Armstrongs*)

239

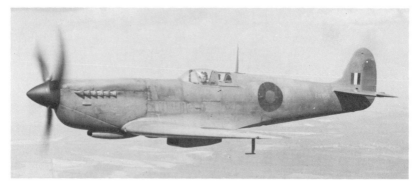

Spitfire PR.XI EN654, with Merlin 61 engine.

Photographic Reconnaissance

One of the Spitfire's most important duties, mostly non-combatant, was obtaining air intelligence of enemy positions by photographic reconnaissance. This activity had been initiated by Sidney Cotton in his Lockheed 12 in 1938 as an undercover civilian enterprise. The first PR sortie was made from a French base in November 1939 by a converted Spitfire I and from then on specific variants were developed under PR mark numbers. The first were the PR.IV and PR.VII, both converted from the basic Mk V. In the PR.IV the wing torsion box forward of the main spar was sealed to form integral fuel and oil tanks to promote increased range; the clean leading edge and curved windscreen (replacing the armoured glass) enabled the speed to be raised to 382 mph. Speed was the essential factor so as to get the pictures and return to base without heroic combat. Conversely, the PR.VII had a normal wing with 0·303 guns, with an extra fuel tank only in the rear fuselage. Its shorter range was compensated by its ability to fight its way home. Various arrangements of the F8, F24 and F52 cameras were fitted, with refinements such as lens dust-flaps and heating for high-altitude operations.

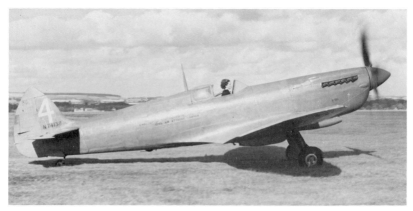

The Spitfire PR.XI used by the US Civil Air Attaché to the United Kingdom. It is seen being taxied by Lettice Curtis of the ATA. (*Flight International*)

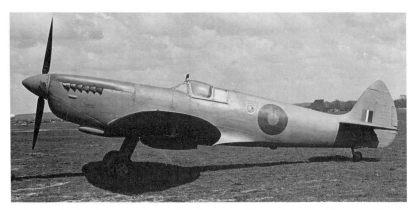

A pressurized and unarmed Spitfire PR.X converted from a Mk VII airframe and fitted with a Merlin 61.

The superior high-level performance of the Spitfire IX with its two-speed two-stage Merlin 61 series engine led to the PR.XI version with an advantage of five mph more than the standard IX. To suit varying requirements a 'universal' camera-mounting system was devised. The PR.X which oddly followed the PR.XI differed in having a pressure cabin and the 16 produced were converted from Mk VII airframes. The PR.XIII was a development of the armed PR.IV but with the Merlin 32 low-level engine. There were 26 examples converted from various Mark airframes by Heston Aircraft.

The appearance of the more powerful Griffon 61 series engines led to the PR.XIX which comprised a Mk XIV fuselage, tail and engine, modified PR.XI wings and the PR.X pressure cabin. By borrowing some camera space in the wings for more fuel tankage the capacity was 252 gallons, and drop tanks of 90 or 170 gallons could also be fitted if extreme range was required. A measure of Spitfire development may be gauged by comparison with the fuel capacity of the Mk I of 85 gallons!

Spitfire PR.XIX PS858, with 170 gal drop tank, on trials at Boscombe Down early in 1945. (*Ministry of Defence*)

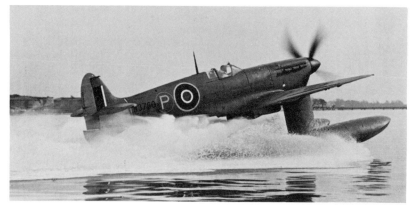

The prototype Spitfire floatplane W3760 on test from Southampton Water.

Special Conversions

In 1940 Spitfire Mk I R6722 was fitted with Blackburn Roc floats in response to a requirement for a fighter floatplane to operate from Norwegian fjords. The vertical stabilizing area was increased by an additional ventral fin. Flotation trials were unsatisfactory and the project abandoned with the sudden end of the Norwegian campaign.

A similar project was revived in 1942 for operation from secret Middle East waters. Spitfire VB W3760 was fitted with Supermarine floats mounted on faired cantilever struts attached to the mainplane spars. Trials were satisfactory after the addition of ventral fin with redesigned rudder. Two conversions with Merlin 45s of VBs EP751 and EP754 were made by Folland Aircraft at Hamble, and later LF.IXB MJ892 was converted with a Merlin 61 but the project was abandoned in 1943 when German forces occupied the Dodecanese islands. Six float conversion sets were sent to the Middle East and three aircraft were used at Alexandria.

Spitfire Mk IX floatplane MJ892 on trial off Hamble.

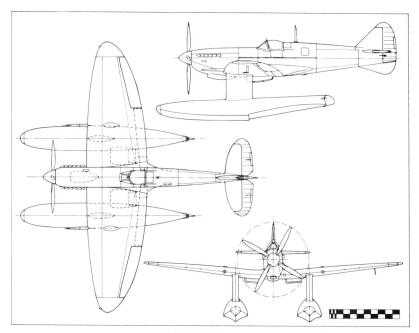

Spitfire IX floatplane

In 1946 a Mk VIII, MT818, was converted as a two-seat trainer under Type 502 with class B marking N32 but later registered G-AIDN. The front cockpit was moved forward to make room for a raised rear cockpit. It was used extensively for overseas demonstrations and subsequently as a private aircraft, under the company designation T8. Up to thirty Mk IXs were converted for overseas sales as two-seat T9 trainers, under Type 509.

Spitfire F.VIII MT818 after conversion to the demonstration trainer N32.
(*Charles E. Brown*)

243

The high-speed Spitfire N17, with variable-pitch propeller, on show in Brussels in 1939.
(*Flight International*)

Overseas Interest and Sales

Before the outbreak of war in September 1939 the exceptional qualities of the Spitfire had drawn a great deal of foreign interest especially from those countries who feared attack from other quarters. The display of the Speed Spitfire N17 at the Brussels International Salon of Aeronautics in July 1938 and of a specially-finished Spitfire I, K9814, at the Paris Aero Show in the following November helped to create a reputation unsurpassed by other exhibits. The first country believed to have made enquiries for Spitfires was Estonia which sent a military commission in July 1938 to Woolston and to Eastleigh for flying demonstrations.

Danish Air Force Spitfire F.IX 407 (*Hans Kofoed*)

A Portuguese Spitfire F.I.

Spitfire F.22s for the Egyptian Air Force.

Indian Air Force Spitfire T.9 HS534. The pupil occupied the front seat.

Following came Yugoslav, Belgian, French, Turkish and Swiss delegations, all of whose pilots flew Spitfire I K9791, allocated by the Air Ministry on special dispensation.

One result of these demonstrations and flight trials was a call for variable-pitch propellers. Orders were placed by France, Greece, Turkey, Portugal and Switzerland, but all failed to materialize (except the two Turkish aircraft delivered to export factors at Christchurch, Hants) on the basis that the British need for Spitfires at the end of 1939 was greater than theirs, although a French ordered aircraft fitted with a Merlin III engine was flown by George Pickering of Supermarine under the marking O-1. It was delivered on 12 July, 1939.

After the War, surplus Spitfires were in demand by various countries for re-equipping their air forces. This was to be expected because of the Spitfire's worldwide reputation throughout the years of major hostilities and the escalating cost of postwar military aircraft, especially the embryo jet fighters. As first-line equipment or as high-speed trainers Spitfires served mainly in Belgium, Burma, Denmark, Egypt, Eire, Greece, India, the Netherlands, Norway and Thailand. Various Spitfires of different vintages have been preserved in many parts of the world as memorials to this great aeroplane's unique career.

Spitfire

Engine. M=Merlin G=Griffon		I M II	LF.VB M 45/46 50	F.IXe M 61/63 63A	F.XIVE G 65	F.21 G 61/85
Span	ft in	36 10	32 2	36 10	36 10	36 11
	m	11·23	9·8	11·23	11·23	11·25
Length	ft in	29 11	29 11	31 0½	32 8	32 8
	m	9·1	9·1	9·45	9·96	9·96
Height (propeller vertical, tail down)	ft in	11 5	11 5½	11 8	11 8¼	11 9¾
	m	3·48	3·49	3·56	3·56	3·6
Wing area	sq ft	242	231	242	242	243·6
	sq m	22·48	21·45	22·48	22·48	22·63
Tare weight	lb	4,341	5,050	5,800	6,376	6, 923
	kg	1,969	2,291	2,631	2,892	3,140
Loaded weight normal	lb	5,800	6,650	7,500	8,475	9,182
	kg	2,631	3,016	3,402	3,844	4,165
Maximum speed	mph	364	357	408	439	450
	km/h	586	575	657	706·5	724
At height	ft	18,500	6,000	25,000	24,500	19,000
	m	5,639	1,829	7,620	7,468	5,791
Climb to 20,000 ft (6,096 m)	in min	9·4	5·6	5·7	7·0	8·0
Range, normal	miles	395	470	434	465	580
	km	636	756	698	748	935
At cruising speed	mph	210	272	324	271	230
	km/h	338	438	521	437	370
Initial rate of climb	ft/min	2,530	4,750	3,950	4,580	4,900
	m/min	771	1,448	1,204	1,396	1,494
Service ceiling	ft	31,500	35,500	43,000	43,000	43,000
	m	9,601	10,820	13,106	13,106	13,106
Armament 0·303-in machine-guns		8	4	Nil	Nil	Nil
0·5-in machine-guns		Nil	Nil	2	2	Nil
20 mm Hispano cannon		Nil	2	2	2	4

A Seafire I taking off from HMS *Victorious* early in 1942. (*Ministry of Defence*)

Seafire

One aspect of naval aviation that had received too little attention before the Second World War was the procurement of British shipborne single-seat fighters. The resurrection of German naval power posed a threat to the aircraft carriers in particular, and the subsequent acquisition of bases on the Atlantic seaboard from which air attacks against Allied shipping could be launched demanded full establishment of an up-to-date seaborne fighter force. There was neither time nor facility to design and develop a specialized type and such was the performance of the Spitfire and the Hurricane that the Admiralty requested some late in 1939. In January 1940 Supermarine produced a design called the Sea Spitfire, fitted with an arrester hook. In addition, one was designed with folding wings, and offered for delivery in October 1940, but the First Lord of the Admiralty, then Winston Churchill, decided against it so the folding-wing Seafire did not materialize for another two years partly because of this decision but more because of the emphasis on the build-up of home fighter defence.

In the autumn of 1941 the Admiralty finally obtained permission to acquire Sea Spitfires and the Air Ministry received a request for the conversion of 400 Mk VC Spitfires, but only 48 Mk VB and 202 Mk VCs were offered. The first aircraft to be fitted by Supermarine with an arrester hook was a VB, AB205, which first flew on 7 January, 1942, as a Hooked Spitfire. It was weighed at Worthy Down in January 1942 under Supermarine Type 340 and later called the Seafire Mk I,* the tare weight being 5,013 lb, and all-up weight 6,591 lb. The next VB airframe to be converted was AD371, again by Supermarine, being weighed at Worthy Down on

---

*The contraction Seafire from Sea Spitfire (c/f Sea Hurricane) was suggested by Mrs Freda Clifton, wife of Alan Clifton of Supermarine.

Seafire IICs over HMS *Indomitable*.

15 February, 1942, under Type 357 and called Seafire Mk II. This aircraft was fitted with a deck arrester hook and catapult spools, the weights increasing to 5,064 lb and 6,642 lb respectively.

Urgency was now put on Seafire production and orders were placed with Air Service Training of Hamble for 48 and with Cunliffe-Owen Aircraft at Eastleigh for 118, all conversions of Spitfire VBs. Supplementary contracts involved the production of arrester hooks which were fitted to Spitfires by RAF Maintenance Units. Known as Hooked Spitfires they were used by the Royal Navy for shore-based training, though some were actually operated from carriers later.

The first Seafire conversion was a Spitfire Mk VB, BL676, during January— February 1942 by AST, being fitted with an arrester hook, slinging points, and ballasted weights in the nose to correct the centre of gravity. It was tested at Worthy Down during March, and was flown by Lt Cmdr H. P. Bramwell DSO, DSC, to Arbroath on 8 May for initial deck-landing trials aboard HMS *Illustrious*. It was re-numbered MB328 as the first of the batch MB328 to MB375. These trials were successful and two variants were scheduled for production, the Seafire IB with Spitfire VB mainplanes and the Seafire IIC with Spitfire VC mainplanes, the suffixes being added from the original Spitfire versions. The design man hours for the Seafire I were 10,130 and for the Seafire II only 3,685 compared to the 339,400 for the Spitfire I, 90,000 approximately for the Spitfire V and 43,830 for the Spitfire IX. BL676 flew on sea trials during March and April 1942 from HMS *Victorious* off the Orkneys and again everything went satisfactorily, the only adverse comment being in relation to the view forward and downward.

Following the first trials of AB205 showing that a Spitfire could be successfully flown off a carrier, fifteen normal Spitfires were flown off HMS *Eagle* on 7 March, 1942, for Malta under Operation Spotter, and all reached the beleagured island safely. These were followed on 20 April by the take-off of forty-seven Spitfire VBs of 601 and 603 Squadrons from the carrier USS *Wasp* under Operation Calendar of which it is reported 46 arrived. On 9 May further reinforcements were sent by the take-off of 47 more from the *Wasp* and 17 from the *Eagle*, of which 59 safely arrived at Malta at a most critical period in the history of the island.*

*Spitfires operated mostly from Ta Kali airfield near Mosta and repeated the successes of the Battle of Britain. The air defence of Malta is a well-known saga starting with the actions of the three Gladiators, *Faith*, *Hope* and *Charity*.

One Spitfire returned to the *Wasp* and subsequently landed safely without an arrester hook, much to the surprise of all concerned because of the then high approach speed of 85 mph. This really proved the potential of the Spitfire, and its success over Malta was another pointer for its use from aircraft carriers. The Admiralty's operational philosophy had been changed from the use of the long-range Grumman Martlet fighter, with which the Fleet Air Arm was equipped, to the short-range interceptor Seafire, whose range indeed was its limitation but showed 50 mph speed advantage over the Martlet.

Type 340 Seafire I

The conversions of the Spitfires to Seafires were required as soon as possible and so the modifications were as few and as simple as possible. The A-frame arrester hook was hinged to the bottom longerons of fuselage frame 15, with legs six feet long. It was operated by a scissors-type snap gear holding the bill of the hook and released by the pilot via a Bowden cable and a lever in the cockpit; however, the hook could be lifted only by ground staff. Because of the extra stress imposed on the aft airframe, local strengthening was incorporated on the bottom longerons at the hook and also to the damping jack hinge-points. To reduce drag the A-frame was faired to the lower fuselage so only the hook's bill was left in the airflow. Slinging points with local strengthening were provided for use by the Royal Navy.

With these modifications, speed was reduced by five mph and empty weight increased by five per cent and so compared fairly favourably with its land counter-part, the Spitfire VB. Only MB328 to 375 were fitted with tropical radiators and oil coolers and supplied complete with both temperate and tropical air intakes. A complete list of the conversions is shown in the Appendices. The first Seafire IB is recorded as being taken on charge on 15 June, 1942, though most of them were routed from AST to Eastleigh for 38 MU and 76 MU and to Glasgow Docks, MB329 reaching the docks with MB330 on 7 July for shipment to HM ships.

The second conversion Seafire, BL687. This aircraft became MB329.

The only squadron to be completely equipped with the Seafire IB was 801 which was embarked in HMS *Furious* from October 1942 until September 1944. As *Furious* had T-shaped lifts, the aircraft could be struck below and with no catapult the lack of spools on the Seafires did not matter. The second squadron to receive them was 842 but not until the summer of 1943 when they were embarked on the escort carrier *Fencer*. Other units to have them on strength were 1 and 2 Naval Fighter Schools at Yeovilton and Henstridge respectively, the School of Naval Air Warfare at St Merryn, RNAS stations at Lee-on-Solent and Stretton and 760 (R) Sqn at Yeovilton.

Type 357 Seafire F.IIC, FR.IIC and Type 375 LR.IIC

The Seafire IIC was a Seafire I modification plus catapult spools, a strengthened fuselage and undercarriage, a Merlin 32 engine and a four-blade Rotol propeller. The prototype, AD371, first flew in February 1942 after being converted by Supermarine, and was delivered to the RAE Farnborough on 25 February for further trials, eventually going to 778 Squadron at Arbroath. To counter these alterations three ballast weights of 27 lb each were fitted in the nose to bring the centre of gravity back to a reasonable position. The production version engine was the Merlin 45 or 46 in common with the Seafire IB to reduce the amount of engine spares needed to be carried aboard ship. With the alterations increasing the tare weight of the Spitfire VC by six per cent and the increased drag from the hook and spools, the top speed of the Seafire IIC was 15 mph less than the Seafire IB. The boost was increased to plus 16 lb/sq in but the same applied to the IB so that the differential remained the same; the Admiralty could not have everything. However, 200 were ordered in March, and the first for the Royal Navy, MA971, was delivered on 2 June, 1942, to 38 MU and on 7 July to RNAS Lee-on-Solent, the same date as the first IB arrived at the docks; MA970, the first of the order, going to the RAE on 19 June for extensive trials. All were fitted with tropical radiators and oil coolers, and alternate temperature and tropical air intakes were supplied but, because of their drag which reduced the top speed by as much as 25

A Seafire IIC caught by a carrier's arrester wire.

250

mph and the rate of climb by 300 ft/min, tropical air-intake filters were rarely used.

The Merlin 45 and 46 engines were found to give the Spitfire and Seafire a mediocre performance at low level where most naval interceptions took place. So when Spitfire L1004 was tested with a Merlin 32 giving 1,645 hp at low altitude in December 1942, the Royal Navy immediately requested the fitting of them in their Seafire IICs. The Merlin 32 increased the top speed at sea level to 316 mph and 335 mph at 6,000 ft and it also reduced take-off run and increased the rate of climb at low altitudes. This engine was therefore essential and transfer of them from Fairey Barracuda II production was ordered. A four-blade propeller was fitted for low-level efficiency, and a Coffman cartridge starting system was also introduced making the starting independent of external power supplies. No engine mounting ballast weights were required, the engine being that much heavier. With this power unit the aircraft as Type 375 was designated Seafire L.IIC. From this time all Seafire aircraft were fitted with propellers having four or more blades.

To improve lateral control, a few Seafire L.IICs had their span reduced which increased the rate of roll and also maximum level speed by about 5 mph. This however lengthened the take-off run and reduced the service ceiling. So the decision to use normal or clipped wings was left to squadron commanders.

One other modification was the fitting of two F24 cameras, one vertical and one oblique. The centre of gravity shift was compensated by one ballast weight. With these modifications the hybrid designation was PR L. II, the first conversion being MB194 in July 1943 by Heston Aircraft, who did all other conversions. By 1944 the designation had been officially changed to FR.IIC or LR.IIC as the operation might dictate.

Various modifications were undertaken on the Seafire IICs, such as the fitting of a bomb rack between the undercarriage legs to carry a 250 lb bomb, and there were trials of Rocket Assisted Take Off Gear (RATOG), initially on MB141/G and MB125. As late as 1947 a Rotol braking propeller was flown on NM938 but it went only into zero pitch. This was an endeavour to eliminate the 'float' on landing rather than shortening the ground run. The career of the IIC was rather short because of the lack of folding wings and so when the Mk III went into production the version was phased out except for a few LR.IICs.

Type 358 Seafire F.III, LF.III, FR.III

Following the preliminary design studies of early 1940 for a folding-wing version of the Spitfire, the first production Seafire IIC, MA970, was fitted with a new set of mainplanes incorporating a double fold to reduce height as well as width for lift clearance and hangar storage aboard all Royal Navy aircraft carriers. The inner wing folded just inboard of the cannon mounting. Each hinge was formed at the top boom of the front spar and at the rear spar, the locking point being at the bottom of the front spar, where a tapered bolt was screwed into appropriate mating lugs. Fairing doors were provided in the top skin to cover the gaps in the fold line at the hinges, these and the main bolt being locked by means of pins operated by cable from a single lever in the wheel bay. Locating spigots were provided at the leading edge, front spar and trailing edge, the gun-heating ducts being provided with a felt butt-joint at the fold. The wings folded gave the aircraft dimensions of 13 ft 4 in wide and 13 ft 6 in high; the folding and spreading operations required a party of five men. MA970 was first flown during November 1942 and then used for further development work, being wrecked in 1944.

The Seafire III went into production as the Type 358, fitted with a Merlin 55 series engine which incorporated an automatic boost control giving the best performance from the engine at all altitudes with a four-blade propeller. A few early ones were fitted with a three-blade type but were modified before delivery. As production progressed a modified undercarriage with strengthened torsion-link oleo legs was fitted as the early ones not so fitted were considered unsuitable for deck landings.

The Seafire III showed a marked improvement in performance over its predecessors, production being initially undertaken by Westland Aircraft. The first 103 were F.IIIs starting with LR766 which was delivered on 8 June, 1943, to Worthy Down for contractor's handling trials, though this aircraft and the following 25 did not have folding wings; some were fitted with them later and so were brought up to the full F.III standard. A total of 1,263 was eventually produced, 913 by Westland and 350 by Cunliffe-Owen. Production issues began with 103 F.IIIs from Westland after which the Merlin 55M engine was fitted instead of the Merlin 55. This new engine had a cropped supercharger impeller giving 1,585 hp at 2,750 ft compared with the 1,470 hp of the Merlin 55 and the type so powered was called the Seafire LF.III. The first F.III was taken on charge by 894 Squadron on 27 November, 1943, followed shortly after by 887, 889, 801 and 880 Squadron, but the first non-folding LF.III was not taken on charge until February 1944.

The final Merlin-engined variant was the FR.III which was the LF.III fitted with two F24 cameras and the final 129 of those built by Cunliffe-Owen were of this variant. At the cessation of the war eight out of the twelve Seafire Squadrons were equipped with them.

A Seafire III with rocket projectiles.

All Seafire IIIs could be fitted with RATOG and could carry either two 250 lb bombs under the wings or a 500 lb bomb under the fuselage, provision was also available for the fitting of a 30-gal drop-tank in place of the 500 lb bomb. PR314 was fitted with two 250 lb depth charges on standard wing racks and flown on 2 March, 1945, and the handling was completely satisfactory; it was also flown on 23 March, 1945, by Lt G. P. Shea-Simmonds, at the request of AAEE with two 200 lb smoke floats, fitted one under each wing and one 45-gal drop tank under the

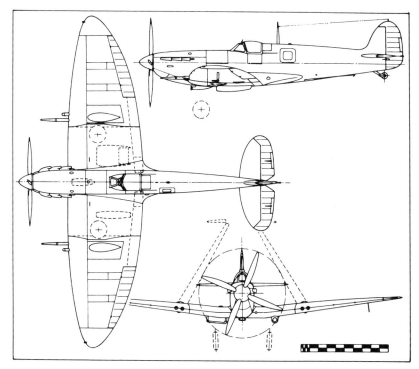

Seafire Mk III

fuselage. It was found that the handling at up to 390 knots was satisfactory but it was noticed that the directional stability had been adversely affected at low speeds and high engine power. SP182 was fitted with a 90-gal drop tank and flown on 31 August, 1945, for general handling trials. It was found that these qualities were poor but not dangerous. The aircraft was unstable longitudinally and was unpleasant for deck landings so the tank was not fitted in service.

Seafire IIIs saw service with most of the FAA units including eight in the Far East and flew in almost all the war theatres including over the main islands of Japan. After VJ day however the Mk III only remained in service until March 1946 when its last two squadrons, 887 and 894, were disbanded.

An order for twelve Seafire IIIs was signed on 31 August, 1946, for the Irish Air Corps, to be numbered 146—157 and all naval attachments removed and so converted to Spitfire Mk VCs. The first was accepted by a representative of the Irish Department of Defence, at South Marston on 24 January, 1947, and delivered to Baldonnel on 17 February, with the last on 27 September, 1947. Most remained in use until 1955 when they were superseded by Percival Provost T.51s and T.53s. Forty-eight Seafire IIIs were transferred to the French Navy and used on their aircraft carrier *Colossus*. On 30 January, 1947, they stated that 450 landings had been made successfully with only the loss of three machines. Thirteen more Seafires, mostly Mk IIIs, were likewise transferred in June 1949 though some of these were the later Mk XV.

Type 377/386 Seafire F.XV

The Royal Navy, having had experience with the earlier Seafires, were looking for improvement in performance, and Supermarine wrote their specification 471 on 29 January, 1943, offering a Seafire with a Griffon engine having a two-speed single-stage blower. Investigations had shown that the requirements could be met with a modified Seafire III airframe. The engine installation would be similar to the Spitfire F.XII but with a cooling system to meet tropical requirements, the fuel systems would be 100 gal internal and 60 gal in drop tanks, the fuselage would be similar to the Seafire III with Spitfire F.XII engine modifications, minor changes to deck arrester hook and catapult spools attachments, Spitfire F.VIII rear-spar attachment, fuselage tail end with retractable tailwheel and also main chassis.

The Air Ministry issued specification N.4/43 for six prototypes to be built by Supermarine, NS487, NS490, NS493, PK240, PK243 and PK245 under Type 377. In June 1943 the Griffon specified was the Mk VI (RG14SM) fitted with a Rotol 10 ft 5 in diameter four-blade propeller, the engine giving an output of 1,750 hp. The Seafire XV followed the Spitfire XIV because it had been decided that there would be no break or mix-up in the different types and each would be numbered consecutively.

The first, NS487, was weighed at the experimental hangar at Hursley Park on 4 December, 1943, and quoted as having an all-up weight of 7,861 lb under Type 377. Orders were placed with Cunliffe-Owen and Westland early in 1944.

On the first few of the 384 XVs, the hook was the A-frame hook of the Seafire III, but later aircraft had a newly designed 'sting' type hook anchored to the fuselage stern at the base of the rudder. The hook was spring-loaded in its housing and, when released, extended aft about 18 inches. On release, the arm and housing of the hook were free to drop into the fully lowered position suitable for engaging the deck cables, and also to pivot laterally within an included angle of about 30 degrees. The lowering of the hook was assisted by an oleo-pneumatic damper which also prevented the hook from rebounding on hitting the deck. After a deck landing, the hook was stowed and its housing locked up manually.

A Seafire XV with sting hook on the *Pretoria Castle*.

A feature of the early Seafire XV rudder was the trim tab which extended aft of the trailing edge. When the 'sting' hook was introduced to reduce the pull of the arrester wire which caused a nose-down pitching moment with the A-frame hook system, a portion of the base of the rudder was sacrificed and to restore the effective area the rudder was enlarged. The resulting outline of the rudder embraced the tab and was slightly taller than before. The hook housing was enclosed in a fairing which joined the lines of the rudder and fuselage, and the whole effect was pleasing. When in flight with the hook locked up, this fairing provided extra fin area.

There was no intercooler on the engine but the external appearance was that of an aircraft having an intercooler radiator, because of the two familiar large radiator fairings. The starboard fairing housed the conventional coolant radiator and the port fairing housed an additional coolant radiator as well as the oil cooler. At this stage the short unused 20 mm gun stub in the leading edge, previously apparent in the universal wing, had disappeared. Another slight change regarding armament was the introduction of Mk V 20 mm guns in place of Mk II. These guns had a shorter barrel and had to be cocked initially on the ground by hand. To prevent deck cables from fouling the tailwheel, a simple tubular guard was attached to the underside of the fuselage just forward of the tailwheel on the last fifty Seafire XVs.

The Seafire XV showed great improvement over the Mk III variants, having a top speed of over 390 mph and a rate of climb of over 4,000 ft/min. Because of the change-over from Seafire III to XV production by both Westland and Cunliffe-Owen, the first production aircraft was delayed before entering service with 802 Sqn in May 1945, even though the prototype NS487 was first flown in February 1944 and the first production aircraft, SR446, was delivered on 26 September, 1944.

Various combinations of modifications resulting from experience gained in earlier trials were assessed to improve the deck-landing characteristics. Four Seafire XVs, NS490, PK240, PK243 and SR448, also the prototype N.7/44, TM379 (navalized Spitfire 21 and prototype Seafire 45), were used in deck-landing trials on HMS *Pretoria Castle* from 20 November, 1944. In the trials report Lt Cdr E. M. Brown specified the differences on each aircraft as (1) NS490 sting-type hook, improved hook damping and propeller fine-pitch stop advanced; (2) SR448 V-frame hook, improved hook damping and strengthening, propeller fined-off; (3) PK243 V-frame hook, propeller fined-off, controllable radiator flaps, stronger wheels and tyres; (4) PK240 V-frame hook, five-blade propeller. To sum up he concluded that the incorporation of the sting hook with improved damping, the larger throttle box, the five-blade airscrew (or the fined-off four-blade in event of production difficulties) and the stronger wheels and tyres, were essential.

The installation of the Rolls-Royce Griffon VI into the Seafire brought with it problems with the M ratio supercharger clutch. This had a tendency to slip at high rpm and high boost and thus was unreliable for take-off and landing on carriers. The XV therefore saw no service from carriers until the fault was remedied early in 1947, after which the engine was very reliable and was used for the Seafire XVII.

Other trials included the fitting of a large-chord sting-hook type rudder on NS490 which was test flown by Lt Shea-Simonds and Lt Cdr J. K. Quill, Supermarine's chief test pilot then serving with the Fleet Air Arm to study the operation of the Seafire under active service conditions, during January 1945, and proved to be effective. SR448 was used for spinning trials in March 1945, NS493 for fuel transfer test from wing tanks, and handling and fuel functioning trials, with combat wing tank, on PK245. Metal elevators on Cunliffe-built PR338 were found entirely satisfactory on test but similar ones on Westland-built PK243 were overbalanced and considered dangerous. It was felt that the whole standard of manufacture of these metal-covered surfaces should be greatly improved and much thought was given to this problem and many tests made.

A report from Jeffrey Quill to Rear Admiral Boyd, the Fifth Sea Lord, in command of naval air services, made various recommendations to improve the Seafire and its *modus operandi*. One of these was that the undercarriage should be strengthened and accordingly long-stroke oleo legs with reduced rebound characteristics were fitted to SR454. Although large-area flaps fitted at the same time proved ineffective for their purpose, the oleo legs were considered a great improvement and were introduced into the Seafire XVIIs which followed the Mk XVs.

Another major modification to a Seafire XV, NS493, was 'put into effect' by Westland and consisted of the cutting down of the aft fuselage to the level of the longerons and the fitting of a 'tear-drop' canopy to improve rearward vision. After tests of several shapes with different refractive indexes, the selected one was fitted to the last Seafire XVs making them almost Mk XVIIs.

Although the XV saw no wartime service it was used extensively afterwards, and during 1949 fifteen were lent by the Admiralty to France with a further 45 to follow, but it is not known how many were actually delivered. A further twenty were 'de-navalized' by Airwork at Gatwick during 1951 under serials G.15-212–231 for flying tests and delivered to the Burmese Air Force at Mingaladon airbase near Rangoon from whence they saw service in 1957/58.

Type 384 Seafire F.XVII

The Seafire XVII was a direct development of the Mk XV and the prototype was a rebuild of the third, NS493. The alterations included the rear-view hood, a curved windscreen in front of the bullet-proof portion, provision for two wing bombs and two $22\frac{1}{2}$-gal wing combat tanks or eight rocket projectiles. A 24-volt electrical system replaced the former 12-volt installation and the XVII was the first Spitfire or Seafire to have it. Rocket assistance for shortening take-off run was provided and, after four minutes burning, the rocket sabots were jettisoned. The long-stroke undercarriage facilitated adoption of the American method of dropping the aircraft straight into the restraining deck cables instead of flying it in.

The F.XVII entered service with 883 Sqn in September 1945 and in 1947 a few were modified to take two F24 cameras, one vertical and the other oblique. Alternatively, a 33-gallon tank could be fitted to give 60 miles more range.

Thus, with a strengthened main spar permitting the greater use of external stores, at last the Seafire was a truly naval aeroplane and what the Navy had really wanted from the first, and the basic Spitfire design had once again proved its unique versatility. However, the conversion process from a land-based aircraft to a true deck-landing fighter had taken a long time and when at last the Mk XVII was in action the war was nearly over, much in the same way that the improved Walrus design, the Sea Otter, had also nearly 'missed the boat'. Only 232 Seafire XVIIs were built. The last was withdrawn from service in November 1954 and the last one produced, SX389, did not leave the Westland factory until 1952, being held there as a pattern for spares.

A Seafire XVII on the approach to HMS *Illustrious*.

Preparing a Seafire XVII for catapulting from HMS *Illustrious*.

A Mk XVIII Seafire was planned, according to minutes of a meeting between Rolls-Royce and Supermarine held at Boars Hill on 10 October, 1945. This variant was to be fitted with a Griffon 36 but all that is known is that one such engine was delivered to Hursley Park experimental shop. Nothing came of this project and Mk XVIII was allocated to the Griffon-powered reconnaissance development of the Spitfire Mk XIV.

Type 388 Seafire F.45

When the basic Spitfire design was re-engineered into the Mk 21 it was natural for the Admiralty to require a navalized version with the attendant performance advantages. Specification N.7/44 was issued and Mk 45 was allocated to the conversion which was sub-contracted to Cunliffe-Owen, Supermarine retaining the design authority, as with all other similar transactions. The reason for the jump in Mark numbers was a decision at a former stage for future Spitfires and Seafires to be numbered consecutively, to make provision for further development of the basic designs. The change of name to Spiteful and Seafang put a stop to this process which came to an end in the Spitfire range at Mk 24.

With the Griffon 61 the Seafire 45 had a speed of 442 mph, some 45 mph faster than previous Marks. The first conversion was TM379 and its 'sting' arrester hook gave it a length of 33 ft 4 in, the greatest yet. Its standard Spitfire 21 wings had no folding joints, and so this type was used mainly from naval shore airbases because it had a swing on take-off through the high power, transmitted through a five-blade propeller. To cure this, Quill tested TM379 on 10 April, 1945, with a contra-rotating propeller, and two other 45s, LA442 and LA444, were fitted with the Griffon 85 driving a contra-rotating propeller, so leading to a second-stage development, the Seafire 46. A few 45s were in fact equipped with this engine and drive combination. With certain modifications such as a larger-chord rudder and elevator the directional stability of the 45 was considered superior to that of the Seafire XV and the Spitfire 21. In diving trials with Seafire 45 LA494, Mach 0·88 was recorded and it was claimed as the Navy's fastest ever propeller-driven aircraft. Sea trials on HMS *Pretoria Castle* involved 239 landings by Mk 45s TM379, LA440, LA441, LA454 and LA480, with only two minor undercarriage failures.

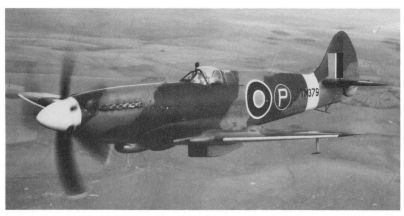

Prototype Seafire F.45 TM379 with four cannon, and the hook housing in the rudder.

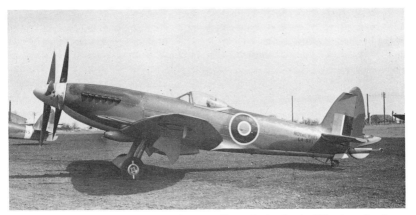

A Seafire F.46 with contra-rotating propeller and sting hook. (*The Aeroplane*)

Type 388 Seafires F.46 and F.47

These were the ultimate in the great development range of the basic Spitfire design. From a recognition point of view the most apparent differences between these and their forebears were the contra-rotating propeller, the rear-view hood (also on the Seafire XVII) and the increased fin and rudder area. The first enabled still more power to be absorbed (Griffon 87 and 88) and in particular eliminated the inevitable torque effect of a 'one-handed' propeller when landing and taking-off, particularly on aircraft carriers. The rear-view hood gave better visibility and in the first F.47 was combined with a smooth curved windscreen in place of the flat panel of the earlier bullet-proof glass.

PS944, the first production Seafire F.47, with contra-rotating propeller. This type was the fastest of the species.

259

Increased fin and rudder area was necessary to balance the forward side area of the 'dual' propeller and the extra long spinner, and additional area was provided in the tailplane and elevators. The fairing on the underside of the engine on the 47 was improved to embrace the air-intake filter and bring the opening of the duct right forward to just behind the propeller. This improved the aerodynamic line along the underside of the aircraft.

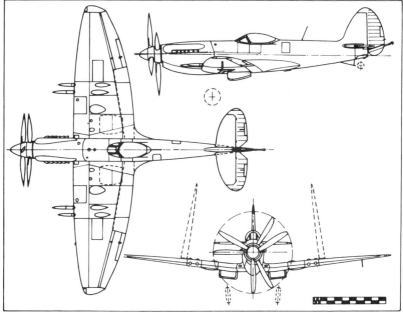

Seafire F.47

Although the Seafire 46 owed its origin to the Spitfire 22 its relationship was soon lost and the first production F.45, TM 383, was converted by Cunliffe-Owen into the prototype F.46, principally by the installation of the 24-volt electrical system and a 'cut-down' rear fuselage to take full advantage of the 'bubble' type canopy. This Mark was an interim type without wing folding and the first production model, LA541, was flown in October 1945, from Vickers' South Marston factory, where it had been assembled from components made at Castle Bromwich. It had the Griffon 86 but the production batch of 24 were fitted with the Griffon 87, except LA545 which flew in March 1946 with a Griffon 88. This engine had the Rolls-Royce combined fuel-injection and transfer-pump system in place of the Bendix-Stromberg induction-injection carburettor, as fitted to the other Griffons. No Seafire 46s saw operational service but were delivered to naval air stations at Anthorn and Chithorn, three to the Empire Test Pilots' School at Cranfield, and some did see service with 1832 Volunteer Reserve Squadron and 781 Training Squadron.

To meet the Navy's requirement a new wing fold was incorporated in the Seafire 47. This time the hinge was outboard of the gun, and only the outer wing folded upwards while the wingtip remained fixed. This was different from earlier Seafires but kept height within 13 ft 10 in although the folded span was 25 ft 5 in.

A Seafire F.47, with long-range tanks, at Boscombe Down. (*Crown copyright*)

At first the wing folding and spreading was done manually and a jury strut was fitted to secure the wings when folded, but later hydraulic power folding and spreading was installed and the strut became unnecessary.

With extra leading-edge fuel tanks, rear fuselage tanks, combat tanks and a 90-gallon drop-tank, it was possible for this version to carry 287 gallons of fuel giving it a range of about 1,000 miles. Another 'best' concerned with the Seafire 47 was a top speed of 452 mph. For reconnaissance purposes some 46s and all 47s had two electrically-heated cameras, one vertical and one oblique, in the rear of the fuselage. The vertical camera aperture in the bottom of the fuselage had a spring-loaded mud flap for protection during take-off. The flap was released in flight.

Seafire F.47 PS945 at RNAS Ford as instructional airframe A2186.

The FR.47 was cleared for all forms of flying at 11,100 lb all-up weight, but for take-off and gentle flying only it could weigh as much as 12,900 lb. The distance between the forward and aft limits of the centre of gravity was only six inches. This characteristic was only achieved after considerable effort to perfect the longitudinal stability which had been found unable to meet the current requirements. This was at the end of 1946 when the first Seafire 47, PS944, had been delivered to the AAEE at Boscombe Down. Another unexpected phenomenon discovered was that the performance of the first two Seafire 47s was inferior to that of the comparative Spitfire 24 because of the new-style air intake close behind the contra-rotating propeller. As this arrangement appeared to set up some aerodynamic interference, the original type intake was restored on later aircraft without impairing the under-fuselage lines.

A total of ninety Seafire 47s was built and, unlike the Seafire 46, did see operational service in Malaya making rocket attacks against bandit hideouts, and in the Korean War where they completed 115 sorties against enemy territory and made 245 marine interceptions. So the Spitfire saga finished where it started—in action, with the Mk I in the Battle of Britain and the Seafire 47 in Korea. The naval variants led via the Seafang to the first operational jet aircraft in the Royal Navy, the Attacker.

Seafire

Engine. M=Merlin. G=Griffon		F.IIC M 45/46	F.III M 55M	F.XV G VI	F.46 G 87	F.47 G 87/88
Span	ft in	36 10	36 10	36 10	36 11	36 11
	m	11·23	11·23	11·23	11·25	11·25
Length	ft in	30 2½	30 2½	32 3	33 7	34 6
	m	9·2	9·2	9·8	10·24	10·5
Height (propeller vertical,	ft in	11 2½	11 5½	10 8½	12 6	12 6
tail down).	m	3·42	3·49	3·26	3·81	3·81
Wing area	sq ft	242	242	242	244	243·6
	sq m	22·48	22·48	22·48	22·67	22·63
Tare Weight	lb	5,215	5,317	6,300	7,100	7,625
	kg	2,365	2,412	2,858	3,220	3,459
Loaded weight, normal	lb	6,665	7,232	8,000	9,400	10,200
	kg	3,023	3,280	3,629	4,264	4,627
Maximum speed	mph	365	359	392	443	452
	km/h	587	578	631	713	727·4
At height	ft	16,000	36,000	36,000	25,000	20,500
	m	4,877	10,973	10,973	7,620	6,250
Range, normal	miles	493	465	430	435	405
	km	793	748	692	700	652
At cruising speed	mph	188	272	255	272	260
	km/h	303	438	410	438	418
Climb to 20,000 ft (6,096 m)	min	5·7	8·1	7·0	7·4	4·8
Initial rate of climb	ft/min	2,950	3,250	4,000+	3,750	4,790
	m/min	899	991	1,219+	1,143	1,460
Service ceiling	ft	32,000	36,000	35,500	41,000	43,100
	m	9,754	10,973	10,820	12,497	13,145
Armament 0·303-in machine-guns		8	4	4	Nil	Nil
20 mm Hispano cannon		Nil	2	2	4	4

Spiteful and Seafang

The quest for improved performance, in particular speed, had always been in the forefront of Spitfire development. The 'idealized' Spitfire represented by Type 356 and identified by Mk 21 was evidence of this policy. But its final consummation involved the introduction of the laminar flow wing. In the event this advanced aerodynamic refinement gave way in the Mk 21 to an improved but more conventional wing of elliptical profile as previously described. The laminar flow wing itself led at last to a new name for a Spitfire development and the resultant aeroplane was called the Spiteful, with a naval version known as the Seafang.

As greater engine powers became available the speed of aircraft continued to rise dramatically and the effects of air compressibility began to be felt. The formation of shock waves, as the airspeed approached the speed of sound, was already familiar to propeller designers striving to maintain propulsive efficiency at very high tip speeds. Aerodynamic researchers had foreseen the increasing drag of aircraft leading to the concept of a 'sound barrier' limiting speed, defined as Mach 1 at sea level. The real barrier proved to be changes in control characteristics as shock waves moved across wing and tail surfaces. Spitfire pilots had observed with interest that the Focke-Wulf Fw 190 sometimes failed to recover from a steep dive under full power as a result of the loss of elevator control at high Mach numbers.

To investigate these problems, a programme of research was initiated at the Royal Aircraft Establishment using both model tests in their new high-speed wind tunnel which had become operational in 1943 and in full-scale flight tests on Spitfires. The flight programme was labelled as 'measurement of tail loads' but was more graphically described by one of the Aerodynamics Flight pilots as 'an attempt to break the world air speed record vertically downwards'. Several pilots took part in the trials, which consisted of diving the aircraft at full power from about 40,000 ft reaching their peak Mach numbers at around 25,000 to 30,000 ft. Towards the end of 1943 Sqn Ldr J. R. Tobin reached an indicated Mach 0·92 flying Spitfire PR.XI EN409, but later trials in 1946 by Sqn Ldr A. F. Martindale in another Spitfire XI produced more accurate static pressure corrections. In consequence, report R & M 2222 records that 'a Spitfire XI has been dived to a Mach number of about 0·90; this is probably the highest Mach number which has yet been recorded in flight on any aircraft in the world'.

A Spitfire PR.XI, flown by Sqn Ldr Martindale, seen at Farnborough after having lost its propeller in a high-speed dive.

Several other types of high-speed aircraft were tested in these RAE diving trials, including the Mustang and Thunderbolt. None was able to reach the speed of the Spitfire because their high-speed drag increased more rapidly. The major reason was in Mitchell's original choice of a thin wing tapering to a nine per cent thickness/chord ratio at the tip joint, thinner than that of all its competitors and contrary to most aerodynamic advice at the time. Since then however there had been important developments in the aerodynamic design of wing-section profiles, particularly by the NACA in America. A whole new family of profiles had been developed, initially with the intention of reducing skin friction by maintaining substantial areas of laminar flow. To achieve this, the greatest thickness of the new sections was located much further aft than those of more conventional wings, which necessitated new structural design.

When these advanced sections were incorporated in the wing design of new types such as the Spiteful it was quickly realized that the theoretical drag reductions were not being obtained in practice. Minute amounts of surface roughness or irregularity, even dead flies sticking to the surface, were sufficient to provoke turbulent flow in the boundary layer. Skin friction drag was not much different to that of the older profiles. But at higher speeds the new sections confirmed the theory that the formation of shock waves and the consequent rise of transonic drag would be delayed, a process later on extended by the adoption of swept wings. Although the thin-winged Spitfire was able to compete adequately with later designs, there were good cases for developing a new wing to exploit the newer aerodynamic principles.

Supermarine specification 470 was written for a laminar flow wing for the Spitfire in November 1942. Unusually, the wing itself was given a Type number— 371—although later this was transferred to the complete Spiteful with the wing. The objects of specification 470 were defined as follow: to raise as much as possible the critical speed at which drag increases due to compressibility become serious; to obtain a rate of roll faster than any existing fighter; to reduce profile drag and thereby improve performance.

The special wing section for the Spiteful was developed with the aid of the National Physical Laboratory. It was designed to maintain laminar flow as far back as possible where there was no interference from slipstream or projecting gun barrels. The maximum thickness was at about 42 per cent of the chord. An aileron reversal speed of 850 mph was aimed at. Wing area was reduced from the 248·5 sq ft of the Spitfire F.21 to 210 sq ft and straight leading and trailing edges were adopted, which eased production as well as facilitating a conventional two-spar wing construction. The estimated weight of the wing was 200 lb lighter than that of the F.21 and a gain of 55 mph in performance was also estimated.

The official specification F.1/43 was issued for a new fighter with a laminar flow wing, and three prototypes were ordered from Supermarine. Its requirements included a contra-rotating propeller. A fuel capacity of 149 gallons with provision for external drop tanks carrying an additional 60 gallons. A rear-view sliding hood was to be fitted and the view over the nose was to be not less than eight degrees. Provision for wing folding for possible naval operation was to be made, and this was probably easier with the two-spar wing than with the single main spar of the Seafires. With the two-spar wing it became possible also to design an inwards-retracting undercarriage, thus extending by some four feet the narrow track of the Spitfire, which had always been the subject of some criticism in take-off and landing. Split flaps extended along the trailing edge from the wing roots to the ailerons, which were metal covered and had controllable trim tabs. The wings

The hybrid Spiteful prototype NN660. It was a Spitfire XIV with new laminar-flow wing.

were made in two sections with detachable tips.

Unlike the original Spitfire design, the Spiteful was notable for the prolific series of wind-tunnel tests made by the RAE and NPL. These were on a whole range of variations such as five- and six-blade propellers, different wing settings, Mach number effects up to 0·82, larger fins, alternative radiator ducts, and so on. One feature of this research was devoted to the evolution of a perfectly smooth wing surface extending even to the production of a complete plastic wing, but although this investigation continued for some time it was never completed.

When the Supermarine laminar flow wing was ready it was fitted to Spitfire XIV NN660, and Jeffrey Quill flew the modified aeroplane as the first prototype Spiteful on 30 June, 1944. After a short period of preliminary trials NN660 was lost on 13 September in a flight from High Post, the Supermarine test airfield in Wiltshire, together with its pilot, Frank Furlong, a former steeplechase jockey who had won the Grand National in 1935. No definite cause was ever ascertained. The second prototype, NN664, was completed to the full production version of specification F.1/43 and flown by Jeffrey Quill on 8 January, 1945. Flight trials to investigate the unsatisfactory features brought to light during the short testing of NN660 continued, such as the 'snatching' of the ailerons and wing drop preceding

NN664, the true Spiteful prototype. (*AAEE*)

265

the stall and a pronounced flick at the stall under high g. It became clear that pushing into the transonic regime was going to need more than simply adopting a new wing section. In extensive research and full-scale flight trials the discovery was made, on a 'tufted' 371 laminar flow wing, that the area in front of the ailerons stalled before the rest, the reverse of the behaviour of the Spitfire wing.

From the multiplicity of modifications and flight trials conducted on NN664 it became obvious that the Spiteful did not, as was hoped, achieve a great advance on the Spitfire in its later versions, but the advantages of the new high-speed wing sections were demonstrated and used in the jet aircraft to follow. For many of these tests NN664 was fitted with a standard F.21 tail including fabric-covered rudder and elevators, and later it was fitted with an enlarged 'stern' which improved lateral control at speeds approaching the stall and also lateral stability. The first production Spiteful, RB515, flew in April 1945 with the original tail but for its fourth flight the enlarged 'stern' was substituted.

RB515, the first production Spiteful, on test.

The first few of the completed seventeen Spitefuls of the 188 ordered were devoted to improving the aerodynamics of the laminar flow wing. With a short air intake, a Griffon 69 engine and a five-blade Rotol propeller, the type was designated F.14; with the Griffon 89 or 90 and a six-blade contra-rotating Rotol, the F.15. The one F.16, RB518, had the three-speed Griffon 101 driving a five-blade Rotol. With a boost of 25 lb, RB518 reached a level speed of 494 mph but at the expense of a suffering engine!

As early as October 1943, Supermarine were envisaging applying the laminar flow wing to the Seafire XV and wrote their own specification 474 under Type 382 for such a development using the Merlin 61. This was on their own initiative but it evinced no response in official places. Later on, however, naval interest was aroused and official specification N.5/45 was issued for a laminar flow fighter for the Fleet Air Arm. Spiteful F.14 RB520 was fitted with a sting-type hook early in 1945 and flew as the interim prototype Seafang. The proper prototype Seafang was completed as VB895 with a Griffon 89, hydraulically-operated wing folding and a contra-rotating propeller, being classified as the Seafang 32. Deck-landing

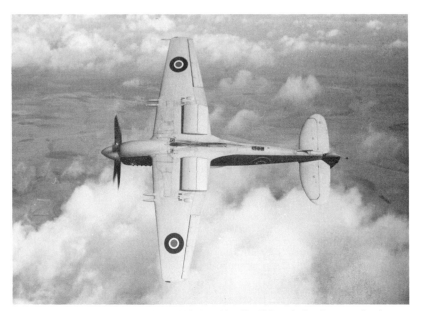

A Seafang 31 with sting hook, deck skid aft and landing lights window in centre fuselage.

trials and simulated landings at Chilbolton and RNAS Ford were made by Lt Cdr M. J. Lithgow, who had assumed test flying for Supermarine. These trials confirmed that the Seafang was suitable for carrier operation with an approach speed of 95 kt with no 'float' on closed throttle and a good pilot's view of the deck. A demonstration of the Seafang by Lithgow to the Netherlands naval authorities was of no avail as they were prevailed upon to order Fairey Fireflies.

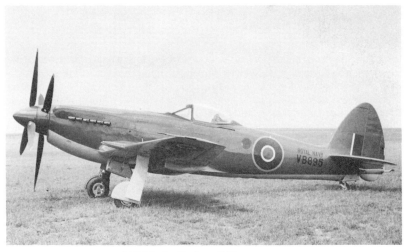

VB895, the Seafang F.32 prototype.

In the meantime, progress in other directions had diverted attention from propeller fighters to jet propulsion for military and naval aircraft with promise of much higher performance although, as will be seen later, there was a long way to go. The Admiralty preferred to carry on with their latest Seafires and interest in the Seafang, and indeed the RAF's interest in the Spiteful waned. A further proposal for a high-speed naval fighter powered by the Rolls-Royce 46H Eagle piston engine was drawn on 20 June, 1944, as Type 391 but was eventually dropped in favour of Type 392 to specification E.10/44, which became the Royal Navy's first jet-propelled fighter. Nevertheless, the Spiteful/Seafang can hardly be called a failure because of the serious contribution to transonic aerodynamics.

Spiteful F.14—One 2,375 hp Rolls-Royce Griffon 69. Single-seat fighter.
Span 35 ft (10·67 m); length 32 ft 11 in (10·06 m); height 13 ft 5 in (4·11 m); wing area 210 sq ft (19·51 sq m).
Tare weight 7,350 lb (3,334 kg); loaded weight 9,950 lb (4,510 kg).
Maximum speed 483 mph (778 km/h) at 21,000 ft (6,410 m); range 564 miles (910 km) at 240-255 mph (386-410 km/h) (Not including allowances); maximum rate of climb 4,890 ft/min (1,490 m/min) at 2,000 ft (610 m); service ceiling 42,000 ft (12,800 m).
Armament. Four 20 mm Hispano cannon with 624 rounds and provision for two 1,000 lb (453 kg) or four 300 lb (136 kg) rocket projectiles, two under each wing.

Seafang F.32—One 2,350 hp Rolls-Royce Griffon 89. Single-seat naval fighter.
Span 35 ft (10·67 m); length 34 ft 1 in (10·4 m); height 12 ft 6½ in (3·83 m); wing area 210 sq ft (19·51 sq m).
Tare weight 8,000 lb (3,632 kg); loaded weight 10,450 lb (4,744 kg).
Maximum speed 475 mph (764 km/h) at 21,000 ft (6,410 m); range 393 miles (632 km) at 220-240 mph (354-386 km/h) (Not including allowances); maximum rate of climb 4,630 ft/min (1,412 m/min) at 2,000 ft (610 m); service ceiling 41,000 ft (12,500 m).
Armament. As for Spiteful.

Attacker

In March 1944 Rolls-Royce, at the bidding of the Government, started the design of a large turbojet engine twice the power of existing types, notably their own Derwent power units of the Gloster Meteor twin-engine fighter. The new engine was to develop over 4,000 lb static thrust and was designated RB.40. Soon after, Supermarine were asked to design a new fighter, to specification E.1/44, around the RB.40 in view of their recent experience with laminar flow wings. However, Joe Smith said he would prefer a smaller engine for his 'Spiteful development' and therefore the engine was reduced in size and power to something over 3,000 lb thrust, re-labelled RB.41 and eventually called the Nene, and the Supermarine fighter became the Attacker in due course.

Drawings for E.1/44 were started a week before the first flight of the prototype Spiteful and only a week later its outline design was submitted to DTD of the Ministry of Aircraft Production, under Supermarine specification 477. Its main features were the RB.41 engine, Type 371 laminar flow wings with the radiators removed and replaced by fuel tanks, increasing capacity to 395 gallons, but retaining the four 20 mm cannon. The cockpit would be pressurized. The Type number allocated was 392.

First trials of the RB.41 in the following October were rather disappointing but with the introduction of intake swirl vanes the new engine came up to the original estimates, in fact the uprating of the official requirement to 4,500 lb thrust was soon reached at an engine speed of 12,000 rpm. The Nene became the outstanding example of the Whittle-type centrifugal compressor turbojet and has since been extensively produced, a copy serving as power unit of the MiG-15.

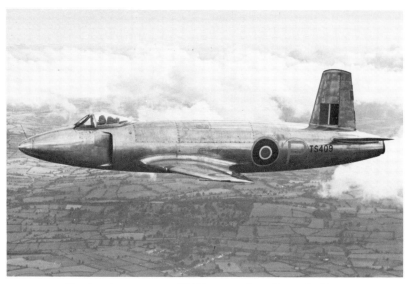

The Attacker prototype, TS409, on test from Boscombe Down.

The Supermarine outline specification was studied by the Ministry, which realized that any teething problems with the laminar flow wing would be resolved on the Spiteful prototype which had not yet flown. Joe Smith received notification in July that three prototypes would be needed and the order arrived on 5 August, with the contract a month later quoting 'jet machines of the Spiteful type'. Serials allocated were TS409, 413 and 416, with the second and third airframes to be 'navalized' but with non-folding wings. After DTD had inspected a partly completed mock-up, the first draft of specification E.10/44 was issued which was essentially Supermarine 477—a case of history repeating itself as with the prototype Spitfire when the Supermarine tender was followed by the official specification based on it.

Progress on the new and in some ways revolutionary design for Supermarine was marred by the loss of the first Spiteful. The second Spiteful was completed as quickly as possible and flew on 8 January, 1945, in an unpainted condition to save time. Some 29 flights were completed by the end of May, most of them by Jeffrey Quill, during which time it was found that the low-speed handling was poor. This did not deter the Ministry and on 7 July, 1945, Treasury approval was obtained for a pre-production order for 24 jet aircraft, six to the original E.10/44 specification and 18 to a later E.1/45 for Royal Navy requirements, the contract of 21 November, 1945, denoting serials ranging from VH980 to VJ118.

The first flight of the E.10/44 prototype was delayed because the Spiteful's handling difficulties had to be solved and so in February 1946 the Admiralty asked for work on the naval version to be suspended and in consequence ordered eighteen Sea Vampire Mk 20s, and the whole contract for all 24 jet aircraft from Supermarine was 'pigeon-holed' for the time being. Work on the three prototypes was allowed to continue.

One of the major delays was aileron development. Flight trials of the second Spiteful revealed that the slotted type of aileron fitted with geared balanced tabs became too heavy at speeds over 400 mph. Accordingly it was decided to reserve the second jet aircraft, TS413 navalized version, for investigation and development of the handling characteristics—an area at that time on the threshold of knowledge of flight approaching the speed of sound. The phenomenon known as 'snaking', a form of directional instability observed during the early history of jet-propelled aircraft, became evident on the first flight trials of TS409 which started on 27 July, 1946, from AAEE at Boscombe Down with Quill as the pilot.

The Attacker, as the new type was later named, was the first individual type to be fitted with the Nene and is believed to have been the first true prototype of a new design flight-tested at Boscombe Down. For initial flights Nene number 13 was restricted to 12,000 rpm giving 4,300 lb thrust but later in engine 28 the

TS413, the first naval Attacker.

270

Attacker TS413 landing on HMS *Illustrious*.

maximum rpm was raised to 12,440 with a thrust of 5,000 lb which then became standard for all production Nenes. The increased power available in TS409 produced a significant rise in maximum speed from 542 mph at sea level to 580 and from 552 at 15,000 ft to 568 mph.

Indicative of the problems that would be encountered by the entry of Supermarine into the jet propulsion arena was the number of modifications made before the first flight trials and delivery to Boscombe. These included alterations to the turbulent air bleeds of the engine air intake—a source of high drag—fuel improvements for accident prevention and to the transfer system between tanks, introduction of spring tabs to elevators and ailerons and mass-balancing of elevators and spring tabs, accompanied by full resonance tests for anti-flutter, an investigation that had become necessary with the increasing speeds and loadings of jet aircraft.

After preliminary trials at the AAEE the E.10/44 TS409 appeared at the first postwar SBAC Display at Radlett in September 1946. The naming of the type came when TS413 was modified to naval standard under specification E.1/45 and was called the Attacker F.1. It was first flown by Mike Lithgow on 17 June, 1947, and differed from the E.10/44 TS409 in the following details. It had a smaller fin and larger tailplane, modified flaps and lift spoilers above the wing, balanced aileron tabs in place of spring tabs, modified air intakes with louvred by-pass air bleeds, extra rear fuel tanks, oleo undercarriage legs, absorption travel lengthened by two inches and, last but not least, a Martin-Baker pilot ejection seat, an innovation in jet fighters necessitated by the near impossibility of baling out normally at the very high speeds concomitant with jet propulsion. Indeed Supermarine, as did other aircraft companies, had made their own attempt to evolve a satisfactory means of escape for jet pilots from the Attacker, none with much order book success except Martin-Baker whose design became standardized.*

*The Supermarine experimental ejection seat was based on a single cordite propellant which soon revealed in trials on a ground rig that to attain the progressive acceleration needed for a smooth ejection over the tail surfaces more than one explosive unit was needed as discovered later by Sir James Martin and painfully proven by one of the authors of this book! The end of the Supermarine attempt was a dangerous fire to the haystack disposed to catch the unoccupied but ballasted seat, needing the attention of two fire engines!

An Attacker on the approach with all drag-inducing aids extended.

On the first flight of TS413 the directional 'snaking' apparent in TS409 was present to a much greater degree and occurred at all speeds. It could be initiated manually by the pilot or by flying through bumpy air. This phenomenon was corrected to a great extent on the second flight by fitting beading from the top of the rudder to the bottom of the tab. The aeroplane was safely flown to 375 knots at 20,000 ft, which represented Mach ·823, and subsequent flying was devoted to the operation and effect on handling of the lift spoilers, in which trials a speed of 506 knots was recorded. After a series of some thirty ADDLs (airfield dummy deck landings) which according to Mike Lithgow, Supermarine chief test pilot, served only to give practice in slow flying, TS413 then went for deck landings on HMS *Illustrious*, beginning on 28 October, 1947, the first being made by Lithgow, followed by Lt Cdr E. M. Brown of the RAE and Lt S. Orr of the AAEE. In the flight test report Lithgow said 'It is considered that the average pilot should have no difficulty in deck landing this aircraft following the method set out in the document'. Lt Orr alone found a tendency to float on approach—a common characteristic of early jet high-speed aircraft in the absence of the inherent braking effect of a large propeller. In the event aerodynamic spoilers proved to be efficient enough, and an engine thrust spoiler for the Attacker in landing, test flown in Vickers Wellington W5518 with a tail-mounted Power Jets W2/700 engine, was not required. Wing lift spoilers were abandoned on the prototype Attacker in favour of drag-producing air-brakes as extensions of the flaps or special extensions from the lower fuselage.

A second series of sea trials was witnessed by officers of the US Navy whose Commodore Shelley commented on the Attacker 'perhaps its most favourable feature as a carrier plane is that the landing gear is conventional' probably referring to the braking effect induced by a tail-down approach and landing with a 'bicycle' undercarriage and tailwheel. In addition, launching by catapult needed a tail-down attitude—a problem in the later Scimitar with its nosewheel undercarriage.

272

Representative of the halting progress being made towards the perfection of jet-propelled fighters after the war and in the early 'fifties was the proposal to use the prototype Attackers as trial horses for installations of engines other than the Nene. Supermarine specification 510 outlined an Attacker Mk 2 as TS409 with a de Havilland Ghost II of 5,000 lb thrust and further design specification 527 envisaged the fitting of either the Rolls-Royce Avon or Tay engines both of over 6,000 lb thrust, as alternatives for comparative trials of engine performances. Other modifications were proposed for experimental purposes, including the fitting of a large ventral fuel tank of 270 gallons capacity on TS413. This naval prototype was lost together with its Boscombe Down pilot, Lt T. J. A. King-Joyce RN, in June 1948.

After the crash of TS413, the original TS409 was brought up to Type 498 standard for trials of the Attacker as a shipboard aeroplane for the Royal Navy. It was announced by the Admiralty in September 1948 that an order had been placed for 60 aircraft, with a hope that all would be delivered by the end of March 1951. Also representative of the official stop-go policy of the period and later was the accompanying comment of the then Deputy Controller of Naval Requirements that the main need was quick production to enable the Navy to acquire jet experience and consequently to accept an aeroplane with a minimum of modifications. This presaged things to come for the swept-wing development of the Attacker, the Swift. TS409 was first flown as a 'navalized' aircraft on 5 March, 1949, and up to 20 April had made 22 flights for general handling assessment, with particular attention to elevator and trimmer angles under various combinations of spoiler and flap openings.

Attacker cockpit mock-up at Hursley Park. On the extreme right can be seen the mock-up of the undercarriageless Type 505 with 75 mm gun and housing in position.

273

Attacker WA493 on board an aircraft carrier.

Flight tests were continued on the revamped TS409 with two objects. One was to give naval pilots ADDL experience before proceeding to actual landings on *Illustrious* and the other to evaluate the air-brake installation, a lack of which had been criticized in previous trials. As already mentioned, highly streamlined jet fighters suffered from a lack of deceleration in the landing regime. Another phenomenon at that time was rudder locking-over under certain conditions of sideslip, especially when the Attacker was fitted with the external long-range tank. It is possible that both TS413 and production WA477 were lost through this cause, the latter with the Supermarine pilot Peter Robarts. As with the Vickers Warwick, the fitting of a dorsal fin cured the trouble and in the case of the Attacker improved directional and rudder control. The decision then was made to fit the dorsal fin to all Attackers retrospectively.

By that time the third prototype, TS416, had been completed using all the knowledge gained from its two predecessors. The wing was set back some 13 in and the air intakes were enlarged resulting in considerably improved handling. But the original type was rushed into production because of a sudden demand for jet fighters in view of the unstable international political situation. Also at that time it was becoming evident that the jet engine promised aircraft speeds previously undreamt of. The world absolute speed record was twice broken by the twin Derwent-engined Gloster Meteor IV, which put an attempt by the Supermarine Attacker out of reach; but Mike Lithgow did capture the International 100 km Closed Circuit Record on 26 February, 1948, with Attacker prototype TS409 flying from the Supermarine flight test base at Chilbolton, Hampshire. He reached 560·634 mph (902·25 km/h) and bettered this the following day with 564·882 mph. In July 1950 Lithgow won the SBAC Challenge Cup with the same aircraft at 533 mph average speed.

As planned, the Attacker prototypes were used extensively for experimental trials or design exercises. Schemes proposed included a two-seat version, the fitting of floats as previously on the Spitfire, and an actual test with RATOG comprising eight rockets disposed in pairs two above and two below each wing for assisted take-off. Under Supermarine specification 512 jet deflection was considered as a means of reducing landing speed but was not pursued.

The first production Attacker, WA469, was test flown by Mike Lithgow on 5 May, 1950, and was followed by R4000 the first Pakistan Attacker in July in an increasing momentum of the flight test programme. During one flight with Attacker WA469 on 23 May, 1950, the purpose of which was to assess behaviour at high Mach numbers and the effectiveness of the dive-brakes, two dives were made and a number of operations of the dive-brakes were made at up to 400 kt. One dive of 430 kt over the airfield at South Marston with the air-brakes open led to a considerable nose-up trim followed by an equally sharp nose-down trim change causing the Supermarine test pilot, L. R. Colquhoun, to bump his head on the cockpit roof. During the nose-up trim change a loud bang was heard and the folding starboard wingtip was seen by both the pilot and the flight controller in the tower, Phil Frogley, to fold up and remain vertical. With hard port rudder the aeroplane was kept straight and with the speed reduced to 270 kt they mutually agreed that a landing should be attempted aided by ground monitoring. The wheels were lowered and a wide left hand circuit was made under rudder control only, the ailerons being effectively locked by the folded wingtip. Final flap was lowered and speed further reduced to 200 kt—considered a safe speed for landing. Vigorous use of the wheel brakes brought the aeroplane to rest some 30 ft from the end of the runway, with a burst port tyre causing it to swing to port. Later Leslie Colquhoun was awarded the George Medal for meritorious flying in hazardous conditions.

Meanwhile the series of deck landing proving trials started by TS413 was continued. Modifications embodied in all aircraft included the new dorsal fin, flat-sided elevators and lighter aileron controls. As a bomb-carrying beam had been built into the design, an additional Navy requirement for bomb-carrying capability was easily met by the provision of the electrical control wiring. In this form the Attacker FB.1 WA529 made its first flight on 7 January, 1952. A further development FB.2 had the Nene 7 engine (later designated 102), an electric

An Attacker being launched by steam catapult. The towing strop can be seen falling away.

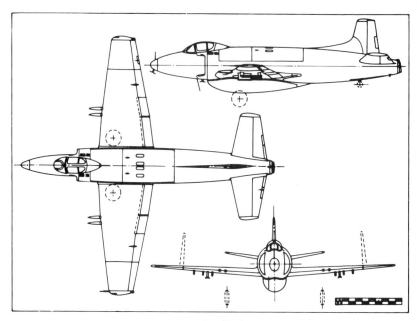

Attacker FB.2

starter, a high energy igniter unit, acceleration control linked to the throttle, a metal-framed cockpit canopy, and provision for six rockets in two tiers under each wing. The first Attacker FB.2, WK319, was flown on 25 April, 1952. Of the 149 Attackers built for the Royal Navy, 84 were FB.2s.

The first operational jet squadron of the Royal Navy was No.800, formed at Ford, Sussex, with Attackers on 17 August, 1951. This was followed in November by 803 and in April 1952 by 890. Each squadron had eight Attackers with reserves but this size of unit was considered by the Navy as too small to be an effective

The first Pakistan Attacker, with 250 gal fuselage and 93 gal wing drop tanks.

276

The first Attacker for Pakistan, seen with two 1,000 lb bombs and eight rocket projectiles.

fighting force and so 890 was disbanded and absorbed into the other two squadrons, thus increasing their strength to twelve front-line aircraft each. Other 'mixed' equipment squadrons using Attackers were 702, 703, 718, 767, 787, and FRUs Brawdy and Hurn. Training Squadron 736 also was fully equipped with Attackers, and after 1954, when front-line Attackers began to be replaced by Sea Hawks, some went to the RNVR Squadrons 1831, 1832, 1833 and 1836.

It was considered that the Attacker might achieve some success in the export market as jet-propelled military aircraft were becoming attractive to the air forces of other countries still operating front-line piston-engined types, but embargos imposed by certain international agreements were in force on such sales of strategic supplies. One sale that did materialize, after protracted negotiations, was 36 Attackers to Pakistan. Supermarine pilots ferried 33 of these out to Pakistan and the other three were flown out by Pakistan Air Force pilots as an exercise, the flying time to Karachi averaging 11 hr 40 min.

Thus the Attacker's last service career was with the Pakistan Air Force. As a pioneering type it had played a vital role in the transition from the piston-engined propeller-driven fighter to pure jet propulsion, and in the process had registered quite a few 'firsts', including the first jet type to enter full squadron service with the Royal Navy. The first emergency ejection of a Service pilot was by Lt P. O. McDermot RN from Attacker WA480 on 20 March, 1951, and the first use of the Martin-Baker automatic ejection seat was by Lt C. W. Bushe RN from WK324 on 15 July, 1953. The Attacker was one of the first aircraft to use a flight recorder of inflight information.

Attacker F.1—One 5,000 lb (2,268 kg) st Rolls-Royce Nene 3. Single-seat fighter.

Span 36 ft 11 in (11·25 m), 28 ft 11 in (8·8 m) folded; length (tail down) 37 ft 1 in (11·3 m); height (tail down) 9 ft 6½ in (2·9 m); wing area 227·2 sq ft (21·1 sq m); sweepback outboard of kink 2·7 deg, inboard 1·7 deg.

Tare weight 8,426 lb (3,822 kg); loaded 12,211 lb (5,539 kg).

Maximum speed 590 mph (949·5 km/h) at sea level; maximum range (with overload tank) 1,190 miles (1,915 km) at 355 mph (571·3 km/h); maximum rate of climb 6,350 ft/min (1,935·5 m/min) at sea level; climb to 30,000 ft (9,144 m) 6·6 min; service ceiling 45,000 ft (13,716 m).

Armament. Four 20 mm Hispano Mk V cannon and 624 rounds in wings, and two 1,000 lb (454 kg) bombs or four 300 lb (136 kg) rocket projectiles under the wings.

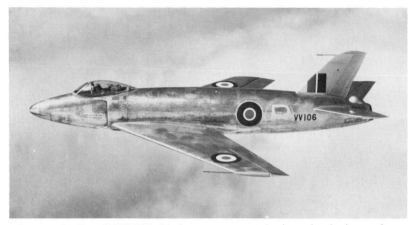

Supermarine Type 510 VV106 with short nose, square wingtips and anti-spin parachute blister aft of the rudder.

Swift and Type 545

During 1946 the Air Staff, perhaps realizing how far behind they were in experience with high-speed jet aircraft, issued advanced specifications for heavy bombers and for two-seat and single-seat fighters. One of the single-seat fighters was the E.41/46, a developed version of the Attacker with swept-back wings to serve as a Gloster Meteor replacement; similarly the E.38/46 was to be a development of the Hawker P.1040.

Two prototypes of each were ordered. The two Supermarine prototypes were serialled VV106 and VV119, both being built at Hursley Park and each fitted with a Rolls-Royce Nene 2 engine. The fuselages were Attacker-type with tailwheel but with wings and tailplanes swept back to an angle of 40 degrees. A maximum design speed of 700 mph was specified. VV106, the Supermarine Type 510, was first flown by M. J. Lithgow on 29 December, 1948, from Boscombe Down. It was the first British jet-engined aeroplane to fly with sweepback on both wing and horizontal tail surfaces. Testing was terminated temporarily by a wheels-up landing by Lithgow on 16 March, 1949, but was resumed again after repair on 10 May.

M. J. Lithgow, then Supermarine chief test pilot, stated in the *RAF Flying Review*: 'Within a few flights I was taking it up to Mach 0·9 without any trouble, which at that time was quite phenomenal, and we realised that Joe Smith, our designer, really had something.' The Attacker fuselage with swept-back surfaces soon showed its superiority in maximum speed over that of the Attacker with Spiteful wings, the top level speed at 12,300 rpm being 630-635 mph at 10,000 to 15,000 ft and a maximum Mach number of over 0·93 was achieved. This limit, as with several similar aircraft, was set by a change in lateral trim (port wing low) which, at that Mach number, required full control-column movement to starboard to counteract it. For most of the initial trials the nose was rounded, but later a pointed nose gave increased speed, a nose pitot head was fitted and the aeroplane painted. At last a Supermarine aircraft capable of exceeding the Spitfire's Mach 0·92 had emerged. During the early trials the cockpit hood was lost in flight after which the hood jettison mechanism was modified.

The new type was demonstrated at the 1949 SBAC Display where it was favourably received, making six flights between 6 and 11 September. During handling trials at Boscombe Down from September to November 1949 it was confirmed that although there was a limit to the maximum usable lift-coefficient in the transonic region, the sweepback so improved the high Mach number drag characteristics that there was considerable improvement in the lift at such high speeds. At the same time however, the trials showed that the sweepback also introduced longitudinal instability prior to the stall. This limited the manoeuvrability at high altitude and the level turn performance was also affected by insufficient power, at 40,000 ft the aircraft being almost confined to straight flight. The aeroplane, by then called Swift, was fairly easy and pleasant to fly and seemed to be free of the dangerous troubles forecast for aircraft having large degrees of sweepback. It had a maximum usable Mach number of 0·93 and was free of serious and expected tendencies towards snaking or 'dutch-rolling' and had light and crisp ailerons, giving a good rate of roll at lower altitudes. The tailwheel layout was not liked by the pilots at Boscombe Down and they were quoted as saying, 'With a tricycle undercarriage and improved elevator control the aircraft should have the makings of a good fighter.' During the early trials in 1949 severe vibration was experienced upon throttling back to low engine speeds. This problem was cured before return for further trials between January and March 1950 by fitting a modified Attacker-type front engine mounting and other modifications affecting the airflow through the intake ducts.

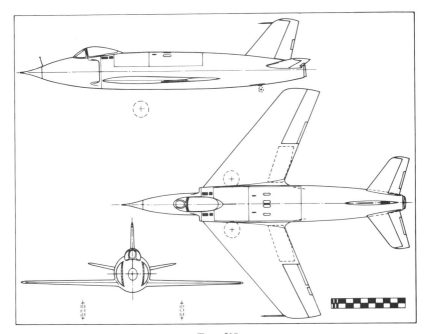

Type 510

Type 510 VV106 with pointed nose probe.

When inspected by RAE in July 1950, VV106 was found to have a poor finish and unsealed gaps at the control surfaces. The RAE report stated 'The aircraft should not be unduly criticized on this score, however, as it is a conversion of a 1944 Attacker and was built not so much to achieve a high performance as to enable flight experience on swept-wings to be obtained as quickly as possible.' Comparative flight tests were made by the RAE between the Swift and the American F-86A Sabre. The Swift's performance at low level was inferior, giving only 520 kt (599 mph) compared to the F-86A's 580 kt (668 mph). At 25,000 ft however, the two aircraft had almost identical performances—617 mph for the Swift and 619·5 mph for the F-86A. The conclusions reached were that the Sabre's good overall finish and the large thrust produced by the American J47 engine at high speeds with the greater efficiency of the intake gave it a superior performance.

Following modifications and adaptation for a naval role, the Swift was first flown, as such, by Lithgow, on 14 September, 1950, in preparation for deck-landing trials and evaluation of a naval swept-wing fighter and was delivered to Farnborough on 20 September by Supermarine pilot L. R. Colquhoun. There it underwent airfield dummy deck-landing tests and measured take-off performance including rocket-assisted take-off exercises. It was flown and cleared with four rocket units, one above and one below each wing, increasing the loaded weight to 12,790 lb. In flight little effect on handling was evident, the stall was unaffected and only slight buffeting was noticeable up to an indicated air speed of 320 knots, to which the aeroplane was restricted at that time for experimental purposes.

On 8 November, 1950, the Swift VV106, flown by Lt J. Elliot RN, became the first swept-winged aircraft to land on and take off from an aircraft carrier, in this case HMS *Illustrious*. Twelve landings and rocket-assisted take-offs were achieved on that day, three by Lt Elliot, the remainder by Lt Cdr D. G. Parker (later Rear-Admiral Parker) of Boscombe Down, and by M. J. Lithgow. On most occasions there was a 50 knot wind down the deck, the carrier speed being about

22–25 knots, and the ship was comparatively stable for all landings. Take-off with only two rockets into this wind was achieved in about 500 ft with only a slight tendency to drop the starboard wing when leaving the carrier.

The approach speed was 124–134 knots indicated air speed and the landings were all good, the rebound characteristics of all oleos being judged excellent. Refuelling, change of rockets and other equipment, was achieved in a short space of time which allowed landings to be made every 20 minutes. Three further landings were made next day, but later, when a fuel-pressure warning light would not go out, the aircraft was flown back to shore. The last take-off, however, was the most frightening because the rockets on one side did not provide the same thrust as those on the other, consequently the aircraft swung rapidly and a wingtip just struck the top of one of the ship's gun turrets. The pilot, Lt Cdr Parker, was sufficiently skilful to maintain control and complete the take-off.

During these trials, the first production Attacker was also undergoing the same exercise thus giving a good comparison between the two. The Swift later returned to the RAE for further tests and then to Supermarine for extensive modifications, including the removal of all naval equipment.

Under Supermarine specification 515 dated 1 December, 1948, a proposal was formulated that the Swift with swept-back wings and tail should be capable of reaching a speed in the region of Mach 1·0. In order to maintain full control of the aircraft at high speed, it was considered that a tailplane adjustable in flight would be very desirable if not essential, and lesser modifications were also proposed, including removal of the elevator spring tab—a potential source of flutter; reduction of elevator chord; provision of elevator power control reproducing light control of a spring tab while retaining the trim tab. With the above scheme,

Swift VV106, the first sweptwing aircraft to be carrier borne, landing on HMS *Illustrious* in November 1950. (*Fleet Air Arm Museum*)

VV119 as Supermarine Type 528 with nose probe and tailwheel undercarriage.

deflection of the rear jet-pipe was also required because of the tailplane attachment. This resulted in VV106 being fitted with an unusual rear-fuselage, the whole of which was hinged to rotate in the vertical plane, adjustable up and down through four degrees either way. During test flying, this variable-incidence tail fitted to Type 517 proved to be a powerful and effective trimmer under all conditions of flight up to the limiting speed of Mach 0·95 which, after the tests, was relaxed considerably. However, the tailplane actuation rate was considered too fast and a modification was made to slow the transition.

Pilots of the RAE Farnborough who flew the Swift in the new configuration liked its improved handling characteristics. One of these pilots, T. Gordon Innes, who was flying it on 14 November, 1952, had an undercarriage failure and made a successful wheels-up landing at Farnborough. The aircraft was repaired and flown again by Dave Morgan of Supermarine on 2 September, 1953. Its flying career ended on 14 January, 1955, when it was allotted to RAF Melksham as an instructional airframe, later being moved to Halton, Cardington, Colerne and to its ultimate resting place at RAF Cosford.

VV119 as Type 535 Swift with nosewheel undercarriage.

The second prototype Swift, VV119, was externally similar to VV106 and, as the Type 528, was first flown by Lithgow on 27 March, 1950, at Boscombe Down. Before this aeroplane could do much flying it was grounded in May 1950 for extensive modifications, the most noticeable being the change to a nosewheel layout after which it became known as the Type 535.

The chief differences from VV106, other than the fitting of a nosewheel, were a rear fuselage of enlarged diameter to accommodate the larger jet-pipe with reheat; a special tail cone to reduce the diameter at its rear, so preserving its aerodynamic shape; larger air-intakes of different shape; provision for wing-mounted guns requiring reduced-span ailerons; cockpit hood reverting from one-piece bubble to a more conventional steel-framed type; no anti-spin parachute fitted, so housing aft of rudder eliminated; a longer nose; and an improved fuel system to increase efficiency and raise capacity to 400 gallons. The wing centre-section area was increased by reducing the sweepback of the trailing edge which was then kinked in planform. As a result of the structural modifications the length of the aircraft was increased by four feet. These modifications were aimed obviously at fighter usage.

Prometheus, Swift VV119, 'star' of the film *Sound Barrier* being flown by Supermarine test pilot Dave Morgan.

VV119, in the new Type 535 configuration and fitted with reheat, first flew on 23 August, 1950, at Boscombe Down, the first use of reheat being a week later on 1 September. This was the only Nene installation to which reheat was applied. Immediately after this the aircraft went to the SBAC Display at Farnborough, the early flying having shown that the elevator buffeting experienced previously had been eliminated, probably due to the less severe changes of contour on the lengthened fuselage.

An order was placed in the following November for two pre-production Swift prototypes and for 100 production aircraft to be fitted with the Rolls-Royce Avon axial-flow engine. Wing fences were added to VV119 and it was flown on 28

December to ascertain their aerodynamic effect. A speed check on the aeroplane with all its modifications was made during July 1951 and level flight figures recorded were 622 mph at 15,000 ft, 609 at 26,000 ft and 583 at 35,000 ft. The two production prototypes were designated Type 541 with serials WJ960 and WJ965.

The test flying of VV119 was taken over from October 1951 by Sqn Ldr D. W. Morgan, who had joined the Supermarine flight test team from the Royal Air Force. Flown by Morgan and others, VV119 assumed the star role under the guise of *Prometheus* in the full-length public feature film *Sound Barrier*, a unique experience for a prototype still on test. Also in 1951 it was used to check the functioning of anti-gravity clothing for pilots, from heights of 30,000 ft down to 10,000 ft. No uncomfortable gravitational effects were reported.

Experiments were made with drag-inducing upper surface flaps but they caused considerable buffeting at high speed and eventually it was found that sufficient braking could be achieved by using the landing flaps only. These were operated by a switch conveniently mounted on the throttle control, and a two-position switch was also provided to give 35 degrees flap or 55 degrees when fully down. This arrangement enabled the aeroplane to be slowed down from top speed to about 160 knots at low altitude in 58 seconds or to glide from 40,000 ft at a rate of 25,000 ft/min without exceeding Mach 0·79.

Although wing drop still persisted on VV119 at high speed, it was less prone to it than VV106 but it did suffer to some extent from the limited effectiveness of power-assisted manual controls at transonic Mach numbers. During 1955 VV119's wings were adapted to accept various combinations of dummy Blue Sky rockets to find in flight the effect on drag, manoeuvrability and general handling, including the influence of pylon length. Flight tests covered normal service speeds of up to Mach 0·95 with two weapons and to 0·90 with four. These tests showed that the choice of any weapon configuration gave negligible change in handling although increased inertia in roll was noticeable. VV119 was finally 'pensioned off' in 1955 and allotted to RAF Halton in September 1955 as an instructional airframe with the maintenance number 7285M.

Development of the Swift was demanded by the outbreak of the Korean War in June 1950, Britain being committed to give support to the South Koreans because of its membership of the United Nations. This situation therefore solved the question of how to develop the Type 535, as the Air Staff had decided to acquire a fully-equipped fighter as a back-up insurance for the Hawker Hunter which at that time was a year away with no guarantee of its success. At the same time it was obvious that the 535 needed more power and, as mentioned previously, the Rolls-Royce Avon was chosen which then was producing 7,500 lb thrust, some 50 per cent more power than the Nene as fitted to earlier types.

Apart from this material difference the first production prototype, WJ960, was almost identical externally to VV119 except that the ailerons were of longer span because of the absence of the wing-mounted guns. It was first flown from Boscombe Down on 1 August, 1951, and various control oscillations were experienced. During the third flight, two days later, Lithgow experienced severe control vibrations due to mechanical rather than to aerodynamic deficiencies and these caused the fuel cock linkage to break thereby closing the cock and stopping the engine. An extremely clever power-off landing was made back at Chilbolton without damage to pilot or aeroplane, a supreme example of the skill of the professional industry pilot in preserving an expensive prototype.

On 8 September, while practising for the SBAC Show, Dave Morgan suffered engine failure on WJ960 and made an equally commendable forced landing on the

WJ960, the first pre-production Swift, accompanied by Spitfire F.22 PK542.

Swift WJ965 under construction in Hursley Park experimental hangar.

approach to Chilbolton. Although the tail was damaged it was repaired and the aeroplane was flying again within three months. The fitting of a variable-incidence tail went some way towards modernizing the type, which first flew with this improvement on 4 February, 1953, when Mach 0·91 was reached but with some aileron flutter which was best stopped by rapid deceleration using the powerful air-brakes.

With production aircraft becoming available, WJ960 went to South Marston where it was used briefly to simulate engine surge experienced on production Swifts but only succeeded three times out of ten flights. It was then withdrawn from service because of its differences from production aircraft.

Swift production at South Marston.

The second production prototype, WJ965, was flown by Dave Morgan from Boscombe Down on 18 July, 1952. It was more representative of the production Swifts in having a modified nose, cockpit canopy and fin. The position of the wing in relation to the fuselage was different and the wingtips followed the then current trend of the Kuchemann curved pattern (as on WJ960). There was also a much larger internal fuel capacity. Spring-tab ailerons were fitted and during the early flights wing and aileron flutter was experienced. This was more severe than with WJ960 and was the result of reducing the wing skin thickness to save weight.

Type 541 Swift WJ965.

There had been much concern regarding the structural integrity of transonic aircraft, particularly over failures suspected of having been caused by flutter. The fatal crash of the D.H.110 at the Farnborough Air Show in 1952 high-lighted this alarm, and WJ965 was grounded so that additional test instrumentation could be fitted for an intensive flight-test programme. The outcome of the tests was the replacement of the aileron spring-tab by a geared tab. With this more rigid system the Swift became the first Supermarine aeroplane to exceed Mach 1·0 in a dive, on 26 February, 1953, so delighting the ground staff at Chilbolton when they heard a sonic bang from a Swift for the first time.

The first production Swift F.1 of the preliminary batch of eighteen was WK194 which with WK195 was built at the Hursley Park experimental shops. All subsequent Swifts were erected and completed at the South Marston factory although many major components were made elsewhere. The first true production Swift was WK196 and it was similar to the pre-production prototypes. It was flown in

March 1953 with fully-boosted controls. Later came a call to double the fire power of the two 30 mm Aden guns but production of the F.1 was too far advanced to incorporate any change. It was halted after the initial batch of eighteen had been completed.

The first Mk 2 Swift, WK214, mounted four 30 mm Aden guns in the lower fuselage, with ammunition stored in the wing roots. The extra space needed was provided by forward extension of the inboard leading edges. The new wing shape introduced by this change in geometry proved disastrous for it so altered the airflow pattern that an uncontrollable manoeuvre known as pitch-up occurred when g was applied at Mach 0·85 or above. If the pilot pulled the control column back hard the nose reared up and instant correction could not prevent the aeroplane flicking over on its back.

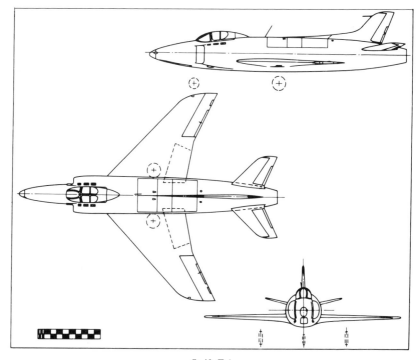

Swift F.1

This was quite unacceptable in a fighter as the time and height taken for recovery would render it extremely vulnerable in combat. Various wing modifications were tried with partial success. Wing fences were added to the upper surfaces and the leading edges of the outer wings were extended forward in the now familiar saw-tooth profile common on sweptwing aircraft. In effect this reduced the surface curvature and helped to prevent airflow breakaway. The final cure however proved to be moving the centre of gravity much further forward than originally intended. Unfortunately this entailed loading a considerable amount of ballast in the nose of the aircraft which crippled the high-altitude performance of the aeroplane. Despite all these trials and tribulations, which it

WK194, the first production Swift F.1

must be said were being shared with other similar aircraft in the exploratory transonic region, the Swift F.1 became the first British sweptwing fighter to go into service with the Royal Air Force. This was with No. 56 Squadron at Waterbeach on 13 February, 1954, followed by the Swift F.2 on 30 August, but only seventeen F.2s were built.

Following the Swifts F.1 and F.2 came the F.3, similar in all respects to the F.2 except that it was equipped with reheat. The first was WK247 and it was demonstrated at the 1953 Farnborough Show with its thunderous take-off under full reheat. Pitch-up was still present but it could now be partly controlled. This was aided by the fitting of vortex generators above and below the tail surfaces, the elevator control at high Mach numbers showing distinct improvement. The number of Swift F.3s built was 25.

The third production Swift airframe, WK198, was then converted from a Mk 1 into the prototype Mk 4 under Type 546. It was fitted with four Aden guns,

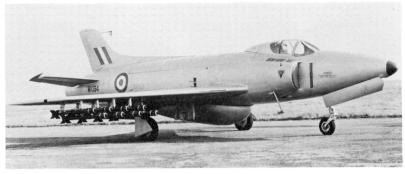

Swift F.1 WK194 at Chilbolton test base, equipped with rocket projectile battery and ventral long-range tank, with pilot's step extended.

A Swift F.3 in the detuner silencing pen at South Marston. This aircraft has kinked leading edge, wing fences and vortex generators on the starboard tailplane.

Swift F.4 WK198 on a test before the World Airspeed Record attempt.

reheat, the saw-toothed wing leading edges, and the long-awaited variable-incidence tailplane. It was hoped that this last feature would help control the pitch-up characteristic. This aircraft was also brought up to the production standards sought by both the Ministry and by Supermarine. It was flown by Mike Lithgow on 2 May, 1953, and on nine test flights subsequently, prior to taking part in the Coronation Flypast at Odiham on 15 July in company with four Swift 1s flown by RAF pilots. Lithgow however suffered compressor blade failure after the Flypast and had to make another of his spectacular power-off landings at Chilbolton. Engine failures in the Swift were causing concern at that time because Hawker Hunters fitted with the same engine were trouble free. Eventually it was found that a compressor blade of a different design had in fact been used in the Swifts' engines and after modification of the blade roots no further failures were reported.

Swift F.4 WK198 over Tripoli harbour at the time of the World Airspeed Record attempt.

The Mk 4 WK198 took part in the 1953 SBAC Show and was then flown to Tripoli in North Africa for an attack on the World's Absolute Air Speed Record. This was achieved on 26 September by Mike Lithgow at a new speed of 735·7 mph. Another attempt produced an average of 743 mph on two runs but on the third run the reheat failed to ignite, so this could not be submitted for promulgation. The normal maximum speed of the Swift Mk 4 with reheat was 709 mph at sea level (683 mph without). Further attempts were called off when it was learned that the American Skyray had flown at 753 mph on one run, and it took the record at 752·94 mph on 3 October.

291

A Swift FR.5 on a photographic reconnaissance over Germany. (*Crown copyright*)

An indication of what might have been achieved by this design, given more time, was when a Mk 4, WK275, was fitted with an all-flying tailplane and datum trimming. Supermarine test pilots reported the resulting handling as superb! Only six F.4s were built, the remaining 35 of the order being converted to F.5s. The production was stopped in 1955 because of the time involved in descending from the standing patrol height of 35,000 ft to 20,000 ft in order to light the reheat.

Because of the unsuitability of the earlier Swifts in the interceptor role and their consequent brief service in the RAF, a decision was made to adapt the Swift FR.5 for low-altitude high-speed tactical reconnaissance, as Supermarine Type 549, to replace the Meteor FR.9. The FR.5 was basically a Mk 4 with a lengthened nose to accommodate three cameras, one mounted in the extreme nose and, for oblique photography, one on each side just forward of the air-intakes. Initial trials of the camera installations were conducted in a converted Swift Mk 1, WK200. The first FR.5, XD903, made its maiden flight on 27 May, 1955, with Leslie

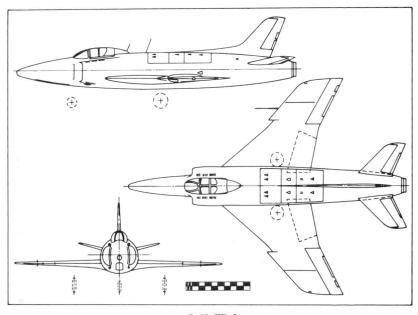

Swift FR.5

292

Swift FR.5s ready for delivery to No.2 Squadron, Tactical Air Force, based at Geilenkirchen in Germany.

Colquhoun as pilot. The next two production aircraft, XD904 and XD905, were equipped with clear-view cockpit canopies and 220-gallon drop-tanks giving each a total fuel capacity of 998 gallons, thus considerably increasing their range of operation. The FR.5 was the first aircraft in RAF service to be equipped with reheat.

In January 1956, Swift 5s began to re-equip No. 2 Squadron of the Tactical Air Force in Germany and were followed later into No. 79 Squadron also of TAF. In the second NATO Annual Reconnaissance Competition, Royal Flush, held at Laarbruch, West Germany, in May 1957, two Swifts of 79 Squadron came first and second competing against a mixed bag of Allied RF-84F Thunderflashes. The low-level mission was a visual reconnaissance with photographic confirmation covering 260 nautical miles below 500 ft. Two years later Swifts repeated the performance. Swifts continued in service in Germany for four years and were finally phased out when 79 Squadron was disbanded in 1960. Production of FR.5s was 59 in addition to the 35 modified F.4s.

An unarmed version designated Swift PR.6 as Type 550 was to have followed to replace the Meteor PR.10 but its development was abandoned.

In August 1952 a design study was submitted by Supermarine for a Swift modified to carry four Blue Sky air-to-air missiles, as well as four Aden guns, with radar guidance equipment. To accommodate the radar the nose had to be lengthened, and the wing span was increased. This project became the Mk 7 with

A Swift F.7, without undercarriage fairings, on wet runway trials at Filton, Bristol.

293

an uprated Rolls-Royce Avon 116 engine of 7,550 lb thrust. For trials of the proposed installation, a Mk 4 Swift, WK279, was modified to the aerodynamic standard required for the Mk 7 and fitted with detachable launchers for the Blue Sky missiles, three of which were successfully launched in October 1955.

The first F.7, XF774, flew early in April 1956 followed in June by XF778—both regarded as prototypes. The first production F.7 flew in August and all three plus WK279 went to Boscombe Down in September for handling trials and to determine limiting speed and Mach number. With pylons only, the maximum permissible speed was 600 kt or Mach 0·92 up to 20,000 ft and, with missiles, the restriction was 580 kt but the same Mach number. Both prototypes were sent to RAF Valley in Anglesey for guided weapons trials, XF778 equipped with cameras in the nose to photograph weapons being fired from XF774 flying in formation, the latter being equipped with the radar guidance system. The remaining F.7s of the total production, excluding the prototypes, of twelve were delivered to RAF Valley and became the first British fighters to be equipped with guided weapons. The Blue Sky missiles were renamed Fireflash. On completion of these trials the unit was disbanded and the aircraft were used for various other experiments such as aquaplaning and braking tests at Waterbeach and Filton.

Type 545

A proposal by Supermarine in February 1951 for a supersonic version of the Swift as Type 545 was made after the relative success of the prototype 510, VV106. This proposal was accepted by the Ministry in March 1951 and in February 1952 an initial order for two aircraft was placed to specification F.105D2. From this emerged a design, again with the compound-sweep wing as on the later Swifts, with 50 degrees on the inner planes and 30 degrees on the outer. The fuselage was area-ruled and the thickness/chord ratio varied from eight per cent at the wing root to nearly six per cent at the tips. By using a thick skin and closely-spaced thin spanwise webs with stringers of maximum depth a better weight/strength efficiency was claimed and proved in structural test rigs.

The incomplete Type 545 at the College of Aeronautics, Cranfield, with serial XA181.

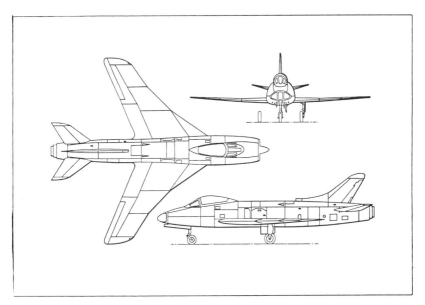

Type 545 which was partly built

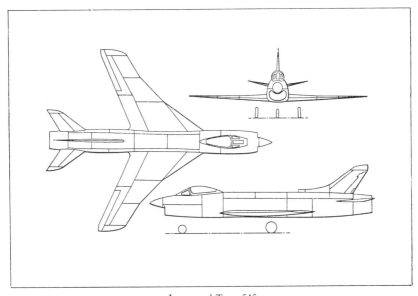

Improved Type 545

Most noticeable difference from the Swift in the external design of the Type 545 was the moving forward of the air intakes to the nose well ahead of the wings, the pitot type entry being initially split by a bullet-shaped centrebody, thus avoiding the need for a bypass bleed. The lower part of the fuselage forebody at the junction with the wings was flattened to improve airflow, with appropriate fillets at the junction. These modifications were intended to avoid the low-speed drag losses encountered on the Swift.

The engine selected for Type 545 was the Rolls-Royce RA.14 with a dry thrust of 9,500 lb and 14,500 lb with reheat. Speed was estimated at Mach 1·3, and Mach 1·68 with a Rolls-Royce Avon RA.35R or RB.106 for the second prototype XA186. The first prototype, XA181, was nearing completion when the project was cancelled, and it survived in one piece as a museum exhibit at the College of Aeronautics, Cranfield.

The main reason for cancellation of the Swift was that orders for interceptors overstretched the available national finances and were incompatible with the end of the fighting in Korea. If both Swift and Hunter production had continued, the peak delivery of 50 fighters a month would have been excessive for peacetime requirements. In fact both programmes were cut back and ultimately the Swift was discontinued altogether. However, the Swift had met its operational requirements and its aerodynamic shortcomings were just being overcome. The Swift FR.5 proved that as a low-level reconnaissance aircraft it could not be beaten even by the Americans.

The fighter reconnaissance Swifts did a great deal of pioneering work flying at low levels under the radar screen. This was very demanding structurally and the Swift's robust construction stood up extremely well. Unique methods devised by the Royal Aircraft Establishment for extending the life of such dive-bombers and tested by Supermarine proved invaluable in the subsequent development of terrain-following techniques and in the integrity of airframe strength under repeated high g dive-bombing manoeuvres. There were no structural failures.

Swift F.7 XF774 with Fairey Fireflash guided missiles.

The Swift F.7 was the first to deploy the guided weapon Fireflash and was also the first British operational aircraft to use a reheated engine, laying the groundwork for the application of the same basic engine to be used in the later Lightning fighter.

		Swift			
		F.1	F.4	FR.5	F.7
Engine – Rolls-Royce Avon		RA.7/105	RA.7R	RA.7R/ 114	RA.7/116
Span	ft	32·35	32·32	32·33	36·08
	m	9·86	9·85	9·85	11·0
Length	ft	41·5	41·45	42·26	43·7
	m	12·65	12·6	12·9	13·3
Height	ft	13·5	13·2	13·2	13·2
	m	4·1	4·0	4·0	4·0
Wing area gross	sq ft	306·2	320·7	327·7	347·9
	sq m	28·45	29·8	30·44	32·32
Tare weight	lb	11,892	13,136	13,435	13,735
	kg	5,394	5,958	6,094	6,230
Loaded weight	lb	15,800	19,764	21,673	21,400
	kg	7,167	8,965	9,831	9,706
Maximum speed at sea level	mph	660	709	713	700
	km/h	1,062	1,141	1,148	1,127
Climb to 40,000 ft (12,192 m)	min	5·16	—	4·69	16·75*
Range	miles	730	493	630	864
	km	1,175	793	1,014	1,390
Initial rate of climb	ft/min	12,300	14,540	14,660	—
	m/min	3,749	4,432	4,468	—
Service ceiling	ft	45,500	39,000*	45,800	41,600*
	m	13,868	11,887	13,960	12,680

*No reheat

Scimitar

Last of the aircraft types designed entirely and built by the Supermarine division of Vickers-Armstrongs (Aircraft), the Scimitar was a single-seat naval fighter powered by twin jet engines. It was evolved through complex stages of development from an official project for an aircraft without undercarriage, designed to operate with a take-off catapult accelerator and a landing 'carpet'. The idea was to save weight and drag, particularly in operations from aircraft carriers. This interesting experiment was the subject of much work by the RAE at Farnborough, but ten years later the project emerged as a conventional type with a retractable undercarriage, but with an advanced feature known as flap-blowing to reduce landing speed.

Ideally, the deletion of the undercarriage promised a considerable gain in performance through reduction of weight, and would have facilitated the high rate of climb demanded by the specification. Powerplant selection depended upon maximum power in a small and comparatively light airframe with small-

297

Mock-up of Type 508 at Hursley Park, with one Rolls-Royce AJ.65 engine above its destined bay.

diameter engines installed closely side by side, thus producing a flat cross-sectional fuselage and ensuring a stable landing on the 'carpet'. The engines selected were the Rolls-Royce AJ.65 axial-flow turbojets later developed as the Avons.

The absence of an undercarriage and its wing mounting also meant that the wing could be made correspondingly thinner structurally, and a seven per cent thickness/chord ratio was adopted for the Type 505, as the aircraft was designated, with bonuses in speed and climb. Swept wings were considered, but at that stage they involved too many unknowns, and a straight form was adopted. The wing section was symmetrical with maximum thickness at 37·5 per cent of the chord, and to avoid tip stalling the aerofoil section was constant over the whole span. Stalling was given special attention and the leading-edge radius was made as large as possible to prevent early breakaway of the airflow.

A V tail of butterfly form was chosen to promote the necessary strength in the fine thickness/chord ratio surfaces and to clear the jet effluxes. It was thought that its high-speed interference effects would be less than those of a normal cruciform tail. Fore and aft control was effected by moving the whole tail but with elevators for additional pitch control and with differential movement for turning, thus replacing a normal rudder. Lateral control was by wide-chord ailerons, with lift spoilers for the approach. Dive-flaps were fitted at one-third chord under the wings to ensure recovery at high Mach numbers by restoring lift and the down-wash over the tail surfaces. To establish the flight characteristics of the type, a fixed tricycle undercarriage was fitted and the cockpit layout was similar to that of the Attacker in that the pilot, from his forward position in the nose, had a good view forwards and downwards, essential for carrier operations. At 40,000 ft the cabin was pressurized to a 33,000 ft atmosphere.

At the time of its design in 1945 the Supermarine 505 represented yet another solution for the layout of twin jet engines in a single-seat fighter. The semi-monocoque fuselage comprised a centre body of basically square cross-section which contained the engine bay with the AJ.65s lying in juxtaposition. The mid-wing spars were attached to the top longerons of the fuselage through bent-up ends with a short strut connection between the elbow thus formed and the bottom longerons, to provide a stress-balancing structure. Cooling of the surrounding skin of the engine bay was by air from the boundary-layer bleeds on the intakes through an annulus around each jet-pipe. Removable panels on the top centre body gave access to fuel tanks, engine accessories and the ammunition bay.

In 1947 the Admiralty abandoned the undercarriageless idea, and Supermarine modified the designs of the 505 to the 508 with a retractable nosewheel undercarriage. Amended operational performance figures included a reduced landing speed, which involved increased dimensions all round. The wing thickness ratio was increased from seven to nine per cent, which, among other advantages, enabled a higher lift coefficient to be obtained to the benefit of the low-level performance and landing characteristics. In conformity the wing area was increased from 270 to 310 sq ft. Both the 505 and the modified 508 were designed with a military version in mind, and the latter could easily be adapted to RAF requirements. At the same time the undercarriageless version could equally have been resuscitated had the naval procurement so required. Structurally, the major difference from the 505 was made by running the main wing spars under the engines to accommodate the undercarriage anchorages, and this changed the centre body to an open boat form, with the engines installed on its floor.

Following the development of a swept-wing version of the earlier Supermarine Attacker, which became the Type 541—the Swift I, Supermarine applied the experience gained to design a swept 508 and reclassified it as Type 525. The

The development Type 508 flying at Boscombe Down as a single-seat fighter. (*Vickers-Armstrongs*)

299

alteration of the wing geometry needed a taller undercarriage positioned further out on the wings. The folded width was also increased, but was still acceptable in carrier lifts, and the overall length of the aeroplane increased to 52 ft as a result of sweeping back the tail surfaces.

Operational criteria in a high-speed carrier-operated aeroplane demanded high-lift devices for approach and landing-on. In the swept-wing 525 these were the NACA double-slotted flaps with extensions under the fuselage, and tapered nose flaps (slats) extending along the leading edges of the wings. In addition, lift spoilers and Attacker-type air-brakes were also provided, as well as dive recovery flaps under the wing at 0·3 chord width.

At first the 'butterfly' tail was retained although swept back, with an adjustable tailplane as in the 508 and the single-engined 510, but structural problems associated with this unconventional design caused it to be replaced later by a normal cruciform type. Little modification was needed to the fuselage of the 508 or of the installation of the Rolls-Royce axial-flow engines, by then called Avon, apart from an increase in fuel capacity needed by later requirements. These resolved into the issue of draft specification N.113D. A contract for two proto-types was placed early in 1951, and later amended to three. Meanwhile the first of the 508 prototypes had been completed and was flown as VX133 by Mike Lithgow on 31 August, 1951, at Boscombe Down. This was followed by deck landing trials on HMS *Eagle* in May 1952, and the prototype 525, VX138, flew in April 1954.

Meanwhile, research into new methods of overcoming turbulence of the boundary layer, either by blowing or by sucking through orifices in the aerofoil surface, were coming into prominence, now made possible by the large quantities of air available from the compressors of jet engines. With their laminar flow experience, Supermarine submitted a proposal to evolve a flap blowing system, or 'super-circulation' as it was called, for the 525.

With a normal flap system the primary object is to increase the lift of a wing and so reduce speed for landing. But large angles of flap deflection can cause separa-tion of the boundary layer when flow breakaway occurs with rapid rise of drag. Skin friction also causes loss of boundary-layer energy, and this can only be regained by adopting some form of energy restoration such as flap blowing. In its simplest form and in the case of the 525 and its development, the Scimitar, this consisted of a device to project a thin jet of high pressure air, bled from the engine compressor, through a narrow slot along the trailing edge of the wing just ahead of the flap hinge. Here the phenomenon known as the Coanda effect took over and bent the jet of air, which tended to follow the contour of the flap, carrying with it local particles of air and thereby neatly rectifying boundary-layer separation. In practice this system of flow control produced a reduction of some 18 mph in approach speed, together with a lower stalling speed and also meant that at a given speed a smaller angle of attack would yield an improved view for deck landing. Control and stability at low approach speeds were improved because of the smoother wake and more stable airflow over the trailing edges. The speed at which they became critical was thus reduced considerably. All these improve-ments were most acceptable in a naval aeroplane.

The first prototype N.113 (as it was to be known until named Scimitar later) was flown under serial WT854 and Type 544 by Mike Lithgow from Boscombe Down on 19 January, 1956, according to his pilot's log. Deck landing trials on HMS *Ark Royal* followed in April, and the other two prototypes were completed and flown later the same year. Although designed as a single-seat fighter, changing oper-ational requirements dictated its future role as a low-level strike aircraft, capable

Type 525 VX138 at Farnborough SBAC Display in 1954.

First prototype Type 544 landing on *Ark Royal* in 1956. (*Vickers-Armstrongs*)

Type 544 WW134, to specification N.113, during proving trials on HMS *Ark Royal* in January 1957. (*Crown copyright*)

of using the under-the-radar LABS attack system (low altitude bombing sortie) and of carrying a nuclear device. In addition, the N.113 had a supersonic speed capability in a shallow dive, a useful attribute in clearing a target zone after a strike. These prerequisites entailed excellent control characteristics and a stout airframe to withstand the buffeting encountered from low-level gusts in high-speed manoeuvres.

At the very high speeds (for the time) which fighters had to fly, lateral, longitudinal and yaw stability became critical. In the case of the Scimitar the rate of roll was very high at moderate Mach numbers, and with the original Fairey powered-controls the ailerons were over-sensitive. This was the first use of duplicated fully-powered-controls in a British naval aircraft. Modification of the system by introducing supplementary hydraulic jacks and differential gearing produced the finer degree of accuracy required. As regards the pitch-up phenomenon experienced in the longitudinal control of the newer generation of high-speed aircraft, various measures were taken in geometrical design to overcome the difficulties apparent at high altitude and high Mach numbers.

Scimitar production at South Marston. (*Vickers-Armstrongs*)

This unwelcome characteristic was caused by the shock-induced separation of the air flow over the wing leading to high-speed tip stall and aggravated by increased downwash over the slab-type all-flying tailplane, that is, with no independent elevator. Introduction of the saw-tooth steps in the wing leading edges, augmented by boundary-layer fences and the adoption of the Kuchemann-shaped wingtips, aided solution of the problem, but perhaps the greatest improvement was made by inverting the whole tailplane, converting a ten degrees dihedral to ten degrees anhedral.

Inertia forces generated during rapid rolls, and particularly in rolling pull-outs, could induce excessive yaw, structurally dangerous to the airframe of aircraft with long fuselages of weight concentration and short stubby wings of relatively lighter weight, as on the Scimitar. Many computer exercises were conducted by Supermarine on this condition, but the advanced engineering already adopted to cover any such strength contingency proved sufficiently sound.

303

These engineering details included high-tensile steel spars and members in major stress areas in the wing and tail, the use of titanium for lower stressed areas where heat resistance was essential, and the introduction of chemical etching to remove surplus metal from wing and tail panels, a method more accurate in terms of panel thickness and certainly quicker and cheaper than conventional machining. In one respect only was the Scimitar airframe in some trouble, and that was from the effect of acoustic waves set up by engine noise on the rear structure, manifested by panel cracking. By using thicker engine skins, steel ribs replacing light alloy ones and synthetic resin bonding backed by foam filling, the problem was sufficiently overcome for a fatigue life of 1,000 hr to be achieved. The Scimitar was not only the largest, heaviest and most powerful fighter the Royal Navy had acquired up to that time, but also was certainly the noisiest!

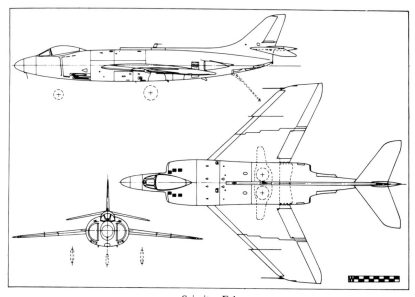

Scimitar F.1

The initial deck landing trials of the Scimitar prototype WT854 were made on HMS *Ark Royal* in April 1956, after a series of simulated deck landings at the RAE Bedford on the runway equipped with arrester gear. At the presentation of the Scimitar to senior Naval and Ministry personnel at Lee-on-Solent in November 1957, it was stated that 148 deck landings and catapultings had been made. The recommended approach speed was 124 kt at a landing weight of 28,000 lb, using the flap blowing. As the attitude on approach was steeper with the blowing on, the nose of the aircraft was lowered to improve the pilot's view. The maximum permissible weight for the steam catapult launch was 34,000 lb at 118 kt.

Naval pilots were trained for deck landings with the Scimitar at Boscombe Down experimental establishment, and a special unit known as 700X Flight was formed to prepare modes of operational practice in what was in effect a new deal in a Naval aircraft of high complexity in systems and equipment. Specialized courses had to be arranged for the instruction of ground personnel and shipboard handling crews. The 700X Flight spent most of its time at Ford Naval Station in

Scimitar F.1 XD216 with long-range tanks and Sidewinder missiles. (*Vickers-Armstrongs*)

Sussex, and 803 Naval Squadron started operational training at Lossiemouth in Scotland in June 1958 before embarking in HMS *Victorious* in the following September. Other squadrons of Scimitars were formed—Nos. 736, 800, 804 and 807, with the expansion of the 700X Flight into 700 Squadron. In addition to *Victorious*, Scimitars were flown from the carriers *Ark Royal, Centaur, Eagle* and *Hermes*, mainly in the low-level strike role, while the contemporary Sea Vixens assumed the interceptor fighter duties. The Scimitar, however, retained throughout its first-line service the four 30 mm Aden guns called for in the original specification.

Scimitar XD212 equipped for 'Buddy' flight refuelling.

305

Scimitar XD216 with four Bullpup missiles. (*Vickers-Armstrongs*)

The Blackburn Buccaneer which was designed for the bombing role with two crew was adopted in 1969 in place of the single-seat Scimitar. This was a matter of naval policy. As it was almost supersonic in level flight, the Scimitar, though much used on weapon trials, could undoubtedly have had a greatly enhanced performance if developed further and would have been a worthy successor to its illustrious forebear—the Supermarine Spitfire.

Scimitar F.I—Two 10,000 lb (4,536 kg) st Rolls-Royce Avon RA24 or RA28, later Avon 200 series. Single seat.
   Span 37 ft 2 in (11·3 m); span folded 20 ft 6½ in (6·16 m); length 55 ft 3 in (16·85 m); height 17 ft 4 in (5·28 m); wing area 484·9 sq ft (45·05 sq m); sweepback 45 deg at 25 per cent chord.
   Empty weight 23,962 lb (10,869 kg); loaded weight 34,200 lb (15,513 kg).
   Maximum speed 640 kt (1,186 km/h) Mach 0·968 at sea level, 587 kt (1,088 km/h) at 30,000 ft (9,144 m).
   Climb to 45,000 ft (13,716 m) in 6·65 min; service ceiling 46,000 ft (14,020 m); normal range 1,422 miles (2,288 km) at 35,000 ft (10,668 m).
   Armament. Four 30 mm Aden cannon and four 1,000 lb (454 kg) bombs or four Bullpup air-to-ground missiles or four Sidewinder air-to-air missiles or other alternatives including four 200 gal (909 litre) drop tanks.

Types 559 and 571

Supermarine design in its own right finally came to an end in 1958 when the office at Hursley Park was closed and the bulk of the staff transferred either to South Marston for work on non-aviation projects or to Weybridge design organization where they continued to work on the TSR2 project as further extension of their experience on the supersonic Types 545, 559 and 571.

Both 559 and 571 followed the philosophy of the integrated weapons system fighter which broadly specified that the airframe and its armament, interception radar, navigational and ground control equipment were to be designed simultaneously with matched performances, integrated into a common system. This concept was already undergoing investigation in the mixed-powerplant fighters as materialized in the form of the Saunders-Roe SR.53 jet-cum-rocket aeroplane. Avro also had a similar project (designation 720) to the Saunders-Roe development of SR.53 which was the P.177. These, together with Supermarine Type 559, were intended to satisfy Operational Requirement OR 329.

Specification F.155T dated 15 January, 1955, written up to comply with the then current requirements, called for a two-seat radar-equipped fighter carrying four missiles. It could not be met without a mixed powerplant of considerable size. For Type 559 the thrust of the two de Havilland Gyron PS.26/1 turbojets was augmented at high speed by reheat and at altitude by two D.H. Spectre Junior rocket motors. To define the performance envelope, the Ministry required an aeroplane capable of intercepting and destroying targets flying at up to Mach 2 at 60,000 ft and when Mach 2·3 was reached at that height to use rocket boost to take it up to 92,000 ft, with the rocket fuel exhausted after 45 seconds, an attack philosophy initiated by the German Me 163 rocket fighters.

An unusual feature of the 559 was the selection of a canard (tail-first) configuration from a number of alternative layouts. It promised a better lift coefficient than conventional design at the stall but the all-moving foreplane was cropped at the tips to avoid the buffeting normally associated with full delta shapes. To prevent any vortices that might have arisen from the foreplane at high angles of

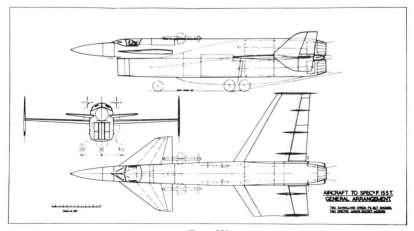

Type 559

307

incidence affecting a centrally disposed fin, the vertical surfaces were wingtip endplates. The wings had integral fuel tanks each carrying 960 gallons. Special attention had to be paid to skin heating because of the high operational speeds and altitudes. Even solar heating had to be taken into account on the pilot's canopy, needing complex air-conditioning.

The development of the fully-automatic control and guidance system was planned to occur in stages in step with the development of the aeroplane, though the instrument and basic control installations would have to be available for the first flight of the prototype. Fully-operational equipment would include facilities for programmed climbs, instrument landings, manoeuvre holding and pre-selection of heading, heights and speeds. More advanced techniques such as mid-course guidance, air interception control and automatic navigation back to base were to follow. The missiles chosen were either the D.H. Blue Jay (later called Firestreak) or the Vickers Red Hebe (development of Red Dean), the former an infra-red seeking device and the latter a semi-active homer operating on a continuous wave transmission.

Although Type 559 started favourite in the F.155T race, all contestants were cancelled by the notorious 1957 Defence White Paper which ordered the abolition of manned fighters in favour of ground-operated missiles. The one requirement left on the military order book for the aircraft industry was for a low-level bomber in the tactical-strike-reconnaissance roles to replace the Canberra.

The main requirements were defined as operation at low-level with tactical strike weapons, a medium-altitude bombing role, and an all-weather reconnaissance role with full photographic capability including night coverage.

For all these duties General Operational Requirement GOR 339 was issued to the Industry and from it emerged the TSR2, a project shared originally between Vickers-Armstrongs Aircraft and the English Electric Company and later assumed by the British Aircraft Corporation when it was formed from the aviation interests of these two firms and others.

Supermarine submitted two project designs to GOR 339 as Type 571, one for a smaller aeroplane of 40,000 lb weight and the larger of 81,000 lb. The former was to be powered by a single Rolls-Royce RB.142 turbojet with reheat and the latter

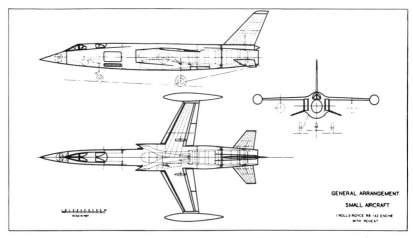

The '40,000 lb' Type 571

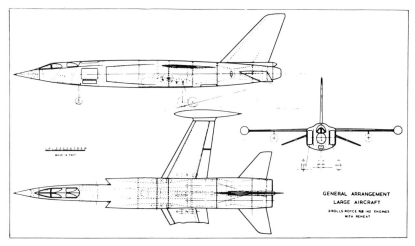

The '81,000 lb' Type 571

with two, also with reheat. Both were to be subject to the integrated weapons system philosophy with a low-level terrain clearance capability achieved by means of sophisticated electronic devices. For this and other operational missions such as LABS these included inertial guidance navigation, sideways and forwards-looking radar, Doppler distance-measuring with unrolling map, and automatic bomb delivery.

A drastic reduction of the size and weight of this sophisticated electronic equipment was promised by the adoption of a design policy of so-called 'miniaturization' of the separate items of auto-control, etc., which philosophy carried through into the TSR2.

Although eventually the larger twin-engined alternative was officially chosen to be married to the English Electric design into the TSR2, Supermarine would have preferred the smaller version of Type 571. It would have followed on nicely behind the Scimitar production line at South Marston as a naval fighter and saved a great deal of the subsequent political wrangling and public money just at a time when Supermarine appeared to have overcome most of their transonic problems.

Type 559—Two 27,000 lb (12,247 kg) st (with reheat) de Havilland PS.26/1 plus two 5,000 lb (2,268 kg) de Havilland Spectre Junior rocket motors. Single seat.
Span 42 ft (12·8 m); length 68 ft 3 in (20·8 m); height 15 ft 3 in (4·65 m); wing area 615 sq ft (57·13 sq m); foreplane area 202 sq ft (18·8 sq m); sweepback 27·5 deg.
Empty weight 41,485 lb (18,817 kg); loaded weight (Red Hebe) 62,190 lb (28,209 kg).
Performance limited by structural heating considerations to a Mach number of 2·5.
Radius of action with internal and external fuel 150 miles (241 km); duration about 32 min.

Type 571. TSR 2—Two (One) 14,000 lb (6,350 kg) st, Rolls-Royce RB.142. Two crew.
Span 41 ft 6 in (12·65 m); small 28 ft (8·53 m); length 77 ft (23·5 m); small 58 ft (17·7 m); wing area 430 sq ft (40 sq m); small 200 sq ft (18·6 sq m).
Internal fuel 4,675 gal (21,252 litres); small 1,948 gal (8,856 litres); loaded weight internal tanks full 81,225 lb (36,843 kg); small 40,220 lb (18,244 kg).
Maximum speed at sea level Mach 1·1 and at 36,000 ft (10,973 m) Mach 2·3 (design limitations).
22,700 lb (10,297 kg) with reheat.

309

Supermarine Sparrow I biplane with 35 hp Blackburne Thrush engine.

Sparrow

In 1924 the Air Ministry offered a prize of £2,000 for the best lightplane designed and built in Great Britain, suitable for flying clubs and the private owner. A contest known as the Two-Seater Light Aeroplane Competition was held at Lympne, Kent, during late September and early October. Supermarine entered a sesquiplane called the Sparrow, the larger upper wing and the smaller lower wing having different wing sections. This was the first landplane they had designed and built since the efforts of the Pemberton Billing company. The engine was the 35 hp Blackburne Thrush, a three-cylinder air-cooled radial, a choice which Mitchell later regretted.

The Sparrow was built of wood, the two-seat fuselage, fitted for dual control, had spruce longerons and plywood covering, and the wings had two spindled spars with built-up ribs and nose ribs and were designed to fold. The aerofoil section of the upper wing was a modified Raf15 known as 'Sloane' and the bottom 'half-wing' had a thin cambered section known as AD1, which presumably was a legacy of the Admiralty Air Department. Interplane struts were of steel tube and both wings had full-span aileron-cum-flaps which could be drooped to vary the wing camber. Wing loading was $3\frac{1}{2}$ lb/sq ft.

First flown by Henri Biard on 11 September, 1924, from Hamble, the Sparrow was registered G-EBJP but it never carried that marking, only the competition number 9 as shown in the illustration. Its colour scheme was a dark blue fuselage and struts, with aluminium doped wings, tail surfaces and engine cowling. It was fitted with a wooden propeller intended to match the engine maker's maximum rpm of 3,500, which was very high for that type of engine and was later held to be responsible for most of its misbehaviour.

The Supermarine staff worked like Trojans testing and retesting the Sparrow, and Biard, who flew it constantly, said 'it was as impudent as its name implied'. One day it would fly properly and the next only a mile or so before its engine stopped. In the fortnight before the start of the competition Biard had nineteen engine failures and other temporary troubles and had sleepless nights and spent his days cursing; but out of it all came success, not the least of which was the emergence of private light aeroplanes exemplified by the D.H. Moth and its contemporaries.

One humourous story deserves to be retold about the preparation of the Sparrow for the contest. The directors of Supermarine, including Mitchell, insisted on a demonstration of the Sparrow before finally deciding to enter. Biard took off, flew the length of two fields when he had the usual engine failure and disappeared from view. When the directors reached the spot after tearing through thick and prickly hedges they found Biard restarting his engine for another try. This process was repeated several times more until they decided it was time to call enough, as the spectacle of chief executives chasing five miles across country was not conducive to preserving the popular image of company directors! What their comments were when the Sparrow was turned round and flown straight back to base without fuss can only be imagined.

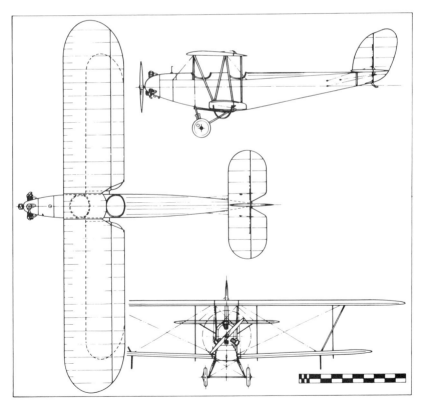

Sparrow I

Late in September a decision was reached to design and make a modified propeller and on 27 September it was fitted on the Sparrow and flown to Lympne. The eliminating trials of the competition began that day with a total of eighteen competitors. The transport tests and folding and re-erecting the aeroplane presented little difficulty but the reliability trials of flying two circuits of the triangular course of 12½ miles, with the pilot occupying first one seat and then the other, was not so easy, as only one entrant, the Beardmore Wee Bee, was successful the first day. Bad weather and sulky engines were the main causes of other failures. After some trial figures of eight before the actual test, Biard did one circuit next day and then after changing cockpits took off and almost as promptly came in again. One of the Supermarine directors wearily went over to ask him why he had landed, all Biard did was to point at the engine where a connecting rod had pierced the crankcase.

Then ensued a frantic race to get another engine fitted before dark, with everyone including Cdr Bird helping. The substitute engine could not be persuaded to run properly in time for the completion of two circuits so the Sparrow was pushed back into the hangar and left there overnight.

The next morning Biard was airborne early in the Sparrow only to have the engine seize up, forcing him to make a landing right among the other competing machines, but the light loading of the aircraft and the expert handling of a professional pilot resulted in no damage to anything. But that was that in the competition as far as the Sparrow was concerned. It was won by Maurice Piercey in the Wee Bee with Cyril Uwins second in the Bristol Brownie.

A Blackburne engine expert was called in to repair the damaged engine but he could only get it to run at full throttle, otherwise it stopped. Even so, Sir Sefton Brancker trusted himself to a solo flight in the Sparrow, brave man. It was entered in the Grosvenor Challenge Cup flown on 14 October and came in fourth at an average speed of 62·08 mph over the course of eight laps of 12½ miles each. The only reason the Sparrow managed to complete the eight laps without engine failure was a new metal propeller which cut the rpm unintentionally from 3,500 to 2,800.

By the end of the year the Sparrow had only managed to fly for about ten hours and it was left in a corner for its future to be decided. After numerous tests and experiments nothing had emerged but proof of the engine's temperamental nature. Mitchell therefore gave it a new engine, a Bristol Cherub III of 32 hp, and changed it from a biplane to a high-wing parasol monoplane as the Sparrow II, with the primary object of flight-testing aerofoils of differing sections.

The Sparrow II was duly entered for the 1926 *Daily Mail* Two-seater Light Aeroplane Competition which was held at Lympne in September. This was an important event because it presaged the eventual private ownership of hundreds of small aircraft and encouraged thousands of budding aviators to join flying clubs. The contest saw the first major public appearance of the de Havilland Moth, the Avro Avian and the Blackburn Bluebird, although the merit of none of them was disclosed under the formula devised for the competition nor indeed by the stewards' peculiar interpretation of the rules. The idea was good and credit accrues to the *Daily Mail* as sponsors but the execution left much to be desired and the Sparrow's was no exception to the ill fortunes that befell many of the competitors. Anyway, Biard must have had premonitions that anything might happen during the out and home circuits scheduled over six days with a total of nearly two thousand miles with twenty-three landings at the Lympne base. His experiences in the King's Cup of 1924 in the Seagull must have been in his mind.

The Sparrow II as a monoplane for calibrated tests of different aerofoils.

Biard was last but one to take off on 12 September, with the weather worsening and in a very strong wind with heavy rain squalls. He lost his way and found himself at Hastings vainly trying to fly into the wind and, as he feared he would have insufficient petrol to go on to Brighton and return, he turned back and arrived at Lympne much earlier than he should have done without completing the course. As it happened, he had not crossed the starting line properly and so his flight did not count as an attempt, although the petrol consumed would have to be regarded as used up in running up and engine tests. Biard however decided to press on but came to grief later in the day when he had to make a forced landing near Beachy Head and was thus eliminated from the competition because each course had to be completed before 8 pm on the day allotted. He landed at Beachy Head because his observer had noticed that one of the pins which held the struts of the wing had worked itself nearly out of its socket and had it come out the wing might have come off, which, as Biard summed up by saying, 'would have been very annoying'. Biard and his observer climbed out, but the wind blew the machine over on one side, so they righted it and put the pin back in place. By then it was near nightfall and so they stayed there, spending an uncomfortable night.

The following morning they tried to take off but found it impossible; they then dumped the lead-shot ballast and tried again, unsuccessfully. Then they set the engine flat out, with each one holding on to a wingtip, guided the machine over the rough turf several yards up the slope of Beachy Head and turned the nose downhill for take-off. The passenger, one of Biard's favourite mechanics, did not want to leave the lead shot behind so volunteered to carry it four miles across country to Pevensey. Biard had to leave him and then ran the Sparrow downhill till she picked up enough speed to take off and so eventually arrived back at Lympne.

The competition was won by the Hawker Cygnet flown by Flt Lt P. W. S. Bulman and only three other machines finished. The Sparrow also competed in the Steward's Prize, which was for the eliminated aircraft, on 17 September and again that day in the Grosvenor Cup Race but was unplaced in both.

313

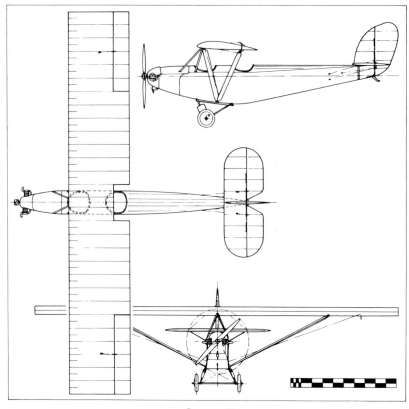

Sparrow II

In 1927, under Air Ministry contract 730450/26/49, the Sparrow II was used for flight comparison trials of identical wings with four different aerofoil sections. These were the Clark Y, T64, Raf30 and SA12 (a development of the Raf30), and the object of using the Sparrow monoplane was that the wing was mounted well above the fuselage thus reducing interference effects to a minimum.

The tests were made at Worthy Down, with Biard at the controls and E. H. Mansbridge of Supermarine design staff as the observer. Maximum speed, minimum flying speed, and time to reach 5,000 ft with intermediate times at intervals of 500 ft were carefully recorded. The total flying time amounted to 10 hr 45 min.

For these tests the engine speeds were kept constant at 3,100 rpm for all high-speed tests and 3,000 rpm throughout all the climbs at a fully-loaded aircraft weight of 943 lb. The results showed that with the Clark Y the machine was slightly tail heavy, with the Raf30 considerably tail heavy, but with the SA12 the machine was in excellent balance and was capable of climbing and gliding 'hands off' and was more pleasant to fly. With the T64 the machine was considerably tail heavy and it was noticeable that when landing the machine appeared to drop out of the air quite suddenly when about five feet off the ground, thus confirming the known characteristics of this aerofoil section. The Raf30 wing was marginally

314

better on recorded speeds while the SA12 had much the best climbing times. As a result of these tests the SA12 was chosen for and used on the Nanok (Solent). After that the Sparrow II was dumped in a shed at Hythe following more problems flying it there on to a nearby narrow road. In May 1929 it was given to the Halton Aero Club. As far as is known, no photograph exists to prove that the Sparrow II ever had its registration G-EBJP painted on, but reports indicate that the aircraft survived until 1933.

Sparrow I—One 35 hp Blackburne Thrush. Two-seat dual control.
Span (upper wing) 33 ft 4 in (10·15 m); length 23 ft 6 in (7·16 m); height 7 ft 5 in (2·26 m); wing area 256 sq ft (23·78 sq m).
Empty weight 475 lb (215 kg); loaded weight 860 lb (390 kg).
Maximum speed 72 mph (115·8 km/h); landing speed 27 mph (43·4 km/h); ceiling 11,000 ft (3,353 m).

Sparrow II—One 32 hp Bristol Cherub III. Two-seat dual control.
Span 34 ft (10·36 m); length 23 ft (7·01 m); height 7 ft 5 in (2·26 m); wing area 193 sq ft (17·93 sq m).
Competition weights—empty 605 lb (274 kg), loaded 1,000 lb (453 kg).
Maximum speed (Raf 30) 65 mph (104·6 km/h); minimum flying speed (Clark Y) 30 mph (48·2 km/h); best climb to 1,000 ft (305 m) (SA12) 4 min 5 sec.

Type 179 'Giant'

Oswald Short of the aircraft firm Short Brothers, having seen the German Dornier Do X, decided that he could do better and prepared a similar design which he submitted to the Air Ministry's Director of Technical Development, Air Commodore A. Chamier, who showed interest but took no action. Undaunted, Oswald Short then made a direct approach to the Chief of the Air Staff, Sir Hugh Trenchard, who agreed eventually to recommend it to the sum of £60,000, exclusive of embodiment loan items, engines and armament. Around this, design specification R.6/28 was written, and this was of necessity circulated to other aircraft firms, including Supermarine, who received a request to tender on 17 November, 1928, for a large multi-engined all-metal boat seaplane. Supermarine's tender was declined but Shorts were given the go ahead to build the Sarafand to the specification.

Another specification, 20/28, received by Supermarine on 18 May, 1929, was for a civil version of the R.6/28 to carry 40 passengers. This time Supermarine's tender was successful, though it took almost a year before the contract was drawn up for one aircraft at a cost of £86,585. This was approved by the Air Minister, Lord Thomson, but his valuable support was lost when he was killed in the R 101 airship disaster in October 1930.

The first drawings for the Supermarine R.6/28, dated 31 January, 1929, were for a high-wing monoplane with a thick Raf 34 aerofoil section, powered by six inline engines in three nacelles and driving tractor and pusher airscrews. The nacelles were supported above the elliptical wing on pylons, with four machine-gun positions. Sponson-type floats were attached directly to the underside of the wing and would have made the water behaviour of the seaplane comparable with

The original layout of the Supermarine Type 179 with tandem rows of Bristol Jupiter
engines and passenger cabins within the wing.

that of a modern trimaran. Triple fins and rudders were selected. This design
somewhat resembled Oswald Short's Sarafand except that the monoplane
arrangement had been selected. The span was 160 ft, length 102 ft and height 29 ft,
and the mainplane area was 3,520 sq/ft.

The first general-arrangement drawings for the civil 20/28 were dated 15 July,
1929, and Mitchell had changed to radial engines, arranging them in three tandem
pairs driving tractor propellers, with a hull modified forward of the wing. In
parallel with this design he produced drawings of the same date as that of the
R.6/28 configuration but modified by mounting the wing floats on struts and
altering the tail unit after certain wind-tunnel tests. It is not known which design
was offered but probably, because of the higher efficiency of inline engines, these
were selected to power the new aircraft in preference to the newer type radial
engines.

The engines chosen were to be six steam-cooled 850/900 hp Rolls-Royce
Buzzards. An experiment, ending in August 1930, was made on a one-quarter
scale model to investigate the mechanism of the steam cooling, using the leading
edge of the large wing as a condenser. Particular investigation was needed into the
displacement of the air in the wing caused by the steam cooling. The resulting
Supermarine report proved that this system of cooling was feasible.

On 29 October, 1930, Major H. J. Payn, then a Supermarine executive,
reported that the Type 179, as the design was classified, had an all-up weight of
65,000 lb—a reduction of 9,000 lb from the figure of 74,000 lb loaded as previously
quoted to the Air Ministry. The weight was later quoted as 72,500 lb.

The Air Ministry *Report on the Progress of Civil Aviation 1930* under the
heading 'Mediterranean Flying Boat' stated '. . . being built with idea of increasing length of flight stages on routes such as through the Mediterranean. Luxurious
accommodation will be provided for 40 passengers, while detachable bunks are
being fitted in order that sleeping accommodation may be available for half that
number'. It was also stated that the aircraft 'Will be entirely of metal with the
exception of fabric covering to trailing portion of wing.' The all-up weight was

quoted as approximately 35 tons. The Type 179 would obviously have been operated by Imperial Airways had it been completed.

On 12 June, 1931, the design had been changed to a four-nacelle layout, with the two inners having two engines apiece driving fore and aft propellers and the two outers with a single engine each driving a tractor propeller; all were mounted on streamlined struts. In this changed configuration the 40 passengers were to be accommodated entirely within the hull, thus dispensing with the leading-edge seating and enabling the wing thickness to be reduced inboard.

Component weights quoted, as well as the above all-up weight, were: 2,780 lb for one outer nacelle and mounting complete, 5,630 lb for the weight of one inner nacelle and mounting complete, 550 lb for the weight of one wing float and mounting, and 6,300 lb for the weight of petrol and tanks. This design still had triple fins and rudders but by January 1932 these were changed to a single fin and rudder although with a small tailplane added above the main tailplane as seen here in the general arrangement drawing. On 7 April, 1931, the aeroplane, constructor's number 1316, was registered as G-ABLE and the keel was laid shortly afterwards. It was called the 'Giant'.

From the 1929 and 1931 Schneider successes, Rolls-Royce had accumulated additional engine data on the Rolls-Royce Buzzard (the basis of the racing R engine) so it was not surprising that the power of the engine had been increased during November 1931 to 1,030 hp at normal rpm and climbing. It was then called the Buzzard MS (moderately supercharged). The introduction of these engines entailed reconsideration of the proposed steam-cooling system. With the original radiator area of 2,400 sq ft, or 2,880 sq ft corrugated surface area, the following data were estimated in a report dated 4 December, 1931: horse power dissipated

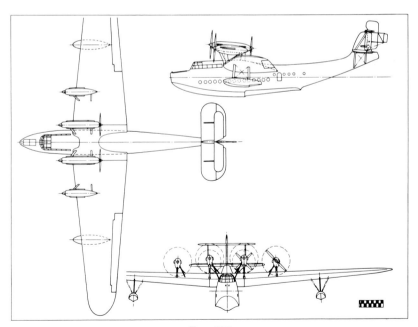

Type 179

317

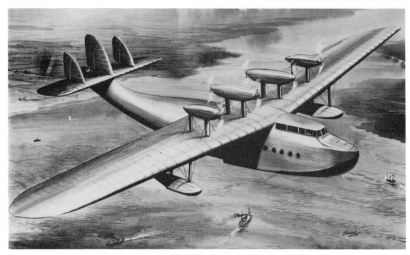

Drawing of the Type 179 with Rolls-Royce Buzzard engines.

by 'Giant' steam-cooled wing 1·0 hp per sq/ft; heat to jackets 490 hp per engine; total horse power to be dissipated 2,940; area required 2,940 sq/ft. The report continued 'It is considered that provision should be made for dealing with 10 per cent of the above horse power by means of honeycomb radiators fitted if found necessary after preliminary trials'.

By 5 January, 1932, the aircraft shape had changed again, each main engine mounting strut being replaced by a smaller centre strut and longitudinal struts replaced the bracing wires previously considered. There was again a redesigned tailplane and rudder of increased areas.

The hull of the Type 179 under construction.

318

When the aircraft had reached the stage as seen in the photograph, which was dated 19 January, 1932, the Government cancelled the contract on the grounds of economy and the work already done was scrapped. In 1961 the registration G-ABLE was re-issued to a Cessna 170A.

At a subsequent meeting of Vickers Joint Design Committee held at Weybridge, attended by the three designers, Mitchell, R. K. Pierson and B. N. Wallis, various points concerning the experience gained with the 'Giant' project were discussed, some at great length. One of these was on wing design with thick aerofoil sections and it was agreed that interference from wing roots, struts and in particular from multi-engine mountings was more responsible for poor performance, as shown up in wind-tunnel tests, than the choice of aerofoil sections. With the 'Giant' wing alone the wind-tunnel results were as predicted but with the engines in position there was a considerable decrease in lift readings. Alterations to engine position and incidence gave much better figures. With regard to the steam-cooling system, Pierson and Mitchell were authorized to visit Rolls-Royce to discuss the subject and later on a similar system with leading-edge condensers was embodied in the Supermarine F.7/30 single-seat fighter.

Type 179—Six 850/900 hp Rolls-Royce H (later 1,030 hp Rolls-Royce Buzzard MS in December 1931). Seven crew and up to 40 passengers.

Span 185 ft (56·4 m); length 104 ft 6 in (31·85 m); height 32 ft (9·75 m); wing area 4,720 sq ft (438·5 sq m).

Empty weight 49,390 lb (22,403 kg); loaded weight 75,090 lb (34,060 kg); fuel 2,175 gal (9,887·5 litres); oil 105 gal (477·3 litres).

Maximum speed 145 mph (233·35 km/h) at sea level; alighting speed 72·5 mph (116·7 km/h); normal range 700 miles (1,127 km) but 1,300 miles (2,092 km) under above fuel load at 108·5 mph (174·6 km/h); maximum rate of climb 750 ft/min (230 m/min) at sea level; service ceiling 11,000 ft (3,353 m); endurance about 12 hr.

Data for design at July 1931, and estimated performance.

Types 316–318 B.12/36 Bomber

After Hitler's statement to Anthony Eden and Sir John Simon in March 1935 that the German Air Force already equalled the Royal Air Force in striking power, the Air Staff reacted quickly and issued specification B.12/36 in July 1936 for a high-speed four-engined long-range strategic bomber. From the tenders received, contracts were awarded to Supermarine and Short Brothers for two prototypes each, L6889 and L6890 from Supermarine and L7600 and L7605 from Short Brothers. It seems odd now that these two firms, who were specialists in seaplanes and flying-boats, were expected to build the heaviest bomber in the world.

B.12/36 required that design, construction and satisfactory operation of all services must proceed with the greatest possible speed, which obviously implied that existing materials and technology should be used. The pilot should have an excellent view in all directions (including aft), and the armament should comprise nose and tail multi-gun turrets, together with a retractable ventral 'dustbin' turret for protection against beam and under-belly attacks. A crew of six was specified, with accommodation for a reserve member with rest stations and for twenty-four armed troops, for which duty a level floor and an adequate number of push-out emergency exit windows were to be provided. The largest bombs to be carried in the B.12/36 were to be 2,000 lb armour-piercing type. As C. H. Barnes says in his definitive book on Shorts aircraft*, the divided bomb compartments limited the size of the bombs to 2,000 lb, nothing larger, which reduced the capability of what became the Short Stirling and might have similarly affected Supermarine's B.12/36 had it been produced.

Another requirement was that the airframe had to be 'broken down' by means of bolted or screwed joints into components small enough to fit into the existing packing-cases used by the Air Ministry. These in turn were based on the existing capacity of the standard-gauge railway wagons. Another requirement was that similar components had to be interchangeable. Finally, the bomber had to be able to use the existing grass airfields, and to have a catapulting capability for short take-off. In the extreme case of having to 'ditch' it had to be able to stay afloat for several hours. The span had to be less than 100 ft to enable the aircraft to fit into existing RAF hangars.

Model of the Type 317 to heavy bomber specification B.12/36.

These requirements were no deterrent to Mitchell, and his tender was sent to the Air Ministry in September 1936, under Types 316–318, with provision for five alternative engines, the Bristol Pegasus XVIII and Hercules HE1 SM, the Rolls-Royce Kestrel KV 26 and Merlin F, and the Napier Dagger E 108. The detailed Supermarine specification 455 is of more than usual interest, because it represents Mitchell's final thoughts on advanced aircraft design—B.12/36 was in fact his last design, as he died shortly after. What he would have done with the high-speed aeroplane, given the jet engine, is a matter for speculation. In addition, the estimates for Supermarine's B.12/36 have miraculously survived and are appended to give an inner look at the technical requirements of British bomber philosophy in 1936.

The single-spar wing of the B.12/36, as developed by Supermarine over a number of years and used in the F.7/30 and Spitfire, made multi-tier storage of bombs unnecessary. Bombs could be slung in a single tier in the fuselage and in the wing aft of the spar. This bomb installation took up space in the wings normally unused and also enabled the design of a smaller fuselage. The wing bomb-storage scheme also had the advantage of distributing the load over the span and so would have reduced the wing bending moments in flight and thereby

*Shorts Aircraft since 1900—Putnam, London.

320

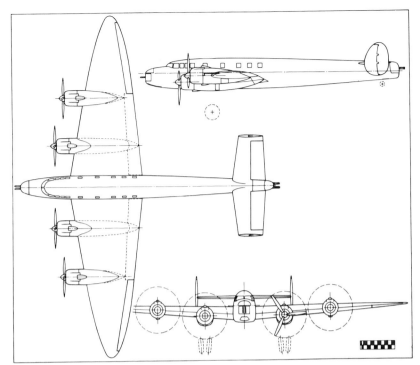

Type 317 (B.12/36)

the weight of the wing. A comparison of volumes as put forward by Supermarine to press their case was as follows: fuselage 2,180 cu/ft; wing outside fuselage 1,900 cu/ft; volume of bombs and attachments in fuselage 335 cu/ft. If all bombs had been carried in the fuselage, tier storage would have had to be used and the fuselage would have been 42 per cent larger while the wing size would have stayed the same. The actual bomb load scheduled could be: 29—250 lb 'B' bombs, 27—500 lb 'AS' bombs, 29—500 lb bombs of sizes other than 'AS', or 7—2,000 lb 'AP' bombs.

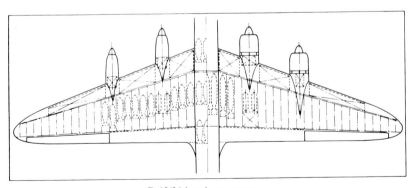

B.12/36 bomb arrangement

321

As already stated, the light alloy wing was of the single-spar stressed-skin type. The spar, having built-up flanges and plate webs, was situated near the maximum thickness of the wing and would resist all bending. Torsion was resisted by the metal nose portion from the spar to the leading edge over that portion of the wing inboard of the outermost bomb installation. Outboard of this point, the whole wing section was torsionally resistant as far as the false spar supporting the aileron. An important structural feature was the incorporation of the fuel tanks in the wing structure as portions of the metal leading edge. This feature resulted in a weight saving of approximately 1,000 lb as the effective weight of the tankage was very small and the petrol load which relieved bending was a large proportion of the all-up weight (about 30 per cent). The wing section was of the NACA 2200 series. It was found advisable to use a four-wheeled two-unit chassis in order to reduce the space necessary for retraction. The wheels were arranged in pairs side by side beneath the inboard nacelles, the units swinging backwards into the rear portion of the nacelles to retract completely. A single fin was chosen to increase the tail gunner's range of vision. Provision was made for the carrying of 26 men and equipment as alternative load.

Power-operated gun turrets were to have been developed by Supermarine or in conjunction with Nash and Thompson Limited. The Supermarine type shown on the drawing could accommodate either two or four Browning machine-guns and was arranged to give the gunner the maximum of comfort and the widest possible view by locating the guns between his knees instead of in front of his face. The nose and tail turrets were interchangeable and each contained four magazines of 1,500 rounds each. The retractable ventral mid-turret contained four magazines of 1,000 rounds each. The low position of the gun mounting permitted a small diameter turret, eliminated gun slots in front of the gunner and enabled the moment of inertia of the turret to be reduced, thus improving rotative acceleration.

At a design conference held on 12 January, 1937, with a view to interchangeably accommodating the Hercules or Merlin engines, the design was reconsidered. It was stated that the landing condition would not be adequately met. To improve this the wing area was increased from 1,240 sq/ft to 1,358 sq/ft and the flaps increased from 14 per cent chord to 17 per cent. The following items were also redesigned. Twin fins and rudders were proposed, to give less weight and greater aerodynamic efficiency but slightly inferior view for the rear gunner. In view of the fact that the Hercules required more fuel than the Merlin engines, it was considered reasonable to provide fuel half way between the two engine requirements, 2,290 gallons. This would mean that the aeroplane would attain 3,000 miles range at 282 mph instead of 302 mph mean cruising speed when fitted with the Hercules. Details as amended are shown in Table II for three of the engine types as originally tabulated in Table I, the other two are presumed to have been abandoned. It is surprising how quickly designs were changed and especially in the case where the engines were being developed; for instance, the main performance figures had changed yet again by 7 September, 1937, as in columns 4 and 5 of Table II.

B.12/36

Table I

		Bristol Hercules HE1 SM	Rolls-Royce Merlin F	Napier Dagger E 108	Bristol Pegasus XVIII	Rolls-Royce Kestrel KV 26
Maximum power	BHP	1,300	1,035	1,000	945	855
Maximum	RPM	2,750	3,000	4,400	2,475	3,000
Height	ft	12,500	16,000	Sea level	Sea level	15,000
	m	3,810	4,877	Sea level	Sea level	4,572
Maximum loaded weight	lb	54,715	51,855	49,364	49,792	47,460
	kg	24,818	23,521	22,391	22,585	21,527
Maximum speed	mph	370	355	330	330	330
	km/h	595	571	531	531	531

Span 93 ft (28·35 m); length 71 ft (21·64 m); height on chassis 19 ft (5·79 m); wing area 1,240 sq ft (115·2 sq m).

Cruising with maximum load 14,000 lb (6,350 kg) bomb load and range of 2,000 miles (3,219 km) at ⅔ power.

Optimum speed	mph	306	287	266	270	270
	km/h	492	462	428	435	435
Height	ft	18,000	21,000	16,000	21,000	20,000
	m	5,486	6,401	4,877	6,401	6,096
At 15,000 ft (4,572 m)	mph	300	275	265	258	258
	km/h	483	443	426	415	415
Service ceiling	ft	34,000	36,000	32,000	30,000	32,000
	m	10,363	10,973	9,754	9,144	9,754

Table II

		Bristol Hercules HE1 SM	Rolls-Royce Merlin G	Napier Dagger E 108
Maximum power	BHP	1,330	1,100	1,100
Maximum	RPM	2,750	2,850	4,400
Height		Sea level	Sea level	Sea level
Tare weight	lb	25,440	24,539	23,310
	kg	11,539	11,131	10,573
Maximum loaded weight	lb	55,745	52,611	50,681
	kg	25,286	23,864	22,989
Maximum speed	mph	360	345	325
	km/h	579	555	523
At height	ft	14,500	18,000	17,000
	m	4,420	5,486	5,182

Span 97 ft (29·6 m); length 73 ft 6 in (22·4 m); height on chassis 17 ft 3½ in (5·5 m); wing area 1,358 sq ft (126·2 sq m).

Cruising with maximum load 14,000 lb (6,350 kg) bomb load and range of 2,000 miles (3,219 km) at ⅔ power at 15,000 ft (4,572 m).

Speed	mph	299	278	267
	km/h	481	447	430
Service ceiling	ft	33,000	30,000	30,000
	m	10,058	9,144	9,144

However, the basic design of the airframe and wings was settled and drawings were prepared under Type 316 for all the assemblies and components. A fuselage mock-up was constructed and visited by Wing Commander McEntegart of the Air Ministry on 12 August, 1937, at Supermarine. Basic design assumptions using the Hercules HE1 SM were raised on 15 October. Two figures not quoted previously were a cruising speed of 300 mph at 15,000 ft, and a stalling speed of 78·5 mph. A visit by Supermarine executives to Bristol, on 22 November, helped to finalize certain details as regards the engine and its installation.

After another twelve months the following figures were sent to the Air Ministry, actually on 11 November, 1938, once again differing slightly from the previous figures: top speed 330 mph at 17,000 ft; maximum cruising speed 290 mph at 15,000 ft; range 1,980 miles at 179 mph at 15,000 ft, with 2,000 lb bomb load, at normal all-up weight of 44,000 lb; and service ceiling of 32,000 ft.

At the maximum overload weight of 59,000 lb the following data applied: range 3,680 miles at 202 mph at 15,000 ft and bomb load of 8,000 lb; range 2,360 miles at 208 mph at 15,000 ft and maximum bomb load of 14,000 lb.

To sum up as regards the final configuration in January 1939, Supermarine claimed the following advantages for their B.12/36.

1. Fuel 2,500 gallons or 20,000 lb—considerably more than the whole of the aeroplane structure; 2. fundamentally the most efficient structurally; 3. straightforward to design and construct; 4. minimum maintenance; 5. reduction of fuel tank weight; 6. adaptable to modern requirements of locating as much load as possible in the wings; 7. resulting in a design of small size and low drag and hence high overall efficiency.

The cumulative effect of these advantages resulted in the Supermarine design being lighter, smaller and having a considerably higher performance than any other design submitted to the Air Ministry to the same specification.

The part of the specification referring to the catapulting requirement was gone into quite thoroughly by Supermarine, one of the last schemes being that the

Front fuselage of the Type 317 under construction, spring 1939. (*Crown copyright*)

Completed fuselage of the Type 317 at the Itchen Works (*Vickers*)

aircraft should take-off from a 'rail assister track', similar to those used by the German V 1 pilotless bomber during the latter part of the war.

Design and construction of the two prototype fuselages at Itchen Works were nearing completion when the factory was bombed and both were severely damaged when the German Luftwaffe made a heavy daylight low-level attack on 26 September, 1940.

The Short Stirling prototype, L7600, first flew on 14 May, 1939, but on landing one brake seized and the aircraft was written off. Thus, of the four B.12/36 prototypes ordered, only one, L7605, was of use as a flying test-bed for development. The Stirling and B.1/35 Avro Manchester production lines were well advanced so the Air Ministry decided that Supermarine should concentrate primarily on the production and development of the Spitfire as well as on the Walrus, the Sea Otter and other promising projects.

For comparison the Short Stirling had a maximum speed of only 260 mph, compared with the Supermarine design's speed of over 300 mph, a maximum range of 2,010 miles compared to 3,000 miles at all-up weight of 59,400 lb, and bomb loads of 3,500 lb and 8,000 lb respectively. A total of 2,381 Stirlings was built but a projected production quantity at South Marston was cancelled.

The Vickers design to this specification had a span of 135 ft, wing area 1,520 sq/ft, normal loaded weight 49,520 lb, maximum loaded weight 68,000 lb, was fitted with four Bristol Hercules HE1 SM giving a top speed in MS gear of 262 mph. It would have had geodetic construction and a successor, the Vickers Windsor, to specification B.5/41, was actually built, three prototypes being flown.*

The detailed description of this project discloses the advanced thinking of R. J. Mitchell, particularly when considering his clever adaptation of wing space to house the major bomb and fuel loads to relieve wing bending loads and reduce ultimate weight, a feature of all modern long-range aircraft.

*See *Vickers Aircraft since 1908*—Putnam, London.

Some Supermarine Design Projects

Like most of the British aircraft companies that survived the First World War,
Supermarine were active in submitting many attractive design projects for new
types to meet official specifications or to attract interest from potential operators,
possibly from emergent countries new to air transport. Some of these are outlined
here ranging from the ambitious transatlantic triplane flying-boat of 1919 to the
quarter-scale SST model of the Concorde.

In the military sphere came attempts to harvest the knowledge derived from
participation in the Schneider Trophy International Seaplane Contest from improvements to the single-seat fighter flying-boat as exemplified by the Admiralty
Air Department Baby of the First World War to the ultimate Spitfire of the
Second World War.

The 'unframed' drawings were specially prepared from surviving Supermarine
drawings which were not suitable for reproduction.

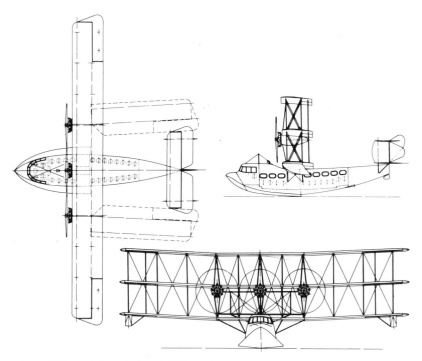

An ambitious triplane design of 1919 as a 24-passenger transatlantic transport flying-
boat with three Bristol Jupiters or Napier Lions as alternative power.

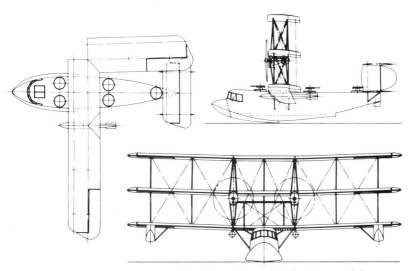

Shark type triplane torpedo-carrier flying-boat with two Napier Lions and five gun positions. Span 76 ft; loaded weight 14,000 lb.

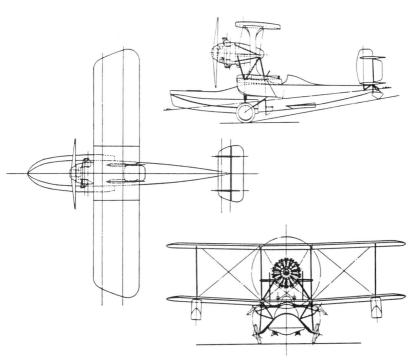

A single-seat fighter flying-boat design of 1921 to DoR type 6 with a Jupiter or Jaguar engine. Span 29 ft, length 24 ft; speed 120 kt at 10,000 ft.

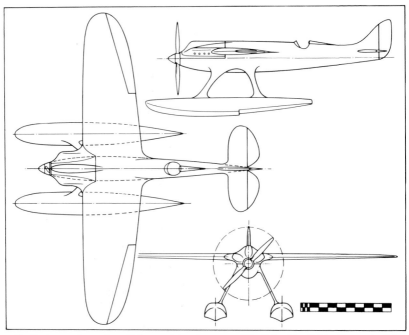

Preliminary scheme for a high-speed development of the Schneider S.4 leading to the S.5 and (*below*) original drawing by Joe Smith for proposed layout of Schneider S.5 as strut-braced monoplane but wire-bracing finally preferred.

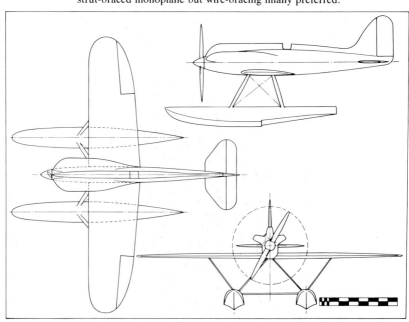

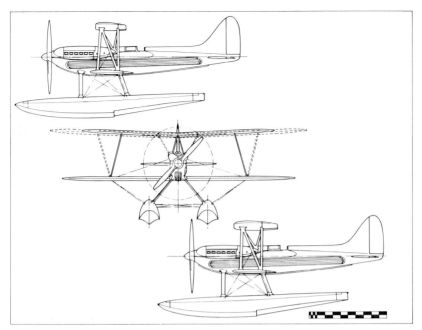

An interesting scheme for adding wing area to a Schneider S.6 to lower alighting speed to 90 mph for experiments.

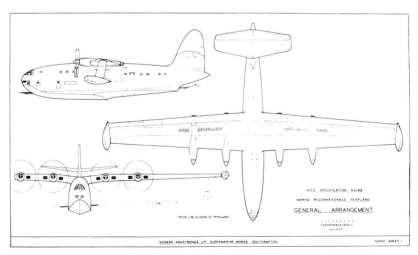

Last Supermarine maritime design to specification R.2/48 with four Bristol Proteus propeller-turbines. Estimated speed 338 kt at 24,000 ft; span 148 ft; loaded weight 117,110 lb; and comparative to Saro Princess. This was Type 524.

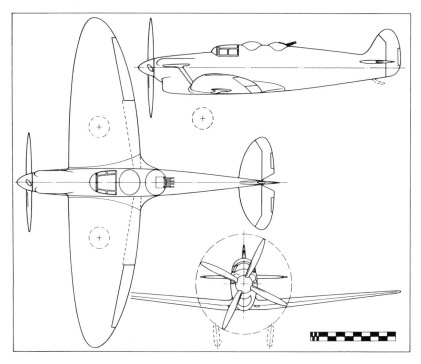

F.9/35 two-seat Spitfire comparative with the Hawker Hotspur. Span 37 ft; length 30 ft 6 in; loaded weight 5,650 lb; speed 315 mph at 15,000 ft; and (*below*) the Mark IV Spitfire proper—the first scheme for a Griffon-engined type. Span 40 ft 6 in, length 30 ft 6 in; weight loaded 8,095 lb; estimated maximum speed 433 mph at 23,500 ft. Six 20 mm cannon.

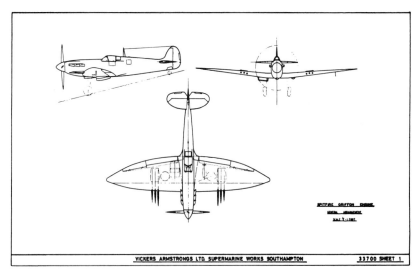

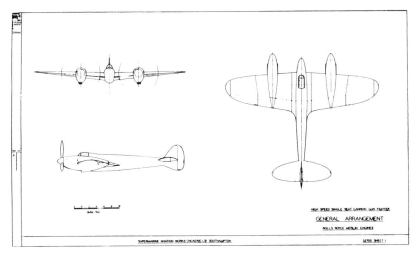

Supermarine drawing of the Type 327 twin-Merlin six-cannon fighter to specification F.18/37. Span 40 ft, length 33 ft 6 in; loaded weight 11,312 lb; maximum speed 465 mph at 22,000 ft.

Type 327 project in mock-up form in 1939 as a twin-engined six-cannon fighter.

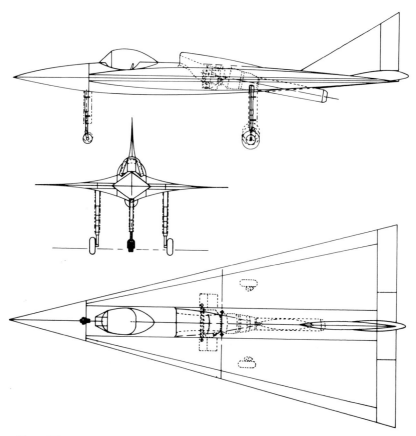

Type 573 quarter-scale SST slender-wing piloted model for Concorde—leading to Handley Page 115.

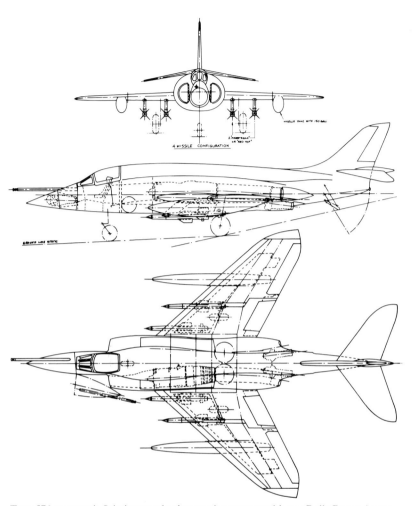

Type 576 supersonic Scimitar as mixed-power interceptor with two Rolls-Royce Avons
and two DH Spectre rocket boosters. Span 41 ft, length 61 ft; weight loaded 51,357 lb;
Mach 1·8 at 65,000 ft.

A very small part of Castle Bromwich Spitfire Mk VB production in 1942.
(*Vickers-Armstrongs*)

Spitfire Production Dispersal

Spitfire production in Southampton suffered much as a result of enemy action in the early part of the Second World War. With the fall of France in 1940 and the evacuation of the British Expeditionary Force from Dunkirk, enemy airfields were established just across the English Channel and air attacks on Southern England, increasing rapidly, culminated in the Battle of Britain. It was a crucial period, the outcome of which largely depended on the production of fighter aircraft in the greatest possible numbers.

The production of Spitfires was originally confined to the Woolston Works, with assembly and flight testing at Eastleigh Airport. A new factory, to be known as Itchen Works, had been completed in 1939 on land reclaimed from the River Itchen not far from the Woolston Works, and was intended initially for Walrus and Sea Otter production; construction of Spitfire fuselages soon began there, the wings being built by General Aircraft and Pobjoy Airmotors under sub-contract.

When the original contract for 310 Spitfires was placed on 3 June, 1936, Vickers Supermarine were restricted to producing fuselages only, together with final assembly and flight testing. Therefore, in effect, dispersed production was established from the start, the main difference between it and the subsequent dispersal programme necessitated by the bombing of the Southampton factories in 1940 was that the original sub-contractors were not controlled by Vickers, as in the later dispersal. This official policy was later severely criticized by Sir Robert McLean, who in 1936 was Chairman of Vickers (Aviation) Ltd. It was claimed by him to have held up the supply of Spitfires at the most critical time.

The programme of sub-contracting was as follows:

Wings—General Aircraft, Feltham, and Pobjoy Airmotors, Rochester; tail unit—Folland Aircraft, Hamble; wingtips—English Electric, Preston; ailerons and elevators—Aero Engines, Kingsmead, Bristol; engine mountings—Singer Motors, Coventry; fuselage frames—J. S. White, Cowes; wing ribs—Westland Aircraft, Yeovil, and G. Beaton and Son; and leading edges—Pressed Steel, Cowley.

This background of sub-contracting caused the planners a great deal of concern. The fuselage, complete with engine and tail-unit, although advanced in design was a straightforward production task; the wings, however, presented a major problem. A design feature of the Spitfire wing was the spar at 25 per cent chord, with a leading-edge torsion-box formed from 14 swg flush-riveted skin, giving a good form to the most important part of the aerofoil. Without this section, wing production could not proceed, and this was one of the main reasons for the initial delay in early deliveries.

The first production Spitfire flew on 14 May, 1938, and was delivered in July to Martlesham Heath. By the end of June, 80 fuselages had been completed but only 12 sets of wings. To help redress the balance 12 wing assembly jigs were built at the Woolston Works in April 1938. One of the major dispersal tasks was to ensure supplies of leading-edge torsion-box assemblies. This applied not only to the sub-assembly system introduced by the Air Ministry before the war but also to the crash programme that had to be devised later when the Southampton aircraft factories were destroyed by enemy action. With hindsight it is now clear that of

The Woolston Works of Supermarine as rebuilt just before the Second World War.

the Vickers aircraft of the time, the Weybridge Wellington and the Supermarine Spitfire, embodying advanced structural philosophies, were unsuitable for the early exploratory break-down pattern of aircraft production. In the case of the Spitfire the worst possible items were chosen for sub-contracting, the wing components.

So by the end of June 1940, although the orders for Spitfires totalled 2,610, only about 800 had been delivered. The new 'shadow' factory at Castle Bromwich, near Birmingham, which had to be taken over by Vickers from the Nuffield motor car organization after their inability to master the intricacies of aircraft construction, had at that time only just completed its first Spitfire. The situation was crucial. Production capacity had fallen far short of the then undefined but predictable needs of Fighter Command.

This predicament had been foreseen by men of vision who had begun to plan their action before the German forces started to move across Europe in the spring and early summer of 1940. In November 1939 the accounts department of Supermarine moved to Deepdene House in Southampton and the tank and pipe fabrication unit to the Weston Rolling Mills. Various other properties were requisitioned in Southampton under powers conferred by the Defence of the Realm Act, as further expansion at Woolston and Itchen was impossible. On 1 December, 1939, Leonard G. Gooch, a young engineer from Supermarine's project office, was appointed works engineer responsible to John Butler, the production manager, to plan a complete production line among suitable premises in Southampton, feeding components into Eastleigh for assembly and flight test. Gooch's plan was put into operation by Gilbert Olsen, a young foreman, whose organizing ability played a vital part in the complex operation of building an advanced fighter aeroplane in a well-dispersed series of unlikely workshops, by people who were not necessarily skilled aircraft workers. This dispersal was virtually completed by 20 September, 1940, with the planners blissfully ignorant that disaster was only four days away.

At 13.30 hr on 24 September the Observer Corps* post at Sandown on the southeast coast of the Isle of Wight reported 17 hostile aircraft at 15,000 ft flying towards Portsmouth. Turning, the formation of Messerschmitt Bf 110 bombers flew up Southampton Water, coming inland over Hamble at 13.32 and peeling off to make individual attacks on the Itchen Works, in the course of which one Messerschmitt was shot down by gunfire. No direct hits were made on the Works but six near misses blew in all the window glass and removed the roof as well as a lot of the asbestos sheeting covering the walls. Several Spitfire fuselages were damaged. A direct hit on an air-raid shelter tragically accounted for a large proportion of the 90 people killed and the 40 other casualties, mostly valued aircraft workers. A red alert had been issued when the bombers crossed the Isle of Wight but inexplicably no sirens sounded and local warnings were given only when the bombs had started falling and the guns had opened fire. The rest of the day was given over to attending to the casualties and clearing the debris. Night shift was cancelled and the following day work began salvaging as much as possible on to 'low loader' transport, but a further interruption occurred when a Dornier Do 17 flew across the Isle of Wight and in broken cloud dived towards the Supermarine factories, turned and made off in the way it had come. The result of

*The distinction 'Royal' was not added to the name of the Corps until later, an honour granted in recognition of its original contribution to the Air Defence of Great Britain.

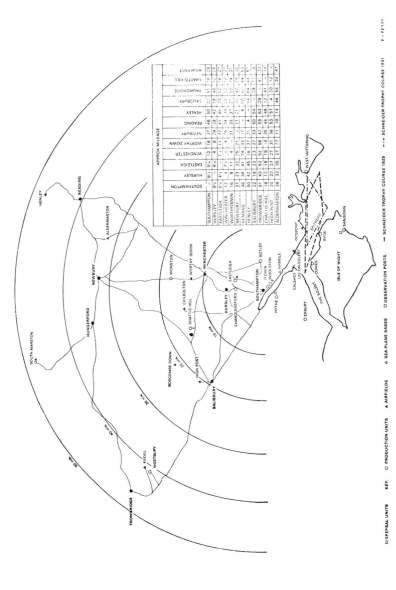

Regional map of Supermarine Southern Division showing main dispersal sites. The 1929 and 1931 Schneider Trophy courses are also shown.

what must have been a photographic sortie became evident next day when the area was again attacked in a mass raid.

This time ample warning was given. At 16.00 hr on the 26th the sirens sounded as the enemy aircraft left their bases in France, indicating that the 'C' stations, later known as radar, were working properly. Crossing the Isle of Wight over the Needles, 55 Dornier Do 17s and 10 Heinkel He 111s, with fighter cover of Messerschmitt Bf 109s and 110s, flew in over Hythe. The Heinkels attacked from the northwest, flying out over Hamble, while the main force approached from the west dropping over 70 tons of bombs, completely destroying the Woolston Works and finishing off Itchen in a single 'carpet-bombing' attack. The enemy formation turned over Botley and flew southwest, the Observer Corps post at Exbury, just inland from Calshot, reporting a big dog-fight overhead. One of the Heinkels was shot down by a Hurricane of 229 Squadron and in crashing it demolished the church of St Barnabas in Southampton. Two Messerschmitt 110s were shot down over the Isle of Wight, and four Hurricanes and two Spitfires were lost.

The Vickers-Armstrongs Supermarine factories at Southampton were a shambles. Several aircraft had been completely destroyed, many others were damaged as were all parts of the factories. The second prototype Sea Otter was on fire. A bomb had exploded right in front of the two prototype B.12/36 four-engined bomber fuselages, reducing their length dramatically. They had been moved to Itchen from K shop, Woolston, to await the wings which were behind schedule. Thirty-seven workers had been killed in the works and 52 others (also including key workers) in the surrounding area, with many injured. The German target maps had been incorrectly marked, indeed the Thorneycroft shipbuilding works had been identified as Avro Aircraft, but the German aircrew had known their real targets better. Spitfire production ceased in the Supermarine Southampton factories which were abandoned for the rest of the war. In the Battle of Britain this enemy sortie had been one of the most effective against vital war production.

Hardly had the dust settled and the 'all clear' sounded at 17.16 hr when the sirens blared another warning at 17.28. A single hostile aircraft flew up the Itchen at 20,000 ft to Chandlers Ford, turned and re-crossed the Supermarine factories site to Hamble, where it turned again and flew across the Observer Corps post at Exbury near where it was shot down by fighters, crashing south of Gurnard in the Isle of Wight. One set of air photographs did not arrive at German headquarters in France!

The loss of a major fighter production complex at the height of the Battle of Britain was extremely serious. It presented a challenge to Supermarine, and history now records that however disastrous the situation at Southampton might have been, it was not allowed to become so. This was evident from the production figures for Spitfires which followed the raids. For the week ending 28 September it was 34, only six less than the week before, and this was followed by weekly figures of 32, 31 and 25 until 26 October when production was normalized at 42. This miraculous recovery was a masterpiece of planning foresight and the application of sheer hard work to meet the urgent needs of the time.

On the evening of the second raid the man most concerned in the situation arrived in Southampton to lend his substantial weight to recovery, Lord Beaverbrook. As Minister responsible for aircraft production to Winston Churchill, the Prime Minister, he was extremely powerful and had enormous energy. His often ruthless approach to a problem was much criticized but he got things done. No obstacle was too large for him and no person too influential to suppress if he so

338

The Woolston Works after its complete destruction by the Luftwaffe in September 1940.

The Itchen Works a short distance up-river from the Woolston Works. This was also a German target in 1940.

decided in the national interest. He saw for himself the chaotic state of the Supermarine factories and made a characteristic decision. Spitfire production would be dispersed over Southern England, the Minister having powers to remove all obstacles. The following day he sent a number of businessmen, who had been seconded to his Ministry from industry, to assist in the organization of the first completely dispersed aircraft production programme ever undertaken in this country and probably anywhere. There was to be not one production line but four, each turning out one quarter of the planned total. Even in the unlikely event of one dispersed complex being completely destroyed, production would still continue in the others and any shortages could be supplemented by the other units. Flexibility both in planning and application was to be of prime importance.

Tragically, the one man whose experience would have been invaluable was not available. Gilbert Olsen, who had so brilliantly organized the initial Spitfire dispersal units in Southampton under Gooch's plans, had been attending a meeting in Conrad Mann's inspection office at Itchen Works. There had been a discussion about dispersed production at Seaward's Garage in Southampton and he had left, presumably to return there, just as the guns opened fire during the first raid on the 24th. When his car was later found in the car park it was realized that he had lost his life in the air raid shelter that had suffered so cruelly.

No time was lost in putting the Beaverbrook plan into operation. The fourth floor of the Polygon Hotel in Southampton was requisitioned the day after the raid for the works manager and his staff to begin planning the dispersal. The following day was devoted to searching the town for likely factory units, apart from those already occupied under the pre-raid dispersal. At this stage it became clear that the whole operation was going to resemble a gigantic jig-saw puzzle, with all the pieces coming together in the right place at the right time. Gooch, accompanied by Richard Kellet as requisition officer, had the job of planning the exercise and their aides set about combing the southern area expanding fanwise northwards, with Southampton as the apex of an inverted pyramid, for promising sites for Spitfire production. Salisbury, Reading and Trowbridge were eventually chosen as the centres, with High Post, Henley and Keevil airfields for final assembly respectively.

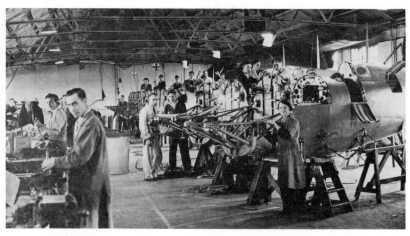

Spitfire fuselage assembly in Seward's Garage, Southampton, in 1939.

340

Chattis Hill dispersal factory in July 1941. The works are in the coppice near the racehorse training tracks which provided camouflage for aircraft take-off marks. The town of Stockbridge is at top centre.

A second airfield was found necessary for the Salisbury complex and it was created next to the final assembly hangars being built at the Chattis Hill racing gallops of Atte Persee, the racehorse trainer. For camouflage purposes these hangars were erected in a long belt of trees with only those required for floor space or taxi tracks removed. The rest of the trees were bent apart by ropes when the pre-fabricated structures were dropped into place and when released to their normal position the factory just disappeared from view.

The dispersal plan worked well. Within six weeks 35 different units had been established and of these 16 were working day and night shifts and the rest soon after. Eventually Spitfire production was spread over 65 units in the South of England, of which 46 were manufacturing and the others had a supporting role—such as stores, offices and transport, and one odd one, which was for rivet sorting by the Women's Volunteer Service, for in production rivets tended to become mixed in both size and type. This mundane task was an important contribution to efficiency and to safety through reliability.

One of the first major tasks of dispersal was to ensure supplies of leading-edge torsion-box assemblies, the component that had caused so much trouble and delay in the prewar Air Ministry scheme. Jigs salvaged from Woolston were sited in the Hants and Dorset bus garage in Southampton, the Anna Valley Motors garage in Salisbury and the Tasker steam-roller works in Trowbridge, each supplying the wing assembly units to each production centre. Trowbridge subsequently became the main supplier when the Southampton jigs were moved out as the threat of invasion increased, while Salisbury became the centre for the

341

so-called 'bowser' wings for the photographic reconnaissance Spitfires. Armament was not fitted to the PRU types so the entire leading edge was sealed to become an integral fuel tank—hence the term 'bowser'.

Apart from the delay in early Spitfire production attributable to the problems of wing construction, further hold-ups were caused by the slowness of delivery of embodiment loan items such as instruments, armament, and the miscellaneous accessories that go to make up Service equipment, the subject of separate Government contracts. There had been also the considerable support given by Vickers to the 'shadow' aircraft factory at Castle Bromwich. As stated previously, its first Spitfire delivery was not made until the middle of 1940 when the Battle of Britain was imminent, but Vickers' massive investment in it had probably drained resources from Southampton at a critical time.

Castle Bromwich eventually became the major producer of Spitfires, principally of Mks II, V, IX and XVI, reaching a peak of 320 a week in June 1944. Its total of different operational types was six, whereas the Southern area with its many smaller units was much more flexible in its approach with as many as five distinct types in production at one time, eventually reaching a total of 30 a week. It was this versatility that enabled Joe Smith, Mitchell's successor as chief designer, to give full rein to his talent for developing something that was inherently good, the original Mitchell design, with the result that the Spitfire remained in the front line in one form or another throughout the war.

Indicative of the precise planning exercised in the organization of the Southern area was the building of the photographic reconnaissance Spitfires in the Reading centre, ideally situated between the PRU bases of the RAF at Benson, Mount Farm and Heston. High Post Salisbury produced the oddest modification of all when they fitted beer barrels to the bomb racks of a Mk IX, more or less as a joke for the troops in Europe after 'D' day. The plan to put beer in long-range tanks

Spitfire LF.IXs and LF.XVIs nearing completion at Castle Bromwich in 1944.

Operation XXX in 1944—beer for the troops in Normandy by courtesy of a Spitfire Mk IX.

was abandoned when it was found later that the practice contaminated fuel, so Strongs, the Romsey brewers, supplied complete barrels of Triple 'X'. This modification was given a fictitious number to conceal the operation from more official or officious eyes.

One story concerning the requisition exercise conducted by Richard Kellett with aides Carleton Dyer, Joseph Cowley and Arthur Whitehead, all delegated from the Ministry of Aircraft Production, is sufficient to illustrate the problems involved. One of the Salisbury units selected for requisition strongly objected, since they would lose a lucrative contract for repairing military vehicles. They suggested to the Dean of Salisbury that a Spitfire factory just outside the Close would render the Cathedral very vulnerable to enemy action. The Bishop, taking the case up with the Minister concerned, received the typical Beaverbrook reply 'there will be no cathedral if we don't get the airplanes'!

The lessons of Southampton were not lost on Vickers-Armstrongs' giant shadow factory at Castle Bromwich. This was situated near Birmingham in the Midlands target area and easily identified from the air by the steam plumes arising from the cooling towers of the local power station and of course by the adjacent aerodrome, from which Alex Henshaw achieved such legendary fame in his breathtaking flight-testing of the production Spitfires.*

In fact, according to Stanley Woodley, works manager at Castle Bromwich and later superintendent at Vickers' South Marston factory, the Birmingham location was bombed before Southampton, probably because the shadow factories had been shown by the British Government to General Milch, then commander of the embryo Luftwaffe before the war, to impress him with our potential offensive capacity!

*Sigh for a Merlin—Alex Henshaw, John Murray, London.

343

Spitfire IXs awaiting delivery at Castle Bromwich, Birmingham, in May 1944. Three Vickers-Supermarine built Lancasters are also ready for delivery.

Among the Castle Bromwich dispersals were to be found some unlikely sites for aircraft production. For instance, there was the carpet factory at Kidderminster, the old prison at Worcester, silk stocking and celluloid doll factories at Leicester, the Midland Red bus depot at Shrewsbury (which had to be abandoned in a hurry because of flooding from the River Severn), Dudley Zoo, and an old iron foundry at Wellington; even the Mersey Tunnel at Liverpool was considered at one time but was abandoned because of the disruption that would have been caused by the continuous passage of military transport through the tunnel on the way to the docks.

APPENDIX I
Supermarine Type List

Original Type No.	Revision No.	Engine(s)	Purpose	Remarks
P. B. Glider	P.B.0.	—	Glider	First design
P. B. Monoplane	P.B.1.	Valveless rotary	Pusher	Unsuccessful
P.B. Monoplane	P.B.3.	Two-cylinder JAP	Pusher	Short hops only
P.B. Monoplane	P.B.5.	N.E.C.	Pusher	Not flown
P.B.1.	P.B.7.	Gnome	Flying-boat	At 1914 Olympia
P.B.1. (Mod)	P.B.9.	Gnome	Flying-boat	As above but engine in hull
P.B.2.	P.B.11	Austro-Daimler	Flying-boat	—
P.B.3.	—	(2) Austro-Daimler	Flying-boat slip-wing	Not built
P.B.5.	P.B.21*	(3) Austro-Daimler	Flying-boat slip-wing	Not built
P.B.7.	P.B.19*	Sunbeam Salmson	Flying-boat slip-wing	Two ordered by Germany
P.B.9.	P.B.13	Gnome	Single-seat scout	Probably 1267—
P.B.11	P.B.15	Gnome	Pusher Gunbus	'Seven-day bus'
P.B.13	P.B.17	Rotary	Single-seat scout	Probably 1374
	P.B.19 see P.B.7	—	—	Improved P.B.9
—	P.B.21 see P.B.5	—	—	—
—	P.B.23E	Le Rhône Clerget or Gnome	Single-seat scout	No.8487 only
—	P.B.25	Monosoupape	Single-seat scout	9001–9020 only
—	P.B.27	Inline	Submarine-stowed flying-boat	Not built

*Unconfirmed.

345

P.B.29E NightHawk	(2)Austro-Daimler	Quadruplane	One only
P.B.31		Submarine-stowed flying-boat	Project
P.B.31E NightHawk	(2) Anzani	Quadruplane	1388–1389

Type	Engine(s)	Remarks
A.D. Boat	Sunbeam Nubian	1412 flown 1916
A.D. Boat	Hispano-Suiza	1412 flown 12 March, 1917
A.D. Navyplane	Bentley A.R.1	9095 built only
N.1B. Baby	Hispano-Suiza/Sunbeam Arab	N59 and N60
Patrol Floatplane	Sunbeam Arab	Developed Navyplane N24—25
Channel I	Beardmore	Postwar conversion of A.D. Boat
Channel II	Siddeley Puma	As Channel I
Sea King I	Beardmore	—
Sea King II	Siddeley Puma	—
Sea Lion I	Hispano-Suiza	G-EBAH only
Sea Lion II	Napier Lion IA	G-EALP for 1919 Schnieder
Sea Lion II	Napier Lion II	Sea King II re-engined
Sea Lion III	Napier Lion III	Sea Lion II rebuilt as N170
Sea Urchin	R-R Condor	Schneider biplane for 1924
S.4	Napier Lion	Schneider monoplane 1925
S.5	Napier Lion	Schneider monoplane 1927
S.6	R-R 'R'	Schneider monoplane 1929
S.6B	R-R 'R'	Schneider monoplane 1931
Commercial Amphibian	Eagle VIII	G-EAVE
Sea Eagle	Eagle IX	Three built
Seal I	See text	—
Seal II	Lion	N146 only
Swan	(2) Eagle IX / (2) Lion IIB	N174/G-EBJY only
Scylla	(2) Eagle IX	N175 only
Seagull I	Lion II	N158 only
Seagull II	Lion IIB	Tank in top centre section. First prod.

Type	Engine(s)	Remarks
Seagull III	Lion V	RAAF. Production
Seagull IV	Lion V	Handley Page slots
Sparrow I	Blackburne Thrush	G-EBJP only
Sparrow II	Bristol Cherub III	G-EBJP as monoplane
Sheldrake	Lion V	N180
Scarab	Eagle IX	12 built for Spain
	Lion	
Seamew	(2) A S Lynx IV	N212 and N213
Air Yacht	(3) A S Jaguar VI	G-AASE only
	(3) A S Panther IIA	
Southampton I	(2) Lion V	N218
Solent/Nanok	(3) A S Jaguar IVA	G-AAAB/99 only

Vickers Sequence

Type	Purpose	Engine(s)	Remarks
178	Misc. Drawings		
179	Monoplane Flying-boat	(6) R-R Buzzard	Design Feb 1929
			Design Aug 1929.
180	Civil	(4) —	G-ABLE partly built
181	G. P. Amphibian	Bristol Pegasus	Design Oct 1929
182	G.P. high-wing monoplane	—	Design Feb 1930
183	G.P. low-wing monoplane	—	Design Oct 1930. For Canada
184	Southampton II	(2) R-R FXII	Design Dec 1930. For Canada
			Design Jan 1931.
			Metal planes – N253
185	Southampton X	(3) Bristol Jupiter XFBM	Design Feb 1931
186	S.6A 1929 Type floats modified for use on 1931 aircraft		Design Feb 1931
187	S.6B1931 Type floats redesigned		Design Feb 1931
188	Southampton X	(3) Jupiter XIF	Design Feb 1931
189	Southampton I	(2) Jupiter XIF	Design Mar 1931
190	Southampton II	(2) Kestrel IIIMS	Design Mar 1931 Prod.
221	Southampton IV/Scapa	(2) Kestrel IIIMS	Design Jul 1931. Scapa
			(P) S1648 and production

No.	Type	Engine	Notes
222	Floats for Vildebeest.		Design Nov 1931
223	Seagull V	Pegasus LII	Design Mar 1932. Into Type 228
224	F.7/30	Goshawk II	Design Mar 1932 (P). K2890 only
225	Seagull type	Kestrel	Design April 1932. Civil type
226	Southampton IV	(2) Pegasus	Design April 1932
227	Southampton V	(2) Pegasus	Design May 1932. To R.24/31
228	Seagull V	Pegasus IIL 2.P	Design June 1932.N-1/N-2
229	Southampton IV	(2) Kestrel III	Design June 1932, with S.S. spars
230	Southampton V/Stranraer	(2) Pegasus X	Design June 1932. (P) K3973 Stranraer
231	Bomber Transport	(2) Pegasus X	Design Sept 1932. To C.26/31
232	Monoplane Flying-boat	(4) Goshawk	Design Sept 1932. To R.2/33
233	Southampton II	(2) Hispano-Suiza 12 Nbr	Design Dec 1932 Turkey-bomb installation
234	Southampton II	(2) Hispano-Suiza 12 Nbr	Design April 1933 Turkey-torpedo installation
235	Southampton IV	(2) Junkers Jumo	Design Sept 1933. R.24/31 with Jumo
236	Walrus I	Pegasus IIL	Design Sept 1933
237	Southampton V/Stranraer	(2) Pegasus IIIM	Design Jan 1934 (P). K3973 re-engined
238	Biplane Flying-boat	(4) Perseus	Design April 1934. To R.2/33
239	Monoplane Flying-boat	(4) Merlin	Design April 1934. To R.2/33
240	Coastal Landplane	—	Design May 1934
300	Spitfire (P) and I	Merlin C/II	K5054 and 1st production aircraft
301	Vildebeest Development floats for Vincent		Design November 1934
302	Flying-boat	(4) Perseus PRE-IM	Design November 1934. For Imperial Airways
303	Scapa Development	(2) R-R F12	Design December 1934, Monoplane, biplane and sesquiplane
304	Stranraer R.24/31 Dev	(2) Pegasus X	Design July 1935. 17 built and 40 Canadian
305	F.9/35	Merlin	Design Aug 1935. Two-seat fighter
306	Atlantic Mail Boat	(4) Vulture	Design Sept 1935
307	Seagull V	Pegasus VI	Design Sept 1935. K4797
308	High-performance Flying-boat	(2) Vulture	Design Oct 1935. To R.12/35

Type	Name / Description	Engine	Notes
309	Sea Otter I.	Mercury XXX	Design Nov 1935. To S.7/38. Production
310	Walrus Development	Perseus XI	First flown in K8854
	High-performance Flying-boat R.2/33 replacement	(4) Hercules or Taurus or Vulture	Design Dec 1935
311	F.37/34	Merlin E	Design April 1936
312	F.37/35 Spitfire	Merlin E	Four 20 mm cannon
313	F.37/35	(2) Goshawk B	Single-seat fighter
314	R.1/36	(2) Vulture	Flying-boat
315	Walrus	Pegasus VI	Design Sept 1936. Argentine
316	B.12/36	(4) Hercules or Merlin	Design Sept 1936. Mock-up
317	B.12/36	(4) Hercules	Design April 1936. Partly built
318	B.12/36	(4) Merlin	Design April 1936
319	Two-seat Fighter	(2) Vulture	Design Aug 1937. Dev. of F.11/37
320	Walrus	Pegasus VI	Design Sept 1937. Turkey
321	Supermarine Mk IV Gun Turret		Design Sept 1937
322	S.24/37 'Dumbo'	Merlin 30 Exe	Two R1810/1815 only Original design
323	Spitfire N17	Merlin II (special) and XII	Design Dec 1937. K9834
324	F.18/37	(2) Merlin	Tractor fighter
325	F.18/37	(2) Merlin	Pusher fighter
326	Walrus Dev./Sea Otter	Pegasus VI	Design June 1938. Cabin top 2nd Exp. aircraft
327	Cannon fighter	(2) Merlin	Design Aug 1938. Six 20 mm cannon
328	R.3/38 Flying-boat	(4) Hercules	Design Sept 1938
329	Spitfire F.II	Merlin XII	Design Sept 1938. Production
330	Spitfire F.III	Merlin XX	N3927 and W3237 only
331	Spitfire F.VB	Merlin 45/46	2 Cannon and 4 Browning guns
332	Spitfire FN gun installation in wings	—	Design Apr 1939 Estonia Nil
333	N.9/39 Two-seat fighter	Merlin	Fleet fighter
334	S.6/39	(2) Mock-up only	Fixed guns
335	Spitfire F.I	Merlin XII	1939 Greece. Nil
336	Spitfire F.I	Merlin XII	1939 Portugal. Nil

No.	Aircraft	Engine	Notes
337	Spitfire F.IV	Griffon IIb 1,720 hp	1939 DP845 only
338	Spitfire F.I	Merlin XII	Design Nov 1939. FAA
339	NAD 925/39	—	Design Dec 1939. Project. Single-seat FAA fighter
340	Seafire F.IB	Merlin 45/46	(P)AB205 and production
341	Spitfire F.I	Merlin XII	Turkey 15 ordered, two delivered
342	Spitfire F.I	Merlin XII	Roc Floats. R6722
343	Spitfire F.I	Merlin XII	Design May 1940. Long-range
344	Spitfire F.III on floats	—	Supermarine floats
345	Spitfire F.I	Merlin	Design May 1940. 13.2 mm guns
346	Spitfire F.I	Merlin	C wing 20 mm guns
347	S.12/40	Perseus	Developed into Seagull ASR.I
348	Spitfire F.III	Merlin XX	2nd Prototype – W3237
349	Spitfire F.VC	Merlin 45/46	W3237 and production
350	Spitfire F.VI	Merlin 47	(P) X4942 and production
351	Spitfire F.VII	Merlin 61	(P) AB450 and production
352	Spitfire F.VB Trop	Merlin 45/46	X4922 and production
353	Spitfire PR.IV	Merlin 45/46	Design Sept 1941. VB converted
354	Spitfire	Merlin 46	Design Sept 1941
355	Spitfire	Merlin 45	Prototype W3760
356	Spitfire F.V Special	Griffon 61	DP851 and production
357	Spitfire F.21,22,24	Merlin 45/46	(P) AD371 and production
358	Seafire F.IIC	Merlin 55/32	Folding wings – MA970, and prod.
359	Seafire F.III	Merlin 61	Design March 1942. JF299 prototype
360	Spitfire F.VIII	Merlin 61	Design March 1942. JG204 – Production
361	Spitfire F.VIID and VIII	Merlin 61	F.IX with CR propeller – (P)MH874
362	Spitfire F.IX/XVI	Merlin 64	Design Apr 1942. MD191 and prod.
363	Spitfire PR.X	Griffon IIB	Design May 1942
364	Spitfire F.XII Trop	Griffon 61	Design May 1942
365	Spitfire LF.VIII Trop	Merlin 61	Production and Civil
366	Spitfire PR.XI	Griffon III	DP845 prototype and production
367	Spitfire F.XII	Merlin 32	F.VB converted Prod
368	Spitfire PR.XIII	Merlin 61	Heston project. Malinowski wing
369	Spitfire F.VIII	Griffon 61/65/83	JF316 F.VIII conv
370	Spitfire F.XIV	Merlin 61	Design Oct 1943
371	Spiteful (Laminar)	Griffon 61	Design Jan 1943. NN660 F.1/43
372	Spitfire F.VIII (semi-laminar)	Griffon 61	Design Jan 1943
373	Spitfire F.XIV	Griffon 85	F.XIV with CR propeller. DP851

No.	Name	Engine	Notes
374	Spitfire PR.XI	Merlin	Design Feb 1943. Mk IX conv'd
375	Seafire LF.IIC	Merlin 32	Design Feb 1943. (P) L1004 and prod.
376	Spitfire VIII	Merlin	Design Feb 1943. CR propeller
377	Seafire F.XV	Griffon VI	Design Mar 1943. (P) NS487
378	Spitfire F.IX Trop	Merlin 61	Design April 1943
379	Spitfire F.XIV	Griffon 75	F.VIII with Griffon
380	S.24/37 Dumbo	Merlin 32	Design April 1943 2nd prototype
381	Seagull S.12/40	Griffon RG29	Design Sept 1943. (P) PA143
382	Seafang 31/32	Griffon 65	Design Oct 1943. (P) VG471
383	Spiteful	Merlin 61	Design Nov 1943
384	Seafire F.XVII	Griffon 6	Design Nov 1943. (P) NS493 and prod.
385	Spitfire F.IX seaplane	Merlin 61	(P) MJ892 only
386	Seafire F.XV	Griffon 6	Design Nov 1943. Rear view
387	Spitfre PR.X	Merlin 64	Pressurized, production
388	Seafire F.45–47	Griffon 61	Design 1943. (P) TM379
389	Spitfire PR.XIX	Griffon 65	(P) SW777 and production
390	Spitfire PR.XIX	Griffon 66	Pressure cabin production
391	High Performance Fighter	46H	Design June 1944
392	Attacker E.10/44	Nene B41	Design June 1944. (P) TS409
393	Spiteful F.XIV	Griffon 69	Design Aug 1944, single prop.
394	Spitfire F. and PR.XVIII	Griffon 65/67	Design Nov 1944, production
395	Seafire F.XVIII	Griffon 35/36	Design Nov 1944
396	Seafang F.32	Griffon 89	Seafire XVII development. Design Nov 1944. (P)VB893
397	Attacker 2nd (P)	Nene	Folding wings for foreign sales
398	Attacker F.1/FB.2	Nene 3	Naval Prod (P) TS413 and prod.
399	Sea Otter ASR.II	Mercury 30	Design Dec 1944
500	Revised version of 392	—	Design Oct 1945
501	Spitfire Exp	Merlin 66	Powerplant Development
502	Spitfire T.8	Mercury 30	1 converted. MT818/G-AIDN only
503	Sea Otter	Griffon	3 converted. G-AIDM Civil
504	S.14/44 ASR	(2) AJ.65	Design March 1946, civil project
505	Naval Jet Fighter	Merlin 55	Project. No undercarriage
506	Seafire F.III	Pegasus VI	12 converted for Irish Air Corps
507	Walrus II		For Amsterdam

No.	Type	Engine	Remarks
508	N.9/47	(2) Avon RA.3	(P) VX133 Type 505 with undercarriage
509	Spitfire T.9	Merlin 66	21 converted
510	E.10/44 Mod	Nene 2	(P) VV106 only
511	F.44/46	(2) Avon	Night Fighter
512	Allotted to Technical Office		
513	Attacker F.1	Nene 3/4	(P) TS416. Improved intakes
514	E.10/44 mod	Nene 2	Project
515	Attacker F2	Ghost	Project TS409 to be converted
516	Naval Attacker	Nene	Project
517	Swift	Nene 3	2nd 510 to 535 VI tailplane
518	Spitfire T.XVIII	Griffon	Not converted
519	Attacker	Nene II	Project
520	Swift	Avon	VV119 projected conversion
521	HP.88	—	Special fuselage similar to 510
522	N.9/47	—	Strike aircraft
523	F.3/48	(2) Avon	Interceptor fighter
524	R.2/48	(4) Proteus	Marine Reconnaissance Flying-boat
525	N.9/47 3rd P	(2) Avon	(P) VX138. Dev into 544
526	F.3/48	(2) Avon	525 with sweptback wing
528	Swift 2nd Prototype	Nene 3	(P) VV119 modified
529	N.9/47 developed	(2) Avon RA.3	(P) VX136
530	Seagull ASR.I	Griffon 57	Prod. None built
531	Swift	Nene 3	VV119 with VI tail and nose u/c, to 535
532	E41/46 Dev	Ghost	TS409 to have been modified
533	34 mm Vickers cannon		Recoil-less gun
534			Design only – no drawings
535	Swift	Nene 2	(P) VV119 with tricycle u/c
537	N.9/47	(2) Avon	Strike
538	Attacker F.1	Nene 3	36 to Pakistan
539	N.9/47	(2) Avon	Trainer and Variants designs
541	Swift F.1-F.3	Avon RA.3	(P) WJ960 and WJ965. Fighter 510 with two 30 mm Aden guns
542	Attacker	Nene 3	On floats. Project only
543	Fighter	BE17	Undercarriageless
544	Scimitar F.1	Avon	(P) WT854 N.II3D and production
545	Swift development	Avon RA.14R	(P) XA181. Not completed
546	Swift F.1 to F.4	Avon RA.7	(P) WK194. Production

No.	Designation	Engine	Notes
547a	Swift two-seat (F.1)	Avon RA.7	With nose extended for radar and two or four 30 mm Aden guns as trainer
547b	Swift two-seat (F.4)	Avon RA.7	Night Fighter project as above
548	Swift Naval (F.4)	Avon RA.7R	Interim version project
549	Swift FR.5	Avon RA.7R	To OR 308. Production
550	Swift PR.6	Avon RA.7	XD943 not completed
551	Swift F.2	Avon 105	WK199 only
552	Swift F.7	Avon 116	(P) XF774 with Blue Sky
553	ER134T Experimental Research	RB.106	Supersonic M:2·4 at 36,000 ft
554	OR 318	Avon RA.14	Advanced Jet Trainer of Type 545
555	N.9/47 3rd (P) N113P	(2) Avon	N113P with method of lift augmentation
556	544 Dev	(2) Avon 7R	D.H.110 competitor. Red Dean missile
557			Project
558	N113 P Mk 2	(2) RA.24	Project
559	Canard to GOR 339/F155T	(2) Gyron PS.26/1 and (2) Spectre Junior rocket motors	Supersonic fighter Project
560	Scimitar F.1	(2) Avon RA.24	51st Production 544 denavalized
561	Scimitar Dev	(2) Avon RA.24	Low-level atomic bombers
562	Scimitar Naval	(2) Avon RA.24	101st A/C Single-seat
563	Scimitar Swiss AF	(2) Avon RA.24	141st A/C Two-seat
564	Scimitar Naval	(2) Gyron Junior PS43	Two-seat as 563 developed
565	Scimitar RAF	(2) Avon RA.24	Single and two-seat denavalized Strike
566	Scimitar Naval	(2) Avon RA.24	Single and two-seat Strike with Sperry control system
567	Scimitar Naval	(2) Avon RA.24	Single and two seat
569	Guided powered bomb	(4) RB.93/4 Soar	For carriage by V-bombers
571*	Projects to GOR 339	RB.142 or (2) RB.142	See pages 307–9
572	Scimitar RAF	(2) Avon RA.24	Denavalized tactical reconnaissance
573	Quarter-scale SST	—	Model for Concorde
574	Scimitar	(2) Avon RA.24	Project
575	Scimitar	(2) Avon	For RCAF
576	Supersonic Scimitar	(2) Avon and (2) DH Spectre rocket motors	Mixed-power interceptor

* The twin-engined version was evolved in collaboration with English Electric to become the TSR2 of which a preproduction batch was built although only XR219 was flown.

The Pemberton Billing P.B.1 in 1914 after rebuilding with forward cockpit and twin pusher propellers. It still did not fly. See pages 14–15. (*T. Grubb*)

APPENDIX II

Production

Pemberton Billing

1. Monoplanes. Three types built or converted during 1909 but none successful.
2. P.B.1/P.B.7—flying-boat exhibited at 1914 Olympia.
3. P.B.9/P.B.13—The 'Seven Day Bus' of 1914 probably allocated serial 1267.
4. P.B.11/P.B.15—probably 1374 which was allocated to a P.B. Boxkite under C.P. 34377/15.
5. P.B.23E—8487 only under C.P.62042/15. Classified in one report as the P.B. School Machine.
6. P.B.25—9001-9020(20) built under C.P.134727/16.
7. P.B.29E—One only, no known serial number.
8. P.B.31E—1388 and 1389 allocated but only 1388 built under C.P. 130778/16. 1389 cancelled.

Other Firms' Aircraft

1. 1580-1591(12). Short S.38 with Maori III engine, under contract C.P.50249/15.
2. N2760—2789(30). Norman Thompson NT.2B with 200 hp Hispano-Suiza engine, under contract AS34279, N2785 to 2789 not completed.
3. N3300—3374(75). Norman Thompson NT.2B. All cancelled before production began.
4. N9170—9199(30). Short 184 with Sunbeam Maori III engine, under contract AS11686/18. Only N9170—9181(12) confirmed as built.

A.D. Flying Boat

1. 1412—1413(2). To contract CP.109611/15.
2. N1290—1299(10) ordered under AS1449. N1290 built only, having been taken over from J. Samuel White & Co Ltd under AS14609. Remainder cancelled in March 1918.
3. N1520—1529(10) ordered under AS5388/17, N1526, 1528 and 1529 became Channel Mk Is G-EAEM, G-EAEL and G-EAED respectively. N1525 fitted Wolseley Python and Wolseley Viper.
4. N1710—1719(10) ordered under A.S.20798. N1710, 1711, 1714, 1715 and 1716 became Channel Mk I G-EAEE, G-EAEK, G-EAEJ, G-EAEI and G-EAEH respectively.
5. N2450—2499(50) ordered under A.S.18936. N2450—2455(6) built only, rest cancelled. N2451 to G-EAEG and N2452 to G-EAEF.

Total built 29

A.D. Navyplane

1. 9095—9096 ordered but only 9095 built, 9096 cancelled.
2. N1070—1074(5) ordered with 140 hp Smith engines, but cancelled.

Supermarine

1. N24—25. Supermarine Patrol Seaplane, but cancelled when design almost complete in 1917.
2. N59—61. N.1B Baby under contract A.S.3929. Only N59—60 completed, N60 to Grain as spare. N61 not completed but believed hull used for Sea Lion I.

Channel

All conversions of the A.D. Flying Boat.

G-EAED (N1529), G-EAEE (N1710), G-EAEF (N2452) to Bermuda in November 1920, G-EAEG (N2451) to Bermuda in May 1920, G-EAEH (N1716) to Norway as N9 May 1920, G-EAEI (N1715) to Norway as N10 May 1920, G-EAEJ (N1714) to Bermuda May 1920, G-EAEK (N1711), G-EAEL (N1528) to Norway as N11 and G-EAEM (N1526) to Norway May 1920.

Four, F-38, F-40, F-42 and F-44 delivered to Norwegian Navy between May and July 1920. F-38 crashed 12 July, 1920, and replaced by N10 ex. civil airline. All Mk Is though F-40 and F-44 converted to Mk IIs later.

Three to Japan during 1922 by the British Aviation Mission for the Imperial Japanese Navy.

One to Royal Swedish Navy in 1921 as 46.

One, G-NZAI, to New Zealand as a Mk I, but converted to Mk II later.

Mk II conversions. G-EAWC to Venezuela and British Guiana in 1921, possibly G-EAWP sold abroad late 1922 to Chile, another to Venezuela, but serial not known.

Sea King

Mk I. One only, high-speed flying-boat.

Mk II. A developed Mk I first flown December 1921, converted to Sea Lion II during 1922.

Sea Lion

Mk I was modified N.1B Baby, registered G-EALP August 1919, damaged beyond repair Swanage Bay 10 September, 1919.

Mk II ex. Sea King II registered G-EBAH won Schneider Trophy contest on 12 August, 1922.

Mk III Sea Lion II, G-EBAH, bought by Air Ministry under contract 409868/23 dated 8 March, 1923, numbered N170, but also carried civil markings G-EBAH. Came 3rd in 1923 Schneider Trophy context.

Sea Urchin

One aircraft ordered by Air Ministry, but not proceeded with because of technical difficulties.

Commercial Amphibian

One only, G-EAVE, built for the 1920 Air Ministry Competition for seaplanes (amphibians), where it came second.

Sea Eagle

Three built as G-EBFK, G-EBGR and G-EBGS for the British Marine Air Navigation Co Ltd during 1922/23 and used on the Channel Islands route from 1923 to 1928.

Scylla

N174 ordered under contract 248426/21 for a five-seat military boat seaplane but only completed as a taxi-ing machine.

Swan

N175 ordered under contract 331411/22 for a commercial amphibian machine to specification 21/22 and first flown on 25 March, 1924. Later registered G-EBJY.

Seal

Mk I believed to have been allocated to the Commercial Amphibian.
Mk II first flown May 1921 and allocated serial N146. On 4 July renamed Seagull.
One exported to Japan during 1922 in company with the three Channels.

Seagull

N146 prototype converted from Seal Mk II under contract 366547/20.
N158—159 Mk II built under contract 317009/21, dated 7 February, 1922, with revised tankage arrangement.
N9562—9566(5) Mk II built under contract 357965/22, dated 18 September, 1922.
N9603—9607(5) Mk II built under contract 402282/23 dated 10 February, 1923. N9605 was converted into a Mk IV and to G-AAIZ. N9603 and 9606 not confirmed.
N9642—9654(13) Mk II built under contract 425115/23 dated 21 June, 1923. N9653 to G-EBXH and N9654 to G-EBXI.
A9-1 to A9-6(6) Mk III exported to Australia during 1926.
One, no serial, exported to Japan.
N-1/K4797, Mk V, built as a Private Venture, first flown on 20 June, 1933, converted to prototype Walrus.

Total built 32 (excluding the Mk V)

Sheldrake

One only, N180, built under contract 466409/23 using a Seagull II hull and as an experimental development of the Seagull.

Scarab

Twelve, M-NSAA to M-NSAL, ordered by Spanish Government in February 1924 and built during that year. One crashed before delivery and it is assumed only 11 were despatched.

Sparrow

One aircraft only built for 1924 Air Ministry Light Aeroplane contest, registered G-EBJP but flown as 9 in 1924 contest as a sesquiplane.

Converted to Mk II for 1926 Two-Seater Light Aeroplane Competition but not successful in either. Used under Air Ministry contract 730450/26/49 for aerofoil trials.

Seamew

N212—213(2) built under contract 600444/25 and specification 31/24. N212 tested at Felixstowe

Schneider Racers

S.4—N196—197(2) ordered under contract 618379/25 dated 20 August, 1925, for 1925 Schneider Trophy race. N197 allocated civil registration G-EBLP. N196 not built.

S.5—N219—221(3) to AM specification S.6/26, N219 ordered under contract 674204/26; N220—221, S.5 (modified), under 747192/27 for the 1927 Schneider Trophy race.

S.6—N247—248(2) to AM specification S.8/28 and ordered on 3 May, 1929, under contract S27042/28 for the 1929 Schneider Trophy race and modified into S.6A for the 1931 race. N248 preserved at the Southampton Mitchell Museum. N247 and 248 converted to S.6A under I.T.P. 30013/30.

S.6B—S1595—1596(2) built for the 1931 Schneider Trophy race. S1595 preserved at the Science Museum.

Southampton

N9896—9901(6) First production order under contract 516531/24. Produced during 1925 as Mk I with wooden hulls. N9896 converted to Mk III prototype under contract 516531/24.

N218, experimental to AM specification R.18/24 and built under contract 616014/24 with a metal hull as the prototype Mk II.

S1036—1045 and S1058—1059(12) ordered in July 1925 under contract 601035/25. Built as Mk I during 1926.

S1121—1128(8). Ordered under contract 664492/26. Instructions to proceed dated 6 March, 1926, with instructions that S1127—1128 to be fitted with metal hulls and so became the first production Mk II. S1122 fitted with Kestrels.

S1149—1152(4) built under contract 719081/26 for the Far East Flight as Mk IIs.

S1158—1162(5) ordered in December 1926 and built under contract 718920/26 as Mk IIs during 1927. S1159 to RAAF as A11-1 (or A11-2).

S1228—1236(9). Ordered early 1927 under contract 765929/27 and delivered during 1927. S1235 used temporarily by Imperial Airways as G-AASH.

One Mk II ordered for Japanese Navy and delivered during 1928. Bought by Mitsubishi. Believed to be that later registered J-BAID and operated Osaka–Beppu route in 1930s.

S1248—1249(2). Added to the above contract, the aircraft with sweptback mainplanes.

HB1 to HB8(8). For Argentine Naval Air Force fitted with 450 hp Lorraine 12E engines. Five wooden-hulled plus three metal-hulled delivered during 1929.

N251 ordered under contract 826424/28 dated 5 April, 1928, to be fitted with a special hull built by S. E. Saunders Ltd.

N252 ordered under contract 786295/27 on 28 June, 1928, as part of original contract for three experimental Southamptons N251—253, built as Southampton Mk X fitted with Jupiter XFBM engines.

N253. Hull from S1149 fitted to metal planes ex. contract 632526/25 and wingtip floats ex. contract 865877/28 converted under contract 931284/29 and re-numbered K2888. Fitted with Kestrel IV engines.

S1298—1302(5) ordered under contract 837553/28 as Mk IIs.

S1419—1423(5) ordered under contract 922543/29 as Mk IIs.

S1464 ordered under contract 38000/30 as Mk II and delivered to No.201 Squadron.

S1643—1647(5) ordered under contract 105491/31 as Mk II and delivered to No.201 Squadron.

S1648 ordered to specification R.20/31 on 31 July, 1931, and under contract 124775/31 as an Improved Southampton, built as Southampton Mk IV but renamed Scapa.

K2888—2889(2) Mk II. K2888 renumbered from N253 and K2889 also assumed renumbered.

K2964—2965(2) (K2964 as Mk III?)

N3—N8(6) ordered by Turkey fitted with Hispano-Suiza 12Nbr engines and delivered in their class B registrations during 1934.

During the period 1929–33 twenty-four metal hulls were produced to replace the wooden ones of the Mk I aircraft and for replacement purposes.

Total built 83—79 production and four prototypes (This excludes the Scapa prototype).

Service Use

Equipped No.201 Squadron (Calshot), 203 Squadron (Iraq), 204 Squadron (Cattewater), 205 Squadron (Singapore), ex. Far East Flight, and No.210 Squadron (Felixstowe and Pembroke Dock). First entered service with No.480 (Coastal Reconnaissance) Flight at Calshot in September 1925. The Flight became 201 Squadron on 1 January, 1929.

Nanok/Solent

One aircraft only built for the Danish Navy as the Nanok serial 99 in 1928, not delivered. Registered G-AAAB for the Hon A. E. Guinness and renamed Solent.

Air Yacht

One aircraft only, G-AASE, designed initially to specification 4/27 for armed reconnaissance but completed as a luxury yacht for the Hon A. E. Guinness and first flown in February 1930.

Type 179 'Giant'

One aircraft, G-ABLE, ordered under contract 13135/30 on 29 March, 1930, to specification 20/28, but cancelled 19 January, 1932.

Scapa

Prototype Southampton IV S1648 first flown 8 July, 1932, attached to 202 (FB) Squadron, specification R.20/31 issued to cover it.

Twelve ordered under contract 277617/33 to specification 19/33 as K4191—4202 fitted with Kestrel III engines and as Type 221.

Served on Nos.202, 204 and 240 Squadrons, K4192 of 204 Squadron swerved to avoid buoy on take-off and hit a destroyer on 18 November, 1935, and was written off.

Three replacements ordered under contract 394125/35 as K7304 to K7306.

K7304 delivered 30 April, 1936, and converted to instructional airframe 2191M on 26 August, 1940; K7305 to DTD 8 June, 1936, but struck off charge 16 October, 1939; K7306 delivered 31 July, 1936, and later to 228 Squadron but when used by Bawdsey Research Station on radar experimental flight on 13 August, 1938, it went into the sea off Felixstowe.

Total built 15

Stranraer

R.24/31 tender submitted by R. J. Mitchell turned down, but privately proceeded with and contract No. 262922/33 placed for a prototype, K3973, later powered by two Pegasus IIIM engines. Delivered 24 October, 1934.

Seventeen ordered under contract 419705/35 to specification 17/35 as K7287—K7303 on 29 August, 1935. First delivered, K7287, 16 April, 1937, to No.228 Squadron, last delivered, K7303, 3 April, 1939, to No.209 Squadron.

Served on 209, 228 and 240 Squadrons and at RAF Calshot and MAEE Felixstowe.

Forty built by Canadian Vickers at Montreal, and powered by Pegasus XXII engines. C/ns CV184—190, 204—236. Ordered under four contracts and built as 907—916, 918—923, 927—938 and 946—957 for the RCAF. First delivered, 907, on 9 November, 1938, and last five, 953 to 957, delivered on 26 November, 1941. Served with the following RCAF Squadrons; No.4(BR), 5(BR), 6(BR), 7(BR), 9(BR), 120 and 166 Squadron. No.5(BR) was the first operational unit with Stranraer when designated 5(GR) Squadron. Fourteen given Canadian civil registrations, 907 to CF-BYI (re-engined with Pegasus X in December 1946), 909 to CF-BYL, 910 to CF-BYE, 913 to CF-BYF, 914 to CF-BYH, 915 to CF-BYJ (re-engined with Wright GR-1820-205A Cyclones in April 1949), 919 to CF-BYA, 920 to CF-BXO, 921 to CF-BYD, 923 to CF-BYG, 936 to CF-BYK, 948 to CF-BYB, 949 to CF-BYM and 953 to CF-BYC, of these four, CF-BYI, CF-BYJ, CF-BXO and CF-BYM served with Queen Charlotte Airlines Ltd.

One, 920, preserved at the RAF Museum, Hendon.

Total built 58.

K9676—9681(6) ordered May 1936 but cancelled.

F.7/30

One aircraft, K2890, built under contract 189222/32 and specification F.7/30 and first flown on 20 February, 1934. R. J. Mitchell's 'unsuccessful' machine, from which the Spitfire was evolved.

B.12/36

L6889—6890(2) prototypes ordered to specification B.12/36 but destroyed by bombing 26 September, 1940.

S.24/37 'Dumbo'

Two prototypes, R1810 and R1815 ordered 17 May, 1939, under contract 976687/39. R1810 first flown February 1943, R1815 not long afterwards. Used for trials on the variable-incidence wing. R1810 had Merlin 30 and R1815 Merlin 32.

Seagull V

24 supplied to Australia as A2-1 to A2-24 and ordered under specification 6/34 on 27 August, 1934. A2-1 first flew 25 June, 1935, last, A2-24, first flew 28 April, 1937. Two, A2-3 and A2-4 converted as VH-BGP and VH-ALB respectively. VH-BGP and Walrus VH-BLD used by Amphibious Airways of Rabaul, New Britain, to the Solomons and Sohana until withdrawn in 1954. VH-ALB now stored at the RAF Museum, Hendon.

Walrus

Prototype, K4797 Ex N-2 and N-1 Seagull V. Purchased by Air Ministry under contract 362547/34.

K5772—5783(12) ordered under contract 391700/35 and specification 2/35 with Pegasus IIM2 on 18 May, 1935. K5772 first flew on 18 March, 1936. K5774 and K5783 to New Zealand. First delivered 28 March, 1936, last delivered on 12 July, 1936.

K8338—8345(8) ordered under contract 391700/35 but changed to contract 472708/35 with Pegasus VI, specification 2/35 and Requirement 29/35. K8338 first flown 17 August, 1936, delivered 19 August, last delivered, K8345, 25 September, 1936.

K8537—8564(28) ordered under contract 472708/35, Requirement 117/35 and specification 2/35. K8537 first delivered 28 September, 1936, last delivered was K8563 on 3 June, 1937. K8558 to New Zealand for HMS *Leander*. K8540 fitted to take Towed Target Gear.

L2169—2336(168) ordered under contract 534422/36, specification 37/36 and Requirement 47/36 dated 10 July, 1936. L2169 and L2170 delivered 25 June, 1937, last delivered, L2336, on 18 September, 1937. L2301 to L2303 to Eire as N-18 to N-20. L2222, 2236 and 2285 to New Zealand as NZ151 to 153. L2271 fitted during 1940 with a 20 mm Oerlikon cannon. L2330 to 3SFTS Canada 20 December, 1943. L2301 became EI-ACC of Aer Lingus, later as G-AIZG and sold for scrap in 1963, later renovated by RNAS and now on display at the Fleet Air Arm Museum, Yeovilton. L2263 to 2267 to Portugal as 97 to 101.

N-9 to N-14(6) to Turkey. N-9 first flew 4 February, 1938, last, N-14, on 2 March, 1938, as Type 320, but not delivered.

N-15 and N-16 to Argentina as M-0-9 and M-0-10, delivered aboard *La Argentina* at Barrow 5 January, 1939, as Type 315.

P5646—5670 and 5696—5720(50) ordered to specification I/P3 under contract 974377/39 dated 23 January, 1939. First flown 25 September, 1939—9 May, 1940. P5664 to VH-BLD.

R6543—6557 (15) ordered under contract B. 21120/39 and first flown between 18 May and 1 August, 1940. R6554 to R6557 not delivered. 11 built.

All the foregoing were Mk I wooden-hulled aircraft and built by Supermarine, a total of 285 Walrus between 1936 and 1940.

R6582—6591(10) under revised contract B.43393/39 built by Saunders-Roe at Cowes.

W2670—2689, 2700—2729, 2731—2760, 2766—2798, 3005—3051 and 3062—3101(200) under contract B.43393/39. All Mk I (wooden) except for W3010, 3047, 3051, 3076 and 3078 Mk II (metal hull). Five to New Zealand, W2700 as NZ157, W2707 as NZ154, W2724 as NZ155, W2740 as NZ159 and W3021 as NZ160. Others, W2705, W2707(NZ154), W2755, W2768, W2783 included, served with the Royal Australian Navy and W2706, 2708 to 2710, 2767, 2788, 3012—3013 and W3016—3017 with DAE in Egypt as ASR aircraft with the RAF from February 1944. W3089 to Royal Canadian Navy.

X1045 and X1046 ordered to the Standard Walrus specification but fitted with a Saro wooden hull as Mk II by Supermarine. X1045 first flown by Sqn Ldr L. S. Ash on 2 May, 1940. Later flown by Flt Lt G. Pickering, who reported that performance was very similar to the standard production Walrus but the hull was smoother and much quieter. No record discovered of X1046 and assumed not built. X1045 was the prototype Mk II.

X9460—9484, 9498—9532, 9554—9593(100) Mk I to W9558, X9559—9593(35) Mk II. To RNZAF X9512 as NZ158 and X9567 as NZ156. X9513, X9516 and X9520 used on HMAS *Australia II*. X9499, 9518, 9525, 9554, 9557-8, 9560(7) cancelled.

Z1755—1784, 1804—1823(50) all built as Mk II. Z1768, Z1771, Z1775, Z1781 and Z1814 to RC Navy, Z1781 to CF-GKA in 1948.

HD804—837, 851—878, 899—936(100) 70 built as Mk I. 30 Mk II HD878, 902—908, 910, 912, 914—915, 917—918, 920—923 and 925—936. HD909 to RC Navy. HD916 to G-AJJD, HD917 to G-AJJC and LN-SUK. HD874 used by Australian National Antarctic Research Expedition.

2-0-23 to 2-0-30 (8). Exported to Argentina during 1947 and first flown under Class B as N-33 to N-40. Five of them believed to be X9564, X9571, X9573, Z1758 and HD823.

Production by Saunders-Roe was 461 of which 190 were Mk II.

Walrus—Total built 746 (of which 191 Mk II)

Sea Otter

K8854—8855 prototypes to specification 5/36 and under contract 493798/36 as Type 309. K8855 destroyed at Woolston Works by enemy action 26 September, 1940.

90, BL112—151 and 167—216 ordered from Blackburn Aircraft but order subsequently cancelled.

100, BT316—347, 357—401 and 415—437, ordered from Blackburn Aircraft but order subsequently cancelled.

250, JM738—773, 796—837, 861—885, 905—922, 943—989, JN104—142, 179—205 and 242—257 ordered from Saunders-Roe under contract Air/1806 as ABR.I. built as ASR.II from JN249. JM738 first flown about 7 January, 1943.

100, RD869—899, 913—935 and 948—993, ordered from Saunders-Roe under contract Air/1806/CB20(b). Only RD869 to 922 built as ASR.II (Naval), the rest being cancelled. RD920 first sting hook production received from Saunders-Roe 11 November, 1946. RD869, first delivered 21 September, 1945, RD922, last delivered 13 July, 1946.

50, VF354—374 and 407—435, ordered from Saunders-Roe under contract Air/5068 but the order was cancelled.

Total of 592 ordered but only 292 built.

Civil and Exports

Eight to Royal Danish Air Force, 801 to 807 (ex JM809, JM833, JM958, JM975, JM978, JM980 and JM807) and JM943 delivered in May 1948 but JM943 not given a Danish serial number. First four landed Kastrup 19 December, 1946, for No. 1 Luftflotille, later 721 Squadron, serving until 1952.

Eight, 18-1 to 18-8 to Dutch Naval Air Arm during 1949/50, later in 1950 re-serialled 12-1 to 12-8, as Type 507 and under Vickers contract C.517/49. Used for air-sea rescue. All ex-RAF, 18-1 JM977 (G-AKRF), 18-2 JM818 (G-ALVB), 18-3 JM966 (G-AKYH), 18-4 JN107, 18-5 JN141, 18-6 JN142, 18-7 JN186 and 18-8 JM984 plus three others in 1950, JM764 (G-AKID), JM826 (G-AKIC) and JM827 (G-ALTX) for spares.

Six to French Customs Administration (Indo-China) believed as N-82 to N-87, first flown after recondition as G.15-82 to G.15-87 between April and July 1950 and delivered by sea to Saigon. Of these G.15-82 was JM797, G.15-84 was JM953 and G.18-85 was JM879, all of which were fitted with the Rotol Hydraulic variable-pitch propellers. The other three were; JM741, JM873 and JM884.

Two, VH-AJN and VH-AJO, ordered 21 July 1949 and first accepted 9 November, 1949 by Qantas Empire Airways. Both were ex RAF, JN188 and JN242, at a price of £18,000 the pair reconditioned.

One, VR-SOL, converted and exported to the Shell Petroleum Co Ltd (later to British North Borneo) passing its ARB test on 14 March, 1949, flown by L. R. Colquhoun.

The following were all bought from the Government by other concerns than Vickers-Armstrongs and are listed in British Registry sequence:

G-AJFU (JM747); G-AJFV (JM959) received C of A 21 April, 1949, and exported to Burma as XY-ABT; G-AJFW (JM957); G-AJFU and FW were bought by British Aviation Services Ltd in March 1947 but not converted and scrapped at Blackbushe in 1950.

G-AJVR (JM966) bought by J. M. McEwan Gibb but not converted and re-registered G-AKYH and converted at Squires Gate, Blackpool, and sold abroad 17 October, 1949.

G-AKIC (JM826) and G-AKID (JM764) bought by Ciro's Aviation Ltd in 1947 but not converted.

The following were bought by BSDM on 30 October and 30 November, 1947, and registered:

G-AKPN (JN139), G-AKPO (JN114), G-AKPP (JM989), G-AKPR (JN197), G-AKPS (JN187), G-AKPT (JN138), G-AKPU (JN137) and G-AKPV (JN194) and sold via J. Patient to Egypt on 17 February, 1949.

G-AKRF (JM977) was sold abroad on 4 June, 1949; G-AKRG (JN134) bought by R. L. Whyham and converted but stored and finally scrapped at Burnaston in 1957.

The last two G-ALTX (JM827) and G-ALVB (JM818) were sold abroad on 6 March, 1950, and 3 October, 1949, respectively, after having been bought by Autocars (Worc) Ltd and Essex Aero Ltd. These last two aircraft actually went to the Dutch Navy, G-ALVB being serialled 18-2 and later 12-2.

Spitfire

In compiling this list of serial numbers the authors have had access to the Supermarine production records up to December 1943 (which had not been available previously), the Air Historical Branch of the Air Ministry and Vickers-Armstrongs archives. The reference taken is that the aircraft was first flown in that particular Mark designation, even though it had changed before being delivered to the Services, *i.e.* in some cases by having an engine change; this applying especially to the Mk V to Mk IX conversions; in other cases by the introduction of modifications between first flight and official delivery.

More than 10 per cent of the total listed had their designations changed at least once.

K5054, prototype Type 300, to specification F.37/34, and under contract 361140/34 dated 1 December, 1934. First flown 5 March, 1936, initially with a Rolls-Royce Merlin C engine, later fitted with a Merlin F and later still with a Merlin II. Delivered to the RAF 23 October, 1937. Crashed at Farnborough 4 September, 1939, after the aircraft had been brought to Mk I standard.

310, K9787—9999 and L1000—1096, ordered 3 June, 1936, under contract 527113/36 as Mk I. All built at Southampton to specification F.16/36 and operational requirement OR17. K9787 first flew at Eastleigh 14 May, 1938. First delivered, K9788, 19 July, 1938. Last delivered, L1096, 7 September, 1939. K9834 converted to High Speed Spitfire N17, Type 323, under contract 817241/38, later converted to PR.II standard. First 74 to K9960 fitted with Merlin II, remainder with Merlin III. First 77 to K9963 fitted with two-blade fixed-pitch propellers, remainder with three-blade two-speed propellers. First 49 batch costed at £8,783 each, next 26 fixed price of £5,782 each, next 31 at £5,768 10s, remainder at £5,696 each. Many conversions, trial installations etc, L1090 shipped to USA in September 1939, K9991 to Portugal September 1943. L1004 fitted with Merlin 32 and cameras as PR.XIII.

Six countries placed orders under Vickers contract numbers as follows;
Estonia—12 to C.186/39   Contracts cancelled and
Greece—12 to C.315/39   advance payments refunded.
Portugal—15 to C.972/39
Switzerland—three to C.638B but contract not accepted.

France—one to C.590/39 and supplied as O-1 on 12 July, 1939, having first flown under Class B registration N-21 and with production number 251.

The Supermarine production numbers were 1—250 and 252—311.

Turkey—Two to C.1060/40 but see P9305—9584 serial batch.

200, N3023—3299, ordered under contract 527113/36 and built at Southampton as; N3023—3072, 3091—3130, 3160—3203, 3221—3250, 3264—3299, N3296—3299 not included on Supermarine production list, though N3297 completed as Type 330 Mk III to contract B23634/39 with a Merlin RM3SM(XX), later to Type 348 and later fitted with Merlin 61 as Mk VIII prototype. N3296 and 3298—3299 delivered as sets of parts to Castle Bromwich on 24 January, 1940. First delivered, N3023—3026, 8 September, 1939, last delivered, N3293—3295, on 20 January, 1940. Production numbers 312 to 507(N3295) and from this batch the production numbers were not in sequence.

196 Mk I and one Mk III.

1,000, P7280—8799, ordered under contract B.981687/39/CB/23(c) on 12 April, 1939, as Mk IIA from Castle Bromwich. Built as;
P7280—7329, 7350—7389, 7420—7449, 7490—7509, 7520—7569, 7590—7629, 7661—7699, 7730—7759, 7770—7789, 7810—7859, 7880—7929, 7960—7999, 8010—8049, 8070—8099, 8130—8149, 8160—8209, 8230—8279, 8310—8349, 8360—8399, 8420—8449, 8460—8479, 8500—8531, 8533—8536, 8540—8541, 8543—8549, 8561—8563, 8565—8577, 8579—8580, 8582—8584, 8586—8599, 8601—8602, 8605, 8608, 8641—8679, 8690—8698, 8701—8702, 8704—8706, and 8725—8729. 921 Mk IIA/IIB. P7301 trial installation of meteorological oblique cameras for Seafire L.IIC by Heston Aircraft during 1942. P8532, 8537—8539,

8542, 8560—8561, 8564, 8578, 8581, 8585, 8600, 8603—8604, 8606—8607, 8609, 8640, 8699—8700, 8703, 8707—8724, 8740—8759 and 8780—8799. 79 Mk VA/VB.
First delivered, P7280, 27 June, 1940, last delivered, P8799, 21 July, 1941.

200, P9305—9584, ordered 29 April, 1939, under contract 980385/39 as Mk I from Southampton. Built as;
P9305—9339, 9360—9399, 9420—9469, 9490—9519 and 9540—9567 (183) Mk I. P9568—9584(17) cancelled 9 June, 1940. P9566—9567 to Type 341 for Turkey as N-22 and N-23, delivered 8 May and 4 May, 1940, respectively. P9544 to Portugal October 1943. P9547, 9553—9561 and 9565 built as Type 341 but converted back to Mk I RAF standard on the production line. P9551 and 9552 built as PR. 'D'(PR.III) under contract S.B.2415/CB23, P9551 delivered 21 September, 1940, to Malta 27 January, 1941, but missing 2 February, 1941; P9552 delivered 22 February, 1941, to PDU but missing 10 May, 1941. Both of these are included in the total of 183 Mk I. The 179 true Mk Is were built at a fixed price of £5,120 each, the PR.'D's at £6,500 each under SB.2415 dated 18 January, 1940.

450, R6595—7350, ordered 9 August, 1939, under contract 19713/39 as Mk I from Southampton. Built as;
R6595—6644, 6683—6722, 6751—6780, 6799—6818, 6829—6840, 6879—6928, 6957—6996, 7015—7044, 7055—7074, 7114—7163, 7192—7231, 7250—7279, 7290—7309 and 7333—7350. 343 Mk I and the remainder were converted on the production line as; R6722 Mk VA floatplane, R7207—7210, 7213, 7217—7218, 7220—7223, 7225—7227, 7229—7231, 7253—7256, 7258—7261, 7263—7264, 7266—7275, 7277, 7279, 7291, 7293, 7295, 7297, 7299—7309, 7333, 7335, 7339, 7341—7343, 7345, 7347, 7349—7350, 65 Mk VA. R7158, 7161, 7192, 7195, 7219, 7224, 7228, 7262, 7265, 7276, 7278, 7290, 7292, 7294, 7296, 7298, 7334, 7336—7338, 7340, 7344, 7346 and 7348 were 24 Mk VB. R7029—7034 were six PR.C.V, R7035—7044 and 7055—7056 were 12 PR.IV. R7252 was the first of 18 produced at Chattis Hill and first flown 27 March, 1941. Thus total of 432 built at Eastleigh.
First delivered, R6595, 9 May, 1940, last delivered, R7350, 24 April, 1941. Production halted at R7022 and X4009 to 4997 were then manufactured before R7023 to 7350 to confuse the enemy. R6920, 6987, 7027, 7071, 7123, 7146 and 7159 to Portugal during 1942/43. R7120 fitted with first pressurized cockpit, R6700 fitted with Merlin 61 as Mk IX.

450, W3109—3970, ordered 22 February, 1940, under contract 19713/39 as Mk V from Supermarine. Built as: W3109—3138, 3168—3187, 3207—3216, 3226—3265, 3305—3334, 3364—3383, 3403—3412, 3422—3461, 3501—3530, 3560—3579, 3599—3608, 3618—3657, 3697—3726, 3756—3775, 3795—3804, 3814—3853, 3893—3902 and 3931—3970. 424 Mk VB the remainder as follows: W3237 prototype Mk III, and 25 Mk VA W3109—3114, 3119, 3121, 3123, 3130, 3136, 3138, 3169, 3184—3185, 3213—3214, 3216, 3240, 3323, 3364, 3366, 3369, 3374 and 3379.
W3109 first delivered 8 May, 1941, from Chattis Hill; W3119 first flew from Eastleigh 23 April, 1941, and despatched to Wright Field, USA; W3175 first built at High Post Aerodrome and first flew 27 April, 1941. Last delivered, W3970, on 20 October, 1941. W3760 fitted with Folland floats in 1942. Three converted to PR.XIII: W3112, 3135 and 3821. Eight to the French Air Force; W3229, 3322, 3328, 3426, 3619, 3899, 3931 and 3957. Three to the Portuguese Air Force; W3518—3519 and 3803.

500, X4009—4997, ordered 9 June, 1940, under contract 19713/39 as Mk I from Supermarine. Built as: X4009—4038, 4051—4070, 4101—4110, 4159—4188, 4231—4280, 4317—4356, 4381—4390, 4409—4428, 4471—4505, 4538—4562, 4585—4624, 4641—4685, 4708—4722, 4765—4789, 4815—4859, 4896—4945 and 4988—4997. All Mk I except: eight Mk V PR.C; X4499—4505 and 4538. Four Mk VA: X4663, 4665, 4667 and 4669. Four Mk VB: X4664, 4666, 4668 and 4670. The following were Mk I (PR Type C): X4332—4335, 4382—4386 and 4491—4498 all delivered to the Photographic Development Unit (PDU) but these are included in the total of 484 Mk Is built. Six were delivered to Portugal in 1942/43: X4339, 4617, 4719, 4855, 4857 and 4920. X4780 crashed before delivery.
All built at Eastleigh except X4498—4505 and 4538.
Conversions: X4472 to PR.VI and X4615 to prototype PR.XIII.
First delivered, X4011—4012, 26 July, 1940, last delivered, X4994, 18 March, 1941. X4942 second Spitfire with pressurized cockpit.

500, AA718—AB536 ordered 19 July, 1940, under contract 19173/39 as Mk I, but changed to Mk V, from Supermarine. Built as:
AA718—767, 781—815, 833—882, 902—946, 963—982, AB118—152, 167—216, 240—284, 300—349, 363—382, 401—430, 450—469 and 487—536. 315 built as Mk VB. The remainder were: 81 PR.IV, AA781—815, AB118—132, 300—319, 421—430 and 466; 87 Mk F.VC, AA878, 963, 968, 976—977, 980, AB139, 167, 169—170, 174, 178, 182, 188, 191, 196—197, 202, 204, 208, 210, 212, 214, 216, 248, 252, 254, 262, 349, 365, 367—368, 371—372, 374, 377, 380—381, 417, 452—453, 455—465, 467—469, 489, 491, 493, 495—497, 501, 505, 507—512, 514—516, 518—522, 524—526, 531—532 and 535—536. 16 Mk VI: AB176, 198, 200, 211, 498, 503, 506, 513, 517, 523, 527—530, 533—534. One F.IX, prototype, AB450. Conversions included: AA739 to PR.XII, AB197 to second prototype F.IX, AB450 to prototype F.VII, AB456—460 (5) to F.IX. AB499 to Mk VII Special, and AB487 fitted with liquid oxygen trial installation by Heston Aircraft.
First delivered, AA718, 31 August, 1941, last delivered, AB535—536, 26 February, 1942. Fifteen, AB262, 264, 329—332, 334—338, 341, 343—344 and 346 were shipped on the ss Cape Hawk to Gibraltar and transferred to the aircraft carrier HMS Eagle where they were re-assembled. The carrier sailed about half way to Malta and all the aircraft were flown off and landed in Malta safely on 7 March, 1942.

500, AB779 to AD584, ordered 22 June, 1940, as Mk I but changed to Mk V from Vickers-Armstrongs, Castle Bromwich, under contract 981687/39. Built as: AB779—828, 841—875, 892—941, 960—994, AD111—140, 176—210, 225—274, 288—332, 348—397, 411—430, 449—478, 498—517 and 535—584 all Mk VB.
Conversions: AD354, 389, 501 and 556 to PR.XIII.
AB780 first delivered 25 July, 1941, and last delivered, AD583—584, 23 November, 1941.

300, AR212—621, ordered as Mk IA from Westland Aircraft at Yeovil under contract 124305/40 in August 1940. Built as: AR212—261(50). Mk IA, AR274—298, 318—347, 362—406 and 422—461(140) Mk VB, AR462—471, 488—532, 546—570 and 592—621(110) Mk VC.
Conversions: AR319 to PR.XIII.
First delivered, AR212, 18 July, 1941, last, AR620—621, delivered 7 September, 1942.

BF271, 273, 274, 335 and 336 incorrect numbers. BF applied in error for BS but changed later, except for BF274, which retained its serial throughout. It became the prototype Mk IX and was delivered from Supermarine on 20 December, 1942. It was converted by Vickers in 1948 as a T.9 for the Netherlands and was delivered as H-98 on 23 March, 1948.

1,000, BL231 to BM653, ordered as Mk III (Merlin XX—eight Browning guns) under contract 981687/39 on 24 October, 1940, from Vickers-Armstrongs at Castle Bromwich. Built as: BL231—267, 285—304, 311—356, 365—391, 403—450, 461—500, 509—551, 562—600, 613—647, 655—699, 707—736, 748—789, 801—833, 846—864, 887—909, 918—941, 956—998, BM113—162, 176—211, 227—274, 289—329, 343—386, 399—430, 447—493, 508—543, 556—597 and 624—653, all Mk VB.
Conversions: BL446, 526, BM447 and 591 to PR.XIII. BL676 to first 'Hooked Spitfire' by Air Service Training 10 January, 1942. BL773 became a 'Queen' Spitfire and BM156 was used for negative g trials. First delivered, BL231, on 23 November, 1941, last delivered, BM653, 16 May, 1942.

800, BP844 to BS152, ordered 24 October, 1940, as Mk I from Supermarine under contract 19713/39, but order changed to Mk V and later amended to include other marks. 598 built only. BS683—721, 745—772, 799—831, 849—877, 890—935 and 950—976(202) being cancelled.
Built as: BP844—892, 904—937, 950—993, BR106—143, 159—205, 226—256, 282—330, 344—393, 410—435, 459—499, 515—549, 562—605, 621—670, 977—987 and BS104—152. Of these 339 were Mk VC and the remainder were as follows: 104 PR.IV BP879—892, 904—937, BR410—435 and 641—670. Ten VB BP844—853. 70 F.VI BR110, 162, 164, 167, 173—175, 178, 181, 186, 189, 191, 193, 197, 200, 205, 243, 247, 250, 252, 255, 286—287, 289, 297—298, 302, 304, 307, 309—310, 314, 318—319, 326, 329—330, 541, 563, 567, 569, 571, 575, 577—579, 585, 587—588, 590, 593, 595, 597—599, 979, 983—984, BS106, 108, 111, 114—115, 117, 124, 133—134, 141, 146 and 149.

First production HF.VII, three only BS121, 142 and 150.

72 F.IX: BR549, 581, 592, 594, 596, 600—605, 621—640, 977—978, 980—982, 985—986, BS104—105, 107, 109—110, 112—113, 116, 118—120, 122—123, 125—132, 135—140, 143—145, 147—148 and 151—152.

BP985, BR114 and BR234 modified locally at Aboukir during 1942 for high altitude operations (but no pressure cabin). They shot down three Ju 86P-2s between 42,000 ft and 45,000 ft over Alexandria, first on 24 August, 1942, the other two in September, after which no more were sent over. BR202 used for LR fuel tank trials and BR372 fitted special split braking flaps by Heston Aircraft and later with an under-fuselage bomb rack. First delivered, BP844 and 845 on 4 February, 1942, last, BS151 and 152 on 26 August, 1942.

300, BS157 to BS559, ordered 24 October, 1940, as Mk IB from Supermarine under contract 19713/39, but order changed to Mk V and Mk IX. Built as; BS157—202, 218—255, 271—319, 335—367, 383—411, 427—474, 489—515 and 530—559. Mk IXs (205) except the following:

BS158, 160—169, 171, 174—175, 178, 181—182, 184, 186—188, 190—191, 193, 197, 199, 201, 218—226, 228, 230—238, 291, 293, 295, 298, 300 and 305 Mk VC (52). BS355—358, 360—367, 489—496, 500 and 503—505 Mk IV PR (24). BS228, 245, 253, 359, 427, 436—437, 442, 448, 453, 460, 465 and 472 Mk VI F (13). BS229 Mk VII F, BS497—499 and 501—502 Mk XI PR (5).

120, BS573—618, 634—659 and 677—724 ordered 24 October, 1940, under contract Air/71 as Mk III from Supermarine but cancelled 26 April, 1941.

DP845 and 851. Two prototypes fitted with Griffon engines to specification F.4/41 and ordered under contract Air/821 dated 26 May, 1941. Both designated Mk IV, which is different from the PR.IV designation already mentioned in previous contracts, but completed as DP845 prototype F.IV and F.XII. DP851 prototype F.20, later to F.21. DP845 fitted with Griffon IIB, IV and VI in that order.

200, EE600 to EE867, Mk V ordered from Westland in September 1941 and built as Mk VCs. EE600—644, 657—690, 713—753, 766—811 and 834—867 under contract 124305/40. First delivered, EE601 and 602, 21 October, 1942.

185, EF526 to EF753, added to above contract in October 1941 and all built as Mk VC. EF526—570, 584—616, 629—656, 671—710 and 715—753. Delivered from 2 February, 1943, last delivered on 5 November, 1943, was EF753. At least 30 were delivered to the USAAF in North Africa, most being taken on charge 29 February, 1944.

500, EN112 to EN759, ordered from Supermarine as Mk VC on 23 August, 1941, under contract B19713/39. Order amended to Mk IX and later different marks added. Complete list:

EN112—156, 171—207, 221—270, 285—315, 329—370, 385—430, 444—483, 490—534, 551—583, 601—637, 652—695, 710—759, 60 cancelled EN686—695 and 710—759. All built as Mk IX except: EN153, 155, 262, 264 and 386—389 (8) PR.IV, EN176 and 189 F.VI, EN192, 285, 297, 310, 457, 465, 470, 474, 477, 494—495, 497, 499, 505—506, 509, 511—512 and 604 (19) F.VII, EN149—151, 154—155, 260, 263, 330—332, 337—338, 341—343, 346—348, 391, 395—396, 407—411, 413—430, 504, 507—508 and 652—685 PR.XI (81) and EN221—238, 496, 601—603 and 605—627 (45), first production F.XII: the remainder were 285 F.IX. First delivered, EN112, 17 November, 1942, last, EN683, on 15 August, 1943. EN465 and 470 modified for liquid oxygen injection.

905, EN763 to ER200, ordered from Vickers-Armstrongs (Supermarine), Castle Bromwich, on 23 August, 1941, as Mk VC and as an addition to contract B981689/39. Produced as: EN763—800, 821—867, 888—932, 944—981, EP107—152, 164—213, 226—260, 275—316, 327—366, 380—417, 431—473, 485—523, 536—579, 594—624, 636—669, 682—729, 747—795, 812—847, 869—915, 951—990, ER114—146 and 159—200. EN830 fitted with DB605A after being captured by Germans. 27 converted to Seafires, EP751 and 754 to Mk V seaplane. First delivered, EN763, 6 April, 1942, last, ER199, delivered 4 September, 1942. 905 built in 132 days or 6·86 aircraft every day, 48 per week, in wartime conditions. EN948 used for ground ejector-seat experiments postwar.

750, ER206 to ES369, ordered as above and part of the same contract but as Mk IV. Order changed and produced as: ER206—229, 245—283, 299—345, 461—510, 524—571,

583—626, 634—679, 695—744, 758—791, 804—834, 846—894, 913—948, 960—998, ES105–154, 168—214, 227—264, 276—318 and 335—369. All Mk VB/C, first delivered, ER206, on 29 August, 1942, last, ES368, delivered 20 December, 1942, though the previous last, ES367, was delivered 14 December, 1942, thus, ignoring this one, Castle Bromwich produced 1,655 Spitfires in 233 days, giving a production rate of 7·1 Spitfires per day or approximately 50 per week during 1942, just from this one factory.

800, JF274 to JG695, ordered from Supermarine under contract Air/1877 as Mk VIII on 23 January, 1942. Built as follows:
JF274—300, 316—364, 392—427, 443—485, 501—528, 557—592, 613—630, 658—676, 692—716, 740-789, 805—850, 869—902, 926—967, JG104—124, 157—204, 239—275, 312—356, 371—387, 404—432, 465—500, 527—568, 603—624 and 646—695. All Mk VIIIs except JF316, 318—320 (4) prototype XIVs, JF317 and 321 classified as Mk VIII converted, thus 796 Mk VIII.

989, JG713 to JL395, ordered from Castle Bromwich as Mk VB on 1 January, 1942 as addition to contract B.981687/39 and built as V/IX as follows; JG713—752, 769—810, 835—852, 864—899, 912—960, JK101—145, 159—195, 214—236, 249—285, 303—346, 359—408, 425—472, 506—551, 600—620, 637—678, 705—742, 756—796, 803—842, 860—892, 922—950, 967—992, JL104—140, 159—188, 208—256, 301—338 and 346—395. Total of 976 Mk VB/VC and 13 Mk IX but at least 70 others converted to Mk IX later. Majority were for overseas delivery. Some, like JK174, 176, 181, 184, 257, 258, 273 and 331 were lost en route. These eight were lost when the ss *Silver Beech* was torpedoed and sunk on its way to Australia on 14 April, 1943. First delivered, JG713, 10 December, 1942, last, JL395, delivered 21 April, 1943.

South Marston built Spitfire F.21 LA226. (*Vickers-Armstrongs*)

300, LA187 to LA582, ordered from South Marston under contract Air/1951/CB.23(c) in 1942 as F.21s but changed to Castle Bromwich, still as F.21s, on 24 April, 1944, as addition to contract B.981687/39. 120 built as F.21s, LA187—236, 249—284 and 299—332. First, LA188, delivered 6 September, 1944, last, LA332, delivered 2 January, 1946. LA333—346, 358—395, 417—457, 480—519 and 536—582 cancelled. Order reinstated for 75 Seafire F.45s, LA428—457, 480—519 and 536—540 also 42 Seafire F.46s LA541—582—*see* Seafire list. LA187 built at Castle Bromwich, LA188 to LA332 at South Marston (C/n SMAF/4333—4339, 4341—4342 and 4344—4453 but not in sequence).

70, LV643—756, ordered from Supermarine on 21 April, 1942, in addition to contract B919713/39 fitted with Merlin 61 engines. Built as L.F.VIII, LV643—681 and 726—756. 54 sent to India, nine LV644, 647, 649, 652, 657, 672, 727, 740 and 750 to Australia, six to Casablanca on the ss *Argyll* arrived 13 June, 1944, only LV674 staying in the UK. First delivered, LV643, 4 November, 1943, last, LV753, delivered 4 June, 1944.

680, LZ807 to MA906, ordered from Castle Bromwich 28 February, 1942, as Mk VC as addition to contract 981687/39, delivered as 300 Mk V and 380 Mk IX, LZ807—848, 861—899, 915—956, 969—998, MA221—266, 279—315, 328—369, 383—428, 443—487, 501—546, 559—601, 615—657, 670—713, 726—767, 790—819, 831—863 and 877—906. Mk V were: LZ807—830, 834—835, 844—848, 862—888, 893—899, 918—956, 969—988, MA261—266, 279—315, 328—368, 383—397, 644—657, 670—704, 850—863, 877 and 880—906. Of these LZ816, 888, 893, 947—956, MA299—315, 683, 690, 693, 854, 860 and 884 were converted to IXs off the production line and others, including LZ889—892, 894—899, MA298, 643, 645—646, 651, 655, 657, 671 and 687, were converted to IXs later. First delivered, LZ807 and 808, on 28 March, 1943, and last, MA906, delivered 1 July, 1943.

426, MB761 to MD403, Mk VC ordered from Supermarine on 12 May, 1942, under addition to contract 19713/39 and built as: MB761—808, 820—863, 875—916, 929—976, MD100—146, 159—199, 213—256, 269—303, 315—356 and 369—403. F.VII MB761—769, 806, 808—828, 883—887, 912—935, MD100—108, 110—146, 159—190 (116). LF.VIII MB959—976, MD109, 214—256, 269—303, 315—356, 369—403 (174). F.IX MB807. PR.X MD191—199, 213(10). PR.XI MB770—793, 888—911, 936—958(71). F.XII MB794—803, 829—863, 875—882(55). First delivered, MB761, 4 July, 1943, last, MD401, delivered 21 February, 1944.

Spitfire Mk IXC MK210 after flying the Atlantic from Newfoundland to the United Kingdom on 20 September, 1944. The aircraft was modified at Wright Field, Ohio, and fitted with a Packard-built Merlin 266. (*AAEE*)

2,190, MH298 to ML428, Mk V/IX ordered from Castle Bromwich on 28 May, 1942, under contract 981689/39 amended. Built as: MH298—336, 349—390, 413—456, 470—512, 526—568, 581—626, 635—678, 691—738, 750—800, 813—856, 869—912, 924—958, 970—999, MJ114—156, 169—203, 215—258, 271—314, 328—369, 382—428, MJ441—485, 498—536, 549—589, 602—646, 659—698, 712—756, 769—801, 814—858, 870—913, 926—967, 979—999, MK112—158, 171—213, 226—268, 280—326, 339—379, 392—428, 440—486, 499—534, 547—590, 602—646, 659—699, 713—756, 769—812, 826—868, 881—926, 939—967, 981—999, ML112—156, 169—216, 229—277, 291—323, 339—381, and 396—428. All Mk IX, 2,144 except the following 46 Mk VC MH298—311, 564—568, 581—596, 600, 605, 637—646. First delivered, MH298, on 1 July, 1943, last delivered, ML427, on 29 April, 1944. MJ892 converted to a seaplane, MK210, fitted with two wing tanks with 500 gal fuel and flew the Atlantic in 1944. MJ556 installed with first Packard-Merlin 266 engine as LF.IX, later Mk LF.XVI.

700 Mk VIII, MT502—MV514, ordered from Supermarine on 27 July, 1942, under contract 6/AIR/1877/C.23 as: MT502—527, 539—581, 593—635, 648—689, 703—748, 761—802, 815—858, 872—915, 928—969, 981—999, MV112—156, 169—208, 231—273, 286—329, 342—386, 398—441, 456—487 and 499—514. 585 built as Mk VIII, except the

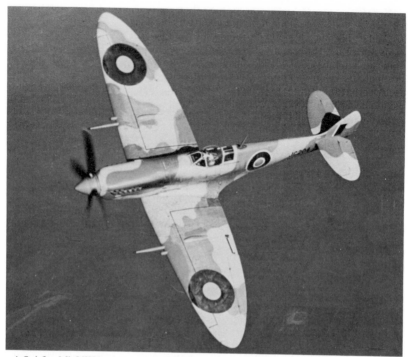

A Spitfire Mk VIII in standard configuration with original planform but powered by the Merlin 61.

following built as FR.XIV: MT847—858, MV246—273, 286—320 and 347—386 (115). First delivered, MT504, on 23 March, 1944, last, MV514, on 22 October, 1944. MT818 converted to T.8 as N32, later G-AIDN.

600, Mk IX NG757 to NH611, ordered from Castle Bromwich on 1 December, 1942, under contract B981687/39 as amended. The first 232 were cancelled. NG757—798, 813—856, 868—890 cancelled 15 November, 1945,(109), NG891—913, 926—968, 979—999, and NH112—147 cancelled as F.22s on 18 August, 1945, (123). The remainder 368 were built as Mk IX, NH148—158, 171—218, 230—276, 289—326, 339—381, 393—438, 450—496, 513—558 and 570—611. First delivered, NH148, on 28 April, 1944, last delivered, NH611, on 14 June, 1944. NH403 used for towing a Messerschmitt 163B Komet from Wisley airfield.

225, NH614 to 929, ordered from Supermarine on 1 December, 1942, under contract Air/1877 as 142 Mk VIII and 83 Mk IX, but order changed and built as 23 Mk VIII, 191 Mk XIV and 11 Mk XVIII as follows: NH614—661, 685—720, 741—759, 775—813, 831—875 and 892—929. Mk VIIIs were NH614—636, Mk XVIIIs were NH847—856 and 872. First delivered, NH614, from Chattis Hill on 9 November, 1944, last delivered 17 May, 1945.

70, NM814—855 and 879—906, ordered from Supermarine (Chattis Hill) on 29 December, 1942, under contract Air/1877/CB.23(c) as FR.XIV. Only 10 built, NM814—823, at Aldermaston, except NM821 at Chattis Hill. NM814 first delivered on 31 March, 1945, and NM823 last delivered on 24 April, 1945.

100 PA838—961, Mk IX ordered from Supermarine on 9 April, 1943, under contract Air/1877/CB.23(c) but built as PR.XIs PA838—871, 884—913 and 926—961. PA838, first delivered 3 November, 1943, last delivered, PA961, 24 February, 1944, from Aldermaston.

368

800, PK312 to PL499. LF.IX ordered from Castle Bromwich on 2 June, 1943, under contract B981687/39, which was altered several times but ended as: PK312—356, 369—412 and 426—435 F.22, PK436—468(33) cancelled, PK481—525, 539—582, 594—635, 648—677, 680 and 715 F.22 (263), PK678—689 and 712—726 (less 680, 684 and 715) (24) completed as F.24 at South Marston, PK727—754, 769—811, 828—868 and 883—926, (198) cancelled 15 November, 1945, as F.22, PK991—998, PL123—169, 185—228, 246—288, 313—356, 369—408, 423—466 and 488—499 Mk IX (282). First delivered, PK313, 17 March, 1945, last, PK677, delivered 11 February, 1946. F.24 first delivered, PK679, 25 October. 1946, last, PK726, 5 November, 1946. Mk IX first delivered, PK991 and 992, on 10 June, 1944, last, PL498, delivered 1 July, 1944.

600, PL758 to PM676, LF.VIII ordered from Supermarine on 2 June, 1943, under contract Air/1877CB.23(c). Changes to the contract gave a final production of 351 aircraft only. 219 PR.XI were built as: PL758—799, 823—866, 881—925, 949—998 and PM123—160. First delivered, PM758, on 21 February, 1944, last, PM160, on 1 March, 1945. The following were cancelled: PM161—168, 184—228, 245—288, 302—347 and 367—404 (181).

It was envisaged that PM419—462 and 478—495 (62) should be built as Spitefuls, but order changed and only PM462 was produced, as a PR.XIX. A further 123 PR.XIX were built as follows: PM496—519, 536—581, 596—637 and 651—661. First delivered, PM496, on 19 May, 1945, last delivered, PM661, on 31 May, 1946. The final 15, PM662—676, were cancelled, PM671—676 at one time being scheduled as Spitefuls.

One prototype, PP139, ordered under contract Air/2601CB.23(c) from Supermarine and produced as the true Mk F.21 prototype at High Post Aerodrome. Compromised a Sunderland Mk III serial number in the range PP135—164.

200, PS684 to PS935, H.F.VIII ordered from Supermarine on 17 July, 1943, under contract Air/1877CB.23(c). Contract changed to 121 Spiteful PS684—725, PS739—781 and 795—830, but cancelled and 79 Spitfire PR.XIX built as: PS831—836, 849—893 and 908—935. First delivered, PS831, on 27 November, 1944, last, PS935, delivered 18 May, 1945.

1,500, PS938—PW250, Spitfire F.21 (Victor) ordered from Castle Bromwich and South Marston factories on 6 June, 1943, under contract B981687/39 as PS938—987, PT100—145, 160—203, 220—267, 281—325, 335—380, 395—436, 451—498, 523—567, 582—627, PT639—683, 697—738, 752—795, 818—859, 873—915, 929—970, 986—999, PV115—160, 174—215, 229—270, 283—327, 341—385, 399—445, 458—499, 520—567, 581—625, 639—680, 697—739, 752—797, 820—865, 879—919, 935—984, PW112—158, 173—196, and 221—250.

Many amendments and cancellations affected this contract and the results are as follows: PS936—957 Seafire F.47, but PS938—943 and 958—987 cancelled on 18 August 1945. Only PS944—957(14) were completed with 36 cancelled. 688 Mk IXs between PT335 and PV359 were built at Castle Bromwich. Five, PV288, 295, 307, 327 and 349, were converted on the production line to LF.XVI. First delivered, PT335, 28 June, 1944. 307 F.22 cancelled 18 August, 1945 were; PT163—203, 220—229, PV360—385, 399—445, 458—499, 520—567, 581—583, PW123—158, 173—196 and 221—250. The remaining 380 were also cancelled in 1945. 200 Griffon Seafires cancelled 18 August, 1945, were: PV734—739, 752—797, 820—865, 879—919, 935—985 and PW112—122.

50, RB140—189, F.XIV ordered from Supermarine on 14 August, 1943, under contract Air/1877/C23 and delivered as F.XIV. RB140 serial number clashed with that of a Kirby Cadet in the range RB112—140. First delivered, RB141, on 12 November, 1943, last, RB189, on 3 March, 1945. All believed built at Eastleigh.

373, RB515 to 987, F.21 (Victor) ordered from Supermarine on 14 August, 1943, under contract Air/1877/CB.23 as: RB515—557, 571—615, 628—669, 683—725, 739—783, 796—843, 857—898, 912—953 and 965—987. Spitfire order cancelled and amended to Spiteful F.XIV. Only RB515—525, 527—531 and 535 built.

100, RK798—819, 835—868 and 883—926, LF.IX ordered from Castle Bromwich on 25 October, 1943, under contract B981687/39 amended. First delivered, RK799, on 16 August, 1944, last delivered, RK925, on 11 October, 1944. 35 were shipped to USSR commencing 12

369

October, 1944, to Murmansk. LF.XVI RK840, 842, 849, 859, 865—866, 868, 883, 888, 891—893, 895—897, 902—905, 910, 913, 918, 921, 925—926(25).

406, RM615 to RN221, Mk XIV ordered from Supermarine on 23 October, 1943, under contract Air/1877/CB.23 and built as 22 PR.XIX RM626—647 and 384 Mk XIV RM615—625, 648—656, 670—713, 726—770, 783—825, 839—887, 901—943, 957—999, RN113—160 and 173—221. First delivered, RM615, on 1 April, 1944, last, RN220, delivered 16 May, 1945.

73, RR181—213 and 226—265, HF.IX ordered from Castle Bromwich on 16 November, 1943, under contract B981687/39. Built as Mk IX (50) except the following built as LF.XVI: RR205, 212—213, 226—227, 229—230, 234, 236, 240, 242—243, 245, 247—250, 255—257, 261, 263 and 265 (23). First delivered, RR181, on 17 August, 1944, last, RR264, on 18 October, 1944. RR233 deleted from contract, collided with SM212 at Castle Bromwich 19 October, 1944, and not rebuilt.

1,500, RV370 to SM698, F.21 ordered from Castle Bromwich on 20 January, 1944, under contract 981687/39. RV370—415, 428—469, 483—526, 539—580, 593—615, 627—653. 668—699, 713—758, 773—815, 828—859, 873—905, 918—959, 971—999, RW113—156, 168—209, 225—258, 273—315, 328—359, 373—396, SL541—579, 593—635, 648—690, 713—747, 759—798, 812—857, 873—915, 928—959, 971—999, SM112—150, 170—213, 226—258, 273—316, 329—369, 383—427, 441—488, 503—548, 563—597, 610—648 and 663—698. The following were built only, under contract Air/5161: 197 Mk IX, 594—595, 625—635, 648—665 (SL660—665 were over-delivered but Air Ministry included them in their total), SM135—150, 170—177, 240, 425, 441—463, 486, 504—506, 508—510, 513—515, 517—537, 539—548, 563—597, 610—645, 647, 663, 666, 668—669. 366 LF.XVI. RW344—359, 373—396. SL541—565, 567—571, 573—579, 596—602, 604—605, 608—611, 613—618, 620—624, 666, 668—676, 678—681, 685, 687—690, 713, 715, 717—721, 724—725, 727—728, 733, 745, SM178—213, 226—239, 241—258, 273—316, 329—369, 383—424, 426—427, 464—485, 487—488, 503, 507, 511—512, 516, 538, 646, 648, 664—665, 667 and 670—671. SL563, 601, 604, 615, 617, 690, 715, 719—720, 745 (10) were over-delivered but Air Ministry included them in the final total. 110 LF.XVIs, SL890 to SM134 were cancelled on 25 April, 1945. 260 F.22s, RV896 to RW343 were cancelled 18 August, 1945. First delivered, RV345, 26 June, 1945, last delivered, SL745, 31 August, 1945. At least 124 LF.IX exported to USSR including SM447—462, 524—537, 539—548, 563—597 and 610—645. The numbers from RW397 to SL540 were allocated, but not to Spitfires.

150, SM812 to SM997, ordered from Supermarine on 12 February, 1944, under contract Air/1877 as PR.XI but built as follows: SM812—842 F.XIV, SM843—845, FR.XVIII, SM858—875 cancelled. SM876—899, 913—938 FR.XIV, 939—956 and 968—997 F.XVIII. 81 Mk XIV, 51 Mk XVIII and 18 cancelled. First delivered, SM813, 23 February, 1945, last delivered, SM997, 19 January, 1946. 23 of the F.XVIIIs and two of the F.XIVs to India.

6, SR395—400, ordered from Supermarine on 18 February, 1944, under contract 19713/39 as F.VII but delivered as PR.X. between 14 and 16 May, 1944, to RAF Benson, except SR396 to No.542 Sqn. SR395 built at High Post, other five at Southampton.

One prototype ordered from Supermarine as SW777 on 27 April, 1944, under contract SB.27489 for a prototype F.21 and completed as a PR.XIX at High Post during 1945.

One prototype ordered from Cunliffe-Owen Aircraft at Eastleigh under contract Air/1877 as SX549, a Mk F.21 on 27 April, 1944, and completed as a Mk F.22 on 8 November, 1944.

1,884, TA738 to TE578, ordered from Castle Bromwich on 19 April, 1944, as 384 LF.IX (Merlin 66) and 1,500 LF.IX (Packard Merlin) under contract B981687/39. TA738—780, 793—840, 854—888, 905—948, 960—999, TB115—150, 168—197, 213—256, 269—308, 326—349, 352—396, 413—450, 464—503, 515—549, 563—598, 613—659, 674—718, 733— 759, 771—808, 824—868, 883—925, 938—959, 971—999, TD113—158, 175—213, 229— 267, 280—325, 338—379, 395—428, 443—490, 515—546, 560—605, 618—649, 660—706, 720—766, 783—815, 829—866, 884—925, 937—958, 970—999, TE115—158, 174—215, 228—259, 273—315, 328—359, 375—408, 434—480, 493—535 and 549—578.
The following were cancelled: TD409 to 951. The rest were built as Mk IX except for:

370

TA739, 741, 759, 809, TB130—132, 136—141, 232, 237, 244—248, 250, 252, 254—256, 269—308, 326—349, 352—392, 394—396, 475—476, 478, 480—481, 492—498, 501—502, 515, 517, 519—522, 525—526, 528, 549, 572, 574, 578, 580—583, 585, 588—598, 613—637, 639, 675, 702, 709, 713—716, 733—735, 737—739, 741—759, 827—829, 832—836, 858—868, 883—908, 910—913, 915—917, 919, 921—923, 989—991, 993, 995—999, TD113—154, 156—158, 176—177, 184—191, 229—267, 280—286, 288—289, 293, 316—325, 338—351, 369, 372, 375—377, 400—408, TE116, 119—120, 174—196, 198—204, 206—210, 214, 228—229, 235, 237, 239—259, 273—288, 291, 300, 302, 310—311, 314, 328, 330, 332, 334—335, 338—342, 344—359, 375—384, 386—408, 434—471 and 473—480. 632 Mk XVI. 850 Mk IX were built of which 600 were exported to USSR. Thus of the 1,884 ordered, 402 were cancelled. First delivered, TA739, on 29 November, 1944, last delivered, TE578 on 23 June, 1945. After the war the following Air Forces received: Belgian four IX, Czechoslovak 41 IX, Danish 14 IX, one XVI, French five IX plus 54 IX direct to Saïgon, Greek ten IX, 47 XVI, Italian two IX, Netherlands eight IX, two XVI, South African 45 IX, and Turkish six IX.

199, TL773 to TM136, H.F.IX ordered from Castle Bromwich under contract B.981687/39 on 25 July, 1944, as TL773—815, 829—870, 884—916, 930—967, 979—999 and TM115—136. All except TM115 were cancelled 30 October, 1944, and TM115 later scheduled as a XVI was cancelled in August 1945.

77, TM163—205 and 218—251, ordered from Castle Bromwich under contract B.981687/39 on 25 July, 1944, as L.F.IX but cancelled 30 October, 1944.

680, TP195—811, ordered from Supermarine as F.21 (Victor) in August 1944 under contract Air/1877/C.23 but delivered as 201 F.XVIII and 6 FR.XIV, the remainder being cancelled. 207 built as TP195—240, 256—298, 313—350, 363—408 and 423—456. The Mk XIVs were TP236—240 and 256. First delivered, TP196, on 10 November, 1945, last delivered, TP456, on 28 February, 1946. 51 to Indian Air Force from 31 December, 1949. The 473 cancelled were TP457—459, 472—507, 519—558, 573—615, 628—659, 675—717, 730—769 and 783—811.

157, TX974 to TZ240, ordered from Supermarine on 23 February, 1945, under contract Air/1877/C.23(c) amended. Built as: TX974—998, TZ102—149, 152—176, and 178—199 FR.XIV (120) and TZ200—205 and 210—240 FR.XVIII (37). First delivered, TX975, on 13 August, 1945, last delivered, TZ240, on 12 January, 1946. Exported postwar: Indian Air Force four FR.XIV and nine FR.XVIII and Belgian Air Force 14 FR.XIV.

100, TZ598—738, PR.XIX ordered from Supermarine on 6 March, 1945, under contract Air/1877/C.23(c) as TZ598—637, 658—692 and 714—738. The last 50 were cancelled 8 June, 1945, the remainder shortly afterwards.

210, TZ747—VA195, LF.XVI ordered from Castle Bromwich on 6 March, 1945, under contract B.981687/39 as TZ747—791, 815—843, 866—898, 921—957, 969—998, VA123—154 and 192—195. All cancelled 18 August, 1945, as F.22.

50, VA201—250, LF.IX, ordered from Castle Bromwich under contract B.981687/39 on 6 March, 1945. The type was changed to F.22 and all were cancelled 18 August, 1945.

150, VN301 to VN496, F.22, ordered from Castle Bromwich in late 1945 under contract Air/5795/C.23(c) as VN301—348, 364—397, 413—439 and 456—496. 54 incomplete airframes, VN301—334 and 477—496, were transferred to Vickers-Armstrongs, South Marston Works, and completed as F.24s, the remainder being cancelled. First delivered, VN301, on 13 April, 1946, last Spitfire delivered to the RAF was VN496 on 20 February, 1948.

135, VN501 to 673, ordered from Castle Bromwich in late 1945 as F.24 but order amended to Seafire F.46/F.47.

Service Units

Squadrons: 1, 2, 4, 5, 6, 11, 16, 17, 19, 20, 26, 28, 32, 33, 34, 41, 43, 54, 56, 60, 64, 65, 66, 67, 69, 71, 72, 73, 74, 80, 81, 87, 91, 92, 93, 94, 111, 118, 121, 122, 123, 124, 126, 127, 129, 130, 131, 132, 133, 134, 136, 140, 145, 152, 154, 155, 164, 165, 167, 185, 186, 208, 212, 213, 222, 225, 229, 232, 234, 237, 238, 241, 242, 243, 245, 249, 253, 266, 268, 269, 273, 274, 275,

276, 277, 278, 283, 286, 287, 288, 289, 290, 302, 303, 306, 308, 310, 312, 313, 315, 316, 317, 318, 322, 326, 327, 328, 329, 331, 332, 335, 336, 340, 341, 345, 349, 350, 352, 400, 401, 402, 403, 411, 412, 414, 416, 417, 421, 430, 441, 442, 443, 451, 452, 453, 457, 485, 501, 502, 504, 519, 520, 521, 527, 541, 542, 543, 544, 548, 549, 567, 577, 587, 595, 600, 601, 602, 603, 604, 607, 608, 609, 610, 611, 612, 613, 614, 615, 616, 631, 667, 680, 681, 682, 683, 691, 695, 1435.
Flights: 421, 1401, 1402, 1406, 1416, 1490, 1563, 1656, 1660, 1663, 1665, 1675, 1687, 1688, 1692, 1695.

Other Units: AFDU, 5 AFU, 9 AFU, 21 AFU, 203 AFS, APS, ACS, ASWD, BCIS, CCFATU, CFS, CGS, CRS, 1CU, 2CU, EASS, EANS, EFS, 17 FTS, GRU, 2ITS, 226 OCU, 237 OCU, OTUs 5, 7, 8, 41, 52, 53, 56, 57, 58, 61, 63, 71, 73, 80, 111, 151, PRDU, 1PRU, 2PRU, 3PRU, 4PRU, 17RFS, TPS.

Many other units had one or more Spitfires on charge and many airfields had their own Station Flight, e.g. The Aboukir Spitfire Flight, part of 103 MU. Of course, mention should be made of the other Maintenance Units, through which almost all the Spitfires were initially issued and to which they went for repair and modification.

Naval Spitfires

The following Spitfires were transferred to Royal Navy charge for type conversion and advanced training, some unmodified, from September 1942, those with (H) following the serial were classified as Hooked Spitfires:

P8707,	P8708(H),	W3328,	W3437(H),	W3457,	W3602,	W3618
W3646(H),	W3769,	W3775,	W3933,	W3967(H),	X4172(H),	X4558(H),
X4660,	X4997(H),	AA739,	AA758,	AA904(H),	AA974,	AB213(H),
AB899(H),	AD113(H),	AD138,	AD187(H),	AD226(H),	AD359(H),	AD360(H),
AD426(H),	AD467(H),	AD501,	AD535(H),	AD578(H),	AD583,	AD584(H),
AR434,	BL383(H),	BL488,	BL489(H),	BL512,	BL562,	BL582(H),
BL613,	BL628(H),	BL759(H),	BL895(H),	BM371,	BM576(H),	EN226(H),
EN821(H),	EN866,	EN898,	EP130,	EP170(H)	and	EP180(H).

One LF.VIII to be fitted with an arrester hook was JG663 and weighed as such at High Post on 5 April, 1944, whilst two others, JG661—662, were at RNAS Crail in April 1944 in company with JG663, for a period of four months.

Others were used but the above illustrates that the Royal Navy also had the equivalent of a few squadrons of Spitfires. The Hooked Spitfires were of any Mark from the Mk VB upwards and officially were classed as being on loan to the Royal Navy for training.

Seafire

Prototype conversion AB205 carried out by Supermarines, as Type 340 first weighed 12 January, 1942.

Seafire Mk I production, Type 340, under contract/aircraft/1863/C.23(c), the first 48 were conversions of Spitfire VBs by Air Service Training, as Seafire Mark IBs, MB328—375 inclusive, renumbered in sequence from the following:

BL676,	BL687,	BL678,	BL694,	AB416,	AB410,	AB413,	AB408,
AB376,	AB261,	AB415,	BL679,	BL689,	AB414,	AB379,	AB409,
AR344,	AR445,	AR446,	AR443,	AR459,	AR442,	AB404,	AB405,
AB406,	AB407,	AB492,	AB494,	EP148,	AR457,	AR458,	EP141,
AR460,	AR461,	EP142,	EP144,	EP146,	EP147,	EP291,	EP293,
EP294,	EP295,	EP296,	EP299,	EP301,	EP302,	EP304,	EP308,
MB328, first delivered							

MB328, first delivered 14 January, 1942, last, MB373, delivered 19 July, 1942. MB125 and 141 used for RATOG experiments at RAE Farnborough. MB138 fitted with Merlin 32 by Heston Aircraft and 300 production aircraft converted. MB194 fitted with trial camera installation by Heston Aircraft and 160 production sets done. MB201 fitted with X and Y Mk XI camera equipment in first Mk IX by Heston Aircraft.

118 Seafire IB converted by Air Service Training at Hamble. NX879—928, 940—967, 980—989, PA100—129 renumbered in sequence from

BL635,	BL260,	BL521,	AD421,	W3212,	AD517,	BL726,	BM596,
AD933,	BL931,	AB902,	BM625,	BL593,	AB908,	BL546,	BL529,
BL301,	BL750,	BL373,	BL958,	AD387,	N/K,	BM377,	AD358,
BL495,	AD579,	EN825,	BL493,	BL414,	BL986,	EN890,	BL420,
BL983,	BL597,	BL846,	AD580,	AD569,	BL675,	AB968,	AB919,
AD365,	BL855,	BL894,	AD566,	BM420,	BM580,	EN839,	AD294,
BL254,	BM631,	BM632,	BL522,	EN763,	N/K,	BL539	BM559,
AA750,	AD510,	AB817,	AD552,	BM314,	AB928,	EN851,	EN912,
BL736,	BL321,	AD271,	AD354,	BL570,	BL639,	BL901,	BM367,
EN864,	AB809,	NX964,	and 965 ex AB967		(to Hooked Spitfire)		
and BM646 allocation cancelled,				AD120,	BL757,	W3372,	BL239,
AD241,	BL930,	N/K,	N/K,	BL434,	N/K	BM541,	BL994,
BL526,	BM570,	AD397,	EN769,	BM626,	AD393,	EN764,	AD394,
AA932,	AD364,	BL695,	BL492,	AD357,	BL770,	EN780,	BL586,
BL928,	EP166,	AD184,	W3371,	BM296,	BL524,	EN910,	BL861,
BM457,	BL730,	BL806,	BL904,	AD252,	BL566.	Delivered between	

20 March, 1943, and 8 July, 1943. (N/K means serial not known). X4989, AB205, BL238, BL818, also Seafire Is but new serial not known. All the above are in sequential order *i.e.* NX879=BL635.

The last 30, PA100—129, were converted by Vickers-Armstrongs Supermarine at South Marston.

Seafire F.IIC. Type 357

AD371 prototype, converted Spitfire F.VB to Type 357 under contract Air/1683/ CB.23(c) by the fitment of an arrester hook, catapulting spools and extra stressing. Used on initial catapulting experiments at Worthy Down.

202, conversions of tropicalized Spitfire F.VC under contract Air/1863/CB.23(c) and Type 357 to production specification Seafire IICP1. MA970—999, MB113—158, 178—222, 235—281 and 293—326 ordered in March 1942, no serial number changes as they were converted on the production line. First delivered, MA971, on 2 June, 1942, last delivered, MB326, on 8 April, 1943. MA970 converted to prototype Mk III with folding wings. MB141 fitted with RATOG by Heston Aircraft to contract Air/2601/CB.23(c), MB307 fitted next and 144 production sets produced by them. MB178 fitted with reversible-pitch propeller.

200, LR631 to 881, ordered from Westland Aircraft in March 1942 as conversions from Spitfire contract B.124305/40. Only 110 delivered as LR631—667, 680—712 and 725—764, remainder of 90 delivered as Mk III as; LR765—769, 783—820 and 835—881. First delivered, LR631 and LR632, to 15 MU on 23 January, 1943.

260 Seafire Mk II ordered from Vickers-Armstrongs (Supermarine) on 29 July, 1942, as MV660—707, 720—761, 774—823, 846—885, 899—941 and 954—990, but order cancelled 20 August, 1942.

60 converted from Spitfire VCs EN686—695 and 710—759 and renumbered in the range NM910—949 and 963—982. Ordered 5 January, 1943, from Supermarines using contract 19713/39 as amended. First delivered, NM911 and 912, on 11 January, 1943, and last delivered, NM982 on 30 March, 1943. NM938 flight-tested with a Rotol braking propeller from 17 January, 1947.

Total 372 Mk IIC plus prototype.

The overall contract being Air/1683/CB.23(c) to specification Seafire IICP.1.

Seafire Mk III Type 358

MA970, prototype, converted from Seafire Mk II under contract Air/2272/CB.23(c) as Type 358 with wing folding incorporated and Merlin 45.

Production authorized under Air Ministry specification Seafire III P.1 fitted with Merlin 55/55 M and ordered from Westland Aircraft and Cunliffe Owen as Type 358.

90, LR765—769, 783—820 and 835—881, delivered by Westland between January 1943 and January 1944 from amended Seafire contract B.124305/40.

200, NF418 to 665, ordered November 1942 from Westland under contract Air/2605/CB.23(c) as; NF418—445, 480—526, 531—570, 575—607 and 624—665 as LF.III, though 28 had fixed wings and were designated LF.III (Hybrid) later called LF.IIc (Hybrid) though most were converted to LF.III standard later and delivered from 5 January, 1944.

200, NM984 to NN330, ordered from Westland as: NM984—999, NN112—157, 169—214, 227—270 and 283—330. Delivered from April 1944 as LF.III except two or three with fixed wings as LF.IIc (Hybrid).

250, NN333 to 641, ordered 5 January, 1943, from Cunliffe-Owen as; NN333—367, 379—418, 431—476, 488—528, 542—586 and 599—641. Delivered as LF.III.

250, PP921 to PR334, ordered from Westland in July 1943 under contract Air/2605/CB.23(c) as: PP921—957, 969—999, PR115—156, 170—215, 228—271 and 285—334. Delivered as LF.III though the last 90 from PR262 were fitted with Merlin 32. PP921 first delivered 6 September, 1944, last delivered PR330 and PR334, 20 January, 1945.

50, PX913—962, ordered 14 August, 1943, from Cunliffe-Owen as Mk III under contract Air/2777/CB.23(c) and built as Mk III and IIIC. First, PX913, delivered 26 February, 1945, last, PX962, delivered 31 March, 1945.

300, RX156 to 530, ordered from Westland in 1944 under contract Air/2605/CB.23(c) but only 160 built, RX156—194, 210—256, 268—313 and 326—353 as LF.III but fitted with Merlin 32. RX354 to 530 cancelled March 1944. First delivered, RX156, 20 January, 1945, last RX353, delivered 9 July, 1945.

200, SP136 to 461, ordered from Cunliffe-Owen under contract Air/2777/CB.23(c) as F.III in February 1944. Only 50, SP136—168 and 181—197 built as F.III (20, SP323—327 and 341—355 as Mk XVII). The remainder; SP198—223, 236—279, 293—322, 356—380, 393—438 and 453—461 cancelled. First delivered, SP136, 31 March, 1945, last, SP197, delivered 24 July, 1945.

Total built; 1,250.

Seafire F.XV Type 386

Six prototypes, NS487, 490, 493, PK240, 243 and 245 ordered 10 March, 1943, under contract Air/2901/CB.23(c) and built as Seafire F.XV by Vickers-Armstrongs (Supermarine) under specification N.4/43. NS493 converted to prototype XVII during construction. Produced at a fixed price of £126,650.

150, PR338 to 522, ordered July 1943 under contract Air/2777 from Cunliffe-Owen and built as; PR338—379, 391—436, 449—479 and 492—506. PR507—522 were cancelled. First 50 with A-frame arrester hooks, remainder with sting-type. First, PR338, delivered 21 March, 1945, last, PR505, delivered 22 January, 1946.

140, SR446 to 645, ordered February 1944 under contract Air/2605/CB.23(c) from Westland, built as: SR446—493, 516—547, 568—611 and 630—645. First, SR446, delivered 31 August, 1944, last, SR645, delivered 30 June, 1945.

500, SW781 to SX546, ordered March 1944 from Westland under contract Air/2605/CB.23(c), built as: SW781—828 and 844—875 with standard fuselages and SW876—879 and 896—921 with rear-view fuselages. 110 built only. SW922—936 and 951—985 cancelled with the rest of the order changed to F.XVIIIs. Delivered from 26 June, 1945.

Total built 390 including five prototypes.

Seafire F/FR. XVII Type 384

NS493 prototype converted from Seafire F.XV to Type 384 and first flown in 1945, originally being designated Seafire F.41 in December 1943.

20, SP323—327 and 341—355, built by Cunliffe-Owen on amendment of original Seafire F.III contract.

213, in range SW781 to SX546, ordered from Westland under contract Air/3853 and built as: SW986—993, SX111—139, 152—201, 220—256, 271—316, 332—370 and 386—389. The following were cancelled: SX390—432, 451—490 and 503—546. SX153 undertook contractor's trials flown by J. K. Quill. First delivered, SX113, 11 July, 1945, last delivered, SX389, 12 October, 1946.

Total built 234 including prototype.

Seafire F.45, F.46 and F.47 Type 388

300, LA187 to 582, ordered from South Marston as Spitfire F.21 but order changed 24 April, 1944, that the aircraft be built at Castle Bromwich. 120 Spitfire F.21s built at Castle Bromwich, 105 cancelled but LA428—457 and 480—499 built at South Marston as fifty F.45s (c/n SMAF/15478 to 15527). LA429, first delivered 1 March, 1945, last, LA499, delivered 10 January, 1946. LA541—564 built as 25 F.46s at South Marston under contract Air/5794/CB.23(c). LA541, first delivered to High Post 5 November, 1945, last, LA564, delivered 9 May, 1947. Three of these, LA549, 557 and 558 being delivered to the ETPS at Cranfield. LA448 used at the RAE 2 December, 1950, on propeller blade crash trial. LA565—582 cancelled.

260, MV660 to 990, ordered from Vickers-Armstrongs on 29 July, 1942, as: MV660—707, 720—761, 774—823, 846—885, 899—941 and 954—990 but order cancelled 20 August, 1942, before production could begin.

1,500, PS938—PW250, ordered from Supermarine on 17 July, 1943. Many amendments but the following were Seafires: PS938—943 cancelled, PS944—957 (14) Seafire F.47 built at South Marston under contract Air/5794/CB.5(b) between 25 April, 1946, and 16 October, 1946. PS958—987, PT163—203 and 220—229 (81) cancelled during August 1945. 200, PV734—739, 752—797, 820—865, 879—919, 935—984 and PW112—122 also ordered as Seafires but cancelled in August 1945. PS948 first with powered wing folding.

Three, TM379, 383 and 389 Spitfire F.21 (Merlin 66) ordered from Castle Bromwich under contract Air/4425/C.23(c) on 7 May, 1944, but contract changed on 15 August for conversion of three Spitfire F.21s to naval type. Delivery to be made as soon as possible to Hursley Park for modification by Vickers-Armstrongs. TM379 and 383 were LA193 and LA195 renumbered on the South Marston production line (c/nsSMAF/4343 and 4340). LA193 and LA195 were produced later. TM389 was cancelled 9 March, 1946. TM379 was prototype F.45, TM383 was the prototype F.46.

600, ordered as Seafire N.7/44 from Vickers-Armstrongs under contract B.981687/39. Order changed on 26 February, 1945, to read Seafire F.45/F.46/F.47, and on 2 March, 1945, contract number was changed to Air/5155 and on 5 March, 1945, to twenty F.45 and 150 F.47 only. By 12 January, 1946, this order was reduced to fifty F.45 only and later finally cancelled.

600, VD490 to VE593, as: VD490—499, 521—568, 582—597, 618—653, 679—696, 714—748, 763—792, 809—856, 869—893, 925—961, 984—999, VE135—162, 176—193, 233—259, 274—296, 328—362, 379—391, 406—447, 462—498, 516—542 and 563—593. These were all cancelled on 1 August, 1945.

135, VN501—673, ordered under contract Air/5795/CB.5(b) from Supermarine 15 November, 1945, as: VN501—528, 542—563, 567—598, 614—645 and 653—673. (50, VN501 to 563 F.46, and 85, VN567 to 673 F.47) but all cancelled.

64, VP427—465 and 471—495 ordered under contract Air/5794/CB.5(b) on 8 April, 1946, as Seafire F.47 from South Marston at a fixed price of £8,900 each. Delivered between 11 November, 1947, (VP428) and 17 November, 1948.

12, VR961—972, ordered 1 October, 1946, from Vickers-Armstrongs, South Marston under contract 6/Air/636/CB.7(b) as F.47s. They were built between 8 November, 1948, and 28 January, 1949, at the same fixed price of £8,900. These were the last Seafires to be built.

Total built 167 (51 F.45, 26 F.46 and 90 F.47).

Seafire Service Units

Second line Squadrons; 701, 715, 718, 728, 736, 738, 759, 761, 764, 766, 767, 770, 771, 773, 775, 778, 781 and 787.
Reserve Squadrons: 1831, 1832 and 1833.
Front line Squadrons: 800, 801, 802, 803, 804, 805, 806, 807, 808, 809, 816, 833, 834, 842, 879, 880, 883, 884, 885, 886, 887, 889, 894, 897 and 899. These Squadrons were based on the aircraft carriers *Argus, Attacker, Battler, Berwick, Chaser, Fencer, Formidable, Furious, Glory, Hunter, Illustrious, Implacable, Indefatigable, Indomitable, Khedive, Land, Ocean, Premier, Stalker, Theseus, Tracker, Triumph, Unicorn, Vengeance* and *Warrior*.

Spitfire/Seafire

Other Air Forces

Argentina (one only): Australia 245 F.VCs A58-1 to 185 and A58-200 to 259, 251 F.VIIIs A58-300 to 550 and 159 HF.VIIIs A58-600 to 758; Belgium 48 Mk IXs and XVIs and 132 FR.XIVs; Burma 20 Seafire F.XVs; Canada at least 10 Spitfires and 35 Seafire F.XVs; Czechoslovakia took over aircraft of 310, 311, 312 and 313 Squadrons RAF, 76 in all; Denmark 36 H.F.IXs and 3 PR.XIs; Egypt 12 F.VCs and 20 F.22s; Eire 12 Seafire F.IIIs and one Spitfire T.9; France 70 F.VBs and 172 F.IXs; Greece 74 LF.IXs; 3 H.F.IXs; 1 PR.XI and at least 8 LF.XVIs; India 150 F.VIIIs, 70 F.XIVs, 10 T.9s also some F.XVIIIs and PR.XIXs; Israel 50 LF.IXs from Czechoslovakia, 30 from Italy and 3 ex RAF rebuilt from crashed/scrap aircraft; Italy 99 F.IXs; Netherlands 54 F.IXs, 3 T.9s and 4 PR.XIs; Norway 47 F.IXs and 3 PR.XIs; Portugal 15 F.IAs and 50 F.VBs; South Africa 139 F.IXs; Siam 30 FR.XIVs; Southern Rhodesia 22 F.22s; Sweden 50 PR.XIXs; Syria 16 F.22s; Turkey 3 F.Is, at least 33 LF.IXs and 2 F.XVIs; United States at least 7 PR.VIIs, 16 F.IXs and 8 PR.XIs (approx 600 were used by the USAAF in the Middle East but only officially on loan from the RAF); USSR 1,186 LF.IXs, 2 H.F.IXs and 143 F.Vs (some passed to China).

Spitfire T.9s for the Royal Netherlands Air Force, in March 1948.

Spiteful

Three prototypes, NN660, NN664 and NN667, ordered 6 February, 1943, as conversions of Spitfire VIIIs. NN660 Spitfire F.XIV fuselage and Type 371 wings. NN664 and 667 prototype Spitefuls.

60 of the 600, PL758—PM676, ordered 2 June, 1943, as PM419—462, 478—495 and 671—676. All cancelled.

121, PS684—725, 739—781 and 795—830 ordered 17 July, 1943, but all cancelled.

21, RB515—531, ordered but only 17 built; RB515—525, 527—531 and 535.

Seafang

One prototype, RT646, ordered but cancelled.

Two prototypes, VB893 and 895, ordered to specification N.5/45 and contract Air/5176 dated 21 April, 1945. VB895 built as F.32 and used by Supermarines and the AAEE Boscombe Down on trials from 30 June, 1946. VB893 delivered 20 December, 1946.

150, VG471 to 679, ordered to specification N.5/45 as; 10 Seafang F.31s VG471—480 and 140 F.32s in place of 150 Spitefuls. Only ten, VG471—480, built as F.31s. VG481—482, 486 and 488—490 built as F.32s. VG483—485, 487, 491—505, 540—589, 602—650 and 664—679 cancelled.

Seagull ASR.I

Three prototypes, PA143, 147 and 152 ordered 9 April, 1943, under contract Air/2964/CB.20(b) and to specification S.12/40. PA143 first flew 14 July, 1948, as an air-sea rescue aircraft. PA147 also completed, but PA152 not completed.

Attacker

Three prototypes ordered, TS409, 413 and 416 as Type 392 under contract Air/4562/CB.7(b) dated 9 September, 1944, as; Jet Machines of Spitfire Type, to specification E.10/44 with a limit of £150,000 which was later increased to £500,000. TS409 navalized to contract 6/Air/2949/CB.7(b). All built at Hursley Park but transported to High Post for final erection and then first flown from Boscombe Down.

24, pre-production, ordered under contract Air/5530/CB.7(b) dated 21 November, 1945, as; six to specification E.10/44, four to E.1/45 without folding wings and fourteen to E.1/45 with folding wings in the serial range VH980 to VJ118. These were cancelled early in 1946, an order for 18 aircraft going to the Sea Vampire Mk 20.

63, WA469 to 537, production ordered in November 1949 to specification I/45/PI/SU and contract 6/Air/2822/CB.7(b) as: WA469—498 and WA505—526 produced as 52 F.1s and WA527—535 produced as eight FB.1s with Nene 3. WA536—537 cancelled. Served in 736, 800, 803 and 890 Squadrons. WA469 first flew on 4 April, 1950, and delivered 1 August, 1950. WA529 used for cold weather trials in Canada. WA473 sole surviving Attacker at FAA Museum, Yeovilton.

24, WK319—342, ordered as FB.2s fitted with Nene 102 and delivered to 800, 803, 736 and RNVR Squadrons as were the following 61 aircraft. This was an extension to contract 6/Air/2822/CB.7(b). First, WK319, delivered 20 May, 1952, last, WK342, delivered 21 November, 1952.

30, WP275—303, ordered as FB.2s under contract 6/Air/6343/CB.5(b). First, WP275, delivered 21 November, 1952, last, WP304, delivered 27 March, 1953.

WT851, FB.1 built as replacement aircraft for WA477 which crashed on production test flight on 5 February, 1951. Delivered 15 May, 1952.

30, WZ273—302, ordered as FB.2s under contract 6/Air/7319/CB.5(b). First, WZ273, delivered 31 May, 1953, last, WZ302, delivered 4 March, 1954.

36, R4000—4035, built for the Pakistan Air Force. R4000 arrived and accepted at Karachi 3 June, 1951, for the last two, R4034 and 4035, arrived on 29 May, 1953.

Total of 185 built (149 for the Royal Navy).

Attacker Service Units

First naval unit to receive the type was No. 787 Squadron, known as the Naval Air Fighter Development Unit, and WA478 was taken on charge on 6 February, 1951.

Other units were; Nos, 702, 703, 718, 736, 767, 787, 800, 803, 890, 1831, 1832, 1833 and 1836 Squadrons, FRU Brawdy/St Davids and FRU Hurn.

No. 800 Squadron was the first naval operational jet squadron, being reformed on 21 August, 1951, receiving its first aircraft, WA496, on 22 August, followed shortly afterwards by No. 803 Squadron on 26 November, 1951. No. 702 Squadron was the Naval Jet and Evaluation Training Unit which was renumbered No. 736 Squadron on 26 August, 1952.

Swift

Two prototypes to specification E.41/46, VV106 and VV119 built as Type 510 and 535 respectively under contract 6/Acft/1031 and ordered 13 March, 1947. One fuselage ex. contract 6/Acft/4562, Attacker.

Two pre-production to specification F105, WJ960 and WJ965 built as Type 541 under contract 6/Acft/5986 dated November 1950.

100 production to specification F105P, under contract 6/Acft/5969/CB.5(b) dated November 1950 between WK194 and WK315 and built as follows: 18 Mk 1, WK194—197 and 200—213, 17 Mk 2 WK199, 214—221 and 239—246 (WK243 used for experimental work), 25 Mk 3 WK247—271, six Mk 4 WK198, 272—273, 275, 279 and 308. (WK198 was prototype Mk 4). 35 converted to FR.5 WK274, 276—278, 280—281, 287—307 and 309—315. Order increased by 58 F.4 WM583—596, 621—656, WN124—127 and WV949—952; XD361 ordered as replacement aircraft later, but all cancelled 20 March, 1956, except WN124 built as FR.5. First delivered, WK197, to Boscombe Down, on 2 July, 1953, last, WK315, delivered 1 September, 1956.

Of the Mk 1s only WK205—213 were used by No.56 Squadron, of the Mk 2s WK221, 239—240, 242 and 245 were used by No.56 Squadron. All of the Mk 3s were flown and all except one, WK248, which was sold to the College of Aeronautics on 10 December, 1957, were delivered straight to RAF Schools at St Athan, Kirkham, Melksham, Halton and Weston as ground instructional aircraft and allotted Maintenance serials in the range 7315M to 7348M, of the F.4s two, WK276 and 278, went to 79 Squadron and two, WK277 and 280, to No.2 Squadron. Of the FR5s, WK287—290, 295, 299—300, 302, 304, 307 and 314 went to No.2 Squadron and WK292—293, 296—298, 301, 305, 309—313 and 315 to No.79.

140 F.4 ordered under contract 6/Acft/8509 in April 1951 as XA957—993, XB102—151, 169—185 and 206—241, to have been built by Short Bros, a further six XF104—109 ordered later but all cancelled.

Swift F.2s await delivery from South Marston.

One prototype Mk PR.6, XD943, ordered under contract 6/Acft/8700 in November 1952 but cancelled 25 April, 1955, when nearing completion.

113 ordered under contract 6/Acft/9463 as 81 FR.5 XD903—930, 948—988 and XE105—116, but only 58 built (23 cancelled from XD978), 32 FR.6 XE133—164 cancelled. XD903 delivered 31 May, 1955; last delivered, XD976, 10 April, 1957. Flown by Nos.2 and 79 Squadrons. Handling Squadron Boscombe Down and AFDS.

75 ordered under contract 6/Acft/9757 as Mk 7 XF113—129, 155—180, 196—217 and 244—253, only XF113—124 (12) built. XF249—253(5) cancelled 19 March, 1954, remainder on 20 March, 1956. First delivered, XF113, 15 November, 1956; to Handling Squadron last, XF124, delivered 8 July, 1957, to GWDS, as also were XF115—123.

Two prototype F.7, XF774 and 780, ordered under contract 6/Acft/9929 in October 1953, as Blue Sky missile launchers.

Total ordered 499: Total built 193 plus four prototypes.

Type 545

Two prototypes, XA181 and 186, ordered under contract 6/Acft/7711 in February 1952, but XA186 cancelled 8 October, 1954, and XA181 cancelled 23 March, 1956, when almost complete.

Type 508 VX133 at Boscombe Down. (*Vickers-Armstrongs*)

Scimitar

Three prototypes, VX133, 136 and 138 ordered under specification N.9/47 and contract 6/Air/1508/CB.7. In October 1950 the contract was changed so that VX138 would be fitted with swept-back wings under contract 6/Air/5772/CB.7. VX133 was built as Type 508, VX136 as Type 529 and VX138 as Type 525. VX138 was lost during test flight at Boscombe Down on 5 July, 1955.

Three production prototypes, WT854, WT859 and WW134, ordered to specification N.113D and as Type 544. WT854 used for flight investigation of inertia coupling possibilities, wing fence development and tests with external stores. WT859 was fitted with supercirculation for flap blowing in January 1957. WW134 was fitted with blown flaps and used initially for the first deck-landing trials, fitted with two Avon RA.24s.

100, XD212 to 357, ordered under contract 6/Air/8812/CB.5(a), specification N.113P.1, Naval Staff requirement NRA.17 and Type 544, after financial approval had been sanctioned in December 1952. 76 built only, XD212—250, 264—282 and 316—333, the remaining 24, XD334—357 were cancelled. XD212 was used for contractor's trials, XD214 and 327 were flown on tropical trials at El Adem, XD216 was flown with Martin Bullpup missiles, XD216, 218 and 229 were flown with different stores including a dummy TMB (Target Marker Bomb), two 200 plus two 150 gallon drop tanks and four 1,000 lb bombs. XD248 was used in late 1967 at Farnborough for braking friction trials. XD219 on air firing trials of the Aden cannon installation (20,033 rounds were fired to 3 February 1958). XD228 was used on rocket launching trials with 24 3-inch rockets, and was also fitted with camera pods on each wingtip. XD229 used on LABS and TMB trials.

One aircraft, XH451, ordered as a Developed Scimitar to specification NA/38 from Vickers Ltd under contract 6/Air/11268/CB.5(b) dated 23 September, 1954. This was to have been a two-seat version FAW (Fighter All Weather) Type 556 fitted with Ferranti Air Pass radar and guided weapons. After a mock-up was made work was suspended on 27 April, 1955, and it was officially cancelled on 25 July, 1955, due to a production order for the two-seat D.H.110.

Total built 82 including prototypes.

Scimitar Service Units

Initial trials were undertaken by No. 700X Squadron, XD220 to 226 being used by them, later redesignated 700 Squadron.

Front line squadrons; 736, 764B, 800, 803, 804 and 807.

Other units; RNAS Hal Far in Malta, AHU Lossiemouth, RNAY Fleetlands, NASU Brawdy, Airwork FRU, AAEE, RNAS Arbroath, RAE Bedford and Farnborough and AHU Tengah/Sembawang.

Flown from the aircraft carriers; *Ark Royal, Centaur, Eagle, Hermes* and *Victorious.*

Castle Bromwich Built Lancasters

200 ordered as Mk II but produced as B.1: HK535—579, 593—628, 644—664, 679—710, 728—773, 787—806.

200 B.1 ordered but only 100 built: PP663—695, 713—758, 772—792.

APPENDIX III

Supermarine Class B Registrations

N- authorized 23 December, 1929, for Supermarine Aviation Works (Vickers) Ltd. Taken over in October 1938 by Vickers-Armstrongs Ltd Supermarine Division.

G.15 authorized 1 January, 1948, for Vickers-Armstrongs Ltd (Hursley Park Division) Supermarine Works. Authorized 25 June, 1956, for renamed Vickers-Armstrongs (Aircraft) Ltd (Hursley Park Division), and 26 September, 1960, for Vickers-Armstrongs (South Marston) Ltd. Authority cancelled 17 October, 1968.

Most of the aircraft did not fly with B-class registrations applied and it has been extremely difficult to compile this register. The authenticity of some registrations is still in doubt. The initial N markings N-1 to N-6 were allocated more than once.

Following the aircraft type columns here the RAF/Royal Navy serials are quoted where known. The country to which the aircraft were exported, or its service, follows with the new serials allocated. The final column shows the date of first flight (f/f), delivery (d/d) or acceptance (acc). Other dates are those on which the aircraft flew with either Class B registration or non-British serial.

B No.	Aircraft	RAF Serial Country		Serial	Date	
N-1	Viastra VI	Renumbered as Vickers O-6			f/f	22.4.31
N-1	Seagull V	Prototype. Renumbered N-2			f/f	21.6.33
N-2	Seagull V	Prototype. To Walrus & K4797				29.7.33
N-3	Southampton I		Turkey			
N-4	Southampton I		Turkey			
N-5						
N-6		Believed allocated to last four Turkish Southamptons.				
N-7						
N-8						

			Final N Series			
N-1	Southampton I		Argentina	HB1		26.6.33
N-2	Southampton I		Argentina	HB2		2.10.33
N-3	Southampton I		Argentina	HB3		
N-4	Southampton I		Argentina	HB4		
N-5	Southampton I		Argentina	HB5		
N-6	Southampton I		Argentina	HB6		
N-7	Southampton I		Argentina	HB7		
N-8	Southampton I		Argentina	HB8		
N-9	Walrus I		Turkey		f/f	4.2.38
N-10	Walrus I		Turkey		f/f	2.2.38
N-11	Walrus I		Turkey		f/f	9.2.38
N-12	Walrus I		Turkey			
N-13	Walrus I		Turkey			
N-14	Walrus I		Turkey		f/f	2.3.38
N-15	Walrus I		Argentina	M-0-9	f/f	25.4.38
N-16	Walrus I		Argentina	M-0-10	f/f	29.4.38
N-17	Spitfire	K9834	Special High Speed			
N-18	Walrus I	L2301	Eire	N-18	f/f	24.2.39
N-19	Walrus I	L2302	Eire	N-19		10.1.39
N-20	Walrus I	L2303	Eire	N-20		17.1.39

N-21	Spitfire I		France	O.1	d/d	18.7.39
N-22	Spitfire	P9566	Turkey		f/f	27.4.40
N-23	Spitfire	P9567	Turkey		f/f	29.4.40
N-24	Spitfire	P9547	Turkey		f/f	1.5.40
N-25	Spitfire	P9561	Turkey		f/f	8.5.40
N-26	Spitfire	P9558	Turkey		f/f	3.5.40
N-27	Spitfire	P9559	Turkey		f/f	14.5.40
N-28	Spitfire	P9560	Turkey		f/f	14.4.40
N-29	Spitfire	P9565	Turkey		f/f	14.4.40
N-30	Spitfire	P9556	Turkey		f/f	15.4.40
N-31	Spitfire	P9557	Turkey		f/f	13.6.40
N-32	Spitfire T.8	MT818	Prototype trainer conversion 1947			
N-33	Walrus II		Argentina	2-0-23		
N-34	Walrus II		Argentina	2-0-24		
N-35	Walrus II		Argentina	2-0-25		
N-36	Walrus II		Argentina	2-0-26		
N-37	Walrus II		Argentina	2-0-27		
N-38	Walrus II		Argentina	2-0-28		
N-39	Walrus II		Argentina	2-0-29	d/d	21.7.47
N-40	Walrus II		Argentina	2-0-30		21.3.47
N-41	Spitfire T.9	MK715	R Netherlands AF	H-97	d/d	22.3.48
N-42	Spitfire T.9	BF274	R Netherlands AF	H-98	d/d	22.3.48

New Numbering System initiated 1 January, 1948

G.15-1	Spitfire T.9	BF148	R Netherlands AF	H-99	d/d	22.3.48
G.15-2	Spitfire T.9	MA848	Indian AF	HS534		3.6.48
G.15-3	Spitfire T.9		Indian AF	HS535		
G.15-4	Spitfire T.9		Indian AF	HS536		29.9.48
G.15-5	Spitfire T.9		Indian AF	HS537		
G.15-6	Spitfire T.9		Indian AF	HS538		
G.15-7	Spitfire T.9		Indian AF	HS539		
G.15-8	Spitfire T.9		Indian AF	HS540		
G.15-9	Spitfire T.9		Indian AF	HS541		15.11.48
G.15-10	Spitfire T.9		Indian AF	HS542		
G.15-11	Spitfire T.9		Indian AF	HS543		
G.15-12	Spitfire PR.XIX	PS925	R Swedish AF (Flygvapnet)	31001	d/d	7.10.48
G.15-13	Spitfire PR.XIX	PS931	R Swedish AF	31002	d/d	7.10.48
G.15-14	Spitfire PR.XIX	PM503	R Swedish AF	31003	d/d	7.10.48
G.15-15	Spitfire PR.XIX	PM498	R Swedish AF	31004	d/d	7.10.48
G.15-16	Spitfire PR.XIX	PS878	R Swedish AF	31007	d/d	5.11.48
G.15-17	Spitfire PR.XIX	PS874	R Swedish AF	31008	d/d	5.11.48
G.15-18	Spitfire PR.XIX	PS923	R Swedish AF	31005	d/d	5.11.48
G.15-19	Spitfire PR.XIX	PS866	R Swedish AF	31006	d/d	26.10.48
G.15-20	Spitfire PR.XIX	PS860	R Swedish AF	31009	d/d	4.12.48
G.15-21	Spitfire PR.XIX	PS863	R Swedish AF	31010	d/d	4.12.48
G.15-22	Spitfire PR.XIX	PS883	R Swedish AF	31011	d/d	4.12.48
G.15-23	Spitfire PR.XIX	PS933	R Swedish AF	31012	d/d	4.12.48
G.15-24	Spitfire PR.XIX	PS861	R Swedish AF	31013	d/d	19.1.49
G.15-25	Spitfire PR.XIX	PS928	R Swedish AF	31014	d/d	19.1.49
G.15-26	Spitfire PR.XIX	PS862	R Swedish AF	31015	d/d	19.1.49
G.15-27	Spitfire PR.XIX	PS871	R Swedish AF	31016	d/d	19.1.49
G.15-28	Spitfire PR.XIX	PS864	R Swedish AF	31017	d/d	11.2.49
G.15-29	Spitfire PR.XIX	PS868	R Swedish AF	31018	d/d	11.2.49
G.15-30	Spitfire PR.XIX	PS893	R Swedish AF	31019	d/d	5.11.48
G.15-31	Spitfire PR.XIX	PS881	R Swedish AF	31020	d/d	15.12.48

G.15-32	Spitfire PR.XIX PS869	R Swedish AF	31021	d/d	4.12.48
G.15-33	Spitfire PR.XIX PS891	R Swedish AF	31022	d/d	15.12.48
G.15-34	Spitfire PR.XIX PS870	R Swedish AF	31023	d/d	19.1.49
G.15-35	Spitfire PR.XIX PS879	R Swedish AF	31024	d/d	19.1.49
G.15-36	Spitfire PR.XIX PM497	R Swedish AF	31025	d/d	19.1.49
G.15-37	Spitfire PR.XIX PM502	R Swedish AF	30126	d/d	11.2.49
G.15-38	Spitfire PR.XIX PM554	R Swedish AF	31027	d/d	12.2.49
G.15-39	Spitfire PR.XIX PS873	R Swedish AF	31028	d/d	12.2.49
G.15-40	Spitfire PR.XIX PS872	R Swedish AF	31029	d/d	12.2.49
G.15-41	Spitfire PR.XIX PM499	R Swedish AF	31030	d/d	12.2.49
G.15-42	Spitfire PR.XIX PM556	R Swedish AF	31031	d/d	24.2.49
G.15-43	Spitfire PR.XIX PM559	R Swedish AF	31032	d/d	24.2.49
G.15-44	Spitfire PR.XIX PM560	R Swedish AF	31033	d/d	24.2.49
G.15-45	Spitfire PR.XIX PM561	R Swedish AF	31034	d/d	16.3.49
G.15-46	Spitfire PR.XIX PS886	R Swedish AF	31035	d/d	16.3.49
G.15-47	Spitfire PR.XIX PS909	R Swedish AF	31036	d/d	17.3.49
G.15-48	Spitfire PR.XIX PS924	R Swedish AF	31037	d/d	16.3.49
G.15-49	Spitfire PR.XIX PS926	R Swedish AF	31038	d/d	17.3.49
G.15-50	Spitfire PR.XIX PS929	R Swedish AF	31039	d/d	17.3.49
G.15-51	Spitfire PR.XIX PS875	R Swedish AF	31040	d/d	13.4.49
G.15-52	Spitfire PR.XIX PS880	R Swedish AF	31041	d/d	13.4.49
G.15-53	Spitfire PR.XIX PS927	R Swedish AF	31042	d/d	13.4.49
G.15-54	Spitfire PR.XIX PS876	R Swedish AF	31043	d/d	20.4.49
G.15-55	Spitfire PR.XIX PS877	R Swedish AF	31044	d/d	20.4.49
G.15-56	Spitfire PR.XIX PS865	R Swedish AF	31045	d/d	11.5.49
G.15-57	Spitfire PR.XIX PS867	R Swedish AF	31046	d/d	11.5.49
G.15-58	Spitfire PR.XIX PS884	R Swedish AF	31047	d/d	11.5.49
G.15-59	Spitfire PR.XIX PS882	R Swedish AF	31048	d/d	11.5.49
G.15-60	Spitfire PR.XIX PS859	R Swedish AF	31049	d/d	11.5.49
G.15-61	Spitfire PR.XIX PS850	R Swedish AF	31050	d/d	11.5.49
G.15-62	Spitfire PR.XIX PM606	Indian AF	HS693	d/d	8.2.49
G.15-63	Spitfire PR.XIX PM562	Indian AF	HS694	d/d	22.2.49
G.15-64	Spitfire PR.XIX N/K	Indian AF	HS695	d/d	22.2.49
G.15-65	Spitfire PR.XIX N/K	Indian AF	HS696	d/d	22.3.49
G.15-66	Spitfire PR.XIX N/K	Indian AF	HS697	d/d	14.3.49
G.15-67	Spitfire PR.XIX N/K	Indian AF	HS698	d/d	14.3.49
G.15-68	Spitfire PR.XIX N/K	Indian AF	HS699	d/d	22.3.49
G.15-69	Spitfire PR.XIX PM570	Indian AF	HS700	d/d	31.3.49
G.15-70	Spitfire PR.XIX N/K	Indian AF	HS701	d/d	24.5.49
G.15-71	Spitfire PR.XIX N/K	Indian AF	HS702	d/d	1.6.49
G.15-72	Spitfire PR.XIX N/K	Indian AF	HS703	d/d	8.6.49
G.15-73	Spitfire PR.XIX PK330?	Indian AF	HS704	d/d	23.6.49
G.15-74					
G.15-75					
G.15-76	Sea Otter ASR.I JN107	R Netherlands Navy	18-4	d/d	18.11.49
G.15-77	Sea Otter ASR.I JN141	R Netherlands Navy	18-5		19.1.50
G.15-78	Sea Otter ASR.I JN142	R Netherlands Navy	18-6	d/d	12.5.50
G.15-79	Sea Otter ASR.I JN186	R Netherlands Navy	18-7		Unconfirmed
G.15-80	Not known				
G.15-81	Not known				
G.15-82	Sea Otter ASR.I JM797	Indo-China	N-82		25.4.50
G.15-83	Sea Otter ASR.I JM741	Indo-China	N-83		28.4.50
G.15-84	Sea Otter ASR.I JM953	Indo-China	N-84		26.5.50
G.15-85	Sea Otter ASR.I JM879	Indo-China	N-85		5.4.50
G.15-86	Sea Otter ASR.I JM873	Indo-China	N-86		7.6.50
G.15-87	Sea Otter ASR.I JM884	Indo-China	N-87		

G.15-88	Spitfire F.22		Egyptian AF	681	d/d	14.6.50
G.15-89	Spitfire F.22		Egyptian AF	682	d/d	14.6.50
G.15-90	Spitfire F.22		Egyptian AF	683	d/d	27.6.50
G.15-91	Spitfire F.22		Egyptian AF	680	d/d	27.6.50
G.15-92	Spitfire T.9	G-ALJM	Egyptian AF	684	d/d	13.4.50
G.15-93	Spitfire F.22		Egyptian AF	685		6.7.50
G.15-94	Spitfire F.22		Egyptian AF	686		5.7.50
G.15-95	Spitfire F.22		Egyptian AF	687	d/d	26.7.50
G.15-96	Spitfire F.22		Egyptian AF	688		26.10.50
G.15-97	Spitfire F.22		Egyptian AF	689		
G.15-98	Spitfire F.22		Egyptian AF	690	d/d	26.7.50
G.15-99	Spitfire F.22		Egyptian AF	691	d/d	22.8.50
G.15-100	Spitfire F.22		Egyptian AF	692	d/d	12.9.50
G.15-101	Spitfire F.22	PK327	Egyptian AF	693	d/d	10.10.50
G.15-102	Spitfire F.22		Egyptian AF	694	d/d	8.2.51
G.15-103	Spitfire F.22		Egyptian AF	695	d/d	12.9.50
G.15-104	Spitfire F.22		Egyptian AF	696	d/d	21.9.50
G.15-105	Spitfire F.22		Egyptian AF	697	d/d	21.9.50
G.15-106	Spitfire F.22		Egyptian AF	698	d/d	10.10.50
G.15-107	Spitfire F.22		Egyptian AF	699	d/d	22.8.51
G.15-108	Sea Otter ASR.1	JM984	R Netherlands Navy	18-8	d/d	14.10.50
G.15-109	Spitfire PR.XI	RB164*				
G.15-110	Attacker FB.1		Pakistan Navy	R4000	d/d	3.6.51
G.15-111	Spitfire F.XIV		R Thai AF	U14-1/93	f/f	15.1.51
G.15-112	Spitfire F.XIV		R Thai AF	U14-2/93		3.10.50
G.15-113	Spitfire F.XIV	RB184	R Thai AF	U14-3/93		16.10.50
G.15-114	Spitfire F.XIV		R Thai AF	U14-4/93		20.10.50
G.15-115	Spitfire F.XIV		R Thai AF	U14-5/93		24.10.50
G.15-116	Spitfire F.XIV		R Thai AF	U14-6/93		4.11.50
G.15-117	Spitfire F.XIV		R Thai AF	U14-7/93		4.11.50
G.15-118	Spitfire F.XIV		R Thai AF	U14-8/93		13.11.50
G.15-119	Spitfire F.XIV	NH714	R Thai AF	U14-9/93		
G.15-120	Spitfire F.XIV	NH698	R Thai AF	U14-10/93		17.11.50
G.15-121	Spitfire F.XIV		R Thai AF	U14-11/93		
G.15-122	Spitfire F.XIV	NH794	R Thai AF	U14-12/93		
G.15-123	Spitfire F.XIV		R Thai AF	U14-13/93		7.12.50
G.15-124	Spitfire F.XIV		R Thai AF	U14-14/93		
G.15-125	Spitfire F.XIV		R Thai AF	U14-15/93		
G.15-126	Spitfire F.XIV		R Thai AF	U14-16/93		
G.15-127	Spitfire F.XIV		R Thai AF	U14-17/93		
G.15-128	Spitfire F.XIV	RB188	R Thai AF	U14-18/93		
G.15-129	Spitfire F.XIV		R Thai AF	U14-19/93		26.1.51
G.15-130	Spitfire F.XIV		R Thai AF	U14-20/93		
G.15-131	Spitfire F.XIV		R Thai AF	U14-21/93		
G.15-132	Spitfire F.XIV		R Thai AF	U14-22/93		
G.15-133	Spitfire F.XIV		R Thai AF	U14-23/93		27.2.51
G.15-134	Spitfire F.XIV	RM692	R Thai AF	U14-24/93		16.4.51
G.15-135	Spitfire F.XIV	NH800	R Thai AF	U14-25/93		
G.15-136	Spitfire F.XIV		R Thai AF	U14-26/93		27.2.51
G.15-137	Spitfire F.XIV		R Thai AF	U14-27/93		
G.15-138	Spitfire F.XIV		R Thai AF	U14-28/93		
G.15-139	Spitfire F.XIV		R Thai AF	U14-29/93		16.4.51
G.15-140	Spitfire F.XIV	PM630	R Thai AF	U14-30/93		27.4.51

*Also PL983, NC74138 & N74138

G.15-
141–170* Spitfire F.XIV MV265 Belgian AF SG103 1.5.51
Spitfire F.XIV MV261 Belgian AF SG104 20.4.51
Spitfire F.XIV NH741 Belgian AF SG105 Acc 9.4.51
Spitfire F.XIV RM674 Belgian AF SG106 Acc 14.3.51
Spitfire F.XIV RM700 Belgian AF SG107 Acc 9.4.51
Spitfire F.XIV NH789 Belgian AF SG108 Acc 9.4.51
Spitfire F.XIV RM707 Belgian AF SG109 20.4.51
Spitfire F.XIV RM879 Belgian AF SG110 Acc 8.6.51
Spitfire F.XIV RM918 Belgian AF SG111 Acc 9.4.51
Spitfire F.XIV MV267 Belgian AF SG112
Spitfire F.XIV NH658 Belgian AF SG113 26.4.51
Spitfire F.XIV NH690 Belgian AF SG114 Acc 14.3.51
Spitfire F.XIV NH702 Belgian AF SG115
Spitfire F.XIV NH710 Belgian AF SG116 21.5.51
Spitfire F.XIV RM790 Belgian AF SG117 24.5.51
Spitfire F.XIV RM792 Belgian AF SG118 28.5.51
Spitfire F.XIV RM817 Belgian AF SG119 Acc 15.6.51
Spitfire F.XIV NH838 Belgian AF SG120 Acc 8.6.51
Spitfire F.XIV TZ142 Belgian AF SG121 Acc 15.6.51
Spitfire F.XIV SM829 Belgian AF SG122 Acc 15.6.51
Spitfire F.XIV NH743 Belgian AF SG123 Acc 8.6.51
Spitfire F.XIV NH742 Belgian AF SG124 19.6.51
Spitfire F.XIV RM795 Belgian AF SG125
Spitfire F.XIV RB165 Belgian AF SG126
Spitfire F.XIV SM930 Belgian AF SG127
Spitfire F.XIV NH904 Belgian AF SG128
Spitfire F.XIV NH918 Belgian AF SG129 31.8.51
Spitfire F.XIV TX992 Belgian AF SG130 31.8.51
Spitfire F.XIV MV359 Belgian AF SG131
Spitfire F.XIV TZ174 Belgian AF SG132
G.15-171 Spitfire T.9 MJ627 Irish Air Corps 158 d/d 5.6.51
G.15-172 Spitfire T.9 MJ772 Irish Air Corps 159 31.5.51
G.15-173 Spitfire T.9 MK721 Irish Air Corps 160 d/d 29.6.51
G.15-174 Spitfire T.9 ML407 Irish Air Corps 161 d/d 30.7.51
G.15-175 Spitfire T.9 PV202 Irish Air Corps 162 d/d 29.6.51
G.15-176 Spitfire T.9 TE308 Irish Air Corps 163 d/d 30.7.51
G.15-177 Attacker FB.1 Pakistan Navy R4001 5.51
G.15-178 Attacker FB.1 Pakistan Navy R4002 d/d 5.8.51
G.15-179 Attacker FB.1 Pakistan Navy R4003 d/d 5.8.51
G.15-180 Attacker FB.1 Pakistan Navy R4004 d/d 13.8.51
G.15-181 Attacker FB.1 Pakistan Navy R4005 d/d 10.11.51
G.15-182 Attacker FB.1 Pakistan Navy R4006 d/d 10.11.51
G.15-183 Attacker FB.1 Pakistan Navy R4007 d/d 12.11.51
G.15-184 Attacker FB.1 Pakistan Navy R4008 d/d 12.11.51
G.15-185 Attacker FB.1 Pakistan Navy R4009 d/d 26.11.51
G.15-186 Attacker FB.1 Pakistan Navy R4010 d/d 26.11.51
G.15-187 Attacker FB.1 Pakistan Navy R4011 d/d 10.12.51
G.15-188 Attacker FB.1 Pakistan Navy R4012 d/d 10.12.51
G.15-189 Attacker FB.1 Pakistan Navy R4013 d/d 28.1.52
G.15-190 Attacker FB.1 Pakistan Navy R4014 d/d 9.1.52
G.15-191 Attacker FB.1 Pakistan Navy R4015 d/d 28.1.52

*G.15-141 to 170. The allocation of RAF and Belgian Air Force serials is known to be
correct but the correlation with Class B registrations is not known. The dates quoted are
for the first flights with Belgian serials.

G.15-192	Attacker FB.1		Pakistan Navy	R4016	d/d 3.4.52
G.15-193	Attacker FB.1		Pakistan Navy	R4017	d/d 3.4.52
G.15-194	Attacker FB.1		Pakistan Navy	R4018	d/d 27.5.52
G.15-195	Attacker FB.1		Pakistan Navy	R4019	d/d 27.5.52
G.15-196	Attacker FB.1		Pakistan Navy	R4020	d/d 27.5.52
G.15-197	Attacker FB.1		Pakistan Navy	R4021	d/d 16.6.52
G.15-198	Attacker FB.1		Pakistan Navy	R4022	d/d 16.6.52
G.15-199	Attacker FB.1		Pakistan Navy	R4023	d/d 2.10.52
G.15-200	Attacker FB.1		Pakistan Navy	R4024	d/d 28.11.52
G.15-201	Attacker FB.1		Pakistan Navy	R4025	d/d 2.10.52
G.15-202	Attacker FB.1		Pakistan Navy	R4026	d/d 28.11.52
G.15-203	Attacker FB.1		Pakistan Navy	R4027	d/d 15.12.52
G.15-204	Attacker FB.1		Pakistan Navy	R4028	d/d 15.12.52
G.15-205	Attacker FB.1		Pakistan Navy	R4029	d/d 15.12.52
G.15-206	Attacker FB.1		Pakistan Navy	R4030	d/d 12.1.53
G.15-207	Attacker FB.1		Pakistan Navy	R4031	d/d 12.1.53
G.15-208	Attacker FB.1		Pakistan Navy	R4032	d/d 23.4.53
G.15-209	Attacker FB.1		Pakistan Navy	R4033	d/d 23.4.53
G.15-210	Attacker FB.1		Pakistan Navy	R4034	d/d 12.5.53
G.15-211	Attacker FB.1		Pakistan Navy	R4035	d/d 12.5.53
G.15-212	Seafire F.XV	SR451	Burmese AF	UB401	
G.15-213	Seafire F.XV	SW799	Burmese AF	UB402	
G.15-214	Seafire F.XV	SR642	Burmese AF	UB403	
G.15-215	Seafire F.XV	SW863	Burmese AF	UB404	
G.15-216	Seafire F.XV	SR471	Burmese AF	UB405	
G.15-217	Seafire F.XV	PR355	Burmese AF	UB406	
G.15-218	Seafire F.XV	SR534	Burmese AF	UB407	
G.15-219	Seafire F.XV	PR455	Burmese AF	UB408	
G.15-220	Seafire F.XV	PR376	Burmese AF	UB409	
G.15-221	Seafire F.XV	PR400	Burmese AF	UB410	
G.15-222	Seafire F.XV	PR423	Burmese AF	UB411	
G.15-223	Seafire F.XV	SW817	Burmese AF	UB412	
G.15-224	Seafire F.XV	PR453	Burmese AF	UB413	
G.15-225	Seafire F.XV	SR462	Burmese AF	UB414	
G.15-226	Seafire F.XV	PR422	Burmese AF	UB415	
G.15-227	Seafire F.XV	PR454	Burmese AF	UB416	
G.15-228	Seafire F.XV	SR470	Burmese AF	UB417	
G.15-229	Seafire F.XV	PR407	Burmese AF	UB418	
G.15-230	Seafire F.XV	PR462	Burmese AF	UB419	
G.15-231	Seafire F.XV	SW899	Burmese AF	UB420	
G.15-232	Spitfire F.22*		Syrian AF	501	
G.15-233	Spitfire F.22*		Syrian AF	502	
G.15-234	Spitfire F.22*		Syrian AF	503	
G.15-235	Spitfire F.22*	PK658	Syrian AF	504	
G.15-236	Spitfire F.22*		Syrian AF	505	29.9.53
G.15-237	Spitfire F.22*		Syrian AF	506	
G.15-238	Spitfire F.22*		Syrian AF	507	21.8.53
G.15-239	Spitfire F.22*		Syrian AF	508	
G.15-240	Spitfire F.22*		Syrian AF	509	12.1.54
G.15-241	Spitfire F.22*		Syrian AF	510	
G.15-242	Spitfire F.22*		Syrian AF	511	
G.15-243	Spitfire F.22*		Syrian AF	512	
G.15-244	Spitfire F.22*		Syrian AF	513	
G.15-245	Spitfire F.22*		Syrian AF	514	26.1053
G.15-246	Spitfire F.22*		Syrian AF	515	
G.15-247	Spitfire F.22*		Syrian AF	516	

G.15-248	Spitfire F.22*	Syrian AF	517
G.15-249	Spitfire F.22*	Syrian AF	518
G.15-250	Spitfire F.22*	Syrian AF	519	8.1.54
G.15-251	Spitfire F.22*	Syrian AF	520
G.15-252	Hovercraft VA-1 XS798	Vickers research as Type 3038
G.15-253	Hovercraft VA-3 XS856	Vickers research as Type 3031

*Converted by Airwork Ltd

GENERAL INDEX

INDEX OF AIRCRAFT AND ENGINES

Supermarine aircraft are listed alphabetically under type names and designations (as Attacker and S.4); chronologically under the heading Specification; and numerically under the heading Type.

397